AF538956

PERSONNEL MANAGEMENT

Edited by
R.K. Malhotra
Nachhattar Singh
S.D. Sharma

ANMOL PUBLICATIONS PVT. LTD.
NEW DELHI - 110 002 (INDIA)

ANMOL PUBLICATIONS PVT. LTD.
4374/4B, Ansari Road, Daryaganj
New Delhi - 110 002
Ph.: 23261597, 23278000
Visit us at: www.anmolpublications.com

Personnel Management

PRINTED IN INDIA

Published by J.L. Kumar for Anmol Publications Pvt. Ltd., New Delhi - 110 002 and Printed at Mehra Offset Press, Delhi.

CONTENTS

PREFACE

A major trend virtually in all areas of business is the increasing utilisation of 'management science' concepts, models, techniques and approaches in the organisations. Rapid advances in management concepts and techniques and changes in the climate in which business organisations, institutional enterprises and governments operate call for a more comprehensive and authoritative information on all modern arts and science of management. The Encylopaedia of Modern Management is an attempt in this direction. The encyclopaedia is designed on the lines of systematic reading—a programmed reading of subjects in a planned sequence.

It is more than a reference work covering over 1000 topics related to management. Each topic has been selected carefully and recognition has been given to new development and innovative approaches. In addition to the new dimensions in the information processing and communications technology, the changes in taxation, employee-employer relations, mergers and acquisitions, enhanced moral responsibilites regarding environment and acceptable norms of business, modern techniques in production, marketing and office administration and new insights of the behavioural sciences into human motivations and group effectiveness are some of the topics covered. Elaborate discussions and illustrations have been given as the complexity of the subject matter demands. The book has been designed so that it may be used by top management, department management, executive, executive aspirant, accountant, teacher, student of business and management and, indeed, all those concerned with the conduct of business. The scope of this treatise differs in many respects from any reference books, handbooks and deskbooks dealing with business management.

The writing effort has been assited by many individuals. We gratefully acknowledge all the contributions made by various individuals which made this encyclopaedia possible. Constructive suggestions to help improve the book are welcome.

Editors

1

AN OVERVIEW

THE effective use of human resources is basic to the success of all societies, organizations, and other groups. The importance of managing human resources effectively has increased in this century as organizations have grown in size, number, and complexity; have developed new technologies and work environments; and have come to be viewed by society as providers of safe, meaningful, and satisfying work as well as monetary reward.

Personnel management in its broadest sense involves all matters in an organization regarding decisions about people. This broad view focuses on three distinct but inter-related topics. The first is that of *human relations*, in which such matters as individual motivation, leadership, and group relationships are covered. The second is the field of *organization theory*, which considers job design, managerial spans of control, work flow through the organization, and so forth. The third consists of the specific kinds of *decision areas* for which the personnel manager or personnel department is directly responsible—the acquisition, development, rewarding, and maintenance of human resources.

The broad definition illustrates that personnel management pervades the organization as well the proper average. Every person in an organization is involved with personnel decisions. The example that all managers in any organization need to know how to train their employees, appraise their employees' performance, and all that. Similarly, non-managerial employees are exposed to performance appraisals, selection interviews when hired, and so on. Thus, whether or not individuals plan to go into personnel work, they become involved with personnel decisions.

We recognize the interdependencies and importance of the three topics included in the broad definition of personnel management. We prefer, however to define personnel management in the narrower sense of the *third* topic. Thus, this text will focus attention on personnel management in terms of the specific kinds of decision areas for which the personnel manager or personnel department is directly responsible. These decision areas are shown in Figure 1. Depending upon the size of an organization, it should be emphasized, there may or may not be a formal personnel department to handle these functions. One individual might perform all personnel functions. Or, in a very small organization, individuals may spend only part of their time on personnel matters and the rest on other types of decision problems.

Human relations and organization theory are very legitimate fields of study by themselves. We consider it desirable, though, to treat personnel management in terms of decision areas. Because human relations and organization theory are so often taught in courses on behavioral science and organizational behavior, covering these topics extensively in this text would be unnecessary for many readers. However, we will draw on behavioral science concepts as we analyze particular personnel problems. In fact, some of the "contingency" approaches to the study of personnel management represent ideas and notions drawn directly from the field of organization theory and behavior.

DECISION MAKING AND SYSTEMS

Fundamental to personnel management is the meeting of organizational objectives. In personnel, these objectives often involve both economic and non-economic "social," "humanitarian" aspects. For example, when the organization's employees are provided with a safe and healthy work environment, "humanitarian" goals are met. Economic goals may be met at the same time, however, since a better safety record may help reduce a firm's workers' compensation costs, Implicit in these statements is that personnel decisions attempt to meet *individual needs* as well as *organizational objectives*.

If any of their objectives are not met or are inappropriate, personnel managers face problems. For example, a large number of accidents might indicate that the firm's safety goals are not being met; on the other hand, a company objective of never having a singly accident would be unrealistic and hence inappropriate.

To overcome problems, personnel managers need to generate possible courses of action involving decision making and devising personnel systems.

Fig. 1, below, illustrates personnel decision making in an organised sector of industry.

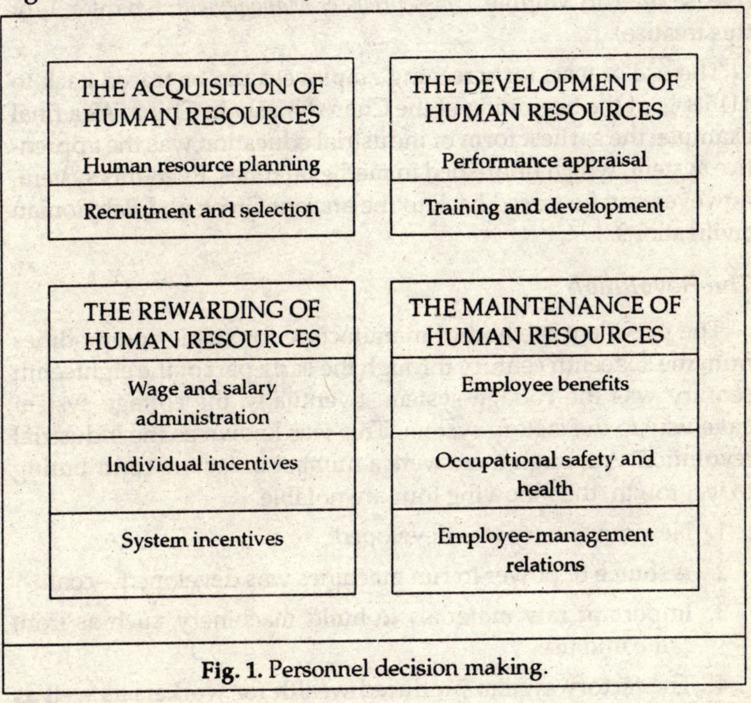

Fig. 1. Personnel decision making.

HISTORY

Personnel decisions can be traced back to primitive societies. Some mechanism had to be developed for the *selection* of tribal leaders. Some consideration had to be given to *sining* youths to hunt or prepare and cook food. Some knowledge had to be developed protect the *safety* and *health* of the group, and so on.

As early as 1750 B.C., the Code of Hammurabi attempted to encourage safety by providing for punishment of individuals who violated safety provisions in constructing building. There are "early illustrations showing workers engaged in the grinding of vermillion (which produces a dangerous dust) wearing a primitive type of breathing apparatus." In a book written in 1473, Ulrich Ellenbog noted the occupational hazards traced by goldsmiths and metal workers and provided advice on how to avoid mercury and lead poisoning. In addition, in 1713, Ramazzini, who is regarded as the father of occupational medicine, suggested that in diagnosis doctors should ask patients about their occupations. (Please refer to Volume 1, *Essentials of Management*, Chapter 1, of this treatise).

The use of tests for screening employees can be traced back to 1115 B.C., at the beginning of the Chan dynasty in China. As a final example, the earliest form of industrial education was the apprentice system, which flourished in medieval times. Even this system, however, can be traced back to the ancient Greek and Babylonian civilizations.

The Revolution

The prevalent method of manufacture for staple commodities from the sixteenth century through the early part of the eighteenth century was the cottage system. Eventually, the cottage system gave way to the factory system. This was known as the industrial revolution. Although there were a number of factors contributing to its growth, the following four are notable:

1. New machinery was developed.
2. A source of power to run machines was developed—coal.
3. Important raw materials to build machinery, such as iron, came into use.
4. The factory system produced wealth for workers as well as the owners of the factories. Individuals could make higher wages in factories than under the cottage system. Thus there was a ready supply of labour for factory production.

The industrial revolution began in England. It was not until about 1860 that mass production technologies flourished in the United States. In spite of the increased wealth that the industrial revolution generated, the factory system had many shortcomings that were detrimental to its workers. Among these were the following:

- □ Rather than performing many tasks, as in the cottage system, work became specialized and *dehumanized.* Workers would labor on the same specialized machine over and over.
- □ Hours of work were extremely long, even for children. The 12- to 14-hour day was commonplace.
- □ Factories were usually unsafe and unhealthy workplaces. Lighting and ventilation were poor, and toxic materials were often touched or inhaled.

With problems such as these, it is little wonder that protests and other pressures arose to improve the factory system. One of the most important pressures for improvement came from labor unions.

The Rise of Modern Personnel Management

In light of the influence of labor, it is ironic that one of the first major thrusts toward modern personnel management occurred in the public sector. Organized personnel work in industry appears to have emerged about 1900. The first employment department (which was only a hiring bureau) appeared at that time. As early as 1902 a national company had a fairly broadly conceived "labor department," which dealt with worker grievances, wage administration, working conditions, employment, record keeping, discharges, education, and improvement of workers and supervisors. This emergence of personnel management has been attributed to two diverse fields of endeavor: (1) the industrial welfare movement and (2) Frederick W. Taylor's "scientific management." Both of these represented responses to the industrial revolution. The industrial welfare movement, derived from religion and philanthropy, led some managements to set such humanitarian objectives as providing their employees facilities such as libraries, financial assistance for education, recreational facilities, and medical care. These functions were sometimes performed by welfare secretaries, who were conceived as a point of contact between the company and its employees. Although the status of "welfare" declined, these types of endeavors continued, and industrial welfare "clearly contained the beginning of personnel administration.... The line from the social and welfare secretaries to the employment manager is a direct one".

The second, and quite different, field that led to the emergence of modern personnel administration was *scientific management,* fathered by Frederick W. Taylor. Taylor's basic objective was to develop more efficient ways of performing work at the lowest level in industrialized organizations—with workers at the shop level. Taylor emphasized (1) researching ways of performing tasks, such as studying jobs in order to eliminate unnecessary motions; (2) applying the best methods devised to all jobs; (3) selecting workers suited to perform the jobs; and (4) training them in the one best method developed. Taylor's work attracted many followers, such as Frank and Lillian Gilbreth and Henry Gantt. The time and motion study methods and other worker efficiency techniques developed and used by Taylor and his followers are still used in industry and taught today in industrial engineering (and other) departments in colleges and universities. Other significant aspects of the early history of the personnel field developed during the period 1910-1920. First, managements suddenly "discovered" labor turnover as a costly proposition and turned to personnel managers to help reduce turnover by the proper selection and placement of workers (along with adequate training). Second, World War I created a labor shortage, which made turnover a calamity and tardiness and absenteeism serious problems. Many organizations developed personnel departments to deal with these problems. Further, in many cases the powers of supervisors, such as hiring and discharging employees, were seriously curtailed by centralizing personnel hiring and giving personnel departments powers to override supervisors' discharge decisions. World War I also triggered the development of the Army Alpha as a group intelligence test for military selection. "It was so constructed as to measure all gradations of intelligence and was by far the most highly standardized test of this sort at that time". The Army Alpha has also been widely used by civil service commissions. Also in the 1910s, many states passed workers' compensation laws, giving employees for the first time the right to be paid for industrial accidents and illnesses by the companies for which they worked. This ended the necessity of workers' going to court to be reimbursed for damages to them on the job.

Beginning in the 1920s, the nature of the labor force began to change considerably. Among the reasons for this change were the slowdown in immigration due, in no small part, to new federal immigration laws passed in the 1920s; the continued rise in educational levels of American workers; and the increase in urbanization. With their knowledge and abilities becoming more fully developed than ever before, workers began to expect and demand more dignified and respectful treatment. In the 1920s many business firms tried to be "good" to their employees, on the assumption that their workers would consequently be more satisfied and work harder. Incorporated into this approach (often referred to as *paternalism)* were such activities as company sponsored canteens and planned recreation programs.

Moving to the 1940s, the spotlight on personnel management was intensified during World War II. With large numbers of persons engaged in active military service, the labor market again became tight. In addition, the need developed for intensive skill training programs for those workers (including many women) who replaced the individuals in the military services. Further, the freezing of wages by the federal government led unions to demand compensation in the form of benefits (such as pension plans) that further enlarged the scope of the personnel department.

Now was the time when the personnel management emerged as science. A brief discussion here, on the pioneers of this science of management will not be out of place here.

THE PIONEERS

Personnel Management is a multifaceted discipline to which distinguished individuals from a number of disciplines have made contributions. Therefore, no two observers of the personnel management scene probably would agree on just who meet the criterion of "outstanding." This lack of agreement is understandable when one considers that the past sixty years have been a period marked by movements and counter-movements, by diverse philosophies and great innovations. It thus is just as significant to include the pioneer of the group dynamics movement as it is to identify the most influential authority in the personnel testing field. Further, although personnel management is ordinarily conceived of as a staff function, two line managers whose work and thought have greatly influenced the personnel function seem also worthy of mention.

When assessing "contribution." it is not always easy to assert categorically that an individual was the creator of an idea, the innovator of a technique, or the founder of a movement. Obviously ideas and techniques come from several sources. For example, Dr. Carl Rogers is considered to be the prime developer of the technique of nondirective counseling, but Freud's work in psychoanalysis is certainly basic to that technique. Also, authorities differ as to who was the father of a particular movement. An example is Kurt Lewin versus J. L. Moreno in group dynamics.

This article invites attention to various individuals who, many persons believe, have greatly influenced personnel management during this century.

In the early part of this period, Dr. Walter Dill Scott (1869–1955) educator and psychologist, was a long-time key figure in personnel management. He set up the World War I Army testing program, and was awarded the Distinguished Service Medal for "devising, installing, and supervising the personnel system in the U.S. Army." His work in testing influenced personnel management significantly in industry and government.

Dr. Walter Van Dyke Bingham (1880–1952) is considered by many to have been the dean of American personnel psychologists. He worked with Walter Dill Scott and others in the testing field on the Army testing program in World War I. His "Aptitudes and Aptitude Testing," 1937 and "How to Interview," 1931, written with B.V. Moore, were long regarded as standard texts.

Dr. Warner W. Stockberger (1872–1944) was the first Personnel Director (1925–38) of the U.S. Department of Agriculture and of the Federal Government. He was also the first President of the Society for Personnel Administration, Washington, D.C. (1937). An early pioneer in Federal personnel management, he had a keen appreciation of the human factor in management. His work, which included training of many personnel workers who ultimately moved on to other Federal agencies, influenced the character of Federal personnel management generally.

Dr. Leonard D. White (1891-1958) was an internationally recognized figure in public personnel administration. A teacher at the

Univ. of Chicago, a scholar, writer, thinker, idealist, and practitioner, he is credited with many "firsts." He was the author of the first text on public administration, which also contained considerable information on personnel management; he was the first to teach public administration in a university classroom; he pioneered in starting the Junior Civil Service Examiner Examination, which attracted liberal arts and social science majors to careers in the Federal Government.

Dr. White's work on organization and personnel management was influenced by the scientific management movement. Some of his students, principally Herbert Simon, later challenged Dr. White's adherence to "principles" of organization. The work of behavioral scientists presented many insights about management and organizational behavior, ones which Dr. White and others in his era had not explored.

The first intensive human relations esearch study was the Hawthorne Experiments conducted at the Hawthorne plant of the Western Electric Co. (1924–32) with the help (1927–32) of a research staff of the Harvard Graduate School of Business, directed by Dr. G. Elton Mayo (1880–1949). Whereas Frederick W. Taylor and his contemporaries in scientific management viewed management and organization primarily from the standpoint of engineering, Dr. Mayo and his staff applied socio-psychological techniques to managerial problems, From this research, a new theory of human behavior in organizations was created.

The Hawthorne experiments led to, among other things, the creation of employee counseling programs in the 1930s, a phase of personnel management which is operative (albeit in a less elaborate form) in many organizations today.

In his "The Human Problem of an Industrial Civilization," 1933 and his "Social Problems of an Industrial Civilization," 1954. Dr. Mayo has given a scholarly interpretation of the significance of human factors in our industrial culture. His thesis related to the advantages to be derived from involving the worker in the decision-making process. He questioned strongly the "rabble hypothesis"—that materialistic goals are the only motivating force and that authoritarian leadership is essential to get the lazy to work and to keep the grasping in line. For all of us, he said, the feeling of security and certainty derives always from assured membership in a group; if this is lost, no monetary gain, no job guarantee, can be sufficient compensation.

Another solid contributor to the personnel field is Dr. Ordway Tead (1892–1972). Dr. Tead taught personnel administration, and at Columbia, 1917-18, he was in charge of war emergency employment management courses of the War Department. He continued at Columbia as a lecturer in personnel administration during 1920-50, and from 1951-56 was Adjunct Professor of Industrial Relations. He was also a faculty member of the Department of Industry at the New York School of Social Work, 1920-29.

Dr. Tead's writings, which stress democratic principles of management, have not been dimmed by more recent research. His better known works are "The Art of Leadership," 1935 and "The Art of Administration," 1951. He also co-authored with Henry C. Metcalf a pioneer personnel textbook, "Personnel Administration: Its Principles and Practices," 1920.

Dr. Chester I. Barnard (1886–1961), an eminent industrialist, was president of the New Jersey Bell Telephone Co. and later of the Rockefeller Foundation. In his much-quoted classic, "The Functions of the Executive," 1938, Dr. Barnard analyzed and stressed the socio-psychological and ethical aspects of managerial organization and functions. His book is an early, if not the first, recognition of the import of the informal as well as the formal organizational structure. He viewed organization as a social system.

This view necessitates a high degree of cooperation as opposed to emphasis upon authority and order-giving; the relegation of economic factors as motivators to a secondary role; the individual's identification with the organization based on a strong belief in its codes, as opposed to compliance imposed from without.

Dr. Barnard was also one of the first management authorities to stress the communication responsibilities of executives, to analyze the role of status in organizational endeavor, and to develop systematically an analysis of incentive systems in organizations.

Charles P. McCormick (1896-1970), late board chairman of McCormick and Co., Baltimore, was the founder of multiple management, which involves the establishment of several boards—senior, junior, factory, and sales—as a means of securing employee participation and developing executives. Hundreds of companies now use this means of securing participation, manager development, problem solving, and morale building.

Among the leaders of the more current period, Dr. Kurt Lewin (1890–1947) is regarded by many social psychologists as the founder of contemporary Group Dynamics. Dr. Lewin tested his ideas about groups after he left Germany in 1932 and settled in the United States, carrying on his pioneer studies on group leadership at the University of Iowa, and later at M.I.T. and the University of Michigan. Results of his studies pointed up the direct relationship between production and participation in the decision-making process.

Dr. Lewin should be credited, too, with being the father of sensitivity training. In this work he pioneered in the use of unstructured discussion groups which function without a leader and without procedures or agenda.

A distinguished disciple of Dr. Lewin, Dr. Leland P. Bradford. established in 1947 at Bethel, Maine, the first "sensitivity" or human relations laboratory. Since that time his efforts have spawned such training at many universities and other organizations. This development has been a significant contribution to group leadership, with a tremendous potential for organizational health. Dr. Bradford was Director, National Training Laboratories, National Education Ass., Washington, D.C. 1947–1970 (in 1967 renamed the NTL Institute for Applied Behavioral Science, located in Arlington, Va.).

An early summation of the work at Bethel is contained in Bradford's "Explorations in Human Relations Training: An Assessment of Experience, 1947-53". A comprehensive account of laboratory training is given in a joint work with Jack R. Gibb and Kenneth D. Benne. Dr. Bradford also launched for N.T.L. "The Journal of Applied Behavioral Science" in 1965.

Using sensitivity training concepts, Robert R. Blake and Jane S. Mouton developed a system of leaderless training laboratories in the early 1960s. Managers thus are enabled to receive feedback from their peers about their leadership style based on the Managerial Grid concepts. Today, managers all over the world are being challenged through training to develop a 9-9 (team management) leadership style. Blake and Mouton also have developed a comprehensive system of organization development.

A long-time giant in the field is Dr. Carl R. Rogers (1902–1962). An internationally recognized psychotherapist, encounter group facilitator, and human relations theorist, he is credited with introducing the non-directive method of counseling and interviewing. In Roger's "person-centered" approach, the client is in charge of the pace, content, and direction of the interchange. The term "non-directive" is now used to refer to any similar approach used by any power figure: e.g., a teacher, counselor, consultant, manager, etc. To do this successfully, one must be willing (and able) really to listen to the other person, try to understand the other person's position without being judgmental, accept the other person as he/she is, Roger's work has also spawned the term "Rogerian" to indicate the non-directive person-centered approach to interpersonal relations. A prolific and profound writer, his major works are "Counseling and Psychotherapy" (1942), "Client Centered Therapy," (1951), "On Becoming A Person" (1961), "On Encounter Groups," (1970), "Freedom to Learn" (1969), "Becoming Partners" (1972), and "On Personal Power" (1977). He is at this writing Resident Fellow at the Center For Studies of The Person, La Jolla, California.

Norman R. F. Maier (1901–1977), an industrial psychologist at the University of Michigan, was a prolific writer, researcher, teacher, trainer, lecturer, and consultant. His unusually creative work emphasized the importance of group decision, employee participation, problem solving and creativity, causation, motivation, and frustration. As a practical trainer of supervisors, Dr. Maier Stimulated the wide use of "group-in- action" training methods (principally role-playing exercise) by training specialists. His "Principles of Human Relations," 1952, "Psychology of Industry," 1946, "Supervisory and Executive Development: A Manual for Role Playing," 1957, "The Appraisal Interview," 1958, "Creative Management," 1962, and "Problem Solving Discussions and Conferences," 1963 have enriched the personnel and training field.

Dr. Rensis Likert (1903–1981), Director, 1948–1972, of the Institute of Social Research, University of Michigan, conducted highly significant human relations research since the 1940s. He has pointed out that the concept of equating high morale with high productivity is much too simple. In fact many kinds of combinations are possible. Dr. Likert's research demonstrates the value to productivity of (1) "supportive" as opposed to threatening supervision and (2) "participative" as opposed to "hierarchically-controlled" management. In general, supervisory attitudes—that is, those which are "employee centered" as opposed to "production centered"—are basic to productivity. Dr. Likert's findings cast doubt on the long-range success of organizations which use people for short- range goals. His book, "New Patterns of Management," 1961, reports his basic findings and conclusions. In "The Human Organization: Its Management and Value," 1967, a direct link to the prior work, Likert looks at management systems and advocates that organizations use "System 4", or participative-group, for greater profitability and employee satisfaction.

We must also recognize that the contemporary scene can boast a good number of other top-fight thinkers, writers, and researchers. Examples are Carroll Shartle (Ohio State) who conducted highly significant studies in leadership, narrowing the description of a leader's behavior to two dimensions—"initiating structure" and "consideration." Later, Fred E. Fiedler (University of Illinois) developed a "Leadership Contingency Modes" which emphasized the importance of the situation rather than the "best" leadership style.

Douglas McGregor (1906–1964) of M.I.T., is to be credited with having authored one of the most original, seminal, and quoted management books in the past quarter century—"The Human Side of Enterprise". Here he developed his ideas on leadership theory, motivation, his management by objectives, presented as "Theory X" and "Theory Y". He elaborated on his ideas in "The Professional Manager," 1967, edited posthumously by Caroline McGregor and Warren G. Bennis, stressing the means of achieving the goals presented in the earlier work.

Warren G. Bennis, educator, trainer, consultant, and former President of University of Cincinnati, was a close colleague of McGregor. He has drawn on the great mass of current behavioral science findings, and has developed ideas explaining causes and consequences of change organizational behavior. Bennis is a leading theorist in the field of organization development.

Chris Argyris (Harvard) advanced the "Immaturity-Maturity Theory," which suggests that organizations all too often keep workers passive and thus stunt their psychological growth. Argyris, in general, has been concerned with making organizations "healthy." A significant book deals with "intervention theory," a behavioral science-consultant approach to helping organizations to diagnose better their ailments and thus to solve their problems in an in-depth way.

Frederick Herzberg (Case Western Reserve University and University of Utah) developed, while at Case, the popular and practical "Motivation-Hygiene Theory," i.e., hygiene factors depend on the environment and merely prevent job dissatisfaction whereas satisfiers or motivators derive from the job and produce positive effects on productivity. Herzberg's work forms an important support for the concept of job enrichment.

Herbert A. Simon (Carnegie) merits high recognition for his analysis of organizational behavior from the standpoint of decision-making, particularly its non-rational character.

All these scholars and practitioners are representative of the continually expanding field of personnel administration, influenced markedly by behavioral science research.

In the 40 or so years since the end of World War II, the personnel department has continued to grow in many ways. Most importantly, it has been faced with an increasingly expanding and complex technology. Among such technological changes, computerization and automation stand out as probably the most important to the personnel manager. Computers have created problems that personnel managers face today (for example, retaining displaced employees), but they have also become an important record-keeping and problem-solving tool. The automation of production processes has not only required layoffs and retraining, it has also created quite different social systems in which different types of interpersonal relationships and human problems have arisen. In addition, in some instance automation has resulted in jobs becoming so routine that employee dissatisfaction has resulted.

Over the period the concept of personnel management underwent a dramatic change. Economic, social and technological changes influenced the concept of personnel management in many ways. A brief note concerning the changing concept in the light of information technology is kindly contributed by a colleague as follows.

THE CONCEPT OF A PERSONNEL SYSTEM

In recent years there has been a lot of talk about professionalism in personnel. In fact, many of the traditional staff function, such as accounting, market planning, and education, are developing the hallmarks—such as professional societies, publications, and academic degrees—of a profession. In the field of personnel many different magazines and books are published. Numerous meetings and seminars are held. And in some schools today it is even possible to get a degree in personnel. Yet despite all the trappings of a profession, I really doubt whether sufficient attention has been paid to the tools and techniques of personnel. In short, I don't think present-day tools and techniques are good enough to enable us to accomplish personnel's basic mission.

I conceive this basic mission to be *a huge balancing act*. Personnel is charged with the job of balancing the demand for people with the supply of people, of balancing the corporation's need for certain skills and experience with the manpower market's supply of these skills and experience. Everything personnel does has an effect on one side of the balance or the other. Its policies in wage and salary administration, benefits, safety, even in cafeteria management are all primarily designed to maintain an adequate workforce. When the need arises, its policies in hiring, transferring, and retraining fill the gaps in the workforce. Personnel provides an interface between the organization and all the potential employees in the manpower market at large. And anything that affects this market tilts the balance and may require translation by personnel into policy changes within the company. To top it off, personnel has to perform this balancing act at the lowest possible cost.

Yet no matter which aspect of this complex balancing act we examine, we find that good personnel management requires fast, accurate information. Professional management demands hard factual data to make decisions, but personnel still flies by the seat of its pants in many situations. It doesn't compare well generally with other staff units which have modern methods for storing and retrieving information, and as a result it cannot answer questions as well as they can.

The man in charge of inventories can say exactly how many machine tools he has on hand, but can personnel say, for instance, how many people in the company have more than three years experience on a certain machine tool? The financial expert can plot meticulously the rate of return on his investments, but does personnel know what the effect of lowering the retirement age would be on salary costs or the make-up of the workforce? The purchasing man can state exactly what he is getting and how much it costs. But does personnel know what it costs to hire and train a man, and whether he is being trained correctly for the needs of the company 20 years from now?

It is clear, I think, that personnel in its present shape cannot provide top management with information that is as valuable as that generated by some other staff groups. Perhaps this explains way personnel people often have to take a back seat in management decisions and are sometimes pictured as being low men on the totem pole. And others besides top management have cause to complain about old-fashioned personnel methods, too.

In a large organization, the individual employee may fear that he will be lost in the shuffle when promotions are passed out. He may feel that nobody knows his talents and that because of red tape in personnel he has little exposure to job opportunities. We have all heart statements like "The only reason Joe was promoted was because he was in the right place at the right time." Yet if we had some way to search each employee's skills, job history, tests, and appraisals quickly we could be more sure that when job opportunities arose all qualified employees would be considered.

Perhaps the biggest problem for personnel is inside its own shop. The traditional personnel function of recruiting, counseling, placement, and benefits can get bogged down by traditional methods of handling personnel data. What personnel man has not had the experience of putting aside his regular work to answer a question from outside of personnel only to find after several hours of searching that the data were incomplete and probably inaccurate? What he needs is a way to handle personnel information more easily, a way which will free the personnel staff to do more creative and professional work.

Most professions accomplish their basic mission with sophisticated tools and techniques. In order for personnel to accomplish its basic mission of balancing the supply and demand for manpower it must have fast, accurate data. What we need is a *personnel data system*.

A personnel data system is a way of storing information about people so that it can be quickly retrieved. We can learn a lot about such a system by examining the information that goes into it. Most of the data which we put into a personnel system is already sitting in our files. However, if the files are organized in the traditional manner, these data are probably scattered among the files of many different departments, such as medical, payroll, personnel records, and benefits. These files could be combined into one easily accessible record. The traditional system of organization can result in an astounding amount of overlap. In one study of personnel records and reports, it was found that over 2,000 elements of personnel information were being maintained, but after elimination of redundancies only 145 unique elements remained. Not only is it expensive to store such data, but it is very difficult to use it to answer general questions. If we wanted information on, say, the relationship between medical history and salary, we might have to remove it from several files and process it by hand.

To systematize the data we must define the component blocks of data and then make it possible to integrate them. A component block might consist of educational data which would be further broken down into two different data fields such as year of graduation and schools attended. In one study conducted in cooperation with 15 companies it was discovered that there was little variation even from one company to another in the basic items of information needed to describe an employee. In most of these companies, 145 to 160 items were needed. These are the elements we put into component blocks. Integrating the blocks means that we should have some easy way to get information from any block and combine it with others. This probably means using a computer with magnetic tape drive or disk storage units.

The ultimate goal of a personnel system is to combine its data with that of financial, manufacturing, and other systems to create a total management information system. This total system could be used to answer general questions like "How long will it take to put a new product on the back dock?" To answer such a question, we would have to know the resources of the company—machines, raw materials, workers, management, and cash—plus how they would fit together in a master delivery schedule using PERT or some other technique. The day of the management information system may not be here yet, but it is surely coming. And the people who are systems-oriented will benefit most from it.

I can give an example of a personnel system that was tested in one of IBM's product divisions. This division had 15,000 employees and kept the following five types of data on each of them:

1. *Employee profile,* which contains personnel data about the employee such as his home address, marital status, number of dependents, and so forth.
2. *Employment history,* which shows the jobs the man has held within the company, his salary over the years, and his appraisals.
3. *Resume and significant achievements* including pervious employment, publications, and patents.
4. *Education data* with major and minor fields of concentration.
5. *Skills data.*

These five blocks of data are used to provide regular reports to management in the way of salary administration and headcount reports and any number of special reports such as benefits analysis, education planning, placement resumes, and appraisal scheduling. Once a year most of the basic data kept on a man are printed out and given to him for review and audit. This lets him know what basic personnel information is kept on him and assures him that his qualifications for advancement are known. Any number of reports can be produced with this system. However, one can never completely exhaust the different uses for the data. I can illustrate this point with examples of the use of simulation in manpower planning and the use of skills inventories.

Simulation is a technique that has become very popular in the last few years. It is an attempt to build a model of a real system so that when we make a change in part of the model, the resulting effects on the rest of the model will accurately mirror what would happen if that change were made in the real world.

Physical models used in simulation have been around a long time. We have all seen pictures of airplane models being used in wind tunnel tests. More recently, researchers have used abstract models consisting of mathematical equations or computer programs. The workforce simulator at one IBM plant is an example of a computer program model, used to evaluate our manpower plans.

Management in many organizations must continually review and evaluate alternative manpower plans. These include such aspects as hiring, transferring, and retraining, which may arise from changing workloads or technological advances. Decisions in this area are now based more on experience than on quantitative knowledge about the probable results of the alternatives. The workforce simulator is a tool for rapidly gaining information on different approaches under varying conditions. An attempt to provide such information without simulation would not allow for the many interactions of the factors involved.

The plant faced two major problems which were attacked with the aid of the simulator. One problem was the result of a limited hiring policy and rapidly changing technologies. As new products based on new technologies were brought into production, a different skill mix was needed among our employees. Sometimes we would have a surplus in one skill and a deficiency in another. What we really wanted to know was who should we hire today to begin what kind of training next week so that we would have the right kind of people on the job next year.

Complicating this question was an uneven distribution of tenure in our plant. The average age of our employees at the location was greater than our companywide average, and many of these employees were hired during a period of rapid expansion in World War II. As a result, this plant will probably lose through retirement large numbers of direct and indirect employees in key areas in the next 5 to 10 years. In order to fill the jobs of the key indirect employees we had to start transferring and promoting the right kind of people now.

Management often needs quantitative data to make decisions, and a simulator can give those data for different alternatives. Hopefully, it could supply the necessary data so that management would have an accurate means of weighing the alternatives and making the best decision. However, I should stress that this was a gross planning model and not an optimizing technique nor a short-range personnel selection tool.

The model itself involves two separate concepts: (1) a phase approach to allow interaction of different workforce factors and (2) a matrix structure for consideration of job levels over a period of time.

In the phase approach, we consider the overall gain and loss of employees in the workforce. We state as a policy decision what the mandatory retirement age will be. On top of that we add an estimate of attrition due to reasons other than retirement. Factors for entering new personnel are added, and provisions are made for internal transfers of employees due to promotions or retraining. When all of these assumptions are put together, we can get a picture of the changes that take place in the level of workforce.

In the matrix concept, we have a description of the job levels of the workforce over a period of time. Each column of the matrix represents a different time period, such as a year or every five years. Each row of the matrix represents a different job level. We used as many at 15 job levels for the 4,000 indirect employees. At each intersection of row and columns, we have one job level represented at a certain point of time. The purpose of the simulation is to watch what happens to the number and the make-up of the people at different job levels under different manpower policies over a period of time.

A simulation is started by entering the policy assumptions and data about the current employees' age, experience, education level, test scores, and so forth. By starting with data about current employees, which is readily available from our personnel data system files, we know that at least the start of the simulation depicts the situation as it actually is.

Once the input data are in our model, we can start them through the different phases to see how the organization structure varies under the policies. In the first two phases, we observe the loss of manpower from the organization caused by retirement and attrition. In the third phase we have told the computer what the workload requirement will be so that we know how many positions we will have to fill at some future date under certain policies.

A workforce simulator, therefore, is an example of an imaginative use of a personnel data system to provide top management with the type of data needed for long-range planning. It can tell us the effect of different manpower policies without our having to try them out in actuality. The particular simulator described is pretty crude compared with those used is science and engineering; however, we are learning as we go along and will no doubt develop more sophisticated models in the future.

Another use of a personnel system is the skills inventory, which is becoming more and more necessary as our technologies change faster. In today's dynamic business world, technology is expanding so fast that it is shrinking the development cycles and cutting manufacturing lead time. Management must be able to bring its forces to bear on the uses of new technology or risk losing a market. People are the main thrust of those forces. Knowing their capabilities and their skills is absolutely a must. To a personnel man, it might seem quite enough to say that a man is a staff engineer in a department responsible for electronic components. To the laboratory manager who must assign this man to another development project, this description leaves many questions unanswered. What actually did the man do? Did he design, analyze, test? Did he work on solid state components? What can he do? What does he want to do?

In order to solve this problem we developed and tested lists of skill terms. The employee chooses the terms which best describe his work experience. These lists were built through discussions with a statistically sound sample of people intimately associated with each particular field. On each list a space was provided for write-in entries so that the list does not confine the individual to the vocabulary of the system but allows for flexibility in the vocabulary.

Designers of the system set out to determine what management looks for in people. It was evident after thorough analysis of written requisitions and interviews with management that the following categories of information were needed:

1. General field of work.
2. Specific areas within that field.
3. Products which were worked on.
4. Experience with specialized instruments and machines.

5. Foreign languages.
6. What work the man would like to do.

In designing the system, an effort was made to attain the highest degree of flexibility in search, maintenance, and output operations. The master skills tape is created from cards punched from data-collection sheets. When the master tape is established and each time an employee record is changed, a profile is printed out. The employee and his manager each receive a copy of the profile with a request to review it for accuracy and validity. Other copies are maintained in the personnel department.

We are also able to produce a skills-frequency listing. This lists all employees by a particular skill and may be used to provide quantitative skills data on how many people we have in certain categories without instituting a special search. If line management wants to know, for example, how many people we have in the company that design cryogenic circuits, we are now in a position to say exactly what the number is.

Of course, the most immediate value of a skills inventory is the assistance it gives to individual placement. The system is flexible enough for the manager to indicate on a single requisition what attributes the individual must have in order to qualify for the position, as well as a series of other qualifications that represent alternatives, any one of which will satisfy the requisition. The former situation is called the "must" condition; the latter the "or" condition. The computer searches and picks out the individuals who fill the requisition. It prints out sheets with the name, department, job code, and any "or" conditions which the individual matches. One can determine at one glance the most qualified individuals in terms of experience. It must be emphasized at this point that the manager, not the computer, makes the final decision. Thus the job of the computer is to narrow the field to potential candidates, just as the personnel manager would do; only the machine does this faster and probably more objectively without overlooking anyone. The skills inventory, I feel, will be one of the most useful tools in our kit in future years.

In the not-too-distant future, the personnel man could also have a visual-display device like a small television screen sitting on his desk. Attached to it would be a remote-inquiry unit that could communicate with a distant computer. If the president of the company should ask for a person with certain qualification, the personnel man could key in the information on a typewriter-like device, push a button, and within seconds the names of people with the right qualifications would appear on the screen.

If he decided to look at an employee's file more closely, he could check off a name with an electronic pen, push another button, and see his complete job resume appear on the screen—or push a button and see his picture appear. If this person did not satisfy him, he could easily bring back the original list. Or maybe it is a report or compilation that he needs. These, too, can be programmed into the machine so that a push of the button will cause files to be scanned and reports prepared.

This may seem to be a little farfetched to some. However, the equipment I have described exists today and is operable. It is not technology that is holding us back; it is our own vision and imagination. If we are really serious about turning personnel into a profession, then we should adopt a more professional attitude toward tools and techniques. I believe that if personnel is to accomplish its basic mission, it must create and use a personnel system.

One of the serious problems in large organizations is the antithesis between centralized policy-setting and management on the one hand, and on the other hand, the decentralization of individual actions. Although the desire to decentralize personnel action is often advocated, it is extremely difficult to do so unless there are easy and rapid communication channels between the policy and management echelons and the action-taking echelons. Because these communication channels are so frequently blocked or unavailable, there is a tendency for the level of approval to creep upward to higher echelons with a loss of flexibility and adjustment to individual needs. I believe that the advent of modern information processing has made it possible to achieve a level of both centralization and decentralization, which was not possible previously.

I would like to introduce this subject by telling a true story involving the late Walter Van Dyke Bingham. Dr. Bingham was one of the early psychologists who served in World War I and helped develop the old Army Alpha and Beta tests. In World War II, Dr. Bingham was called back to the Adjutant General's Office as the chief civilian advisor on selection and classification. Many of us young fellows tended to look on Dr. Bingham as a somewhat elderly gentleman who, while undoubtedly wise in the lore of testing, was not really quite up on the latest techniques. In those days, Eleanor Roosevelt wrote a newspaper column called "My Day." Early in World War II she published a column in which she talked about the poor practices of the Army in assigning and classifying its personnel. She cited the case of a brilliant young lawyer she was acquainted with, who had been inducted and, according to her, completely misassigned into a machinist's training organization for which she said he was totally unfit. In a refined way, she took the Army to task for its bad performance in assigning personnel. This article greatly distressed Dr. Bingham, and he felt that Mrs. Roosevelt was uninformed regarding the work of the Adjutant General's Office, and particularly the Personnel Research Section. Because Dr. Bingham had so many acquaintances from his World War I days, he was able to call on Frances Perkins, who at that time was Secretary of Labor, and suggest to her that Mrs. Roosevelt might like to know more about Army personnel practices. Mrs. Perkins assured Dr. Bingham that Mrs. Roosevelt certainly would, and acted as an intermediary to invite Mrs. Roosevelt to the Adjutant General's Office. I remember one day when Mrs. Rooselvelt arrived, and Dr. Bingham escorted her into our temporary building and explained what we were doing and the efforts being made to develop tests and procedures to assure the proper assignment and utilization of personnel. Generals hovered about, and Dr. Bingham was at his gentlemanly best. A few days later Mrs. Roosevelt wrote another "My Day" column, in which she praised the Army and talked about the excellent efforts being led by Dr. Bingham and his psychologists. Now, either fortunately or unfortunately, both of her articles, in my opinion, had a considerable degree of truth to them. While we psychologists were trying very hard to devise sound classification methods, the Army also had quotas for many different kinds of assignments and training schools. These assignments had to be made in accordance with schedules, and since induction stations were scattered throughout the country and training was likewise scattered many places, the best each local assignment officer could do was to fulfil the assignment he had at a particular time. As a result many inductees were mal-assigned. Today this is no longer necessary because we have abundant, high-speed communication and the possibility of transmitting information through netted computer-based personnel systems.

An office known as the Management Information Office is established at most major commands and is the interface point between the Personnel Data System and the functional area users. The Management Information Office is responsible for maintenance, processing, distribution, and analysis of data contained in the Personnel Data System for Officers and the Interim Personnel Data System for Airmen.

The personnel organization at the base level is standard throughout the Air Force, with the manning level at the Consolidated Base Personnel Office varying with the number of base personnel being serviced. It is responsible for maintenance, processing, and distribution of data in the personnel system. It also provides the interface between the PDS system for officer and airmen personnel operations.

The traditional separation of military personnel functions has been reflected in the creation of a two-part automated data system, the Personnel Data System for Officers (PDS/O) and the Personnel Data System for Airmen (PDS/A). These systems receive data from the Military Personnel Center, the Major Commands and the Consolidated Base Personnel Offices, the majority of data being introduced at the base level. The users of personnel data are also located at these three echelons and receive products from the system for use in accomplishing their management and personnel operations tasks. Almost the only use of personnel data by Air Force agencies in the Pentagon is for management purposes; at the other levels more use of the data is made for operational than for management purposes; but both are necessary.

The present officer personnel data system evolved from a model implemented. This prototype provided the operational experience and preliminary data base necessary for implememting an improved model. The present system uses computer processing at the Military Personnel Center and the Major Commands and punched card equipment at the bases. At each echelon a different kind of computer capability is used for personnel data processing.

The Personnel Data System for Officers was designed and implemented to process personnel data on large number of Air Force officers. Some of the characteristics of the system are:

1. A larger data base with standardized data elements.
2. Use of disc files at the MPC.
3. A remote inquiry capability at the MPC.
4. Standardized computer programs for processing data within and between echelons.
5. Standardized computer programs for inquiry purposes.
6. Standardized procedures for processing data.
7. Standardized hardware at the Major Commands.

Due to the limited equipment capability of the bases, the data for the system have been specified in terms of 80 column cards. The Uniform Officer Record includes 10 basic cards and, in addition, the system requires six transaction cards and eight types of miscellaneous cards.

The information in the data base falls into the three groups shown below.

Personnel Data System for Officers

Uniform Officer Record Information	*Transaction Information*	*Miscellaneous Information*
Strength Data	PDS Availability Data	Grade Spread Summary
Organizational Data	Accession/ Levy/ Allocation	Name-Service No. Change
Service Data		
Assignment Data	Reassignment Request	MAC Add-on
Availability Data	Projected Promotion	Personnel Accounting Symbol
Education Data	Projected Separation	MPC Local Data Series
Dependent Data	Projected Integration	MAC Local Data
Aeronautical Data		CBPO Local Data
Rated Qualification Data		CBPO Suspense Data
Rated History Data		
Previous Duty Data		
Current/ Previous Duty Title		

The main purpose of PDS/O is to assist the functional managers at the Pentagon, the Military Personnel Center, the Major Commands, and the bases in carrying out their specific missions. Included in these functional areas are officer assignment, retirements, promotions, separations, and, to a limited degree personnel analyses. In addition, such items as the monitoring of flying status, regular appointments, and selection for in-service schools are considered part of the personnel missions. In general, the system has been designed to bring about improvements in: (1) availability of timely, accurate and compatible data, (2) assignment actions, (3) personnel accounting, (4) notification of individual moves, (5) the selection process, and (6) stability in the personnel force, so that the most suitable men for the available jobs may be selected at minimal cost.

The personnel data system described above is a very important step forward in the expeditious and efficient handling of individuals within general management policies, but there are other developments which promise to make such systems even more useful in the assignment and career management aspects of personnel actions. Recently at SDC we have been working on an automated counseling system. While this work has been oriented toward the public school situation, it is easy to see that it could be easily adapted to the military counseling and assignment environment.

Two programs were written—one to review the student's record and provide the counselor with an appraisal automatically, and another to conduct an automated interview with the student.

The selection of each question depends both on the student's previous answers and on the information about him that has been previously stored in the machine. After a number of questions and answers, the interview will terminate in a schedule of suggested courses that is uniquely tailored to that student. Thus, student will be aided in selecting their subjects by answering a series of questions presented by the computer. This system should relieve the counselor of much routine work and at the same time be sufficiently sensitive to extraordinary responses so that the student needing expert help will be directed to the counselor for individual attention.

To help the counselor in preparation for either an automated or live interview, programs have been written which use the same rules as an experienced counselor in analyzing the information in the student's cumulative folder. This program was designed to simulate a specific counselor who was asked to "think aloud" as he analyzed twenty student cumulative folders prior to counseling interviews. Analysis showed that most of the pre-interview logic, as well as the interview itself, is specifiable and capable of being programmed. The pre-interview program accepts data similar to that which is normally found in the cumulative folder, such as grades, aptitude test scores, and biographical information. By making various comparisons of these data, the program prints messages for the counselor which are unique for each student. Messages regarding different students might be:

1. Student's grades have gone down quite a bit. Ask about this in interview. Possibly there are personal problems.
2. This student should be watched closely. He will probably need remedial courses.
3. Student is a potential drop-out.
4. Should be headed for college. Encourage student to explore widely in academic areas.
5. Low counseling priority. No problems apparent.
6. Student should improve verbal skills. If not, student may not be able to attain desired academic goals.

In continuing the application of information processing technology in vocational counseling under field conditions, our study team is now in the process of conducting an extensive survey of vocational education installations, including state employment agencies and private and municipal vocational guidance projects. When the survey is completed, a sample field site will be selected for a detailed analysis of counseling procedures, and then a computer-based man-machine counseling system will be developed by a team that will include the counselors at the selected field site.

The computer-based system will have a data base containing student information—with an input-output system for updating and retrieving information. Computer programs in the system will provide appraisals of student data, interviewing procedures, tracking of student performance and identification of students who are experiencing difficulty.

PERSONNEL DECISION MAKING

In this text we conceive personnel functions as centering on decision making. The purpose of this section is to (1) describe this decision-making process as it exists in an interrelated systems sense and (2) indicate how the approach mentioned at the beginning of this chapter—contingency views—may aid such decision-making. Action, evaluate the merits of each, select one or more of these alternatives, and implement the alternative (s) chosen. If the firm's safety objectives are not being met, for example, personnel management might.

- ☐ Generate such possible courses of action as increasing expenditures for safety training, instituting a safety contest, or replacing the firm's present safety director with a more effective one.
- ☐ Evaluate the costs and probable effectiveness in reducing the number and seriousness of accidents, etc., of each alternative.
- ☐ Select one or more of these alternatives (say expanding safety training).
- ☐ Actually implement this course of action by setting up a particular training program.

A schematic model of this decision process is shown in Figure 2.

Personnel decisions such as these are not made in isolation. Rather, like all management decisions, they affect and are affected by other management decisions and actions and by forces outside the organization. Looking at decisions in such an interrelated sense is often referred to as taking a systems view of decision-making.

The word *system* has been defined in many different ways. We will consider a system to represent a complex of elements interacting with each other to form a unified whole. Scholars have classified systems into two "pure" types: closed and open. Closed systems, theoretically, are isolated from any external environment and over time become more and more disorganized.

Open systems, on the other hand, consist both of elements mutually interacting within the system and of those that mutually interact to varying degrees with their external environment. Fur-

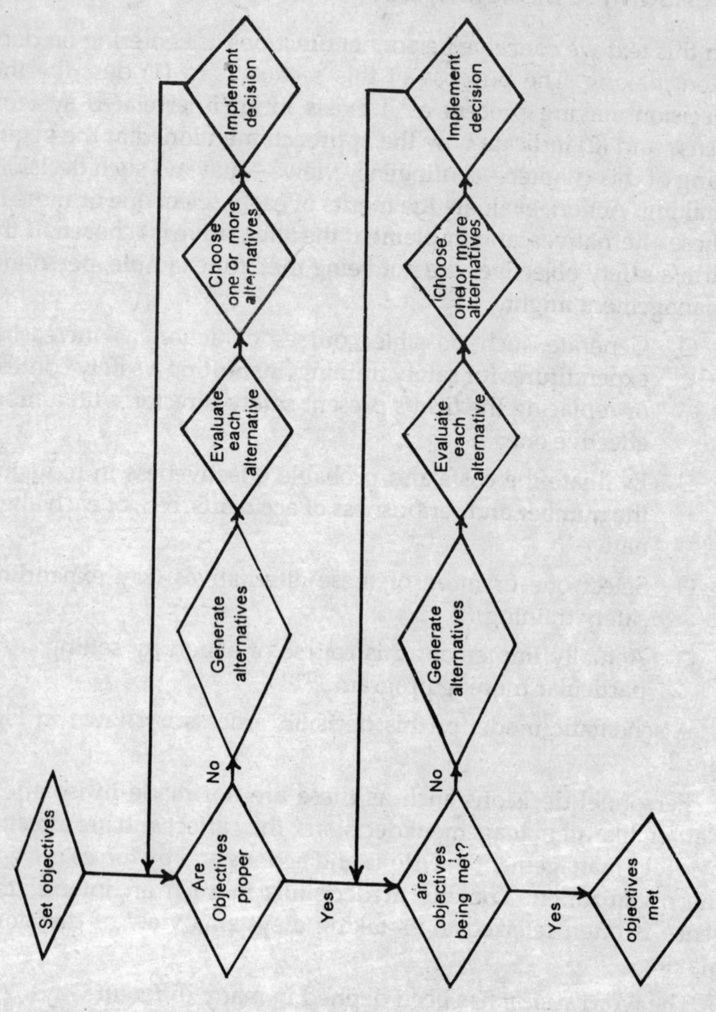

Fig. 2. Diagram showing decision making process.

ther, they may exhibit tendencies toward increasing order rather than disorder. These systems are of much greater concern to personnel managers, because their organization, their own and other departments, groups within such departments, and individuals within such groups all represent systems "open" to varying extents and in mutual interaction with their environments. By *mutual interaction* we mean situations in which one change in a system or its environment will lead to another, which in turn will influence the one originally modified.

For example, within an organization, establishment of a new retirement system by the personnel department may influence certain production managers to retire sooner, which may, in turn, make it necessary for the personnel department to develop a speeded-up training program for their replacements. Or, with respect to a firm's external environment, the personnel department may raise the educational requirements for a particular job. This action may lead to job applicants increasing their salary demands, which would, in turn, require personnel to modify starting salaries for that job. From these two examples, we can see that when viewed in systems terms, there is considerable interdependence among decisions made in the different personnel functions already described. Also, personnel operates interdependently with other departments in the firm, as well as with the firm's environment. These relationships are illustrated in Figure 3.

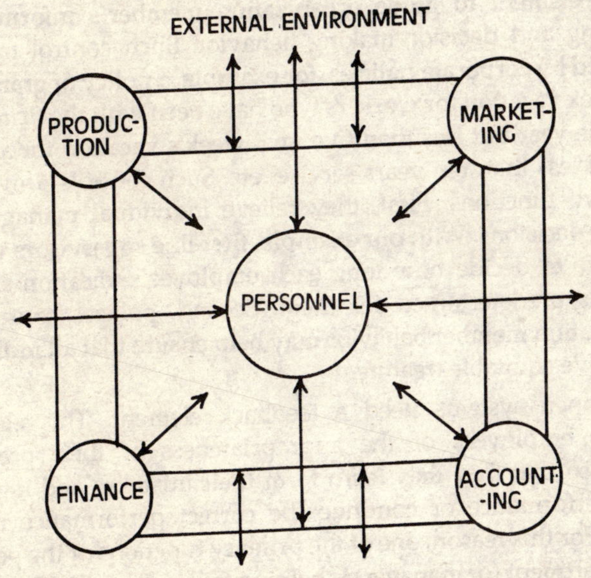

Fig. 3. Personnel decision-making system.

Personnel decision-making in a systems sense may also be thought of as comprising several different kinds of elements. Essentially, the systems view conceives of decisions as transforming informational inputs into outputs or courses of action. For example, personnel managers may be required to transform information about job applicants into an output recommendation, such as to hire the individuals, not hire them, or run a further background check on them. Informational inputs are especially important to personnel managers because the environment with which they are in mutual interaction is a probabilistic one, and they need to be able to predict future events to some extent. The entire human resource forecasting function, for example, provides management with information upon which to base recruitment, selection, and other decisions. The use of statistical data concerning the probable on-the-job success of job applicants obtaining certain psychological test scores provides another example of the need for and value of predictive information in the selection function.

Personnel management also requires the establishment of a control element to guide organization member's information-gathering and decision-making behavior. Such control may be provided by corporate policies, for example, a policy of granting a one-week vacation for workers who have been with the firm more than one year but less than five, two week's vacation for at least five but less than ten years service, etc. Such controls provide at least two functions. First, they relieve individual managers of making decisions. With our example, first-line supervisors would not have to decide how long each employee's vacation should be—it is predetermined for them. Second, policies controlling organization member behavior may help ensure that all individuals receive equitable treatment.

All open systems need a feedback element. This element informs employees of the appropriateness of their previous actions so that they may learn form their mistakes and improve their performance or continue the correct performance in the future. For this reason, one of the primary functions of the personnel department (or manager) is helping to develop a viable performance appraisal system for the organization. Under such systems, the organizational member's performance is periodically reviewed by their superiors, and information is often fed back to them to help them improve their performance.

To function properly, those engaged in personnel management need to have a memory element to store past information that can guide them in making future decisions. Data may be stored in the human mind, in the organization's manual files, or in computerized information storage and retrieval systems. The last, of course, is being used more and more frequently, as our computer technology continues to improve in cost and effectiveness.

From this discussion, we can see that personnel management centers around interdependent decisions in which information plays a critical role.

Contingency Views

In years past many management theorists tended to overgeneralize about the ways in which management should manage. Some, for example, stressed the importance of maintaining effective human relations in organizations, while others prescribed organizational behavior characterized by formal rules and relationships, a rigid hierarchy, a "rational" decision-making process in which personnel desires and feelings would be ignored, and high degree of worker specialization.

More recently, those studying management have taken more balanced "contingency" views of the ways in which organizations, including personnel functions, should be managed. Contingency views all begin with the premise that there is no single type of organizational structure, design, or decision-making process that is best for all organizations in general. Rather, they emphasize that the effectiveness of any particular management decision depends on the specific conditions faced by a particular organization existing in a particular environment. Contingency views are important to personnel decision making because they do not ask the unanswerable general question "What personnel techniques are best?" Rather, they focus attention on a much more answerable specific question: "Under what conditions or contingencies will which personnel decision-making approaches be most appropriate?" In this section, we focus attention on some of the more important contingencies found to have important implications for personnel decision-making.

Degree of certainty. One important contingency in determining what types of management systems are most effective is the degree of certainty under which they operate. When an organization is operating under high environmental uncertainty, on the other hand, human relations orientations seem more appropriate. In view of Burns and Stalker, certainty and uncertainty are opposite poles of a continuum, with degrees of certainty existing in between. They referred to the most appropriate form of organizational structure at the certainty end of the continuum as *mechanistic* and that most effective at its polar opposite of uncertain as *organic.* The mechanistic form of structuring in its pure form has several characteristics.

- ☐ A precisely spelled out definitions of rights, obligations, and methods for each organizational member.
- ☐ A hierarchical structure of control, authority, and communications.
- ☐ A tendency toward a high degree of task specialization for employees.

On the other hand, the organic structure in its pure form is characterized by such human relations—behavioral science orientations as:

- ☐ A movement away from the idea that responsibility is a limited area of rights, rules, obligations, methods, etc.
- ☐ A more lateral form of communication to individuals considered as colleagues rather than precisely defined orders received from the top down in the organization.
- ☐ In general, a more democratic, flexible, free-flowing internal environment as opposed to a more authoritarian one that emphasizes orders, commands, rights, rules, regulations, and other bureaucratic features.

Several comments are in order concerning environmental certainty, the organic-mechanistic framework, and personnel management. First, the organic-mechanistic continuum is quite logical in relation to certainty-uncertainty when one gives it a little thought. When organizations operate under fairly certain conditions, it is possible for them to spell out clearly specific rules of behavior for their members to follow. On the other hand, when operating conditions are not very certain and the organization does not know what the future will bring, it is difficult to prescribe behavior, and the organization is almost forced to give more decision-making latitude to its members to handle uncertainty as it arises. For example, psychological tests cannot be developed to guide the personnel manager's selection of job applicants who will be successful on any particular job five years in the future if organizational conditions are so uncertain that management is unsure of what the jobs will entail at that time. Rather, under such conditions personnel managers may only be able to make an intuitive appraisal of job applicants' future performance based on their own experience and judgment.

Second, historically the organization's technology has been emphasized as a key factor contributing to the degree of certainty it faces and hence the appropriateness of organic as opposed to mechanistic management styles. Today, however, it is recognized that uncertainty and technology are not the only variables that may influence the organization's choice as to where to operate along the organic-mechanistic continuum. For example, the following internal and external variables have been considered important with respect to this decision: the education and skills of organization personnel; the firm's customers, suppliers, and competitors; manager personalities; and the perceptions of and tolerance for ambiguity and uncertainty of organization members.

Third, we should emphasize that different organizational units within a firm may be exposed to different degrees of uncertainty, and hence desire to take a more organic or mechanistic approach to management than other units within the organization. Organizations often attempt and are able to protect their "core technologies" from uncertainty—for example, by decoupling or making independent their manufacturing process from the direct influence of customer demand by introducing inventories. On the other hand, there may be no way whatsoever to reduce uncertainty in a firm's research department. Finally, and of special importance to us, is the fact that with such wide differences in organizational climates, we will find different types of personnel decision-making techniques most appropriate under different conditions.

Change. A second key contingency influencing the types of personnel decision-making approaches that will be effective under different conditions is the degree of change faced by an organization or one of its units. Some organizational situations are relatively stable or static, while others are highly dynamic.

The degree of change existing in organizations has certain basic implications for personnel decision making. First, formal policies, procedures, and programs must be updated more frequently in dynamic organizational situations than in static ones. All other factors being the same, the more frequent the updating is required the more costly it will be for the organization, up to a point. These costs may be relatively high or low, depending upon the particular programs or policies needing updating. To the extent that updating costs are substantial, there will be pressures in organizations to choose more organic types of personnel systems, where there will be a lesser degree of formalization and greater latitude to make decisions for individuals dealing with personnel problems.

For example, in a relatively static environment, the personnel manager may supervise the development of a formal training program for new employees in a department, which can be used over and over again because organizational conditions do not change much.

On the other hand, a formal program for new employees in a highly dynamic research and development department, for instance, may become obsolete in a few months, and its development costs may not be justified in terms of usage. In such a department, it might well be much more feasible to have the department head or a senior employee conduct the necessary training for new employees on a more flexible basis, changing the content of the training informally as organizational conditions change.

In a related manner, the updating of personnel procedures may help create human problems, leading managers in dynamic operations to avoid formalization for this reason as well as on a pure cost basis.

Size. Another important contingency in personnel decision-making is organizational size. Increased attention has been given to this variable, although it has been defined in many different ways and care must be exercised in its discussion.

We will focus on one facet of the complex phenomenon of size: the number of employees who will be exposed to any particular personnel technique or program. With respect to this variable, two general observations may be made:

1. The number of persons exposed to a personnel technique or program may vary widely within any given firm, depending on the particular employees involved and the technique or program in question. For example, the number of blue-collar job applicants given a psychological test in a large manufacturing company during any given year may be much greater than the number of its management trainees who are exposed to a computer-assisted instruction program in that same period.
2. For any particular job, firms employing smaller numbers of people will generally need to expose fewer people to any given personnel program or technique than firms employing more people on that job. For example, assuming the same selection procedures and employee turnover, a small commercial airline would not have to train as many newly hired flight attendants as the nation's largest airline in any given year.

Information systems has found an unshakable place in decision- making process. This worlds machines have, due to technological changes and need to process the vast amount of data in a short time, become indispensable. Their contribution to decision-making process in the personnel management systems cannot be over emphasized.

INFORMATION SYSTEMS AND MANAGEMENT OF MANPOWER RESOURCES

A man's job has significance and importance to him: it determines his standard and style of living; it shapes his planning for the future; and, if he is in the right job, it increases his chances for personal satisfaction along with material reward. A man's job is also significant and important to his employer, for it represents an investment as well as a potential source of profit. Part of that investment is in dollars, but the far more vital factor is the investment in the human resource represented by the individual assigned to the job. If a person is in the right job, he sees a challenge, responds by growing in intellect and mastery of the task, and effectively produces the desired results. Thus both employee and employer benefit by sound matching of an individual and a job. This business of placement, of assigning a specific individual to a specific task, is generally termed "the selection process."

Throughout industry today, two broad changes are occurring with regard to jobs. The first is the gradual disappearance of certain types and styles of jobs. The second is the rapid introduction of brand new jobs—jobs nobody deemed of even five years ago. These trends force managers to ask themselves (1) where they can best use the resources represented by veteran employees whose jobs no longer exist; and (2) where in the organization are the employees with the background to successfully fill the new jobs.

Just how do most people arrive at their present jobs? They may arrive at their positions or lines of work by plan and design. Early in life such a person may develop a particular skill or demonstrate a particular interest. Chances are that counseling at home or at school encourages his interest in that skill, and points him toward a particular field. After such a person undergoes formal specialized education., he begins a career that, to a great extent, he has anticipated. Others travel a different route. For one reason or another, they gain exposure in a variety of fields. They may change college majors once, twice, or even three times before attaining degree. Their work records show a similar series of changes to jobs of different types and with varying levels of success. Modern corporations need people of both types. Complex technology creates a continuing demand for specialists highly trained in a particular field. At the same time there is evident need for individuals with sufficient background and flexibility to adapt to and adequately discharge the duties of those jobs still to be developed.

These trends create management decision-making problems. There is often some difficulty in picking the right man to fill a long- existing and standardized job. And picking the right man for a job that never before existed is considerably more of a problem. Almost invariably these needs force modern management to decide whether to go outside the organization for new employees or to search within the organization for people who can be retrained to fill the new job. Most companies prefer to retrain available employees. This preference puts the selection process squarely in the picture, for now the manager must identify specific individuals who should be considered. He may know what qualifications and experience he intends to use as a criteria, but where can he look to discover who has these qualifications and experience? The obvious answer is the personnel file; but, like most obvious answers, this one has its weaknesses.

This grab-bag method gives little assurance that any job is being filled by the best available candidate. Sooner or later those qualified individuals who have been overlooked are likely to lose their drive and desire to perform for the company and lapse into indifferent performance. Or they may retain their ambition but take it, along with their qualifications, to another employer. Neither result benefits the company that overlooked their potential.

The next step is an analysis of the information needs spelled out by the managers surveyed, using the answers to the third and fourth questions. The survey results showed that we were recording and gathering much if not all the information we would expect to be useful in the selection process. But we could only guess how much of it was being used. The manner of gathering and processing convinced us that much available information was never even considered. There is evidence that people needing specific available information did not know the information existed or, if they did, simply could not afford the time required to locate it.

The matching of skills to the qualifications descriptions could become a major task, even with machine methods, depending on how far we expect the machine to carry the matching step. Our general view is that the computer should be relied on for preliminary matching but not the actual selection of a specific job, for some aspects of selection will always require the human element. The way a man speaks, the way he dresses, and the way he listens are among the attributes that may be important in a specific selection. So the most we expect from the machine is a rough screening of the available work force to identify available, eligible candidates. Using the computer for this screening offers definite advantages to the manager who must make the actual choice. First, it minimizes the possibility that a qualified candidate will be overlooked. Second, by speeding up the preliminary screening, it increases the time available for making the final choice.

What are we asking for specifically? To begin with, we want a new language that is completely user-oriented. This language must be designed for and geared to the needs of the user. It should be uncomplicated, easy to learn, easy to use. The language should avoid the vocabulary of the computer specialist in favor of the vocabulary of the managers in accounting, personnel, production control, and similar areas. It must be structured to allow such users to retrieve, manipulate, and display the information they desire. The language must be dynamic rather than static, and it must have the ability to grow and be adapted to meet the ever changing needs of its management users.

Once we agree that a new language can be written, we can start thinking about the data base. Each element in the data base should be made up of a group of characters that cannot be divided further and still have independent meaning. a dictionary must be provided which shows each data element and its specific definition. This system should be so designed that new data can be entered into and extracted from the data base by use of the new language. And our users—by means of data elements, numbers, or some other device provided by the data processing professionals—should be able to retrieve a single data element, a complete record, or a collection of files simply by feeding an appropriate language statement into the computer.

The filing system for the data base must also be user-oriented. It should be designed to facilitate storage and retrieval of large blocks of data. We want our users to be able to do this without having to develop an extensive knowledge of the file organization used in the system.

There must be a control device for the data base. Obviously, personnel records of any scope contain certain material of a sensitive nature. Therefore the system should include security passwords which the data processing group would assign to users departments so that confidential elements would be available only to persons holding the security password.

Another goal in the design of the system is efficient utilization of the equipment. However, the most important goal is the creation of a man-machine interface that makes retrieval of information easy and fast. The word "fast" represents the first mention of the time factor for the system. "Real time" in this system will be defined to mean the time period which the user establishes as the limit within which the response to his inquiry must be received if the information is to have any value. The total of real time effectively utilized will have a direct bearing on the user-cost of the system.

You may question the practicality of the system requirements outlined. Perhaps such a system demands too much from electronic data processing as an aid to managers who must make the most of their available man-power resources. But consider this observation that resulted from my work on the project described. Manpower always has been and always will be the most precious resource of any society, nation, or corporation. Today, managers complain that manpower is becoming their most expensive resource. The truth is that manpower is expensive only when it is misused.

Better EDP systems and better methods for utilizing such systems can and will enable business and industry to improve its management of human resources. Obviously, business and industry would benefit by this. But more important, the society served by business and industry stands to be better served when its most valuable resource is more effectively applied.

And of utmost importance, the individual himself will benefit. For when he finds the task that presents the challenge that stirs fullest development of his capabilities, he makes his greatest contribution and attains the fullest reward of satisfaction and achievement of his own potential.

THE PERSONNEL DEPARTMENT

The personnel department in organizations is in a unique position. If well managed, it may become involved in a wider range of activities than any other function in the organization. At the same time, every person in the organization is a "personnel person," in the sense that each is dealing with personnel decision problems on a day-to-day basis. For example, first-line supervisors training or disciplining their employees, encouraging them to follow safety standards, and so forth, are engaged in personnel decision-making.

In this chapter, we will focus attention on several key facets of the operation of the personnel department and consider some of the more important problems it faces. This chapter is divided into three sections. First, we will make some observations about individuals occupying personnel positions and the work that they perform. Second, we will view personnel as a staff department and show what roles it performs and what problems it may face assuming such roles. Third, we will turn our attention to the power and stature of today's personnel department.

The Personnel Manger and Personnel Work

Personnel work is heterogeneous. The people who perform it have many different backgrounds and serve many different functions. Such differences are not hard to explain, considering the diversity of personnel work. Training and development activities call for backgrounds in learning theory and psychology; backgrounds in both psychology and engineering would be useful in safety management, whereas labor relations work is highly legalistic and economic in orientation.

There is also considerable diversity with respect to degree of specialization in personnel work. Some people doing personnel work are generalists, who deal with many diverse problems and work with many different people on a day-to-day basis. For example, the personnel manager in a geographical division of a supermarket chain might be engaged on any single day in such activities as placing a newspaper advertisement for clerical help to work in a new store, explaining pension rights to employees who are about to retire, or handling medical insurance claims for other employees.

At the other extreme, in many larger organizations we find (in addition to personnel generalists) a number of highly specialized personnel professionals. For example, in one company there were about 30 managers and professionals in the firm's corporate headquarters, each performing specialized personnel functions. One individual dealt with nothing but wage and salary administration; another, who was not a manager, spent much time developing training materials for the firm's management development programs; and so forth.

Two final observations concerning degree of specialization in personnel work are in order. First is that the top personnel manager of any operating unit must be a generalist. The specialists mentioned in the last example all reported to managers who were under the direction of a generalist personnel vice president. This individual was responsible for all personnel work undertaken in the company just as the super-market personnel manager was responsible for all personnel work in a geographical division.

The second observation is that this discussion should quickly dispel the notion held by some individuals not familiar with personnel work that they would like to get into personnel because they like dealing with people. As we have seen, the supermarket personnel manager had many daily contacts with people. The individual developing training materials, however, spent many weeks at a time working on projects, often alone, and with only moderate interaction with others. Thus, people with quite different interests and personalities may find satisfaction in some type of personnel work.

That the personnel manager's focus of attention will vary as the firm goes through such cycles may be illustrated by a few examples. As a new product is introduced, manufacturing processes need debugging and personnel may be required to help industrial engineers set methods and time standards. Once the product has reached the growth stage, considerable effort is needed to recruit and train additional workers. At the decline stage, on the other hand, personnel may aid displaced workers in finding other jobs in the firm, and in some cases may encourage workers who are unable to be relocated to take an early retirement.

Although there has not been a great deal of research on the personnel department's role in life-cycle analysis, certain hypotheses of a contingency nature may be made. In some industries, such as department stores, there are relatively few if any major "products" being developed, although such industries may experience growth, maturity, and decline. therefore, the life-cycle type of analysis may not be highly relevant for personnel managers in such operations. At the other extreme, however, explicit recognition, even to the extent of developing special types of organizational structures to meet project life-cycle needs, has occurred in industries such as aerospace. Here, during the life cycle of many projects, such as a five-year ballistic missile project, "the bulk of the engineering efforts required might be expended during the first two years... [and then] ... at a later time, the number of production man hours required for the project would be at its maximum."

The important point to be gained from this discussion is that personnel managers should be familiar enough with their organization's operations that they can plan ahead to meet the human resource requirements of all phases of product life cycles. Unfortunately, some surveys have shown that majority of corporate personnel managers have not known such key operational variables as what the dollar volume of their company's sales was or what their firm's profit level was. In light of this, it is not surprising that one chief executive officer of a firm "when asked what qualifications he would like to see in his personnel director, replied, 'The ability to read and understand the company's financial statement.'" Another aspect of personnel work that has not received sufficient attention is the impact of economic conditions on the personnel department. Historically it seems that interest in personnel management often been highest when economic conditions are good or expanding and labor is in short supply. When conditions are poor or contracting and there is an oversupply of labor, however, the interest in personnel management often appears to fade.

Three reasons for such conditions can be put forth. First, much of the work of personnel cannot be shown directly to affect sales and profits. The absence of a production worker or a salesperson, on the other hand, often can be seen to result directly in reduced production or sales. In bad times, therefore, persons in marketing and production are more likely to be retained than are those in personnel. Second, organizations may believe that they can hire more freely in bad times because of the oversupply of labor. Therefore, they may be less concerned with such personnel functions as recruitment, selection, and training and development. Third, there may be a real decrease in the need for certain types of personnel work. For example, if a firm is not hiring, it may make sense to curtail its recruiting activities. Similarly, if workers have been laid off, there may not be much of a need for training and development programs, particularly if the retained workers are experienced.

In spite of poor economic conditions from time to time, however, the personnel department's scope of activities has continued to expand historically. Even in poor times, most established personnel programs are not completely eliminated—they are only cut back.

PERSONNEL ADMINISTRATION

Personnel Administration is best understood in terms of its three elements. First, it is a specialized body of knowledge developed primarily over the past 80 years. Second, it is a viewpoint, and hence expresses a philosophy or a value set. Third, it consists of specialized methods, tolls, and techniques through which its viewpoint is implemented. A central principle is that people are an organization's most important asset.

Definition

Personnel administration may be defined as a well-wounded, planned, executed, and evaluated approach to employee recruitment, use, and development. It draws on a number of related disciplines (especially the behavioral sciences), psychology, sociology, anthropology, law, economics, education, and industrial engineering to name a few. The role of personnel administration in a business organization has undergone historical change from that of mainly record keeping, to employment, to providing for the employee's welfare, to a comprehensive approach to human resource allocation and utilization.

Objectives

The overall task of personnel administration is to study and develop new ways in which human beings can be integrated effectively into the various organizations of our society. This requires that human resources be efficiently utilized, that positive working relationships be promoted among all members of the organization, and that maximum individual development be provided for and encouraged. Hence, its objectives are economic, social, and personal. It is not a series of human relations gimmicks, although admittedly in its earlier history, instances of exploitation, insincerity, and employee manipulation could be evidenced. today, such questionable practices occur ever less frequently as the concept of human dignity increasingly influences personnel thinking.

Personnel administration contributes as much to profit as do other line activities. It is not a practice to be engaged in during times of profit making and full employment only to be discarded during difficult economic periods. On the contrary, god personnel practices can be even more advantageous to the organization when the profit squeeze is on.

Organizational Relationships

The term Personnel Manager is actually a misnomer. In a sense, all persons of management status are personnel managers (they manage people). Their results are achieved through the work of others. In small organizations, the personnel function is centralized. In large or geographically dispersed organizations, the personnel function is often decentralized from the parent organization but still locally centralized. In both, it will be a staff department activity, providing advice and expertise to line managers and top management.

This centralization of personnel activities has resulted from attempts to relieve line managers of some of the more routine chores, to utilize specialists in personnel who can advise and guide the line organization, and to assure a consistency and continuity in personnel practices. Early development and wide dissemination of good personnel polices by a company are ways of further ensuring consistency, but more important, they bring line management actively and with understanding into their personnel development role.

Personnel administration is a relatively late specialized area of general management, in contrast to production, engineering, marketing, and finance. But the need for it is as old as human organizations themselves. Thus, the owner and sole worker in a retail shop in the 1840s who, because of press of business, decided to employ one other person had engaged in the following personnel activities. First, he had to determine what the new employee was to do and what type of person he wanted (job analysis and hiring specification). He perhaps put a sign in his window or ran an and in the local paper (recruiting). Assuming he had more than one applicant for the position, he had more than one applicant for the position, he had to decide which applicant was to be employed (appraisal and selection). Starting wages had to be decided on (bargaining or wage surveying). Some training will have been needed for the new employee (on-the-job or apprenticeship training). As the new employee made progress, the owner will have had to evaluate his or her advancement in order to adjust wages and furnish further training (merit rating).

Approaches and Techniques

Personnel administration may be divided into three major areas. These are evaluation, motivation, and development of human resources.

Evaluation is made of the needs of the organization (organization charts and job analysis), of the human resources of an organization (performance appraisal and manpower inventory), and of how well the company is matching needs and resources (productivity indexes,employee attitude surveys, turnover ratios). It considers the company's long-range as well as immediate objectives (manpower/womanpower charts).

Motivation includes financial and non-financial incentives. It includes wage payment plans, both indirect as well as direct incentive plans. Fringe benefits and employee services are important indirect financial incentives. Non-financially, the establishment of an appropriate fit between the worker and the work, the worker and the work group, (group dynamics), and the work environment (safety and human engineering) are all basic to motivation.

Development would include, chronologically, presenting the job and orienting the new employee, on-the-job training, and preparation for advanced positions, managerial and technical. Day-to-day supervision and an open multi-directional employee communication system are important. Development will probably utilize intra-organizational, as well as external aids.

The above categories are somewhat artificial. In actual practice, an effective personnel program requires elements of all three. For example, good executive development programs require appropriate evaluation of what executives need and how well existing personnel are meeting these needs. It also must include a compensation structure which attracts and encourages the development of individuals who have the potential to assume executive positions. It involves, of course, continual training—both within, as in job rotation, and outside, as in attendance at formal educational institutions or management development institutes. Hence, personnel administration is best conceived and implemented as a total system.

Recent Developments

Personnel administration may be said to be conservative in contrast with marketing research, product development, and advertising. Effective personnel administration, however, results from the creativity we find in these other areas. It is appropriate and desirable that the most recent developments in personnel administration have derived from personnel research: research not only with respect to the effectiveness of internal personnel procedures, but in terms of the successful practices of other companies.

In the past two decades, large-scale changes have been taking place in personnel administration. In the area of philosophy and policy, a new emphasis on humanism and human resources has replaced the prior focus on human relations. The scope and areas of involvement of the personnel function have broadened considerably as new problem areas for resolution have emerged both in the organization and in its relationship to environment. There has been an increasing recognition among top managements of the vital role that personnel administration can and should play in the managing of change in organizations. A strong movement toward professionalization within the field has gathered momentum. And finally, the tools, methods, techniques, and approaches of the field have undergone important examination and refinement through increasing research, both from within the discipline and in response to pressures from state and Federal regulatory agencies. Each of these is considered in greater detail herein.

Technological advances, new social values and life styles, and a changing labor force have all combined to render the traditional value set of personnel administration increasingly inadequate to the challenge of the times. Thus, the challenge to today's personnel administration is not only fair treatment of employees, but the worker's expectation of *meaningful work* that uses their talents and interests and provides opportunity for individual advancement as well.

As a result of the changing business environment, new problem areas have emerged in the world of work to which personnel administration must now address itself. With the increasing number of multinational companies, personnel administration is increasingly extending its functions into areas of international operations, primarily in the staffing and compensation function. At home, our growing work force is rapidly changing in composition. Changes already under way include a growing proportion of young people in the labor force, greater numbers of female and minority group members, the fact that white collar workers now exceed blue collar workers, and the rapidly rising educational level of the work force.

Each of these developments presents new challenges and opportunities to personnel administration in its efforts to meet its objectives.

Within organizations, personnel administration has expanded its role in such areas as management development, organization planning, manpower planning, communications, and personnel research. All of these activities have a common denominator, namely, the management of change in organizations. Accordingly, a new identity has emerged for personnel administration–agent of change in the corporation. To meet these new demands, effective personnel practice has increasingly required administrators with advanced levels of education and training, flexible and innovative minds, and men and women with broad understanding, insights, and interpersonal skills. The attainment of professionalization in the personnel function is clear.

Advances in personnel administration, as in all fields, depend on the continuing refinement of existing procedures and techniques and the development of new ones. The behavioral sciences–organizational psychology, sociology, and anthropology—continue to make important contributions towards this end. In employee selection, culture-free measures, work sample tests, and limitation on the content of the interview, are among the important contributors to enhance the accuracy of and reduce discrimination in employment decisions. Promising developments are under way using electronic data processing in the rapid matching of applicant profiles of skills, aptitudes, and interests with actual job requirements. At the managerial level, role playing, in-basket tests, the leaderless group conference are among the more widespread selection techniques in use.

At the managerial level particularly, there has been a noticeable shift in emphasis from management training to management development. Essentially, the difference is one of moving from education in a narrow sense (training) to development, where the individual is prepared for a career in the firm rather than for a specific job. The term *organization development* represents the conceptual approach under which the total human resources of the firm are continually reviewed and renewed. Management games, programmed instruction, sensitivity training, systems-based supervisory training, behavior modeling, and assessment centers are examples of the newer approaches being taken.

Personnel as a Staff Department

Personnel is considered a staff department within the organization rather than a line one. Line operations in firms are normally those that deal directly with the organization's output—sales and production—while staff helps support these functions with professional expertise.

Traditionally, line managers were considered able to exercise command power over their subordinates, whereas staff managers could only advise or counsel line members in an organization. According to this view, in a manufacturing plant of 1500 to 2000 employees headed by a production manager, the latter would wield command power over all supervisors, who in turn would have command power over the production workers reporting to them. Personnel as a staff department, however, would report to the production manager and only have the power to render advice and counsel to the line organization. Such a relationship is illustrated in Figure 4. Personnel managers do, of course, have direct line relationships with their own subordinates and, hence have command power over them.

Of key significance is that this dichotomy of line and staff has been found to be an inadequate way of describing organizational relationships. In actual practice, the distinction between line and staff is a blurred one. In some situations, for example, personnel may technically only provide advice, but the advice would be so overwhelmingly strong that line would have no choice but to make the decision "recommended" by personnel. For example,

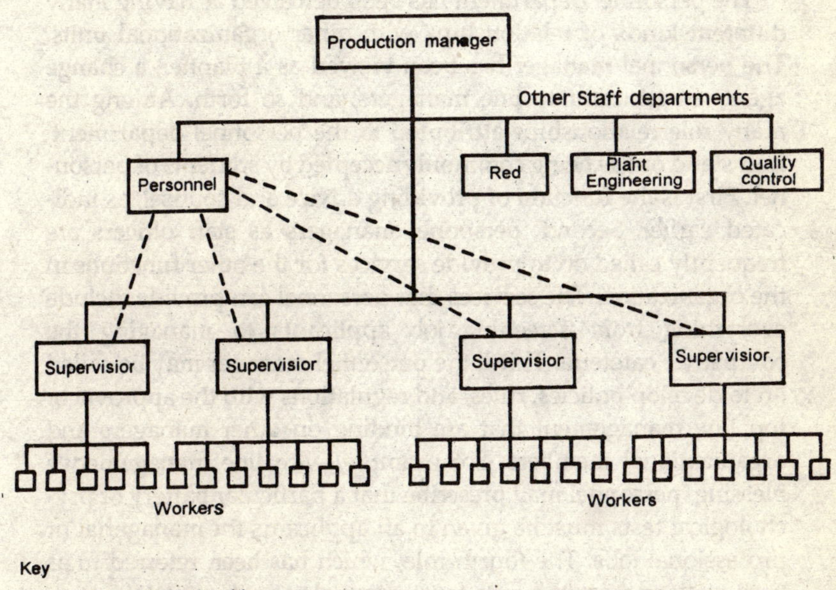

Fig. 4. Line-staff relationships.

suppose the personnel manager depicted in Figure 4 has engaged in research that showed conclusively that a high percentage of newly hired employees performing a particular job who are 35 years of age or older do not have the required manual dexterity for learning how to do the job. Suppose also that the probabilities for success on the job are considerably higher for newly employed workers 30 years or less of age. If personnel management presents this informational input to the production manager and the latter accepts the personnel manager's advice to set up a maximum age limit on this job, who is really making the decision? Overtly, it is the plant manager, but the individual wielding the real power here is the personnel manager. This situation results because the personnel manager has *control over basic information*, a staff characteristic that we will examine more thoroughly later in this chapter.

Personnel Functions

The personnel department has been perceived as having many different kinds of relationships with other organizational units. The personnel manager has been viewed as a planner, a change agent, an educator to line managers, and so forth. Among the many role relationships attributed to the personnel department, four stand out as being commonly accepted by students of personnel. First is the function of providing advice and counsel, as indicated earlier. Second, personnel managers as staff officers are frequently called on to provide services for the other functions in the organization. The services that personnel can provide include everything from screening job applicants to managing the company's cafeteria. Third, the personnel manager may be called on to develop policies, rules, and regulations with the approval of top line management that are binding on other managers and organizational members. For example, with line management's blessing, personnel may prescribe that a particular battery of psychological tests must be given to all applicants for managerial or professional jobs. The fourth role, which has been referred to as both *audit* and *control,* calls for personnel to look at certain company performance standards, compare actual performance with these standards, and attempt to correct any deficiencies between actual and desired performance. For example, the personnel manager may examine absenteeism rates in a production department, observe that the rates are well above acceptable standards set by management, and discuss the problem with the departmental supervisor in an effort to reduce absenteeism.

These four role relationships may lead to interorganizational frictions. With regard to the providing of services, line management may ask staff to provide too many services or services that are ill advised, there may be conflicts over scarce services, or some line departments may want to do certain types of work themselves and resist staff performance of services. To illustrate one of these points—line's asking for ill-advised services—one training director in a good-sized manufacturing operation ran into the following situation: Both her supervisor, the personnel manager, and the latter's superior, the plant manager, would frequently run across articles in professional management or personnel journals suggesting new types of training programs, and bring them to her attention. In many cases, such training programs were theoretically unsound in her opinion. For this reason, the training director considered one important facet of her position the ability to influence line management to say no to the establishment of poor programs such as oversimplified relations training.

Perhaps even more serious than these service-type problems are the *inherently* contradictory roles of advisor and auditor. The personnel manager is expected to be a trusted advisor to line managers. Effectiveness in this role "requires that line feel free to discuss the problems being confronted." The personnel staff, at the same time, is expected to inspect and evaluate line performance. Many observers "contend that it is unrealistic to expect line to confide in a staff helper who also monitors his performance." Following one approach developed to help alleviate such conflict situations, the personnel manager goes directly to line managers whose operation has become out of control and helps them improve their performance. The personnel manager does not communicate the negative information about the line managers to their boss. One author was involved in a situation in which the direct-help, or source-of-help, approach worked quite effectively. This example does not concern staff-line relationships but rather staff-staff relationships, on which we will focus our attention later. The basic principle and psychodynamics involved, however, are essentially the same as would be found in a line-staff relationship, so the following example provides a clear picture of the source-of-help approach.

For years, a large supermarket chain had personnel managers in each of its geographically dispersed divisions administer psychological tests for college degree job applicants. However, it required the field personnel managers to send the tests to a specialized department in its corporate office for test interpretation. This approach worked fairly well until a period in which the labor market got tight. In such cases, the divisional personnel managers could not make any recommendations to their superiors (divisional vice presidents) until after the tests had been sent to and returned from the centralized corporate staff for interpretation—which in some cases took a week to ten days. Thus, no job offers could be made to college graduates on the spot when they made their trip to the division and were tested and interviewed by the divisional management. Top management believed that the whole college recruiting effort could be improved if psychological test interpretation as well as administration were to be delegated to the divisional personnel managers. This would enable the company to tender immediate offers to promising job seekers who might well accept an offer with another firm if they had to wait a week to ten days before receiving an offer from the supermarket chain.

The firm's centralized staff personnel department was asked to develop manuals explaining how its tests should be interpreted, and held training sessions to teach all divisional personnel managers how to interpret the tests.

Even though the interpretation work had been decentralized, the corporate personnel staff was still responsible for ensuring that test interpretation would be handled properly throughout all divisions in the company. This required a control mechanism to be established by corporate personnel. Initially, the divisional personnel managers all were required to send a copy of all their test interpretations to corporate personnel for inspection. Then, if the centralized staff found any division personnel managers who were not making correct interpretations, it would phone the personnel manager who was having problems. A trip would be arranged for one of centralized personnel's members to visit the division and spend a day going over the interpretation problems with the divisional personnel manager. Following the source-of-help concept, none of the divisional vice presidents were told that their personnel manager was performing poorly in test interpretation. They were simply informed that the centralized personnel staff representative was visiting the division to "talk over the new testing program" with the field personnel manager.

With this approach, all division personnel managers were handling the test interpretation properly within a few months. If this approach had not worked and a number of poor candidates had been hired, the divisional vice presidents, of course, would eventually have had to be informed of the situation.

Finally, we should indicate that the policy formulation role may also create line-staff problems. Personnel may generate, with the approval of top management, a new policy that is not completely compatible with other goals set for other organizational units. For example, a new safety policy may lead to lower production per-employee in certain manufacturing departments and hence conflict with the departments' output objectives.

In addition to the conflicts involved in personnel's role relationships, there are certain status incongruencies that may interfere with effective staff-line relationships. By status incongruencies we mean that there are a number of characteristics that individuals possess which gave them status within the company—education, work experience, seniority, and so forth. When two people interact and one of them has more status, according to most indicators, status *congruency* exists and the individuals tend to be aware of the proper roles they should assume in interacting with each other. However, if one individual has, for example, more education but considerably less seniority in the organization, there is status *incongruency* and it may be difficult for the individuals to relate to each other. As one author has pointed out, such ambiguity "tends to result in stress and various other reactions.... For example, a college educated assembler might disturb other assemblers in a department who would then either ignore him or behave in an unfriendly way toward him and thus cause him to be uncomfortable."

The Stature of Personnel Manager

Personnel departments and managers from different organizations differ considerably in the amount of power and stature they hold. One important reason for this is that there is little consensus among firms as to exactly what kinds of work the personnel nel department [illegible] At one extreme, we find "low-status 'personnel' tration, and on the other end, [illegible] wage and salary adminis- same name but deeply involved in the organiz[illegible] carrying the objective setting and the development of its management s[illegible] ture, with all kinds of possibilities in between."

A basic reason for these differences is the degree to which top management gives support to the personnel function. There seems to be almost unanimous agreement among personnel management thinkers that the "leadership displayed by top executives cannot be overemphasized because they are the ultimate determiners of personnel philosophy." From an "organizational climate" point of view, if an organization is assume the audit or control role to ensure that all divisional personnel managers are following corporate policies.

In such situations, the operating personnel managers are "persons in the middle" in the sense that they report directly to their divisional manager yet are called on to follow personnel practices developed by the corporate staff. Their continued employment, merit raises, and possible promotion into a line position in the operating unit are all primarily determined by their immediate superior. On the other hand, possible promotions to the central office personnel department and promotions to personnel management positions in other larger divisions where more responsibilities are called for require them to be in the good graces of the corporate personnel staff. In some cases, the operating vice president may resist certain corporate personnel policies and division personnel managers may find themselves in a conflict situation. In such a position, the divisional personnel manager's proper role has been well described by Osgood, who deals with a situation in which a field personnel manager reports to a district marketing manager:

> He has a mutual responsibility with the district marketing manager for employee welfare...within the district, but he also has the corporate responsibility of keeping the district manager advised about all company personnel matters, including the reasons behind new releases and changes in policy. It is imperative that he make specific recommendations for changes within the district. When he sees that something is being done in his district that is contrary to company personnel [illegible]. He is to tices, it is up to him to appraise [sic] [illegible]ersonnel trouble," but he keep the district m[illegible]ive role in supporting his district manmust [illegible] the point of disagreeing with him about a particular personnel policy and making an active attempt to change it.

There are a number of ways in which an organization may enhance the power and stature of its personnel department. One of the most important of these is the assignment of the personnel manager to a high level in the organizational hierarchy—preferably as a vice president reporting directly to the president of the firm. This action will not only provide status to the personnel department; it will also provide a vehicle for bringing good ideas for personnel programs directly to the organization's top executive officer rather than having them get lost in the organization, as is often the case if personnel reports to low-level executives.

Enhancing the influence of personnel may also be undertaken by what is called the cross-training approach. This approach involves sending out personnel professionals to take over line jobs they can handle while at the same time bringing line managers to take over certain duties in the personnel department. This arrangement not only broadens the experience of the personnel staff, but also gives line managers a better understanding of personnel work. This may render them more supportive of personnel in the future. Such an approach, of course, is feasible only to the extent that the cross-training can be effected without having to provide either individual with too lengthy and costly training.

The Implications

Should personnel continue to gain more decision-making responsibilities and be vested with greater power, two important implications are evident. First, the training of personnel managers will have to be updated. In discussing the impact of automation upon personnel, one authority has stated, "Future personnel executives would have difficulties to perform their functions without a graduate degree in personnel administration, the curriculum of which should include such subjects as linear programming, game theory and organization planning."

The second implication of a more influential personnel department is that it may assume too much power. This can undermine the authority of line managers. For example, in one company the personnel manager and his staff made all the final selection decisions for its largest plant. This gave the supervisors an excellent chance to "pass the buck" to the personnel department if the new employees' performances were poor—even though they performed poorly largely because the supervisors did not bother to train them properly. The supervisors could simply say that the personnel department had given them poor workers and this was why the performance was inadequate. To overcome this problem, the selection process was modified so that personnel continued to interview, test, and make recommendations about all new employees but the supervisors were given the power to make all final selection decisions. Having chosen the new employees themselves, the supervisors could no longer shift the blame back to personnel if a worker's performance was below par.

Even though personnel has been gaining more power and stature, there are dangers in giving it too much power. What is needed most is some type of balance of line-staff power that will meet the objectives of the organization most fully. This balance may be a delicate one. How far to go in either direction must be viewed in situational terms with respect to each decision type and the particular organization with which one is dealing.

2

HUMAN RESOURCE PLANNING

ORGANIZATIONS are in many ways similar to process where there are some inputs and some outputs. They also need material, machinery, equipment, labour (inputs) in order to produce, provide (outputs) and function (growth) successfully. In present day of awareness the labour (manpower) is no less important factor for production, provision and functioning. It is here that the importance of Human Resource Planning ensures that enough competent people with appropriate skills are available to perform the jobs as and when they are needed. In other words Organization undertake Human Resource Planning to enable them to meet their future (manpower) needs in the same way as planning their non-human seeds such as cash management, inventory management etc. (Refer to Volume 6, *Financial Management*, of this treatise).

Human Resources Requirements Planning deals with anticipating staffing requirements taking into account current and likely future demands for skills, and the probable availability of individuals with such skills. The action part of the definition deals with the policies and programs that are used in coordinating supply and demand to attain the goals desired.

While it has frequently been stated that human resources are a nation's and an organization's most valuable asset, there has been paradoxically, relative lack of attention to this critical resource. Financial planning, product planning, physical facilities planning, market planning and the like are probably more advanced in most organization than is manpower planning.

The recent trends to greater emphasis on human behavior and social awareness will probably accelerate interest in manpower planning, in both governmental, institutional, and business organizations. The bureaucratic and mechanistic emphasis on the nonhuman physical systems and economic goals will have to give way, partially, to concern about people as part of systems.

Macro-level Planning

Essential to sound thinking about long-range staffing needs and policies is a realization of the variety of activities and actions, attitudinal and behavioral patterns, and formal and informal decisions by private individuals, organization, and government which make manpower policies in a free and democratic society.

In a general sense, four major conditions account for much of our misuse of human resources: Unemployment, underemployment, inadequate training and development, and arbitrary barriers to employment. The objective of a comprehensive manpower planning effort is to ameliorate these undesirable conditions.

To be effective, human resources planning must eventually be made at the local level, where the people live and work or are looking for work. This means that in addition to the central and state governments, local government must play a role. The Federal Government has number of programs, some with the states and other with local government, which are attacking specific manpower problems—many of which are related to assisting the underprivileged and unskilled groups.

An effective planning effort is, at least partially, dependent on the availability of a supporting information system that contains needed and timely data. On the macro-level, there is some deficiency in this area. One of the major problems in human resource planning has largely been the collection of masses of descriptive data without any scheme for relating and using them, and the use of aggregates and averages that are so general that they mask the useful characteristics of the data.

Our nation's pluralistic, free enterprise system places some obvious constraints on strong central planning and related information banks. In several other nations considerable progress has been made toward achieving a responsive, national manpower planning system with an accompanying information data bank. Without such an approach, the impediments of a segmented and incomplete manpower planning system with an inadequate information base will undoubtedly constrain both macro- and micromanpower planning.

Micro-Level Planning

As recently as two decades ago, the personnel function was primarily engaged in providing largely uncoordinated services to the operating units in the organization. Personnel units are now beginning to have an overriding mission for dealing with the broad people-related activities including the climate of motivation, and are increasingly geared to provide the services needed by top management for effective planning and control.

The nation's manpower in the coming decade can be expected to reflect both the growth in demand for skills and the changes in occupations and their distribution arising out of emerging national goals in a technological dynamic and socially aware society. Even in a stable company, the normal replacement process usually requires some estimate of the organization's future work force. In a large and dynamic organization the needs become considerably more compelling, and the task more difficult.

Human behaviorists have indicated that large and bureaucratic organization have characteristics that have been deleterious to human growth and development. Such characteristics are: impersonality of interpersonal relations, few avenues for improving skills, limited opportunity for expressing opinions, emphasis on conformity and regulations, inflexibility of organizations to change, etc. Part of a human resources planning concept involves an enlightened viewpoint as regards employees, including: treating each person as a unique and valuable individual, providing avenues for improving skills, encouraging the growth and maturation of each individual, primary concern with human rather than physical systems, flexibility within the organization, etc.

The adoption of human resources planning in an organization should not only be based on a desirable social goal, it should also facilitate the organization's economic goals related to:

(1) The need for greater, more creative contributions to productivity in the face of rising costs and stiffer competition.

(2) The need for more broadly skilled managers at the top of the organization and stable executive succession.

(3) The need to plan and assimilate changes in status, work, and relationships of employees.

We shall discuss these goals in more detail later in the chapter.

The kinds of questions to which staffing planning is usually addressed include the following:

(1) What number of employees, by type, are needed to meet objectives?

(2) Are such employees available within the organization?

(3) What number of people, by type, must be recruited by time period?

(4) How should these employees be allocated to the various components of the organization?

(5) What is the best way to recruit and select the required personnel to assure the best quality for the positions available?

(6) What type of education and training is required to satisfy the needs of the organization and the individual?

(7) What kind of career program is available for each individual?

(8) How can the work be designed to provide for a desirable balance between productivity and employee satisfaction?

(9) How can the work environment be developed to provide maximum motivation for the employee and coincide with the organization goals?

From the above discussion, certain principles are suggested.

(1) Management should not overlook the qualifications of its existing employees to fill anticipated work openings. It should think of its employees in terms of their potential rather than only in terms of their existing skills.

(2) Education and training should be thought of as being continuing processes, rather than one-time or spasmodic events.

(3) Human resources planning itself is a continuing activity. It must be sufficiently long-range to be able to provide the proper manpower resources in the right place, in the right amount, at the right time. Because all planning should be approximate in view of uncertainties, the manpower plan should be flexible and adaptable to changes in conditions.

(4) Each organization must tailor its staffing plan to its particular needs and planning process and policies.

(5) Human resources planning is highly dependent on good information. Consequently, a first consideration of the development of a planning program for staffing is the establishment of the informational base which will permit meaningful forecasting.

(6) Planning should not be performed in an ivory tower, but should involve all those affected. Involvement is necessary to assure all meaningful inputs, and to obtain acceptance of the plans.

(7) The plan should be subject to appraisal to determine its effectiveness and to strengthen the planning process.

(8) The planning should be action-oriented to accomplish specific tasks and to attain specific goals.

(9) The plan should emphasize broad and comprehensive goals, rather than minute and excessive details.

Some efforts are currently being made to improve human resources planning by use of a variety of computerized mathematical models. It appears that these efforts have either been of a research nature or are still being evaluated for effectiveness in an operational sense.

GOALS AND OBJECTIVES OF HUMAN RESOURCE PLANNING

Effective human resource planning can help managers meet organizational subgoals as well as wider objectives such as profitability and the needs of employees in the organization. For example, effective planning may

1. Serve to stabilize employment levels when demand for a firm's product is variable, thus reducing the firm's unemployment compensation liability costs due to layoffs, providing more job security to the firm's employees, and

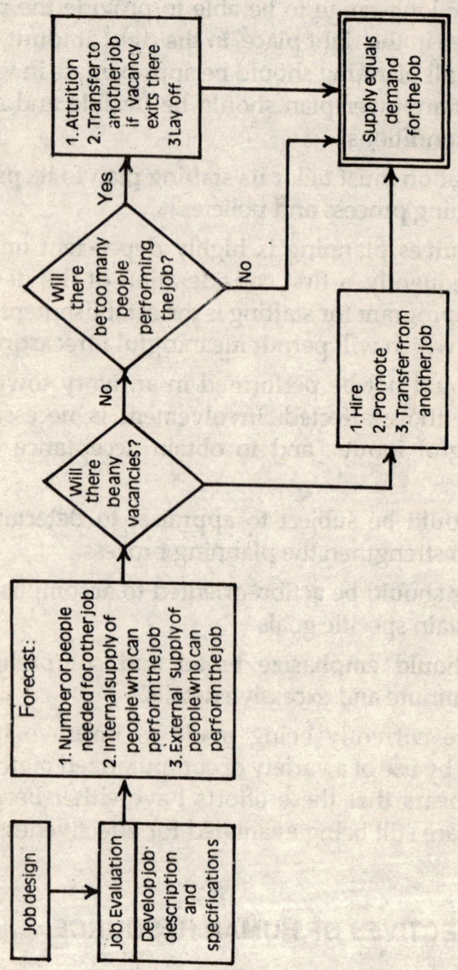

Fig. 1. Human resource planning model for any particular job at any particular time.

minimizing the costs of overtime during periods of peak demand.

2. Prevent young college recruits from leaving the firm after expensive training programs because they lack opportunities for promotion.

3. Reduce the problems of managerial succession by permitting plans for replacements to be drawn up in advance in case key executives resign or die.
4. Make it possible to allocate financial resources so that departments will have the necessary people to produce the firm's desired output.

One example of the way in which human resource planning can provide for employment stabilization involves the use of temporary personnel ("temporaries") by organizations. Although such temporaries have been used primarily to fill in for employees when they are on vacation or ill, many businesses are now finding other creative uses for temporaries which can provide cost savings to firms. Guillet has suggested, for example, that planned staffing may result in using temporary sales personnel during the peak Christmas holidays, thereby minimizing costs associated with overtime pay for permanent employees.

In addition, temporaries may be used "on a long-term basis when employee turnover is high or production low, especially in tedious or routine jobs." Using temporaries may provide savings not only in overtime costs, but costs associated with absenteeism, employee turnover, and recruitment problems, and savings on other benefits as well.

RELATIONSHIP TO PERSONNEL PROCESSES

From a systems view, human resource planning is mutually interrelated with many of the organization's other endeavors in personnel management. The strongest relationship exists between human resource planning and selection. In fact, *all* selection efforts really are an integral part of the whole human resource planning process. Organizations that have either stable or increasing human resource needs must go into the external labor market and hire employees *even though* they generally follow a promotion-from-within policy, as we will see later.

In addition, human resource planning is related to both performance appraisal and training and development. Performance appraisals can pinpoint the skills that will be required for employees to move into higher-level positions via promotion, while training and development efforts may then be designed to provide these skills.

To meet organization goals, human resource planning seeks to ensure that the organization's demand for individuals at any particular time will be *just met* by available human resources. This view assumes that "stockpiling" employees at levels greater than needed and being understaffed are both undesirable. This assumption represents a major difference between planning for human resources and planning for nonhuman resources. Although it is generally unacceptable to stockpile or build inventories of human resources, organizations may find it necessary or desirable to build up raw materials or finished-goods inventories.

It is unacceptable to hold human resource inventories for three reasons. First, human resources are costly and it may be difficult to justify the expense of excess personnel. As the previous example of the employment of temporaries indicated, there are sounder and more cost-effective options available to personnel planners in business firms. Second, excess people are not engaged in productive work, and are likely to be bored and frustrated by the lack of anything constructive to do. Such boredom and frustration can create problems because excess people may make unnecessary work for productive people and may even inhibit the firm's total productive efforts. Third, since human resources (particularly skilled and professional people) may be in short supply, taking productive workers out of the economy's labor pool may be considered socially unacceptable.

It is equally undesirable for an organization to operate with too few employees. As with "stockpiled" employees, individuals may feel frustrated, but in this case because of overwork rather than a lack of productive activity. This situation may also be dysfunctional to an organization's goals. Consider, for example, a department store during the holiday season with a shortage of sales personnel. In addition to the frustrations experienced by employees, such understaffing may also result in loss of employee efficiency. Customers may respond to long lines and excessive waiting by taking their business elsewhere, with resultant loss of sales by the organization. Having too many or too few employees may create numerous problems for organization—problems that can be reduced or eliminated through effective human resource planning.

TRENDS IN HUMAN RESOURCE MANAGEMENT

Unfortunately, the human resource planning efforts of organization have often been inadequate by failing to emphasize the truly systematized approach geared toward meeting overall objectives. As Lopez and others have noted:

> Some organization have perceived manpower planning primarily in terms of budgeting to control labor costs; others have viewed it as a management development technique; still others see it as a table of back-ups and replacements for current employees; and finally, others have viewed it as a means of establishing a human resources informational system and a personnel inventory. Since each of these approaches is necessarily limited in scope, it is a small wonder that the state of the art in human resource planning had limped along quite slowly.

Towards More Sophisticated Human Resource Planning

In recent years, both personnel practitioners and researchers have emphasized some of the basic facets of personnel decision-making: (1) taking systems and contingency approaches, and (2) developing more sophisticated human resource forecasting and planning models. For example, the growth of equal employment opportunity regulations in recent years has increased the awareness of human resource planners of the effects of external changes on personnel systems.

Two observations are in order regarding these more sophisticated approaches. First, more complex planning systems have generally been used in larger firms. Large organizations generally must undertake complex human resource planning and can afford the higher costs of such approaches. Second, although a wide range of human resource models have been developed, some of these models have ignored so many "real life" personnel variables that they have had virtually no practical application. On the positive side, there have been numerous quantitative models that have been very useful to organization. This chapter will focus on the basic concepts involved in some of these more useful models.

Problems Inherent in More Sophisticated Human Resource Planning

Despite these reasons for the growth of more sophisticated human resource planning, such approaches have faced a number of problems. First and most obviously, there is and inherent mathematical complexity associated with efforts to model human resource systems. In addition, however, there are two less obvious difficulties: (1) a lack of certainty surrounding human resource needs in the future, coupled with (2) the existence of an acquisition lead time for meeting those needs.

JOB EVALUATION

Before engaging in human resource planning, management must first define what work is to be performed and determine how tasks can be divided into jobs. The assignment of tasks to jobs is commonly known as *job design*. Even after jobs have been defined, however, current information about their content must be maintained. This information-gathering process, called *job analysis*, serves several useful functions for the organization.

First, since the tasks comprising most jobs will change over time owing to technological innovations or other reasons, job analysis is an ongoing process within the organization. Up-to-date job analysis may provide a firm with an indication of when jobs need redesigning because of task content changes. For example, a firm may purchase newer machinery which reduces the time required to perform the tasks comprising the job by 50 percent. When such situations arise (as they do), job occupants may be assigned new additional responsibilities in order to keep them busy in performing a full day's work.

Second, identifying the work to be performed provides the basis for effective human resource planning. Such planning cannot be done properly by management unless it knows fairly precisely what a "sales", "engineering", "receptionist", or any other type of job consists of. For example, a firm may have hired its present receptionist many years ago when the job consisted of operating a telephone switchboard and greeting visitors. With technological innovations such as automated switchboards and display writers, the tasks performed by that receptionist have changed over the years. Ongoing job analysis would identify those new duties, providing a better understanding of the current responsibilities of the receptionist. Thus, should the present receptionist leave, the organization can seek someone truly capable of filling the job.

Relationship of Job Evaluation to Other Personnel Functions

Accurately describing what each job entails is essential for the recruitment and selection process. Job analysis results in the development of not only job *descriptions* but job *specifications* as well—that is, what characteristics the individual needs to possess to be qualified for any given job. For example, in the case of the receptionist, the degree of typing skills needed by an applicant would be included in the job specification. This kind of specification enables the firm to engage in sounder recruitment and selection procedures.

Job analysis also provides valuable data for performance appraisal. This is so because supervisors can compare an individual's *actual* job performance with the tasks *required* to be carried out as specified in the design of the jobs. In addition, job analysis data provide a basis for training and development efforts in the organization. In order to train individuals to perform particular jobs effectively, we need to define for them (and for the trainers) what tasks employees are expected to carry out.

Job analysis data are also extremely valuable in wage and salary administration. Through job evaluation, jobs in an organization can be compared with each other and differential levels of pay established for jobs calling for greater or lesser skills. Basic to evaluating and comparing jobs for wage and salary purposes is a clear statement of what each job entails.

Finally, job analysis has become increasingly important as the federal government has sought to compel firms to end discriminatory hiring, promotional, wage and salary, and other personnel practices. For example, accurate job descriptions may represent a prime defense against charges of discrimination by proving that a woman performing one job and being paid less than a man performing another is really working at a different skill level.

Job Evaluation in its broadest sense means determination of appropriate base salary or wage rates for specific combinations of duties that are called "jobs" or "positions" in business organizations. In this context, whenever two or more paid individuals are employed by any organization, job evaluation of some kind takes place. The employer tries to recognize, in terms of relative rates of payment, differences among the comparative values of contributions to organization goals made by the jobs among which the total efforts of the enterprise are divided.

In the more limited context used here, "job evaluation" is the generic title applied to those approaches to job rate determination which attempt to systematize the processes that are essential to achievement of equity and employee satisfaction—in so far as wage or salary scales and position rate differentials are concerned. The claim that any "system" of job evaluation is "scientific" cannot be made with accuracy or assurance, despite the fact that many job evaluation systems use numbers in the process of comparing job values or in relating them to wage scales. The knowledgeable practitioner of the art recognizes that the best he can do is to introduce an optimum amount of order into making and recording the human judgments that are essential to construction of more effective wage and salary scales.

History

Although undoubtedly, many individual employers had always sought to bring some order into their wage and salary structures, it was not until the twentieth century, coincident with the growth of increasingly complex business institutions, that general managerial attention has been accorded to systematic job evaluation. Several large companies in various fields experimented with and in some cases implemented job evaluation practices during the 1920. In the majority of these situations, clerical workers and their salary rates were the chief targets for the earlier "systematizers." The inaccurate and hence frequently misunderstood term "salary standardization." was applied to these attempts up to the time that the world was shaken by the Great Depression.

The social, economic, and political climate of the middle and late thirties, including Government encouragement of collective bargaining and the growth of labor unions, forced a majority of larger companies to seek a satisfactorily defensible method of justifying individual job or position rate differentials and the salary and wage scales that placed money values on those differentials. By the end of that decade, few professional personnel administration meeting programs were considered complete without at least one session on orderly salary and wage administration. Imposition of salary and wage controls in World War II and the Korean War intensified the need for and interest in systematic job evaluation. From the middle fifties to the present, there has been continuing research in evaluation methods by employers, educators, and consultants.

The extension of job evaluation up through the very highest positions in the organization was characteristic of the late sixties and early seventies and this will undoubtedly continue. Professional managers have learned to recognize orderly salary and wage administration as a highly useful tool.

Undertaking Job Evaluation

There are four basic techniques generally used for gathering information about different jobs: (1) interviews, (2) observation, (3) questionnaires, and (4) the use of diaries or logs. Each of these four different techniques possesses certain advantages and disadvantages for organizations seeking to analyze jobs.

Interviews. In some cases, job analysts may interview the employee who is performing the job, the supervisor, or both. This technique may be time-consuming, and the danger exists that employees may exaggerate the importance of their jobs. In addition, the persons interviewed may forget certain duties or responsibilities which are an important part of the job, but which are undertaken on an infrequent basis. For example, an assembly line worker may also be required to inventory supplies on a monthly basis. Although this responsibility may be extremely important, it may be overlooked during the interview since it occurs on an infrequent basis.

Observation. A second approach to information gathering in job analysis is having the analyst actually observe the individuals performing a job and record observations while doing so. In some instances this method is very useful, but under certain conditions it becomes more difficult if not impossible. This is especially true with jobs in which some elements of the complete job cycle occur at intervals that are infrequent or unpredictable. In the example of the monthly inventory duties cited above, simply observing the worker may not reveal that this important monthly responsibility is an integral part of the job.

Questionnaires. Probably the least costly method of collecting job analysis data is by using questionnaires. Well-designed questionnaires have been claimed to be "the most efficient way to collect wide array of job data and information in a short time. However, there is the danger that a respondee will either not complete the questionnaire, complete it inaccurately, or take an excessively long time to return it." Although the questionnaire is less expensive generally than interviewing, questionnaires contain many of the same problems: information may not be complete, or it may be inaccurate in describing the actual tasks performed.

Approaches and Techniques

The process of job evaluation starts with the determination and recording of information about all of the jobs or positions to be covered, as such information is related to the appraisal of the difficulty and importance of such positions. This activity is usually referred to as *Job Analysis* and results in a job Description or *Job Specification*. Essentially, such documents contain:

(1) Identifying details such as job title, job location, name of organizational component(s) in which the job is located, and the like.

(2) A brief but informative description of each major duty performed as well as a listing of minor duties assigned.

(3) Indications of the scholastic training or equivalent required, as well as of basic working experience expected for entry into the position.

(4) A description of the precision or decision limits within which the incumbent is required to produce.

(5) Special requirements related to ingenuity, initiative, resourcefulness, and creativity.

(6) Descriptions of elements of responsibility assigned, such as men, money, materials, equipment, methods, markets, and records.

(7) Statements as to the physical effort involved.

(8) Descriptions of the surroundings, hazards, and other unusual or adverse physical conditions under which the work must be performed.

It is essential to recognize that data descriptive of position content contain both fact and opinion. Items of fact can be checked objectively; for example, a worker does of or does not perform a certain duty. However, determining what it takes in skill or training to qualify for performance of the duty can well be a matter of opinion. The best place to start gathering fact and opinion is, therefore, the person of an adequate sample of the people assigned to each position. Suitably trained job analysts then can prepare tentative descriptions and submit them for supervisory approval, and, when feasible after required modifications have been made, secure agreement from the employee or employees whose jobs have been described. *All job evaluation must start with general agreement on the accuracy of the job analysis.*

With respect to clerical employees and others accustomed to recording ideas in writing, questionnaires can be used advantageously to speed the job analysis process. However, these are not customarily used to the exclusion of an adequate sampling of personal interviews. Moreover, the analyst must assure himself that job incumbents who have the same titles actually have the same or similar duties. It is better to err at first on the side of preparing too many job descriptions than, during the evaluation stage, to realize that what are really different jobs have been combined because they happened to carry like titles.

Job Rating. When the preparation of job descriptions has been completed, the process of job rating or job comparison begins. This is the heart of job evaluation. Experience has shown that employees are usually more concerned with equitable comparison of their individual *job rates* with those of fellow workers than they are with the absolute amounts of their salaries or wages. Moreover, mal-alignment of *internal* position values can cause considerable difficulty when it comes to the next step of *external* market rate comparisons.

The actual pricing of the internal job comparison schedule is accomplished by a labor market survey that will reveal how much companies in the local area and in related industries are paying for comparable positions. For such a survey, a relatively few "key" jobs are selected which, it is expected, will have reasonably similar counterparts in other companies and which range from low to high on the comparison schedule. The assurance that the outside rate quotations are for comparable combinations of duties and requirements can be attained by personal interviews with knowledgeable persons from other companies or by membership in properly operated local or industry-wide labor market survey groups, or both.

The results of the "market survey" can be entered on a simple scatter diagram, using cross-section paper, with company key jobs identified at appropriate intervals along the "X", or horizontal, axis (in terms of points assigned to them), and rates paid by other companies for those same jobs entered in the intersecting squares in accordance with an hourly, weekly, or monthly dollar scale on the "Y", or vertical, axis. A regression line representing the central tendency of the rate comparisons can be drawn by inspection or determined by statistical methods. This line permits translation of point values to market rates; it is more likely to be curvilinear than straight.

Selection of a suitable company relationship between the indicated regression line for the "market" and the company wage schedule involves determination of company policy as to whether an average, higher, or lower general wage scale comparison is to be maintained (or bargained for collectively). Federal imposition of minimum wage rates distorts the ascertained values of the low-paid jobs, gradually changing a straight or curvilinear regression line to the shape of a hockey stick. Other aberrations occur if a company has a Federal contract, and must apply "going" rates, which generally become union rates.

Job Descriptions and Job Specifications

Job analysis provides two types of information—job descriptions. We have shown the relationship of job analysis to job descriptions and specifications in Table 1 on the following page.

Job Descriptions. A job description describes the characteristics of the job to be filled. In larger organizations, job descriptions are often written by personnel specialists, while in smaller ones, supervisors usually develop descriptions for the jobs in their departments—if descriptions are developed at all!

In general, job descriptions tend to be less specific at higher levels of the organization. The reason for this is fairly obvious: Lower-level positions, such as ones on a highly repetitive assembly line, are preprogrammed to a much greater extent than, for example, that of vice president for marketing. The vice president's job may involve everything from entertaining visiting dignitaries to supervising the development of marketing projections of a particular product over the next three to five years.

Table 1

The Relationship Between Job Analysis, Job Descriptions, and Job Specifications

Undertaking Job Analysis	*Developing Job Descriptions*	*Job Specification*
1. Interviews 2. Observation 3. Questionnaires (either company generated or PAQ) 4. Combination of techniques	Utilizing data collected through the job analysis, firm develops a one- or two-page summary of the tasks and responsibilities of the job.	The human qualifications needed for performance of the job: 1. Education level 2. Experience 3. Skills 4. Knowledge 5. Abilities

It is also important to recognize that most jobs are more dynamic than their descriptions suggest. First, activities in most organizations will gradually change over time as a result of technological innovations or other reasons (for example, an employee may be given an added duty as a member of the company- wide safety committee). As a consequence, job description need periodic updating. Second, regardless of the description of a job (except possibly highly repetitious production jobs), the personalities of individuals currently filling the position will moderate the job description. Unfortunately, this fact is often not taken into account in organization.

The fact that human personalities may have an important bearing on how jobs are actually performed may also be illustrated by a situation that took place for over two years in the department in which secretary Renu actually worked. Secretary Renu was an excellent typist and could take shorthand. Unfortunately, she often had difficulty reading her own writing! On the other hand, Ram (one of the three secretaries supervised by secretary Renu) could read secretary Renu's shorthand quite easily. As a result of this unique situation, many managerial and professional personnel dictated a letter to secretary Renu which was later typed by Ram. This added responsibility of Ram was obviously not included in the job description, but on several occasions this arrangement helped get the typing done on time.

Job Specifications. Job analysis also provides the basis for developing job specifications. *Job specifications are a statement of the human qualifications required to perform the job.* Among the categories of human qualifications which are often included in job specifications are the following:

- *Educational standards* which may spell out, for example, degrees attained, such as a B.S. in engineering.
- *Experience requirements*, such as two years of general clerical experience for the position. This job requires directing the work of from two to ten clerical employees, and therefore would normally require some prior experience in actually performing clerical duties.
- *Skills requirements*, such as typing 80 words per minute, or being able to take dictation at 100 words per minute.
- *Physical requirements*, which might include such factors as lifting 100 pounds in the performance of the job.
- *Certification or licensing requirements*, such as a practical nursing license in order to work in nursing home, or a license as a registered representative in order to work for a securities firm as a salesperson.

Although job specifications are extremely important for human resource planning, recruitment, selection, and so forth, there are two primary problems with their development. First, some human requirements are fairly easy to translate into specific, well defined skills (for example, typing and dictation). Other human requirements (especially those desired in managerial personnel), such as "Personality," "the ability to get along with others," or "leadership skills," are much more difficult to translate into precise specifications.

Second, accurate job-related specification have become increasingly important. In addition, in the past two decades personnel decision makers have become increasingly constrained by other laws and regulations.

Collective Bargaining. The process of collectively bargaining for job rate differentials and general levels of wage scales is fraught with hazards to rational or logical job evaluation installations. Most labor unions have, perhaps understandably, refused or been reluctant to commit themselves to accepting a management-installed evaluation plan or to joining with management in selecting and implementing such a plan. As a result individual job differentials determined by the internal job comparison schedule can be distorted by successive union attacks, over a long period, on single job rates, and by periodic bargaining positions that change the slope of the entire line representing the relationship between job difficulty and importance and the over-all wage scale.

Other Distortions. Another source of distortion of originally logical rate schedules stems from an otherwise sound practice adopted on installation. When an employer applies the new wage scale, he usually finds that some individuals are underpaid and some are overpaid. The usual practice is to increase the rates of the underpaid individuals to the new flat rates for their positions, or to the minima of their respective new salary ranges. On the other hand, rates of over-paid individuals are not reduced. The theory is that the latter will not participate in future general wage or salary scale increases until their over-payments are removed by the cumulative effects of successive general increases, or until they have been transferred to higher level positions. (These individually over- paid situations are frequently referred to as "red-circle" rates.) However, these inequalities are often perpetuated by collective bargaining provisions or perhaps by unilateral management action aimed at not denying some small pay consideration to holders of "red-circle" rates when most other fellow employees are receiving increases.

There are two sources of salary or wage plan distortion that can be avoided, however, namely, *failure to recognize changes in existing position content*, and *introduction of new jobs.* It is essential that any wage and salary administration activity include constant re-analysis and re-evaluation.

Some Typical Methods of Job Rating

Many individual companies employ several variations of one or more basic methods in order better to satisfy the needs of quite different kinds of employees. On the other hand, no one company should assume, without further validation, that a plan that has been successfully applied in another company can necessarily be taken over and applied in its entirety to the company's own situation.

Ranking. The earliest methods involved simple ranking of all of a certain type of jobs (e.g. production and maintenance or clerical) into a pre-determined number of "grades" or "levels" that progressed from the least to the most difficult and important. For example, from office boy, at the lower end, to assistant bookkeeping supervisor, at the upper end. Individual combinations of duties were identified and placed in various intermediate grades in accordance with what, in the opinion of the evaluator, appeared to be the appropriate order of over-all ranking in difficulty and importance.

Point Plans. A logical improvement over the overall ranking method was the identification of all of the factors that might be considered in the ranking of positions, the assignment of numerical points to the various levels of each of the factors, and the summation of the points so assigned to arrive at total relative job values. In spite of the early application of job grading to clerical work, the first widely known "point rating systems" were applied to factory jobs.

Factor Comparison. Many companies have developed their own point systems or adapted existing methods to their own needs. Eugene J. Benge developed a new approach to the construction and definition of point system scales which, when first practically applied by S.L.H. Burk to factory positions and later to office occupations, and then by E.N. Hay to banking positions, aroused considerable interest and gained broad acceptance under the name "Factor comparison."

The distinctive features of the factor comparison approaches were:

(1) The use of an internal committee of operating executives in pooling their judgments to analyse the "going rates" *for a group of key jobs* to establish values for job factors so that the key jobs can be used as guides to the factor level and to the total evaluation of all other jobs.

(2) The use of key job factor titles to define each factor level, as against the use of verbal definitions in rating of new or changed positions.

(3) The elimination of any maximum number of points or maximum percentage weights. This is essential to the rating of jobs other than key jobs, as well as new jobs to be established in the future. Such jobs may well require either lower or higher factor ratings than those available from the current job comparison schedules or the original key job list.

(4) The detailed rating of key positions in other companies in the labor market on the basis of the inquiring company's evaluation method to assure accurate comparison for wage scale determination.

Summary Principles

In practice, predetermined point assignments are often used, confining detailed factor comparison only to a relatively few key jobs, which are then used as "benchmarks" in assigning points to all other jobs. Following are points which may serve as a guide for companies newly undertaking a job evaluation program:

(1) The pooled judgment of the largest practical, qualified group or groups should be used in the construction of scales and/or in their application.

(2) In selecting the factors (or job elements) to be used, use those that include in total, all of the considerations that make one position more or less difficult or important than another.

(3) The number of factors used should be kept to minimum (perhaps five to eight) and should be so selected and defined as to reduce as far as possible the "halo" effect, that is, pyramiding or overlapping of credits among factors. As indicated in Exhibits V and VI, five factors often used are "Mental Effort," "Skill," "Physical," "Effort," "Responsibility," and "Working Conditions."

(4) The degrees or levels of factors should be defined as objectively as possible by eliminating such relative terms as "rarely," "usual," "normal," "fair," "good," "frequent," and the like.

(5) Within the limits of human fallibility, the same degree of the same factor occurring in different jobs should always be given equal weight.

(6) The point method used should assure that jobs common to the employer and the outside market should carry employer total point ratings which are generally consistent with outside market rate differentials for the same or similar job duties (not necessarily the same job titles).

(7) The method selected and its related procedures should provide for valid, practical checks of results at each successive stage of the process, the check-points to be so arranged as to extend the basis of comparison to increasingly larger groups of positions and broader, pooled judgments.

Development

There is still one area in which much new work must be done to undo a serious mistake that goes back to the quite early days of "Position Classification, Grading and Standardization." Until quite recently, too much weight has been placed on the number of employees supervised or directed through subordinate supervisors, especially as compared to the weight given to the part played by lone professional and scientific workers whose responsibility lies mostly in the areas of technology improvements, creativity, and individual imagination. Many management position evaluation plans have corrected this former failing. In an age of increasingly technical accomplishment we cannot afford to have valuable professional workers enticed away from their important work by inequitably disproportionate salaries awarded largely on the basis of responsibility for large numbers of subordinates.

Finally, it must be recognized that there is nothing permanent to job content, labor-market job differentials, and methods of determining equitable wage and salary rates—except change. Managements must remain alert to the possibility or actuality of change, and, as necessary, revise the processes used in job evaluation to keep up to date with improved methods and new socio-economic conditions that affect sound wage and salary administration.

HUMAN RESOURCE FORECASTING

To make effective decisions, managers need to be able to forecast both what their human resource needs will be in the future and from where these resources will be obtained. As Tichy and others have noted, "the selection, promotion, and placement process includes all those activities related to the internal movement of people across positions and to the external hiring into the organization. The essential process is one of matching available human resources to jobs in the organization." Thus, there is both a "demand" and a "supply" side of human resource forecasting.

From the demand side, the organization will need to predict the number of managers, technicians, and so forth that it will need at particular times in the future. It will also need to forecast what its internal supply of human resources will be. This process involves an evaluation of current organizational members and their potential for promotion or transfer to other organizational positions as they become vacant.

Organizations must also be concerned with forecasting external human resource demand and supply. Such forecasting entails an analysis of both the demand of other firms for various categories of human resources, as well as the supply of these resources in the external labor market. For example, and accounting firm seeking to hire new accountants would need to consider both the external supply of new accountants graduated by business schools five years hence and other firms' demand for those human resources.

A number of forecasting techniques have been developed to deal with organizations' human resource demand, their own internal supply, and external demand and supply. Some of the same forecasting techniques are applicable for each of these different types of situations.

Forecasting the Demand

Length of Forecasting Time. Human resource plans must be updated more frequently in firms operating in more uncertain environments. In addition, the farther into the future that *any* firm makes its human resource forecasts, the greater the uncertainty will be with respect to their accuracy. Some observers have indicated, for example, that long-term forecasts are generally not too accurate, even in firms using reasonably sophisticated human resource planning techniques.

Though it is feasible to develop relatively accurate short-term forecasts for one or two years in the future, intermediate and long-range forecasts may require adjustments owing to the rapid decline in accuracy after longer periods.

Regardless of organization type, length of the planning period, or degree of certainty faced, organizations must focus their human resource demand forecasting on three related factors linked by two conversions. First, and organization must examine both internal and external variables that will enable it to make a reasonably accurate projection of its output. Externally, for example, the nation's birth rate has been declining, with the birth rate per thousand declining from 22.7 in 1980 to 18.4 in 1990 to 15.9 in 1989. This decline has resulted in a smaller potential market for baby food, and in the longer run, declining enrollments in colleges and universities (assuming that a constant percentage of the population continues to go to college). Internally, the baby food manufacturer may have already decided to diversify into other product lines, and may have already begun construction of a plant for producing a new line of products.

Knowledge of such factors will be of value in forecasting product or service demand. For example, the baby food manufacturer must convert birth rate statistics into the number of jars of baby food of each type and flavor it will be to sell each year. Colleges and universities must convert these birth statistics (along with numerous other variables such as the increased demand for adult education) into projections for future student demand in each department for each academic year. In progressive, personnel-proactive firms, the organization's top personnel officer may participate in decision-making regarding the number and types of products produced. When this is the case, the personnel manager may provide valuable data on the available supply of human resources (both internal and external) to meet projected sales levels.

Forecasts for Specific Jobs. When sales forecasts have been developed, they must be converted into specific human resource needs for specified jobs throughout the firm. In some cases, such a conversion may be relatively simple, while in other instances it may be quite difficult. For example, it may be fairly straightforward to predict the number of direct employee hours to build a tire, cure it, inspect it, and so on. Based on previous production data, the firm can simply take the time required in each stage of producing one tire, multiply these figures by sales forecasts, and arrive at a prescribed number of work hours required for production. Compiling such data for the manufacturing of *all* tires produced will enable the firm to calculate the number of direct-labor jobs required at each stage of the manufacturing process.

It would be more difficult, however, for the firm to establish the indirect-to-direct labor hour ratios. For example, the number of setup people required on a production line might increase if the firm's output level increases by 10 percent, but not necessarily by this same percentage. It is even more difficult to project the numbers of clerical workers, managers, technicians, and professionals necessary to accommodate any changes in sales. If, for example, total tire sales increased, the number of first-level supervisors might not increase at all. All supervisors might simply have their span of control increased instead. Even if the number of supervisors increased, their superiors might be able to handle this increase in the same fashion.

Several different forecasting techniques have used to cope with the problems involved in human resource demand forecasting. We will focus our attention on four of these: (1) statistical projections, (2) logarithmic learning curve analysis, (3) one general-purpose computer model, MANPLAN, and (4) the Delphi technique.

Computer Analysis

A number of other quantitative models have been developed to forecast human resource needs. In this section we will describe one such successful computer model: MANPLAN. Such general-purpose models are important, because when they can be utilized by firms, the cost of development is much less.

MANPLAN was developed by General Electric to overcome human resource modeling problems (such as the overwhelming mathematical complexity that can be brought into such planning efforts). General Electric decided to develop a general purpose simulator (MANPLAN) to be made available to users of the GE computer time sharing service. This computer program interrogates its human user for the information it meeds for its forecast, asking such questions as:

1. How many different product lines do you manufacture?
2. How many months does your forecast cover?

3. How many units of refrigerators. washers, dryers, air conditioners, and fans do you forecast for the next 10 months?

Once these questions are answered and fed into the computer, the computer can produce a forecast estimating average human resource levels required to meet product demand. MANPLAN also provides for ranges of possible human resource needs for any period. The personnel manager can use the model to test the impact of various human resource decision-making strategies. For example:

> Possible changes in current manning levels of various employee classifications by means of promotion or downgrading could be tested to locate minimum lay-off strategies...Any number of experiments with various numbers of upgrades or downgrades are permissible until you have finally reached an optimum schedule.

One final merit of MANPLAN is that running the computer model is relatively inexpensive.

Forecasting the Supply

Human resource planning includes both a supply and a demand side. In previous section we discussed the processes and techniques that firms use to forecast their *demand* for human resources. Firms must first develop an understanding of the tasks to be performed and the jobs to be filled through job analysis. Job analysis provides the necessary information for firms to develop both job descriptions and job specifications. It is only after organization understand the nature of jobs to be filled that they can then turn their attention to forecasting their anticipated demand for human resources.

Once an organization has developed a reasonably accurate forecast for each job, it must then determine what qualified personnel will be available to meet this anticipated demand. In this chapter we will discuss the ways in which firms utilize both internal and external labor supplies to meet their anticipated human resource needs.

Ideally, organizations would find an exact balance between their anticipated demand for human resources and the internal *supply* of such personnel. Such ideal conditions seldom if ever exist, however, and organizations often discover that they have either shortages of personnel or overstaffing in individual departments, plants, or the firm as a whole. This imbalance necessitates adopting strategies for either adding needed personnel or decreasing unnecessary personnel through attrition, transfer, or layoff. Now we will discuss strategies for reduction of unnecessary personnel, saving for later chapters the procedures for adding needed human resources through recruitment and selection. We will consider first the forecasting of the internal supply of personnel within the organization.

Forecasting the Internal Supply of Personnel

The same statistical techniques for forecasting the demand for human resources may be used for forecasting the internal supply processes. For example, firms can correlate turnover of various occupational groupings within the firm with age and years of experience with the organization. In addition, a number of other techniques have been developed that are very helpful in forecasting the internal supply of personnel. In this section we will discuss two of these: (1) skills inventories and (2) replacement charts.

The concept of the Skills Inventory—the mechanized, detailed listing of employees interests and talents—is an attractive one. It suggests promotions from within, the efficient use of talent, the quick and easy location of vitally needed or unusual skills, concerned management and, indirectly, high morale.

It can be argued that there is a need for a manpower resources system which will provide for the more efficient utilization of talent, for a significant percentage of all employees who become enchanted with their jobs believe that their talents aren't being utilized to the extent possible. In deed, it is possible to demonstrate that our economy is not suffering from a skills shortage but, rather, from a utilization shortage. Theoretically, a skills Inventory could offer a major contribution. Experience has suggested otherwise.

Management Philosophies

Experience has convincingly demonstrated that significant change in operating procedure which is adopted by a company will fail, unless it has the willing and continuing support of top management. The adoption of a Skills Inventory would be no exception. Attempts to install such registers have indicated that certain kinds of organizational structures and certain types of management philosophies are not conducive to the easy acceptance of the skills register concept.

Probably the least receptive kind of organization is that which is structured on a functional, rather than a project, basis. All similar skills, such as circuit design, stress analysis, reliability, etc., would be in specialized, segregated units and, thus, the location of most skills would be reasonably well known. The need for a skills register would not be urgent and would vary inversely with the degree of the compartmentalization of skills. In such an organization the widely held concept that "a good supervisor should know the skills and interests of all his subordinates" would have good validity.

Where company philosophy endorses the "permissive management" approach a skills register would be more difficult to install. In such organization supervisors tend to be relatively independent and would be more apt to resent a raid by a skills register administrator who was trying to relocate an employee to a different area where the employee's unused skills could be utilized, or where his current skills could be better utilized.

Companies which are "permissive management" oriented often avoid strong, detailed control from the Corporate Office. Yet, if a Skills Register is to be effective, it should be on a company wide basis in order to broaden employee utilization opportunities as much as possible. Without a central authority, backed by strong top management support, semi-autonomous managers could not be expected to embrace an interference with their authority.

If management is quantitatively oriented, and the increasing use of engineers in administrative positions, together with the everwidening reliance upon computers, would indicate a growing movement towards that type of management, then facts and figures to document the value of a Skills Register would be of critical importance. Unfortunately, convincing data on the value of the concept is lacking. Its advocates have to rely too heavily upon noble platitudes, which demanding managers view with impatience.

It is conceivable for management to take the philosophical position that the threat of impersonalized staffing, the fear that the careers of employees will become too dependent upon "randomly" placed holes in IBM cards, will more than negate any possible beneficial effects of a central register of employee abilities.

Implementation Problems

Management philosophies and the related organizational structure of the company are obviously of some importance in determining the degree of success of a Skills Inventory. Even if a friendly climate exists, however, there is no guarantee that it will succeed. The problems associated with the register's implementation are equally formidable.

The selection of the skills and interests to be included is an example. With our "technological explosion" and the tendency for skills to become more and more specialized, the number of specialties being performed by any large sized company can easily exceed a few thousand. Most of the participants in any register would have experience, training and/or interests in from one to possibly as many as ten specialties. Consequently, provisions would have to be designed into the register to accommodate the possible combinations.

Even if the specialties to be incorporated into the register could be agreed upon, a task which would require consultations with all key administrators and supervisors, the problem would be far from solution. Our "technological explosion" is almost daily creating specialties which could not be foreseen as skills in themselves. It is reasonable to believe that it would be precisely in the area of the "unforseeable" that a register would be most useful. Even though the emergence of a new specialty can often not be foreseen, it does not mean that a register, under the skillful administration of a technically capable person, would necessarily fail. Since new skills are most often unique combinations of older ones, a judicious mixing of listed skills could conceivably produce the desired result. However, the register would have to have a very large number of base skills from which to 'draw and it would have to be very ably administered. This has not been characteristic of all registers so far attempted.

A register which contains the proper amount of detail in each of many areas—such as administration, marketing, production, design, research, education, interests, goals—would be a very formidable package to present to all employees for their completion.

It is possible to imagine a recoil action on their part and much persuasion and follow up by those responsible for the establishment of the register. Certainly, orientation and educational meetings would have to be scheduled in order to generate the necessary enthusiasm and knowledge among the company wide participants. It would have to be done skillfully and thoroughly, or the register would fail to get off the ground.

It is easy for register participants to assign quantitative values (i.e. years of experience) to each of their skills, but it is far more difficult for them to determine qualitative values. Few of us know ourselves as well as we think we do, and there are few, if any tests, which can reliably measure such personality traits as dedication, energy, loyalty, drive, creativity and attitudes. A person may have ten years of experience—or he may have two years five times. For the register to accurately portray the real skills of the participants, and thus generate the confidence of the users, the professional assistance of senior psychologists should be available to all participants who are completing the register forms. People often establish unrealistic goals for themselves and wise counsel could forestall disenchantment.

Register system can be used to list the skills of both employees and applicants. It probably would be wise, at the outset, to design a system which could, at least eventually, accommodate both groups of people. Such a system would require the redesign of employment applications, employment requisitions, transfer forms and job description forms in order for the data to be efficiently transferred into storage. Such a massive disruption in routine can encounter serious resistance if it is not intelligently proposed.

Collapse on the Firing Line

Let us assume that the skepticism of top management has been overcome. Let us further assume that a thoroughly professional job was done in presenting the program to all employees and that 100% completed the forms. A great deal of pertinent data is now instantly available. There would still be serious problems to overcome.

For example, if a need develops for an unusual combination of skills and that combination is instantly found, there is no guarantee that: (1) the employee will want to transfer or, (2) the supervisor will be willing to let him go. Few employees are willing to transfer unless it's to their advantage. This generally means an increase in salary, an organizational promotion, or both. Few shorthanded supervisors are willing to release an employee until a trained replacement is on hand. Neither condition is always possible.

There is always the danger of the "crutch effect." If the need for a special skill arises and the proper buttons are pressed and the desired punched card does not drop out, it could easily be assumed that the skill is not present in the company. Most of us, when hard pressed, have a tendency to accept the easy decision. Yet, if the skills register "crutch" were not in effect, a conscientious personal search would have been necessary.

The two problems indicated above the possibility that the employee could not be transferred, once located, and the "crutch effect"—coupled with the necessity to keep the register updated, demonstrate the need for a full time staff to administer the skills inventory. Such a staff would be expensive, because high level technical talent and skill would be required. The past lack of success with registers could persuade management to view such a staff as an unnecessary luxury.

All of the problems indicated above can, of course, be overcome. But study, time and money will be required. The lack of success in the past, coupled with the widely held fear that the skills register is nothing but an impersonalized monster from the "Brave New World," should demonstrate the need for caution.

There are at least two ways in which personnel may benefit from the use of skills inventories. First, however, employees must know of the existence of a skills inventory system, and they must see the system produce positive results. For example, when an employee is promoted as result of the system, the promotion communicates to friends, acquaintances, and *all* employees that there is an ongoing mechanism for filling positions by promotions which includes them.

When employees recognize that the program works, they are assured that they will not simply get lost in the shuffle, especially in large organizations, and be overlooked for a better job when a vacancy for which they are qualified opens. Second, being chosen for a higher-level position can mean the satisfaction of more human needs such as power, achievement, and esteem. As a consequence, skills inventories may serve to meet simultaneously both the firm's objective of finding the best-qualified person and the individual's needs for personal and professional growth and satisfaction.

Manual skills inventories have been successfully utilized for many years. However, when computer capabilities for filing personnel inventories became operational, personnel managers had a tool that permitted data to be obtained quickly for examination of all employees. In the remainder of this section we will consider some of the mechanics of developing skills inventories, the specific goals that skills inventories can help to meet, and some limitations and problems connected with this human resource planning tool.

Steps Designing Skills Inventories. Several steps are involved in designing skills inventories. First, an information-gathering instrument must be constructed which specifies the skills that will be included in the inventory. In some cases, forms are utilized which provide "vocabularies" of words describing skill. The employee simply goes through the list and checks those which are applicable. For example, in one IBM skills inventory, major fields such as photography and reproduction printing as well as numerous subfield vocabularies (for example, movie photography) were included. An even more flexible modification of this technique is to provide the employee with a defined checkoff vocabulary with an open-end provision. In this format, the employee may also list words describing skills not found in the fixed vocabulary.

Step two involves management's decision on how to elicit information from employees. Interviews with individual employees, group interviews, or the questionnaire approach may be utilized. The most expensive of these approaches is the individual interview. It is also the most advantageous, because leading employee through the interview step by step increase the accuracy of the data collected. The third step is the coding of the collected skills data for computer processing. This final stage is necessary for computer storage and retrieval of information.

Advantages of Skills Inventories. Many large firms have reported success with their skills inventories, among them IBM,

RCA Service Company, and Douglas Missile. In addition to the basic objective of quick human resource-job matching, some of the other advantages of such systems are as follows:

- ☐ Often redundant data from the precomputerized human information system has been discovered and corrected during computerization, In IBM, for example, it was found that "over 2000 pieces of personnel information were being maintained but only 145 of these were unduplicated."
- ☐ Valuable special studies may be undertaken quickly by probing the computer skills inventory data on the computer. For example, the RCA system provided for special studies "on a moment's notice—such as military reserve status. payroll data, seniority or the potential effects of possible wage increases."
- ☐ Skills inventories can provide valuable data for utilization in replacement charts (which will be discussed later).
- ☐ Skills inventories can also be an important ingredient of an effective affirmative action program. The federal government has taken a more active role in forcing organization to eliminate discriminatory hiring and promotion decisions. (We will discuss these issues in great detail in Chapter 6.) Information in its skills inventory bank that shows that the firm has taken affirmative action can help protect the firm from court challenges to its policies.

Necessary Conditions for Success. A number of conditions are essential for successful skills inventories. First, firms must have clear-cut objectives and viable procedures when developing such a system. At World Equipment and Machinery, for example, a primary goal of the skills inventory system was to identify candidates for promotion. The firm, however, claimed that the skills inventory was not adequate in identifying individuals for promotion to positions of "significant responsibility" because relevant current skills were not found to be valid predictors of potential at these higher levels. The validity of this claim must be questioned, however, since procedurally this inventory "in many cases, could not accurately represent currently available skills because controls on input were weak."

Other conditions of success for skills inventories include the following:

- ☐ The system cannot be perceived by employees as impersonal. This perception can be overcome if employees see the system working, as we indicated earlier. In addition, carefully explaining the system to all employees *at the very beginning* may help to relieve their concern and anxiety.
- ☐ As with virtually every personnel program, the support of top management is required for a successful skills inventory system.
- ☐ All skills inventory systems need updating from time to time. From a contingency point of view, this need presents extra problems for dynamic organizations in which change is rapid.
- ☐ Also from a contingency perspective, skills inventories may be less successful in firms organized by function (such as engineering, production, and sales) than in those organizes along product line: "All similar skills ... would be in specialized, segregated units and, this, the location of most skills would be reasonably well known" without a skills register.
- ☐ Even when care is taken in limiting access to computer probing, many employees may believe that skills inventories represent an invasion of privacy. Because of the concern that will be felt by some members of the organization, firms must assure that such materials are carefully safeguarded and utilized solely for authorized purposes.
- ☐ Users of skills inventories must decide *how many* skills requirements are necessary to produce a list of qualified candidates. Using too many requirements can result in finding few if any qualified individuals within the firm. For example, *no* employee may fit the job requirements of a Ph.D. degree in physics, five years of experience in solid state physics, the ability to speak fluent French, and willingness to travel abroad!

Conversely, the use of too few requirements may result in a list of too many qualified individuals. If, for example, the description specified only someone with a B.E. degree in engineering and three years of experience, a computer printout of 200 candidates might result. The point is, *the decision of how many biographies are desirable is a matter of judgment*. In the Douglas Missile and Space System inventory, for example, one skills search in a functional area produced between 50 and 60 biographies.

In this section we have indicated that skills inventories provide many advantages to business organizations and their employees. In larger firms especially, skills inventories may foster an "open systems" human resource management approach. Capable employees in one division of a firm are not closed off from promotion opportunities in other parts of the organization simply because they are not known to be available.

FORECASTING THE EXTERNAL SUPPLY AND DEMAND OF PERSONNEL

In addition to predicting its own human resources supply and demand, an organization must also be concerned with demand and supply conditions *externally*—in its own industry and in the economy as a whole. Several comments are in order concerning such external forecasts by organizations.

First, a number of information sources to improve human resources decision making are available for external forecasts that do not exist for internal demand and supply forecasts. Both unions and industrial trade associations publish reports concerning supply and demand forecasts for the labor force.

Second, some of the same types of forecasting techniques useful in projecting a firm's internal human resource demand and supply may be applicable for external human resource forecasting as well. The Delphi technique, for example, can be used to project occupational supply and demand trends. In addition, statistical techniques such as regression or correlation analysis often provide the basis for human resource reports published by the government.

Third, the supply of human resources in the external labor market is generally forecast with special attention to enrollments in various educational institutions and anticipated losses due to retirement, transfer, or death. An analysis of graduation figures and the age distributions of individuals in different occupations is very important.

Finally, firms may employ specific strategies to meet their own human resource needs based on cues derived from external demand and supply conditions. For example, in spite of the disadvantages of stockpiling mentioned earlier, a firm may engage in this practice and offer very high starting salaries to this year's computer science graduates if external supply and demand analysis indicates that the economy's demand for such individuals will start exceeding the supply within the next two or three years. In a somewhat different vein, organizations may contribute to scholarship funds at colleges and universities in order to encourage students to study specific disciplines in which there is a shortage of human resources.

FORMULATING HUMAN RESOURCE PLANS

Once an organization has developed a forecast for human resource supply and demand, it is in a position to deal with either of the following contingencies:

1. The projected number of available employees for any given job is less than the anticipated demand for personnel.
2. The forecasted number of personnel working at any given job is greater than the number of employees needed to perform that job (that is, internal supply is greater than the demand).

In this section we will discuss these two situations and indicate various strategies available to organizations for dealing with these problems.

Filling Job Vacancies

Two basic strategies may be undertaken whenever vacancies are forecast for any job in an organization. First, the firm may hire an outsider to fill the position. This approach falls in the area of selection and will be discussed in the next chapter. The second strategy is to promote or transfer someone already in the organization to fill the position *and to hire*. We emphasize the words "and to hire" because, unless the organization is going to reduce its total number of employees, the job of the individual who is moved into the vacant position will then itself become vacant. In fact, it is common for any such move to kick off a chain reaction of human resource movements within the firm.

If a firm's marketing vice president is retiring, for example, the assistant may be promoted to fill the job. This may in turn lead to the firm's marketing manager for the eastern division being moved into the assistant's job, and so on, until no one within the organization is capable of being promoted or transferred and the firm is forced to enter the external labor market for replacements.

It is important to recognize that such movements may represent lateral transfers as well as promotions on the firm's organization chart. In fact, McCaffrey has noted that in a slow-growth economy "both individual career and organizational needs should or will be met through lateral transfers," and that personnel "can thus maintain, and even increase, the contributions they make to their organization and can continue to earn substantial rewards, without benefit of a promotion." One caution regarding such lateral-transfer or promotion-from-within policies is in order: Such efforts should be accompanied with an effective training and development program in order to prepare organizational members for higher-level positions or those calling for different responsibilities.

A majority of companies adhere to placement-form-within policies. In one study, "almost universally (96 percent), the companies...believed in filling positions from within their own organization. The most frequent estimate was that at all levels of management, at least 90 to 95 percent of managers had come from internal sources." This same study also found that organizations that did *not* place mostly from within were usually *forced* to adopt the "hire" strategy out of necessity. These firms were in rapid-growth situations where there were simply not enough qualified personnel within the firm to fill all the needed job vacancies.

The discussion thus far has referred primarily to managerial and professional promotions and transfers. In non-managerial situations where there is a union contract, management may often be forced to promote from within. The firm may be required to post notices of all job vacancies. Then, members of the collective bargaining unit are permitted to bid for the jobs. Probably the most common decision rule written into labor- management contracts is that employees with the most *seniority* who bid get the Higher-level positions *providing* they possess the skills needed for the job.

It has been suggested that management and professional jobs also be posted. As one author asked, "If this approach works reasonably well for union employees, why isn't it applied to professional staff—such as employees in a research and development laboratory? Scientists and engineers (like everyone else) are concerned about how supervisors are selected, where the challenging jobs are, and how jobs are filled."

On the other hand, many firms do give attention at managerial and professional levels to both the seniority and ability criteria inherent in unionized bidding. Many firms follow this decision rule: "Promote the most able, but if two or more individuals are equally capable, promote the one with the greatest seniority." The primary problem with such a rule is that it may be extremely difficult to determine "the most able" individual. It is difficult to objectively measure executive and professional performance in present positions, and even more difficult to predict the individual's ability to succeed at a different or higher-level assignment. For example, a marketing vice president's performance may be adversely affected by an innovative breakthrough by a competitor.

Finally, in discussing the hire-versus-promote (or transfer) decision alternatives, some of the basic reasons to support each of these strategies deserve attention. Providing promotional opportunities in an organization has the following advantages:

- Many employees may experience greater satisfaction and motivation if they can see promotions awaiting them when they increase their skill and abilities.
- Promoting a known insider rather than a less well known outsider may decrease the risks of making a poor human resource decision. This is true because the firm has a greater amount of valid information on which to base a decision.

On the other hand, hiring from the outside for jobs above those of beginning or "entry port" level can be said to have the following merits.

- At the managerial and professional levels, incumbent personnel may grow "stale" and ultraconservative. Hiring new employees from outside the firm may provide much-needed "new blood" for the organization.

- ☐ The hire-from-outside strategy at these levels does not create the strong need for training and developing managers and professionals, and the firm will not face any upheavals due to promotional chain reactions discussed earlier.

Career Paths

Many of the points which we have just discussed dealt with subjective, judgmental managerial decisions. One reason for this is that both promotional and external job market selection have not been subjected to a high degree of quantification. In recent years, however, increasing attention has been paid to such issues as identification of entry-level positions, job clustering in organizations, *and definition of career paths.* Career path analysis can be useful in human resource forecasting and in feedback that gives employees data about possible career routes they might follow in the organization.

Career Path Analysis. More and more research has been directed toward the flow of human resources through different paths in the organization. One study produced the following findings:

- ☐ The three primary "entry ports" were managerial trainees, clerical positions, and workers in the labor pool.
- ☐ The managerial and professional, clerical, craft, and labor groupings were discrete families between which *no* mobility existed.
- ☐ Management trainees had the greatest probability of all entry-level positions to be promoted, and possessed only two possible career paths.

This type of data is useful to management in several ways. For example, during recruitment of managerial trainees on university or college campuses, the firm could tell applicants that 65 percent of trainees hired during the previous one-year period studied were promoted to professional positions following their initial training program. In a lighter vein, analysis by college football coaching staffs could result in a recruiting pitch to high school players assuring that 90 percent of their players graduate with bachelor's degrees after four years.

Open and Closed System

Roadblocks to promotion is not an uncommon phrase to describe problems that employees may experience within organizations. This statement opens the door to many questions that management should ask when job vacancies exist above entry- port positions in the organization. Are supervisors correct in concluding that one or more of their subordinates do not have the capabilities for greater responsibilities, or that no promotional opportunities will emerge in the near future? Supervisors may be wrong in their assessment of subordinate's capabilities, unaware of promotional opportunities elsewhere in the firm, or trying to "hoard" subordinates for themselves rather than encouraging their promotion elsewhere in the organization.

We have described the use of skills inventories and replacement charts to help create an "open promotional system"—one in which information is developed and transmitted in order that *all* qualified employees will be considered whenever any vacancies do occur. Although both replacement charts and skills inventories are valuable planning tools, certain observers believe that " procedures for bringing candidates up for review...[are]...a problem area which...has been too often overlooked." There are many situations that may lead to a "closed" rather than an "open" promotional system. Some of the key characteristics of closed systems have been discussed by Alfred:

- ☐ In many organization, the system is so structured as to make it easy to hoard good people.
- ☐ It is commonplace for managers to be allowed to hire from within their own departments "without considering others in the organization."
- ☐ A person's chances of being considered for promotion depend too heavily on the immediate supervisor's *opinion* (which may be erroneous).
- ☐ When a promotion has been announced, those who are bypassed are not informed as to whether they were considered, or if they were, why they did not get the job.

As an extreme case of a closed system, Alfred notes that one company had its interdivisional labor flows so cut off that employees "were quitting the company to be rehired by another division."

Underlying the characteristics of a closed system are two basic factors:

1. There is not enough information available in the system.
2. Supervisors have "unnecessary authority" over their subordinates careers.

One way in which companies can lessen the effects of the first factor is to develop a high-quality skills inventory system and indoctrinate its managers in its use and benefits. Managers, for example, should be informed not only that situations will arise in which they may lose good personnel to other departments, but also that the converse will occur. They themselves will also have opportunities to utilize highly qualified talent from other departments.

With respect to the second factor, supervisors in some organizations may well have too much power in controlling their subordinates' careers. This problem can be overcome by having subordinates actively participate in their performance appraisal. In addition, a firm may specify that where career planning is considered, other higher-level members of the organization be included along with the immediate supervisor. Finally, in addition to the use of skill inventories and performance appraisals, job posting provides employees an opportunity to bid on vacancies which are of interest to them throughout the organization.

Open systems for promotion and transfer are congruent with the advantages and limitations of the movement-from-within philosophy itself. Openness provides individuals with greater opportunities for advancement but requires better (and more costly) information generation, transmittal, and retrieval systems. In addition, the organization must be committed to active training and development at all levels in order to ensure that its personnel will become capable of assuming more and different responsibilities.

The Reduction of Unnecessary Personnel

Most organizations have had periods in which more employees were on the payroll than were currently needed. This situation may occur regularly each year, as in toy manufacturing, where demand declines dramatically immediately after the festival season. An excess of employees may also exist when there are recessions in the economy, or when technological changes occur which reduce or eliminate the employee hours needed to perform a particular job. For example, during the severe 1980-1982 recession many firms found themselves with the need to trim not only blue-collar workers, but white-collar personnel as well. This has also occurred in some automated and computerized operations. The addition of word processors to a large office may actually reduce the demand for typists.

In some excess human resource situations, workers themselves have agreed to reduce their work hours each week so that the lesser amount of work could be spread among more personnel, reducing the need for layoffs. This has generally occurred to a greater extent in blue-collar jobs than at professional and managerial levels. However, with declining college enrollments in the mid-1970s, each faculty member in one department of a major university agreed to take a cut in pay so that no one in the department would have to be laid off.

There are three basic ways in which excess human resources may be reduced by organizations: (1) by attrition, (2) by transfer to another job, and (3) by layoff. In the following sections we will discuss each of these.

Attrition. Employees leave organizations by retirement, to accept a better job elsewhere, though death, and so on. Except for retirement, organizations may have no idea of exactly which employees in each specified job will leave the firm. Although the organization may have compiled turnover data by job or department, not knowing exactly who will leave renders the attrition approach highly uncertain.

Transfers. Employee transfers are utilized to fill job vacancies both when the firm's demand for human resources is increasing and when reductions in force occur. If a decreased need for employees in one job category occurs simultaneously with an increased need for employees in another, it may be possible to retrain and transfer people. This strategy has been particularly useful as technological changes such as computerization and automation have simultaneously reduced or eliminated the number of human resources in certain traditional jobs while creating new jobs in other areas. For example, a no-longer-needed typist might easily be trained to use a word processor or office computer. Since management invariably has advance notice of the technological change, it can plan an orderly transition of personnel from one job to another.

Layoffs. It is unusually difficult for firms to predict the need for laying off personnel in the future. However, in periods of declining sales. some human resource projections can be developed and *planned* layoffs utilized in order to avoid organizational chaos. Human resource planning practices are often haphazard, however, as was pointed out by one observer of an economic downturn: "Many organizations are now laying off workers...While some reduction in the work force may be a direct result of loss of sales, some of it was based on an edict from above: cut your personnel by 10% or 15% or some other set figure."

Historically, managerial, professional, and other nonunionized personnel have had little or no protection with respect to who will be laid off (or terminated) in these kinds of situations. However, in recent years the rise of federal and state equal employment opportunity laws have provided protections for employees against discriminatory employment practices. As Hubbart has noted, these laws cover "the full spectrum of employment decisions including the layoff of firing of personnel."

Seniority and Bumping

Seniority system are sacred to labor union agreements. Many union contracts provide that if employees are laid off, they may "bump" the next least senior employees and take their jobs. The latter can, in turn, bump the persons with the next least seniority, and so on, until it is the least senior employees in the unit who actually lose their jobs.

In many cases, some jobs are protected from bumping to the extent that an employee needs certain job qualifications to bump into the next job. Without such protection, production could be reduced drastically, for instance, on a highly skilled job in which it would take inexperienced employees 10 to 20 weeks to reach the standard level of production. For example, in one plant no such protection existed at a time when over 400 workers were laid off. If the union contract had been followed, the lower production of workers newly bumped into positions calling for experience would have resulted in a smaller number of units being processed in other departments.

Had this occurred, fewer work hours would have been required in other departments, and an additional series of bumps would have occurred. These would have shortly meant bumping the newly bumped workers on the original highly unprotected jobs and so forth, until the plant would have been forced to shut down. The ultimate consequence of the contract was realized by both management and the union, and both sides agreed to a modification of the procedure. Only a portion of the called-for bumps into the highly skilled jobs were made each month over a six-month period. This new agreement permitted a fairly high level of production to be maintained on highly skilled jobs, so that additional bumping to other jobs would not occur.

Many types of seniority systems are written into union contracts. Although there are variations, there are three types of "pure" system:

1. *Job* seniority units, where seniority is based on the length of time the individual has been on the job.
2. *Department*-wide units, in which the employee's seniority is based on the length of time worked in the department.
3. *Plant* (or company) seniority, where seniority is based on the length of time the employee has worked in the plant or the firm as a whole.

The choice of units ranging from narrow (job) to wide (plant or company) has a number of implications for human resource planning. First, as seniority units widen from job to department to plant, the number of bumps increases. This increased flow of human resources can be disruptive, and more efforts may be required for training bumped workers. Second, where a number of layoffs or terminations occur, the firm will lose more recently hired employees as seniority units widen.

For example, if a manufacturing plant with 200 workers lays off 50 employees, with a plant-wide seniority system the 50 most recently hired employees would be bumped off the payroll. Contrast this with the same-sized plant under a *job* seniority system. If layoffs were concentrated on one or two jobs, the company might well lose workers with five, ten, or more years of seniority, since they could not bump outside of their own narrowly defined job unit. This raises questions of both an ethical and efficiency nature:

- ☐ Is it fair to have a system in which admittedly qualified employees with long years of service are laid off while younger, less senior people are retained on the payroll?
- ☐ Are the firm's most senior employees in general more efficient and highly skilled? If so, the firm would be losing some of its better people by using narrow units for seniority purposes.

One other point of significance must be considered: With wider units it is much easier for management to request and gain acceptance of transfers by workers from one job to another. Consider an employee who is asked to move into another job where management felt the worker could contribute toward meeting the objectives of the organization:

- ☐ If the worker was in a job seniority unit, transferring to another unit would result in the loss of previously earned seniority. The newly transferred employee would now become the individual with the least seniority.
- ☐ On the other hand, if the whole plant constituted a single large seniority unit, the employee could move to *any* other job in the plant and retain 1966 seniority in the wider system.

Because of these considerations, wider seniority units greatly increase management's probability of obtaining an individual's willingness to move from one position to another.

Determining which type of seniority system is most efficient or fair to the employees depends on many variables. How many employees hold the same job; that is, how many total employees would be in each job seniority unit if this strategy were chosen? How often do layoff occur? What percentage of the total number of employees in the bargaining unit are subject to layoff? Is the firm one in which temporary layoffs are required each year due to uneven demand patterns? Is the firm a technologically stable one, or one where continuing advances in technology require the elimination of old jobs and the creation of new ones.

COMPUTER TECHNIQUES IN HUMAN RESOURCE PLANNING

Personnel management today has a dual responsibility: to develop manpower plans which fulfill corporate objectives; and, within the framework of these plans, to locate most productively the capacities of both present employees and job applicants. Since short-term corporate needs and available manpower are both continually changing, effective decision and action in personnel management depends critically on the accuracy and timeliness of its information on both need and manpower.

In a large corporation that is active in expanding economy, the balancing of manpower need and supply requires a vast quantity of valid information from many points in the organization. Traditional manual methods of recording and retrieving personnel information are particularly inadequate in a corporation that is decentralized, is experiencing a rapid growth in total employment, and has continual demand for a wide variety and depth of skills in many locations. Computer-based personnel data systems can significantly improve the effectiveness of personnel management benefiting both the corporation and individual—by providing at a single, accessible point, up-to-date career-oriented information on both present and potential employees.

An integrated Personnel Data System (PDS) under development for some time in IBM encompasses 115,000 employees in the United States. The corporate PDS evolved from the more specialized personnel information systems which are operational in the various divisions. Similarly, a parallel corporate recruiting information system—IRIS (IBM Recruiting Information System)—has been designed to strengthen recruiting activities of all divisions. Both the PDS and IRIS programs have been built step by step to insure a smooth evolution from decentralized manual recording and retrieving methods to an integrated computer-based system spanning the entire corporation.

While we seek to use all the computer's advanta[illegible] its immense data handling capacity and spee[illegible] primary objective from the first in developing bo[illegible] and our recruiting programs has been resp[illegible] individual—his goals, his needs, his inter- [illegible]ough mechanized personnel data systems, all management levels of the corporation are then given the tools to do a better job in working with their employees. The individual's educational opportunities, career plans, and family needs can and should be considered in planning the systems.

The First Step: Matching

On a broad scale, the personnel specialist's job is to balance the internal corporate demand for people in numbers and in skills with the supply both within and outside the corporation. On an individual level, he must match a particular man with a particular job. In order to accomplish this, Personnel must have immediately at hand enough reliable information on each man in order to evaluate fully his qualifications against the position's specifications. For example, available data on an individual at IBM were formerly more than adequate but were widely distributed in 17 separate records— such as in personnel files at his own location, in the Medical Department, in Salary Administration, and in the Education Organization. A traditional manual system of this type for recording and retrieving personnel data can result in a large degree of overlap, accompanied by a good deal of harmless discrepancy and serious error. In one study of personnel records and reports, it was found, for example, that over 2,000 pieces of personnel information were being maintained but only 145 of these were unduplicated. In mechanizing a personnel data system, then, the first step clearly must be to place all data in a standard format and store all records in an easily accessible form.

Planning for Personnel, and Searching for Them

The PDS now underway at IBM is designed both for personnel planning and for searching personnel throughout the corporation for placement. In planning, the system provides an immediate picture of the corporate population as it is today and, combined with other information sources, indicates what must be done in the future. In placement, the system permits operating management to consider all logical candidates within the corporation as the first step in filling a position.

While special data files will continue to be added, there are presently three basic PDS information files on individual employees:

1. Basic Personnel Profile
2. Personnel Skills Inventory

3. Educational Objectives and Attainment Data

The Basic Personnel Profile contains 80 types of basic data on each of 115,000 employees. These data include: name, address, birth date, marital status, number of dependents, Military Reserve status, when first employed, where located in the corporation, salary, and highest educational level achieved. Besides maintaining the Basic Personnel Profile, each of the more than 200 branch offices, 17 laboratories, and 21 plants in the corporation may also maintain additional computerized personnel records of their own employees, as do the various division headquarters. In general, the amount of profile information increases at the division and location. For example, at the division level we might record a man's patent activity, while his participation in local professional societies may be important only at his particular location. Changes in the Basic Personnel Profile are now made on a monthly basis through our Integrated Teleprocessing System (ITPS). Changes are transmitted to Corporate Headquarters over wire from 24 major IBM locations. Ultimately, the Profile information on an employee will be updated on a real time basis.

The Personnel Skills Inventory records all the career-oriented skills of each employee. These skills are first separated under major groupings: (1) engineering, technical, scientific, (2) marketing, planning, and systems analyst, (3) administrative and staff, (4) manufacturing service and support. Language proficiency and experience with specialized instruments and machines are recorded. Another section is devoted to the specific IBM products that he is familiar with or has worked on. Of his various skills, a man is also asked which are his specialties and what are his preferences.

The Educational Objectives and Attainments file is concerned with the man's formal education, planned and in the past. Thus, is he working towards a master's degree, Ph.D., or a trade school certificate, and in what area? what has he already achieved what degrees has he received, when and at what schools?

Auditing and Validating Data

One of the major values of PDS has been in providing the capacity to audit data directly. For example, as happens in developing information systems for any management area, there were many errors in the original data. While most of these errors were caught before the original information was recorded in the Personnel Profile file, a great deal has been corrected since, either by being pinpointed on the computer (which can detect, for example, that Seattle is not in the Eastern Regional area), or by human review (is a man likely to have graduated from college at the age of eight?).

The overall PDS has been designed and the computer programs developed so that these files can be added to as the need arises. For example, accounting records have always maintained a 7-digit number code for each person. This code has now been added to the profile for each employee so that both Personnel and Accounting can perform the same types of analyses.

Planning that Uses the Information

The scope of planning projects that draw on PDS information, of course, varies widely. A corporate population study might be concerned specifically with employee exposure to draft and military reserve call. Therefore, the computer would be required to print out summaries of employees who are affected. Combined with other data, Personnel and top management are then able to make the necessary decisions on the basis of up-to-date information.

The loss of manpower due to retirement and other forms of attrition can also be observed. With this information, Personnel can indicate to the computer work load requirements in the future so that the number of positions that must be filled can be determined.

Other recent personnel planning projects which have drawn on both PDS and other sources of information include a five-year projection of the corporation's need for personnel in the areas of engineering, mathematics, and physical sciences for various rates of growth.

Reports that Use the Information

In addition to special planning projects, a number of scheduled reports are produced each month by the computer on such subjects as corporate strength (number and location of employees) and analysis of positions and salaries. One of the most important regular monthly reports used in planning is the "Monthly Manpower Transaction Report," which relates a division's current manpower status with its formal objectives. While such analyses are made by each division's own personnel staff and the necessary decisions are made at the divisional level, these reports are helpful in pinpointing possible interdivisional imbalances which may become corporate problems.

Searches for Placing People

Most searches of personnel data for placement purposes occur at the location and division levels. The corporation recognizes that promotional opportunities should be available to all employees; searches normally begin at the location level, then to the division, and finally to corporate. Whenever a qualified candidate can be found at the location or division level, there is usually no need to search the corporate-wide PDS file. For this reason, today much of placement searching at the corporate level is for unusual or highly specialized positions which cannot be filled within a division.

Since the three basic information files can be combined internally in the PDS, corporate Personnel can specify very closely a wide variety of Profile, Skill Inventory, and Education qualifications. The search procedure is designed in general to pinpoint several candidates for each position (rather than the ideal one) so as to leave the final selection to human judgment. When a location or division makes a request for search, printouts of appropriate data of the computer selected candidates are forwarded to the location.

The PDS terminals at Corporate Headquarters are available for the use of other staff functions than the Personnel Department. As a matter of fact, the parameters of the original PDS data base were first reviewed by all staffs. It is planned that Type 1050 terminals will also be available at 30 major locations in the corporation in 1967. These terminals will first be used for retrieval of information from FDS files and later, as the necessary computer programs are developed, personnel data can be updated on a real time basis. Security codes will be assigned both at Corporate Headquarters and for all other users of data terminals on a definite "need-to-know basis." Even today, without terminals outside Corporate Headquarters, firm agreements have been established among all Personnel Departments covering ground rules for searching position candidates in other plants and locations.

MERCK'S MARKOVIAN MODEL

We have found that the reader without knowledge of matrix algebra can gain considerable insight into Merck's research without studying all of the matrix manipulations involved in his paper by understanding certain fundamental notions. In this section, we will present these notions, giving some specific numerical examples from the selection itself.

First, the formulation of problems into matrices (and the use of matrix multiplication) simply represent the application of a mathematical algorithm which can simplify the solution of certain types of problems, which could be dealt with by more familiar methods but which would involve considerably more time and effort. Thus matrix algebra represents a "shorthand" way of handling certain types of mathematical manipulations.

We have found that this point can be illustrated by dealing specifically with Merck's mouse maze problem, while emphasizing first the analogy between the mouse moving from one room (state) to another room (state) and an airman moving from one job- enlistment state to another. For example, an airman moving from the first term "semi-technical" enlistment state in the first time period to the second term "technical" enlistment state in the second time period is directly analogous to, say, the mouse moving from the room 1 state to the room 2 state after one time period (or move).

In illustrating how the *same* solutions as obtained by utilization of the matrix manipulations employed by Merck may be obtained *more familiar means,* let us consider the following. First, examine only the eight possible ways (or paths) by which the mouse, starting in room 1, can arrive in room 3 after 3 moves. As indicated in the table in Merck's selection (see p. 107) they are: from 1 to 1 to 1 to 3; from 1 to 1 to 2 to 3, etc. Then, consider *both* the probabilities (or technically *transition* probabilities) that a mouse in any room will *remain* in that room (or state) or *go to* another room (or state) in any move. Reference to Figure 4 in Merck's paper indicates that the transition probabilities of the mouse moving in any move from room 1 to 2 are .2; and from room 1 to room 3, .2. Since the sum of the transition possibilities for any move *must equal unity* (1.0), the probability of his *remaining* in room 1, therefore, must be: 1.0 minus .2 (room 2 move) minus .2 (room 3 move); or .6. Similar reasoning will indicate that the transition probabilities of a mouse remaining in room 3 in any move are .7; as is also true for the mouse remaining in room 3 in any move.

Knowing these transition probabilities, and considering the 8 possible ways in which the mouse starting in room 1 can arrive in room 3 after 3 moves, we can further illustrate *all* possible path movements, with probabilities assigned to each, that the mouse can take in 3 moves, having started in room 1. These are shown in Figure 1.

Those familiar with basic probability theory will recognize that, in a two-move situation, the chances of the mouse going, say from room 1 to room 2 ($p = .2$) in the first move, and then from room 2 to room 3 ($p = .2$) in the second move simply equal the product of these two probabilities i.e., $.2 \times .2 = .04$. Similarly, in a three-move situation, the *three* transition probabilities on any path in Figure 1 would be multiplied to determine the probability of the mouse's whereabouts after the third move. For example, the probability of the mouse being in room 3 after 3 moves following the path shown lowest in Figure from 1 to 3; remaining in room 3; and then remaining in 3 again—would be $.2 \times .7 \times .7$; or .098. In Figure 1 we have indicated the probabilities of the mouse being in room 3 after 3 moves following each of the eight possible paths that he might take to arrive there. Summing these 8 individual probabilities will give the total probability that the mouse, starting in room 1 will be in room 3 after 3 moves ($\Sigma = .35$). The reader will note that this probability figure is the same as the .350 given in Merck's $[P]^3$ mouse matrix for the mouse starting in room 1 and being in room 3 after the third move.

By developing two more figures, such as Figure 1 (one for the mouse starting in room 2 and the other for his starting in room 3); and by following the same elementary probability multiplications and appropriate summations (as we did above for the room 1-3 case) for all paths on each figure, we could similarly arrive at the other 8 values in this $[P]^3$ matrix.—e.g., the probability of the mouse starting in room 2 and being in room 1 after 3 moves; starting in room 3 and remaining in room 3 after 3 moves, etc. As the reader will observe, this would be cumbersome procedure to arrive at the same values as in Merck $[P]^3$ matrix. Hence, the matrix multiplication, which is based on the same more familiar

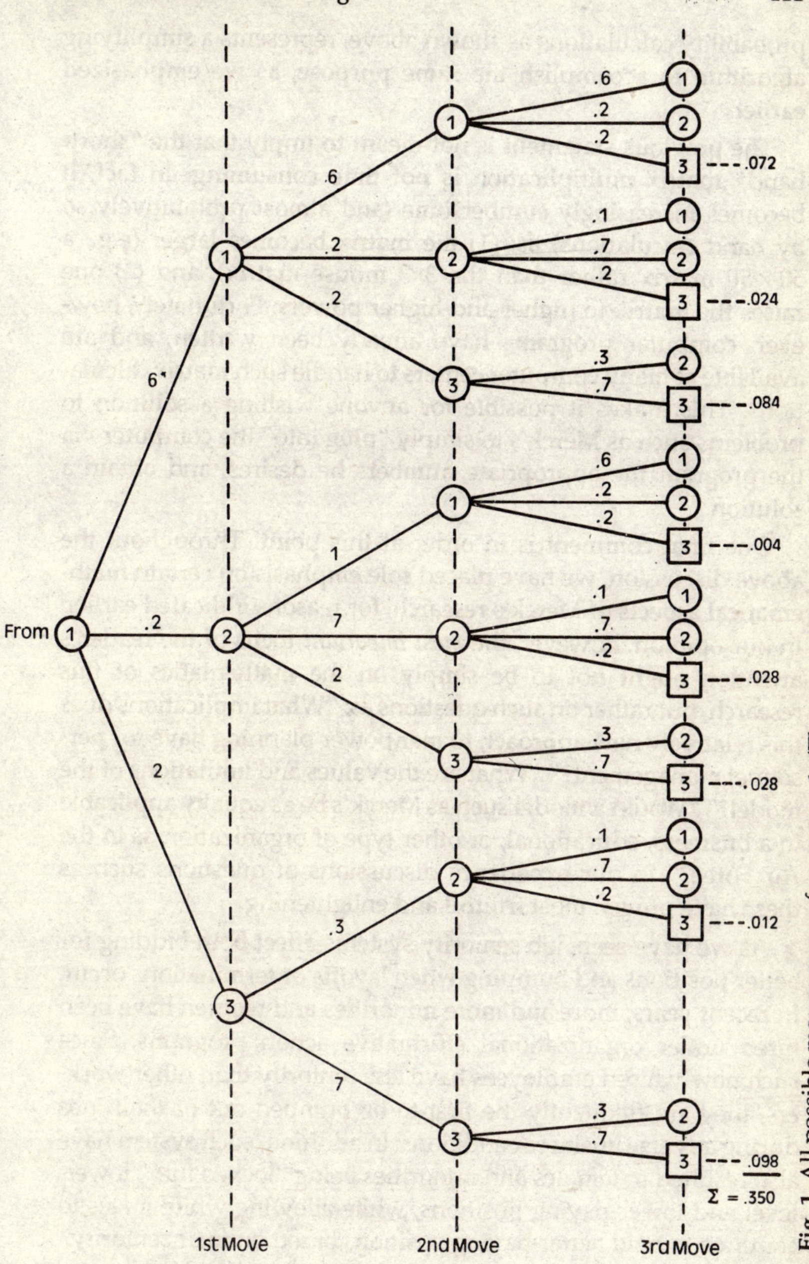

Fig. 1. All possible mouse moves from room 1, (Three moves).

probability calculations as shown above, represents a simplifying algorithm to accomplish the same purpose, as we emphasized earlier.

The previous statement is not meant to imply that the "short-hand" matrix multiplication is not time consuming. In fact, it becomes increasingly cumbersome (and almost prohibitively so by hand calculations) as: (1) the matrix becomes larger (e.g., a 50×50 matrix rather than the 3×3 mouse matrix); and (2) one raises the matrix to higher and higher powers. Fortunately, however, computer programs have already been written, and are available at many computer centers to handle such matrix calculations. This makes it possible for anyone wishing a solution to problems such as Merck's to simply "plug into" the computer via the program the appropriate numbers he desires, and obtain a solution.

One final comment is in order at this point. Throughout the above discussion, we have placed sole emphasis on certain mathematical aspects of Merck's research, for reasons indicated earlier. In our opinion, however, the *most important* focus of the reader's attention ought not to be simply on the mathematics of this research, but rather on such questions as: "What implications does this relatively new approach to manpower planning have for personnel management?" "What are the values and limitations of the model?" "Would a model such as Merck's be as equally applicable in a business, educational, or other type of organization as in the Air Force?" In our experience discussions of questions such as these have proven most fruitful and enlightening.

As we have seen, job seniority systems affect both bidding for better positions and bumping when layoffs or terminations occur. In recent years, more and more minorities and women have been hired under organizational affirmative action programs. Since such newly hired employees have less seniority than other workers, they are frequently the first to be bumped out of their jobs during adverse business conditions. In addition, such system have also resulted in females and minorities being "locked into" lower-level and lower-paying positions, while allowing white males to continue to hold better-paying positions based on their seniority.

This issue has created a conflict between philosophies and mechanisms, each seeking to provide more equitable treatment to the citizens of a democratic society. This issue has also created a dilemma for human resource planning. If traditional seniority systems are allowed to exist, many gains made in EEO will be negated. Conversely, if changes are made in seniority systems, workers hired 25 or 30 years ago under explicit legal agreements protecting them against layoffs as their seniority increased will lose those protections.

There have been a number of court tests involving the conflict between seniority rights and protections under EEO legislation. In regard to promotional opportunities for minority groups and women, at least 30 lower court decisions rendered seniority systems illegal "if they locked racial minorities and women into a lower paying job specialization while white males moved up a better- paying separate seniority ladder."

3

RECRUITMENT, SELECTION AND APPRAISAL

A BASIC problem facing all organizations is that of recruiting and selecting of needed employees. Over the years, many organizations, especially larger ones, have developed more sophisticated recruiting and selection methods, particularly for the hiring of managerial and professional personnel. In recruiting, for example, many firms have carried out analyses and evaluations of sources of different types of potential job applicants, and have maintained professionally trained recruiters in their personnel departments.

In screening job applicants for selection, organizations have developed and utilized many different techniques e.g., weighted application forms; a wide variety of psychological tests aimed at measuring applicants skills, mental abilities, vocational interests, and personality characteristics; and interviewing techniques, such as the patterned and nondirective approaches.

In this chapter are included several sections on objectives, characteristics, methods of selection, Tests, Executive selection and on the whole role of personnel management in recruiting and selection.

Before we go further let us re-capitalate that in the earlier we discussed the planning process, demand and supply consideration of personnel management. Among other things it was discussed how to formulate human resource plans and once the plans are formulated the job analysis and evaluation. In this chapter we will discuss the organisation's search for external candidates for recruiting within the organisation. We shall begin with objectives and basic characteristics of recruiting and selection systems, the conventional and modern techniques covering the recruitment process and then he will consider the selection of personnel including major selection instruments. A selection on performance appraisal and merit rating will follow.

THE OBJECTIVES OF RECRUITMENT AND SELECTION

A basic goal of recruitment and selection is to hire at the least cost as many competent individuals as needed to fill job openings in the firm. The aim of organizations should be to avoid hiring either of the following types of persons:

1. *Underqualified* individuals who will be likely to experience frustration on the job, and who may have to be terminated by the organization.
2. *Overqualified* individuals who will not have an opportunity to fully utilize their abilities, and hence will also experience frustration. In such instances, turnover rates may be high unless these employees can be promoted into higher-level jobs.

In a discussion of employee competence, two questions emerge: (1) How can an organization measure an employee's competence or "success" on the job? and (2) how can recruitment and selection procedures predict just which job applicants are likely to succeed?

In regard to the first question, it may be relatively easy to define success in routine, highly structured jobs such as those on an assembly line. In these instances, *success* may be defined as the number of good pieces of work produced each day by an employee. With managerial and professional employees, however, the determination of successful performance is more difficult. It may be difficult in the case of managerial and professional employees to identify specific, concrete measures by which performance can be evaluated. In addition, successful performance may be beyond their control. For example, a hard-working manager of a local fast-food chain may see unit sales decline suddenly because of competition from a new restaurant in the area. As a result, some firms may use tenure or longevity alone as the measure of success—is the employee still with the firm after two years?

Regardless of the success criterion used, organizations must also seek to develop selection tools that measure what they are supposed to measure. For example, do high scores on a mental alertness test actually predict success on the job? When selection tools actually measure what they are supposed to measure, we say that they are *valid*. In order for a selection tool to be a valid predictor of success, it must also be *reliable*. Reliability means that there is a high probability that an individual who is exposed to the same selection tool at different times would score about the same each time.

Obviously if a selection tool is not reliable it cannot serve as a valid predictor of success. On the other hand, simply because a selection tool is reliable does not necessarily mean that it is also valid. For example, individuals may score about the same each time they take a certain test (that is, the test is *reliable*). However, the test may not predict successful job performance at all (that is, the test may not be *valid*). As we noted at the beginning of this chapter, regulations, legislation, and court decisions have underscored the necessity for having recruitment and selection procedures which are both reliable and valid.

Tow additional points are in order. First, both reliability and validity are extremely complex subjects. With respect to reliability in test development, "traditionally, all measurement error...has been encompassed by the term *reliability*. Today it is recognized that many factors influence and contribute to measurement 'error' and that there is not best way of talking about or estimating test reliability." There are many factors that may influence individuals and cause them to respond differently on the same test at different times. For example, environmental conditions such as lighting may be different, or personal conditions of the individuals, such as mood or physical health, may have changed.

Validity has many facets as well. Ghiselli, for example, has argued that a major factor affecting the validity of many tests involves the reliability of job performance measures themselves. As a result of this problem, *the validity of many tests may well be understated.* Although such discussion extends beyond the purposes of this book, we will discuss several issues relating to the question of validation later in this chapter.

Second, reliability and validity in psychological measurement are used to describe "tests" defined in a very broad and general sense. One can ask whether patterned interviews or weighted application blanks (both will be discussed later in this chapter) as well as tests are valid. In interviewing, for example, we are concerned with interrater reliability—is there a high probability that different rates of an individual's performance in the interview will generally agree with each other?

Characteristics of Recruitment and Selection Systems

In order to meet selection objectives, information-decision systems are often viewed as multistage in nature and invariably involve decision-making under risk. We will now discuss each of these characteristics.

Multistage Process

One convenient way of viewing the recruitment and selection process is to describe it as multistage, consisting of a number of decision points. This process may vary considerably from firm to firm, with organization size being a major contingency. In a small mom-and-pop grocery store, recruitment and selection may involve nothing more than the owner placing an advertisement in the store window, interviewing several applicants, and hiring the person who appears to be the best prospect. In large organizations, however, a multitude of policies and procedures may be developed in order to meet the firm's selection objectives.

Figure 1 depicts a conceptual model of a multistage process that assumes a "successful hurdle" approach for larger organizations. By *successful hurdle* we mean that if applicants do not do well with (or "clear") any of the five selection tool "hurdles," they will be eliminated from the "race" and not considered for selection.

Several observations are in order concerning this model. First, in some cases it may not be possible to make a simple *yes* or *no*

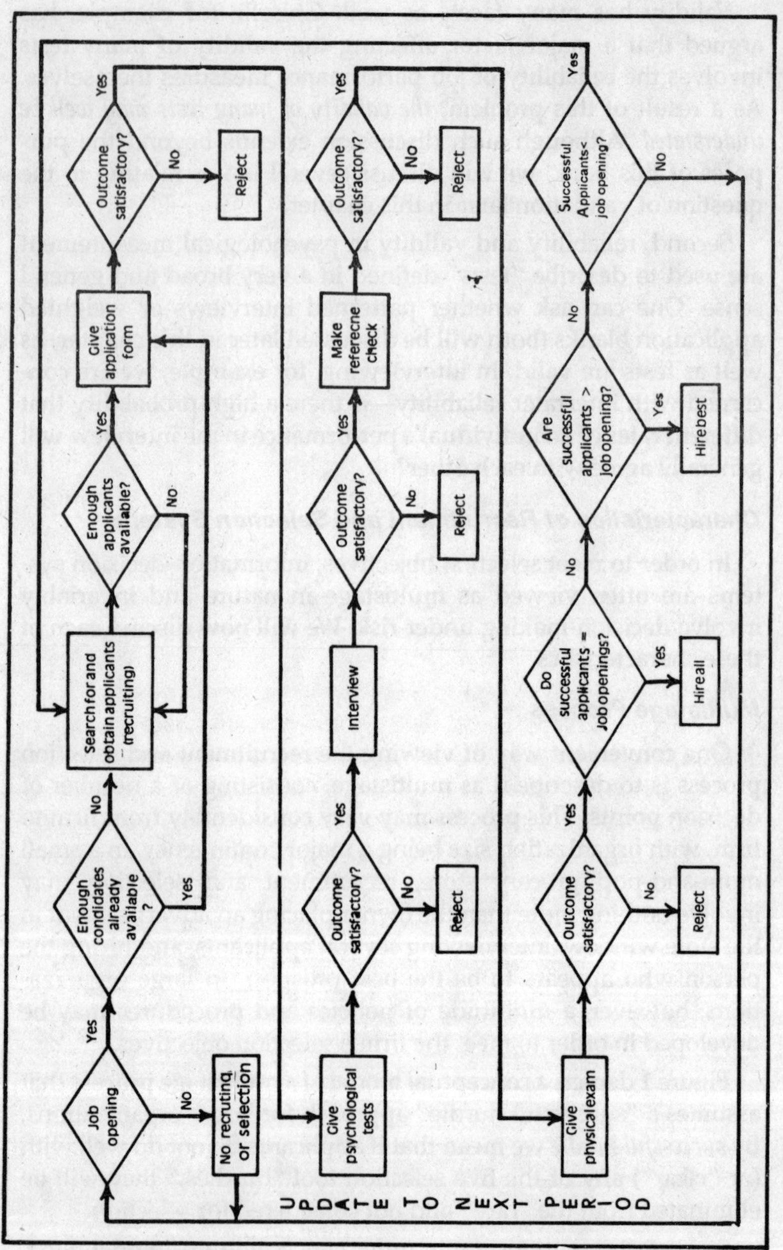

Fig. 1. The recruitment selection process.

decision at a particular decision point. For example, the personnel director may be uncertain about an applicant after reviewing only the application blank, and may decide to have the applicant take some psychological tests before making a final decision. On the other hand, the simple yes-no branching may often be quite simple. For instance, if the organization needs an electronic engineer with a college degree and three years' experience, a quick glance at application forms can easily determine whether candidates have the necessary qualifications.

Second, the sequence of selection tools may not always follow the order indicated in Figure 1. For example, college recruiters may first interview candidates, and then, if the applicants appear promising, encourage them to complete an application form. The information provided on the application may lead to an invitation for a later plant visit and additional interviews. In addition, organizations may also utilize other forms of "screening interviews" early in the process in order to evaluate candidates.

Third, in some cases a firm may continue to put a candidate through the selection process even after the personnel department has decided not to hire that person. This is often true when a managerial applicant is visiting the firm for the day and does poorly on some psychological tests early in the selection process. In order to maintain good public relations, the firm probably will not send the applicant back home immediately but instead will treat the candidate courteously for the remainder of the day.

Finally, even though multiple decisions are involved in personnel selection, some organizations may decide to look at *all* data concerning a job applicant before deciding whether or not to hire. This composite approach is based on the assumption that falling down slightly in one measure may be more than offset by doing extremely well in another.

For example, a firm may have established a cutoff score of 28 on a mental alertness test. However, an applicant who scores only 26 may be considered further because of special work experience that is valued very highly. This composite approach would be utilized in situations where falling down slightly in one measure is not associated with a high probability of failing on the job. Otherwise, high performance in other measures could not be more than an offsetting factor.

THE ROLE OF PERSONNEL IN RECRUITMENT AND SELECTION

We are now fairly aware of line-staff relationships in general. We will now illustrate these in more detail by looking at some of the staff and line activities of a large eastern corporation in recruiting and selecting college graduates. Top line management and the personnel manager of the company have set two basic objectives:

1. The firm should develop a strong affirmative action program to provide equal employment opportunities for all employees.
2. The firm should hire only college graduates for all entry-level management positions, since they would hopefully advance to higher-level positions.

In order to make the second objective congruent with the first, the firm had taken special efforts to expand recruitment efforts at several predominantly black colleges. Each year the college recruiting effort was undertaken with both of these objectives in mind. Each year the personnel department analyzed its previous recruiting efforts, determined which colleges were yielding the best candidates, and decided which colleges should be visited in the current year.

Information on the firm was sent to all campuses, and interview schedules were arranged for interested students. Experienced recruiters from the personnel department visited the campuses selected, interviewed prospective candidates, and asked the most promising ones to submit applications to the firm's personnel department. On the basis of applications received and the recommendations of the recruiters, the "best" candidates were invited to visit the firm for day. During the plant visit, each candidate was interviewed by members of the personnel department and members of line management.

In order to assure that line managers would be skilled in interviewing, the firm had provided training in interviewing techniques for all managerial personnel. Although the personnel department provided line managers with written recommendations about each college student who had visited the firm, the line managers made the final hiring decision.

This example illustrates recruitment and selection as a multi-stage process involving line-staff relationships. In the firm just described, there was no clear-cut distinction between line and staff responsibilities—both participated in the selection process. Further, the personnel department did more than simply advise. Its information and expertise gave it power to actually make many decisions. The recruiters made preliminary screening decisions during their campus visits, the personnel department decided which applicants should be invited for the plant visit, and so forth.

To improve the selection process, the personnel department performed work in another functional area—training. Managers were trained by personnel to interview by use of the technique of role playing, which will be discussed later in this book. This example illustrates again the interrelatedness of personnel activities undertaken and roles performed in relation to line management in the organizational system.

RECRUITMENT OF PERSONNEL

Recruiting involves searching for and obtaining job applicants. Several facets and approaches are utilized for the recruitment of personnel by organizations.

Approaches

Labor markets. In searching for applicants, a firm must be aware of the external labor market, and direct its recruiting efforts for different classes of personnel to the appropriate markets. By *external labor market* we mean those individuals outside of the firm seeking work in some defined geographical area.

Generally, most white-collar, clerical, and other non-management and nonprofessional individuals do not move frequently from city to city. Thus, most potential employees for these positions may be sought out locally. A broader labor market usually exists for managerial and professional employees. These individuals are much more mobile, and may be willing to move any place in the country (or abroad) for another job.

Within each labor market there are persons seeking or willing to accept jobs, and organizations seeking employees. Bringing these groups together entails the use of many different kinds of *media* through which these individuals and organizations may transmit information to each other. If this process were perfect, the "rational individual would maximize his probability of gaining the best job and minimize the costs of search." Similarly, organizations would attempt to hire the most competent individuals at a minimal cost.

In both instances, however, because of imperfect information, individuals and firms are engaged in *decision- making under risk*, Further, both individuals and organizations are inclined to "satisfice" rather than optimize. By *satisfice* we mean that firms will look at applicants until they find a competent one, but will not continue the search indefinitely until they find the "very best" one!

Information Transmission. There are many different types of information transmission media used in recruitment. Many of the more common sources include newspaper advertisements, organization newspaper advertisements, union hiring halls, college placement offices, public and private employment agencies, professional meetings, trade magazines, computerized resume placement services, friends and relatives, and an individual's direct application to an organization. Organizations, therefore, possess a wide variety of strategies in their search for candidates for positions.

Recruitment Decision Making. Three general observations may be made concerning recruitment decision making. First, there is some evidence that the two most common search strategies chosen by individuals are direct application, and through friends and relatives.

Second, many recruiting sources are geared in specific directions so that the firm (and knowledgeable individuals) have some media source guidelines. College placement offices would obviously be used only for positions requiring education beyond high school levels, and generally deal with beginning-level managerial or professional positions. Certain private employment agencies, on the other hand, deal with the experienced managers and professionals, and are often used by individuals who have good jobs but are looking for better ones.

Third, there are a number of contingencies involved in recruitment decision making. One of these is organization size in terms of the number of "exposures." A firm needing to hire 100 to 200 individuals would normally be expected to engage in more extensive and formalized recruiting procedures than if it had only one vacant position. An aerospace firm requiring 70 engineers to work on a new contract and a retail food chain opening a new supermarket in which 90 clerks are needed are two examples of firms in which more formalized efforts would be needed.

In recent years, some firms have turned to more creative and innovative efforts to solve problems with local recruitment efforts in "tight" labor markets. The use of both radio and television advertising to reach prospective candidates has been found to be particularly useful "in situations where competitive hiring needs are more immediate." Some firms have even found it possible to obtain such publicity *free* through the use of professional news releases.

Evaluating Recruiting Performance

One approach a firm can take in evaluating the effectiveness of its recruiting efforts is to first look at a particular medium (for example, newspaper ads) and calculate all the costs associated with it (such as company costs for plant visits and possible moving costs should applicants be hired). Next, the firm obtains an average cost per successful hire for each medium for each class of worker, such as blue-collar or clerical. Finally, the firm selects the medium that provides the most successful hires at the least cost.

Undertaking such evaluation poses a number of problems. First, labor market characteristics and media attraction may change before a firm has a chance to determine whether or not its earlier hires have been successful. Second, since recruiting is part of an interdependent information-decision system, it may be hard to isolate the attractiveness of employment agencies, for example, from the image that candidates gain from interviewers during a plant visit.

One eminent personnel manager has suggested measuring the efforts of different recruiters by comparing their individual efforts by the number of initial contacts made, and the percentage of (1) referrals, (2) invitations for visits, (3) persons actually interviewed, and (4) numbers of offers given, accepted, and refused. One difficulty with reliance on this approach, however, is that some interviewers may make fewer referrals because their standards are higher than others. Is this desirable or undesirable?

In addition, factors beyond the control of the recruiters enter the picture. For instance, different candidates may be interviewed by different managers when visiting the firm, and may come away from their visits with very different images of the organization (a situation which may be completely beyond the control of the original recruiter). These kinds of data must be looked at carefully, and the existence of systems interdependencies must be recognized.

SELECTION OF PERSONNEL

Let us first make some general observations about the decision-making processes in evaluating job applicants. We will then treat each of the five decision techniques indicated in Figure 1: (1) application blanks, (2) psychological tests, (3) interviews, (4) reference checks, and (5) physical examinations.

General Observations

Line management should make final hiring decisions, because they are in the best position to judge whether or not the candidate possesses the necessary knowledge, skills, and abilities to perform the job. However, the personnel department also makes many decisions of an evaluative nature throughout the selection process and influences what the final decision will be. The line manager will not even see certain job applicants because they have already been rejected for employment by personnel.

Selection as a Two-Way Road. In the progression through the stages of selection, several considerations are important. First, the whole selection process should be viewed as a *two-way communication process:* "Not only do companies attempt to assess the qualifications of job candidates but candidates judge the attractiveness of companies as well." It is not only important that the firm obtain necessary information from the candidate in order to make a good selection decision—candidates must also obtain information about the firm in order that *they* can make a good accept-or-reject decision should a job offer be made.

Applicants may be able to obtain financial and overall information about firms from annual reports and other published information. Other information which may be of more significance may be very difficult to obtain. For example, a one-hour interview may not be sufficient to provide candidates with enough information to know whether they will be able to get alone with their potential supervisor. This knowledge is especially important at those organizational levels where there are few clear-cut measures of performance and an individual's future may be strongly influenced by the supervisor-subordinate relationship.

Honesty by Both Applicant and the Organization. We believe that honesty on the part of both candidate and firm is important. With subjective selection techniques, a sophisticated graduating college student may be able to lie through an interview, enter dishonest responses on certain psychological tests, and "con" the company into offering a job not really suited to the applicant's personality. In such instances, the new employee may be unhappy in the job, not excel, and quit or be fired before long. This represents a waste of resources for both the employee and the organization. Similarly, if a firm conveys the false impression that promotions from entry-port to managerial positions at higher levels take about a year, while in reality the average time is three years, the employee may become disturbed by the false impressions and leave the organization or not work as hard.

Decision Making Under Risk. Personnel selection involves *decision making under risk.* As a result, organizations seek to learn as much abut prospective candidates as they can during the selection process. Some firms, for example, are concerned if a managerial candidate for a position involving handling corporate finances is heavily in debt. There may be two reasons for this concern: (1) the individual may have to take a second job to meet these obligations, which may result in excessive stress; and (2) if applicants cannot handle personal finances, how can they manage any of the firm's financial problems in a satisfactory manner?

The more important issue, however, may be the reason for such debt. Is it because the applicant gambles, or is it because a child had a serious illness two years before and all the medical debts have not been paid off? The answer to such a question can provide accurate data for a better decision regarding the suitability of an applicant.

Such probing, however, raises a fundamental issue in personnel selection: Are we infringing on the rights of individuals to have privacy? although some writers have been very much concerned about the individual's right to privacy, we believe that a firm facing a selection decision that may involve thousands of dollars has the right to ask certain personal questions *as long as they are relevant to on-the-job behavior.*

In addition, organizations must be aware that many questions may be viewed as discriminatory by federal and state agencies. Some questions, for example, such as those involving a person's religion, are blatantly illegal.

Two final observations about selection deserve elaboration here. First, organizations will often utilize different selection techniques for managerial and professional applicants than for rank-and-file employees. For example, in selecting managerial candidates, firms may utilize resumes as well as more sophisticated application blanks, require different psychological tests, and devote considerably more time to the interviewing process. Such procedures allow the firm to engage in more careful screening of individuals who will be making may key decisions within the organization.

Second, the sequencing of selection tools has an effect on both costs and information inputs to decision making. With respect to costs, it is much cheaper to have someone fill out an application blank first and be given a physical examination later. This is true not only because of the absolute costs involved, but also because of the probabilistic outcomes of the use of each tool.

Irrespective of costs, there is disagreement as to whether psychological tests (if they are used) should be given prior to or after the interview. Some personnel managers believe that giving an interviewer the applicant's psychological test data may bias attitudes during the interview. On the other hand, one could argue that the interviewer should posses all available information to provide a better basis for decision making. We prefer the latter strategy, even though both test and application form may bias an interviewer (especially if the interviewer is inexperienced). Our preference is based on the benefits to be derived by having these inputs available to the interviewer. This information may provide some indications of a candidate's strong and weak points, and serve as a useful guide for determining what types of questions would be most appropriate to ask during the interview.

Application Blanks

The application form is a quick and inexpensive means of screening out unqualified job applicants. It can also provide valuable information for future use and serve as a test of the applicant's ability to read. write, and follow directions. Typical types of questions on application forms concern prior work experience, names of previous supervisors, educational background, leadership experiences, and hobbies. *Firms must be very careful to avoid questions that could be construed as being discriminatory in nature.* We recommend that if information on age and marital status is needed for insurance purposes, *or* if a firm collects data on race, sex, and so forth, for use in its affirmative action program, *all such information should be collected and maintained separately from application forms.*

The safest strategy on application blanks is to ask only questions of fact that are directly relevant to individuals' ability to perform the job for which they are applying. For example, if clerical skills are an important part of many jobs in an organization, a section of the application blank could contain questions relating to typing and dictation speed.

In an effort to develop application forms that can predict probabilities of success on the job, *weighted application forms* have been used successfully by organizations as far back as the 1920s. Weighted application forms assume that the applicant's personal history is predictive of success on the job, and that statistical analysis can indicate the degree of job relatedness of *specific* application form items to some job success criterion such as tenure. On weighted application forms, those items which are most strongly predictive are given more weight than those of lesser importance. The item weights (which may be either negative or positive) are summed to provide a total score. The firm then establishes a cutoff score, and if a candidate's summed score is equal to or greater than the cutoff score, that person is considered further for selection. If not, the candidate is rejected.

Validated weighted application blanks have provided management with good (probabilistic) prediction instruments for making personnel selection decision. In addition, they may also provide a defense against charges of discrimination should they arise.

From a contingency point of view, the more dynamic the organization, the more frequently weighted application blanks and other selection instruments must be updated and revalidated. Inskeep has expressed the opinion that "weighted application forms are seldom valid for more than two years." Finally, size also represents an important contingency, because a weighted application form must be given to a large enough sample of applicants within a "reasonable" period of time to be statistically sound. Using a sample spread over many years leads to problems in obtaining a sample from a stable population.

Personnel Testing

Personnel Testing refers to the practice of administering psychological tests to personnel in order to secure information useful in their selection, placement, and career guidance. Thus, a major reason for personnel testing is to enhance the accuracy of personnel decisions relative to hiring, firing, promotion, transfer, training, and personnel development. Users of psychological tests believe that a carefully and professionally developed program of personnel testing can and does substantially reduce costly methods of trial and error in personnel administration and reduces the relative incidence of faulty decisions concerning personnel moves. Ideally, then, the end objective of personnel testing is to help in insuring a flow of the *right* people into the *right* jobs at the *right* times.

Psychological Tests

Psychological tests have been used for over half a century as selection tools. Sometimes firms develop tests of their own; in other instances, they purchase tests developed by firms specializing in test design and development.

Tests have been controversial for years. A basic assumption underlying their use is that there are differences in individual abilities, attitudes, and behavior that can be measured and that are related to successful job performance. Unfortunately, this assumption has not proven valid in many cases.

Today there are three basic types of tests available for employers—aptitude and ability, interest, and personality. We are not advocating the use of any particular tests, but simply describing some of these testing devices which are available to organizations today. Before discussing tests in particular, however, we will first consider the issue of test validation, since this concept is basic to the understanding of test usage.

Rationale

A psychological test is best defined as *sample of performance observed under standardized conditions*. A well developed test is one which presents a series of tasks to be performed under uniform conditions by each examine. It is obvious that unless a test is carefully standardized, the behavior required by it will not be comparable from examine to examine. Thus, careful standardization is one of the most important attributes of a psychological test, and constitutes also one of the major advantages of testing over other more subjective personnel assessment procedures such as interviewing. The sampling concept is also important. A carefully developed test samples performance in order to be representative of broader areas of performance. Thus, a personality test designed to measure dominance should be representative of dominant behavior in a variety of situations and circumstances.

This leads to what is by far the most important concept in psychological testing: *validity*. In the broadest sense, the validity of a test refers to the *meaning* that may be attached to different levels of performance on the test. It should be apparent, then, that a test's validity cannot be expressed in a single index or in terms of a single item of information. Validity is *not* an either-or, all-or-none concept. Instead, the determination of the *validity* or the *meaning* of scores on a given test is a never-ending process based on the accumulation of research information over a lengthy period of time. Thus a test may be valid for some purposes and non-valid for others.

Test Validation. Validity, as indicated earlier, refers to the ability of any instrument to measure what it is supposed to measure. Validation of many types of measurement instruments is important in personnel management (for example, weighted application blanks). In this section we will focus special attention on the validation of psychological tests, a major area of validation research.

Criterion validity refers to how well a testing device can actually predict success on the job. Earlier in this chapter, we discussed the problems of accurately defining "successful" performance. The guidelines also recognize the fact that firms may utilize a number of different criteria, to include (but not necessarily be limited to) "production rate, error rate, tardiness, absenteeism, and length of service." In addition, performance appraisals could also be utilized as the criterion of "success." "A standardized rating of overall work performance may be used where a study of the job shows that it is an appropriate criterion."

To demonstrate *content validity,* organizations must show that "the behaviour(s) demonstrated in the selection procedure are a representative sample of the behaviour(s) of the job in question." Some examples of content-valid tests could include a typing test for a position in the secretarial typing pool or a shorthand test for the position of executive secretary. In addition, firms seeking to establish training or experience qualifications as part of their job specifications would also rely upon content validation. In our example of the executive secretary above, a firm requiring "five years of secretarial experience" could be required to establish "the basis of the relationship between the content of the training or experience and the content of the job for which the training or experience is to be required or evaluated."

Construct validity involves a more complex strategy than either of the other two validation procedures we have discussed. It requires an organization to show that psychological tests to identify particular psychological constructs are "validly related to the performance of critical or important work behavior(s)." For example, a firm seeking to hire a crew for a submarine engaged in deep-water or exploration could decide to implement a test aimed at screening out all applicants with claustrophobia. For most jobs, however, the task is not this simple. Because of the relative newness of the field, there is a lack of substantial evidence expanding this concept to employment practices.

Predictive and Concurrent Validation. Two basic types of criterion validation procedures can be used by the personnel manager: *predictive* and *concurrent.* Predictive validation is the more scientific of the two, and requires:

1. Giving "tests" to all job applicants but not using the test scores in hiring any of these applicants.

2. "Hiding" the test scores of the applicants who were hired for some period of time after hiring (for example, six months to two years).
3. At this later time analyzing the relationship between the individual test scores and a criterion measure such as actual performance on the job.

The reason for "hiding" the test results is to avoid *contamination.* For example, if supervisors were told what the subordinates' test scores were, they could be become biased, and treat and rate the performance of those with the higher scores more favorably. If this were to occur, we would have test scores influencing the behavior they are supposed to predict, and there would be no solid basis for scientific validation.

Although predictive validation is most "scientific," it has its limitations. It is expensive and time consuming, and it would pose difficulties for smaller companies. The smaller firm, for example, might not be able to afford the statistical analysis required for validation, and it might take an inordinate amount of time before it was possible to hire a large enough sample size of any particular group of employees to permit statistical analysis. In addition, if a firm administered but did not use the results of the testing in its selection procedure, many individuals who were not competent could be hired.

Because of these problems, organizations frequently utilize the procedure of *concurrent validation:* giving tests to *current* employees and *concurrently* obtaining criterion data, for example, supervisor ratings of performance. This approach permits using the results of this analysis without any of the delay encountered utilizing predictive validation. Further, concurrent validation eliminates the problem of hiring poor performers in order to obtain adequate statistical data.

The procedure is limited, however, by a phenomenon known as *range restriction.* This results because only qualified employees who have remained with the firm are given the tests, and therefore a smaller range of behavior is being evaluated. In addition, the motivation of present employees in taking the tests may be quite different from that of job applicants.

Validation Strategies. With respect to validation strategies, firms have two options: to validate their own testing procedures, or to purchase tests from other firms. There are a number of organizations that develop, provide statistical data on, and sell tests to business firms.

In the latter instance, the firm could simply decide to buy one or more tests developed by firms specializing in this kind of work. *In doing so, firms must be extremely careful that the jobs for which statistical data are available from the test developers are very similar to or the same as those jobs for which the test is to be used.* This illustrates the importance and value of job analysis within organizations. We also hypothesize that the firm's size and resources would represent important contingencies in its decision to purchase or internally validate its testing procedures. For example, smaller firms in particular may lack the resources necessary to undertake elaborate validation studies, and may find it simpler and cheaper to purchase validated tests.

Uses of Personnel Testing

Four major uses of personnel testing are listed and briefly discussed below:

Selection. Personnel testing is most commonly used as an aid in selecting applicants. In using tests for selection, management will want to have evidence that they are valid for predicting job effectiveness defined in terms of such factors as supervisory ratings, productivity, sales volume, low turnover, etc.

Determining Training. Needs. Personnel testing may be used to establish the need for further training or specialized knowledge. Since knowledge or achievement examinations would normally be used for this purpose, management would want evidence that they sample content representative of the skills and or knowledge emphasized in its training programs.

Counseling. Personnel testing is coming to play an increasingly important role in employee counseling. However, since the counseling would usually be undertaken by a professional counselor (e.g. a clinical psychologist), any decision concerning personnel testing would normally rest with him.

Promotion and Transfer. Personnel testing is widely used to aid in decisions concerning promotion and transfer. Since career guidance is an important part of such decisions, the tests must be useful not only in a selection sense but also in a counseling sense, and management will want evidence of their descriptive validity as well as their validity for predicting actual job performances.

It is apparent that different uses of personnel testing involve different kinds of decisions for management, and different kinds of information concerning the tests to be used. It is also obvious that management's use of personnel testing will nearly always involve *institutional* decisions in contrast to *individual* decisions. In other words, management's major purpose is to improve the quality of utilizing its human resources in order to enhance the over-all effectiveness of the organization or institution.

The usual purpose is to maximize accuracy or "batting odds" for selecting and placing persons on jobs in an organization. Management may desire 100% accuracy—all "hits." But it must accept the unfortunate necessity of occasional "misses"–some persons are rejected who could have been successful; others are hired who may actually fail. From the standpoint of the *institution,* management's purpose is to maximize the "hits" and to minimize the "misses." Personnel tests usually help achieve this purpose.

Ability and Aptitude Tests. Many tests have been developed to measure a person's ability to do a specific job, or aptitude (potential ability) to undertake some tasks successfully. Ability or achievement tests can evaluate either a candidate's assumed knowledge or skills. For example, an employee who claims previous meat-cutting experience could be given a written test about various cuts of meat and how to make such cuts. An example of a skills test would be having a secretary take a dictated letter, transcribe it, type it.

Most such tests are for non-managerial jobs, where skills and abilities are more precisely definable. The validity of such tests would, of course, depend upon the content of the test and its relationship to actual behaviors or knowledge of the job. In general, of all psychological tests, the greatest confidence can be placed upon valid ability tests, since they are measuring something fairly concretely.

Although it is not possible to "fake" such tests (interest tests, for example, could be faked), some mental alertness tests may be "culturally biased." For this reason, many firms that produce tests have also developed different norms for ethnic groups. In addition, since some of these tests are so widely used, there may be a test familiarity problem. To help overcome this, alternative forms have been developed for some tests. These are given to job applicants who indicate that they have taken a particular test previously. Most of the well-known tests are relatively inexpensive to administer and interpret, and considerable statistical data concerning their validity are often available from the publishers. This does *not*, however, indicate that firms should not conduct their own validity studies.

How are such tests utilized in personnel selection decision making? Although the current situation is clouded because of equal employment opportunity issues, historically the following principles have applied:

- Mental alertness tests have been given more weight than interest and personality profiles.
- Firms have used either publishers' statistical data or their own validation data to establish cutoff scores.

In some instances, primarily in nonindustrial sales jobs, an *upper* cutoff score may be established on the rationale that an extremely bright person would not find the job interesting. Such upper cutoff scores (in the high forties) have been used on the Wonder-lic test in sales positions with firms in the hearing aid industry, and in the sale of women's lingerie. It must be emphasized that *all* selection-decision rules are ones that improve the firm's *probabilities* of hiring employees who will be successful and rejecting those who would have failed. Thus, we are dealing with selection decision making under risk.

Criticisms of Tests

Personnel testing in industry has often been criticized by those who dispute the use of personnel testing for making institutional decisions. However, most critics argue from the point of view of individual decision making and fail to realize that the "rightness" or "wrongness" of each individual decision must, of necessity, be secondary to the purpose of increasing the odds of accurate personnel decisions for the entire organization. Most critics of testing also choose to ignore or refuse to accept the fact that a carefully developed and validated program of personnel testing will, over the long run, increase relative numbers of correct individual decisions as well as increase the batting odds associated with institutional decisions.

In deciding whether to use testing or not to use testing, management should consider its potential *utility* to the organization. Personnel testing can be expensive. Management must weigh the costs of instituting and maintaining a testing program against the possible gain involved in making more accurate decisions.

We are not suggesting that personnel testing is not often useful; in actual fact, its relative utility is usually very great. We are suggesting, however, that management should diligently seek *evidence* of its utility for the specific uses and for making the kinds of decisions to be asked of it.

Institutional Considerations

It is obvious, then, that a program of personnel testing should not be undertaken without careful thought. In particular, a decision to use or not to use tests should *not* be based on fads, fashions, or personal opinions. Fortunately, a number of institutional considerations can be enumerated which should be taken into account in deciding whether or not to undertake a personnel testing program. These include:

(1) There should be evidence that the present selection program is not achieving maximum effectiveness; e.g. high turnover, low morale, or low job effectiveness may point up the need for "looking into" a testing program.

(2) Management should be able to define successful job performance and to specify explicitly the problems it wants to attack through personnel testing.

(3) Since testing will usually result in setting more rigorous selection and/or promotion standards, management should evaluate its source of supply of candidates. It will want to be assured of a sufficiently large supply to enable optimum use of the personnel testing program. Often, the use of personnel testing will need to be accompanied by improved recruiting

methods and/or more effective and efficient personnel development programs.

(4) Management should confirm the availability of tests appropriate to the jobs and/or problem areas for which it hopes to use them. Ordinarily, the question of test availability will need to be answered by the psychologist with whom the company works.

(5) Management should lay the groundwork for the testing program. The program should not be instituted until everyone apt to be affected by it is fully informed and congnizant of the goals of testing, and the potential gains to be realized as a result of the program.

Interviews

In the past 40 years, numerous reviews of research on selection interviewing have appeared which reflect incongruent findings, low validities when related to job performance, and lack of interrater reliability (comparing the opinions of different interviewers about an applicant). Despite such findings, the employment interview continues to be used by virtually all firms today as an integral part of the selection process. The observations of one researcher in 1949 may well explain the continuing love affair that organizations have with the interview: "The interview remains popular as a selection procedure despite its questionable reliability. Even though the interview were thoroughly repudiated, it would probably not be abandoned: there seems to be a certain human curiosity which can be satisfied in no other way than by 'seeing the man in the flesh."

Prior to 1964, most research on the interview focused attention on the problem of whether the interview *as a whole* is a reliable and valid selection instrument. Although there were some exceptions, in general the findings showed that "unstructured interviews generally had poor interrater reliabilities and that in almost every case in which satisfactory reliabilities were obtained, the interview was structured." Even when studies were able to establish high interrater reliabilities, however, validities were generally poor. Disenchantment with the reliability-validity questions resulted in research focusing on the decision-making process of the interviewers.

Since 1964 studies have identified a number of variables which influence both the reliability and the validity of the interview process, and we have depicted some of these in the box here. Some of the variables identifies as influencing interviewer decision making are: visual cues by the interviewee, body language, interviewer stereotypes of the ideal candidate, prejudices regarding sex and/or racial characteristics, the type of information presented (with negative information weighted more heavily than positive), and so forth. Even the order of applicants interviewed may influence the interviewer's decision. For example, applicants who are interviewed immediately after a very poor candidate may be rated higher than if they had been interviewed immediately after a very good candidate.

The results of studies on these variables affecting decision making led Schmitt to state in 1976: "In conclusion, there is not much in the research of the last half dozen years to bolster the confidence of the personnel interviewer concerned with the reliability and validity of his decisions. There is a good deal of evidence concerning the influence of variables which may make his decision both less reliable and valid."

Although research has failed to resolve the reliability-validity issue of the interview, we believe that many of the problems connected with selection interviewing can be overcome to varying degrees. First, we have noted that a number of studies have shown that structured interviews are more effective than unstructured or less structured ones in resolving the problem of interrater reliability. There are at least two reasons why unstructured interviews may lack such reliability: "Systematic biases and selective perception can affect interviewers in different ways, thus resulting in lack of agreement between them. Further, if the interview is unstructured, entirely different topics may be covered by one interviewer than by another...." Because reliability is a necessary prerequisite for validity, a structured interview appears to be the logical starting point for further research on interviewing.

Second, suggestions have been made that interviewing applicants for specific jobs is more effective than "interviewing in the abstract." As a result, providing interviewers with accurate job descriptions and specifications will help improve interviewer decisions. This suggestion has been supported by one study which found that the availability of job information "reduced the effect of irrelevant attributes on decisions but did not eliminate it."

Third, companies need to take more seriously the issue of interviewer training. Two researchers have suggested that "if interviewers can be trained to perceive more accurately how effectively specific individuals will performs in the job(s) for which they are being considered, any validation problems may be considerably minimized...." These same researchers suggested that the starting point for such training should involve knowledge of the findings regarding those variables affecting decision making which make the interview less reliable and valid. In addition, many of the earlier reviewers of research on the interview have suggested that training in the patterned or structured interview may be a promising way of resolving the reliability (and hopefully validity) problem associated with the employment interview.

There are at least three specific types of interviews available to decision makers: (1) patterned or structured, (2) nondirective, and (3) stress. In addition, firms, especially at managerial and professional levels, usually conduct more than one interview, and these three strategies may be mixed from one interviewer to another. Having considered the research regarding the interview, we will now consider these three different types of interviews.

FACTORS FOUND TO INFLUENCE DECISION MAKING IN THE INTERVIEW

1. Interviewer stereotypes of ideal candidate.
2. Information presented by interviewee: Unfavorable information is weighted more heavily than favorable information.
3. Interviewers' tendency to make early decisions regarding whether to hire or not hire the interviewee.
4. Attitudinal, sexual, and racial similarities between interviewers and interviewees.
5. Contrast of the candidate with other candidates being considered (e.g., following a "terrible" candidate may make even a mediocre candidate appear good!).
6. Visual cues given by interviewee (eye contact, body language, etc.).

7. The amount of information which the interviewer actually has about the job for which the candidate is being considered.
8. Structured interview guides, which increase interviewer agreement about candidates.

The Patterned Interview

For many years, firms have utilized the *patterned interview,* or the planned interview, which "is designed around a common set of questions for each job. The procedure should start with standardized questions. This means the same adequate setting and the same freedom from interference in all interviews. Then, because questions should be the same from interview to interview, they should be specified in writing and given to all interviewers." Often the written questions are given to the interviewer in a form which the interviewer should follow, so that all interviewers will ask basically the same questions in the same sequence to all applicants.

The patterned form asks questions with respect to previous education, previous jobs, and so forth. Claimed advantages of this procedure are that the interviewer works from specific job specifications, knows what questions to ask, and has a definite plan for the interview.

The training aspect of this study raises an interesting question: To what extent was it interviewer expertise (specific training) or the patterned interview itself which led to successful validation? The question must be raised as to whether the same interviewers trained extensively in another technique (for example, the stress or non-directive) would have accomplished more or fewer successful outcomes. However, as we have already noted, research appears to favor the patterned interview because of its increased reliability. Some interviewers, on the other hand, do not like the patterned interview since it constrains them to ask a prescribed set of questions in a prescribed order. This approach provides less opportunity to explore other areas that may be more relevant to the hiring decision.

The Nondirective Interview. An almost diametrically opposite interviewing strategy is the *non-directive interview,* which is used in both counseling and selection interviews. The interviewer attempts to let the interviewee structure direction, plays a very permissive role (not exhibiting signs of favor or disfavor), and hopes that applicants in such a setting will relax and discuss issues that they would not during a more conventional interview. This approach (if done well) requires considerable skill, and will sometimes induce interviewees to discuss salient facts about themselves that might never be revealed in a patterned interview.

The major problem with the nondirective interview is that research has consistently failed to establish either its reliability or validity as a selection technique. In contrast with the planned or patterned interview, interviewers using the non-directive interview do *not* ask interviewees the same basic questions in the same order. Consequently, research has failed to establish interrater reliability.

Stress Interviews. Sometimes firms use *stress interviews* in which they attempt to obtain an idea of the applicant's reactions to stress. This approach may be especially useful when job candidates are applying for positions involving considerable pressure, such as union contract negotiations. What the stress interview does is to make applicants feel uncomfortable through interruptions or challenges in order to see what their reactions may be.

Another means of providing stress is to have more than one job applicant in the room being interviewed by more than one interviewer at the same time. One person, for example, was placed in a situation in which three other interviewees were called together to reach agreement on a managerial decision problem given to them. Two interviewers (one on each end of the table) observed the group dynamics of the problem solving, but made only a few comments during the process. All interviewees expressed the same opinion afterwards: The experience was extremely stressful for them.

Panel or Board Interviews. One variation of the stress interview which appears to have promise as a valid selection tool is the *panel interview,* or *board interview.* This procedure is frequently utilized for selection of police officers and civil service personnel. Drawing on results reported in a number of studies during the late 1970s, Arvey and Campion concluded that "recent research has not been as pessimistic about the validity and reliability as that of prior years. Interviews conducted by a board or panel appear to be promising as a vehicle for enhancing reliability and validity." In addition, these two researchers also encourage the utilization of "directly related job analysis and other information" as a means of improving the accuracy of selection interviewing regardless of which type of interview strategy is followed.

TYPES OF TESTS

Personnel tests may be *capacity or aptitude tests, proficiency or achievement tests, or personality and interest checklists or scales.* Aptitude tests serve to predict success of a person on a job in which he (she) had no (or very limited) experience. Proficiency tests measure skill or other occupational knowledge or ability. Interest and personality measures help to give insights into the kinds of work a person will find satisfaction in doing, and the type of behavior to be expected in his or her relations with other people. Interest and personality measures are usually considered separately from aptitude tests because of their special nature.

All tests mentioned here are available from established test publishers and have been tested in actual employment situations. Because of space limitations, a *selected list* is discussed here, illustrating types of tests found generally useful in selection and placement. Not included here are tests published for the sole use of clients. When such tests are offered to a firm, it is well to inquire into evidence of their validity and have such evidence evaluated by a competent personnel psychologist. The objective here is simply to indicate briefly the general nature of aptitudes and abilities shown by tests of different types and to provide examples of specific tests in each general test category.

Tests of Mental Ability. These measure general intelligence. They may be referred to as verbal ability tests, verbal-linguistic tests, intelligence tests, classification tests, personnel classification tests, or simply "personnel"tests. (it is recommended that the use of the term *intelligence test* be avoided in the employment situation. To many applicants, the idea of taking an "intelligence" test is upsetting.) To others it may be rejuvenating.

Briefly discussed below are some representative tests of mental ability in current use:

Wesman Personnel Classification Text (PCT), alternate forms, The Psychological Corporation. Developed primarily for use in the employment situation, the PCT provides separate measures of verbal reasoning ability and facility in use of numerical concepts.

Adaptability Tests, alternate forms, Science Research Associates. This test attempts to furnish a quick estimate of "general mental ability" by means of a wide variety of items.

Test of Learning Ability, alternate forms, Richardson, Bellows, Henry and Co., Inc. This follows the format of the Army General Classification Tests used and validated during World War II.

Fundamental Achievement Series, (FAS), alternate forms. The Psychological Corporation. FAS-Verbal and FAS-Numerical cover the ability range from basic literacy to somewhat above the eighth-grade level.

Advanced Personnel Test, alternate forms. The Psychological Corporation. Distribution is restricted and test is administered only at specified licensed testing centers. Although not designed for industrial use, it is mentioned here since research in several large companies suggests that it is useful in identifying superior verbal ability among candidates for high-level executive and technical positions.

Tests of Clerical Aptitude

Extensive research indicates that two of the main components for success in clerical work are a minimum level of intelligence, and clerical aptitude—defined by speed and accuracy in perceiving numerical and verbal similarities and differences. For most jobs, the minimum level of mental ability is about the average level of the population as a whole. Where promotability is a factor, higher mental ability is often required. This can be determined from in-plant research.

Successful clerical workers form a highly selected portion of the population in terms of clerical aptitude.

Minnesota Clerical Test, one form, The Psychological Corporation. This is a test of speed and accuracy of number checking and name checking.

General Clerical Test, one form, The Psychological Corporation. This is designed as a general and differential test for use in selecting and up-grading all types of clerical personnel.

Short Tests of Clerical Ability, one form, Science Research Associates. Measures seven skills and aptitudes important in office jobs. Seven separate tests measure abilities in arithmetic, business vocabulary, checking, coding, understanding and following oral and written directions, filing and language (grammar, spelling and punctuation).

The Short Employment Tests (SET), three forms, The Psychological Corporation. Three sub-tests in the battery are: word knowledge or vocabulary–essentially a short intelligence test; numerical ability or speed and accuracy in computations; and clerical speed and accuracy—applicant must locate and verify names in an alphabetic list and read and code the dollar balance associated with the name.

Mechanical Aptitude Tests

In common usage, the term "mechanical aptitude" is applied rather generally to the ability to do any type of mechanical work. This somewhat loose usage has led to the false notion among some personnel managers that anyone they select with high mechanical aptitude, whether on the basis of a mechanical aptitude test or their own judgment, will be able to perform any mechanical job in the plant, given proper training. However, this overlooks both the widely varying nature of jobs labeled mechanical, and the fact that aptitude for mechanical work is apparently not a single trait. Mechanical aptitude also is frequently assumed to include a high amount of manual dexterity. Research has revealed that measures of mechanical aptitude are almost totally unrelated to measures of manual dexterity. Thus, results not better than chance may be expected if a mechanical aptitude test is used to predict success in semi-skilled assembly and operative jobs requiring superior manual dexterity. Because of this lack of relationship, tests of manual dexterity are treated separately from mechanical tests in this discussion.

A number of tests have been developed which have proved to be reasonably valid for various occupations requiring superior mechanical aptitude. The nature of mechanical aptitude has been clarified by a study of relationships among these tests. Studies indicate that mechanical aptitude is apparently a composite of spatial visualization, perceptual speed and acuity, and mechanical information. Because of these findings, spatial tests are included in the present category. However, it is desirable to try out several tests, tapping various factors of mechanical aptitude, in order to achieve maximum efficiency in prediction. Many companies following this procedure have materially improved their effectiveness in selection and differential placement through development of a battery of several mechanical aptitude tests.

Tests of Manual Dexterities

Research has demonstrated that two distinct types of manual dexterity can be measured by currently available tests—variously referred to as *gross* and *fine, manual* and *finger* dexterity, or *arm-and-hand* and *wrist-and-finger* dexterities. It also appears that these two types of dexterity are relatively discrete and unrelated to each other. As a result it cannot be assumed that workers who demonstrate skill in types of packing, wrapping, and sorting that require gross arm-and-hand dexterity are readily transferable to jobs requiring superior wrist-and-finger dexterity. By the same token, workers who may excel in the type of fine dexterity required for small-assembly work may do very poorly if placed on jobs requiring rapid gross dexterity.

Manual dexterities may not be used as indicators of mechanical aptitude. Studies show that manual dexterities are relatively independent of mechanical aptitude as measured by tests of mechanical comprehension and spatial visualization. Also, measures of dexterity have not been found valuable in the skilled trades, where understanding of the processes involved is more important than individual differences in the manual dexterity with which they are executed.

Arm-and-hand dexterity has been found important in such semi-skilled jobs as packing, wrapping, and inspection, and in gross-manual assembly and machine operation jobs. Fine-manual dexterity has been shown to be important in simple jobs which require rapid wrist-and-finger movements, such as power-sewing-machine operation and assembly of small electrical parts; in more complex assembly, requiring both speed and precision, such as watch assembly; and in other occupations in which rapid manipulation of small objects is involved, e.g. office-machine operator, bank teller, and typist. For the later jobs, tests of clerical aptitude and intelligence are generally more useful in selection.

Tests of Proficiency and Acquired Skill

Tests of aptitude may be use to assess the potential for work in which skill is claimed. More frequently it is desired to gauge the actual level of skill of an applicant in relation to present employees and other applicants. Here aptitude tests are not appropriate. Tests to measure job skills are actually achievement tests. They measure the level of skill and knowledge acquired by the applicant or employee prior the time he is tested. Tests of this type are usually referred to as *proficiency tests* or *trade tests.* Proficiency tests may be primarily measures of job knowledge or information, and measures of *job skill.* Oral trade tests, merchandise knowledge tests, and measures of a nature similar to the Purdue tests referred to below are essentially job knowledge and information tests. Measures of job skill are usually work-sample tests such as those to measure proficiency in typing, shorthand, and various machine operations.

Tests of proficiency are of value in three main areas of personnel work: in hiring and assigning, in transferring and promoting, and in training. In selection, they readily disclose the "trade bluffers." In addition to detecting areas which can be remedied by training, proficiency tests are of value in measuring outcomes of training programs. Probably because many tests of job proficiency are tailor-made by companies using them (or perhaps because they are not as widely used as they should be), there is little published material describing them.

Vocational Interest Measures

In addition to aptitudes and proficiency, another factor presumed to be of importance is the basic interest of workers in the occupational field in which they are engaged. Studies have shown that successful workers in an occupation, particularly in the professions, have certain similarities of interests (a characteristic set of likes and dislikes) which can be measured and which differentiate them from other occupational groupings.

The majority of inventories of vocational interests have been developed for use in counseling and guiding students, and have wide use in high schools and colleges. Manuals of a number of published inventories suggest their usefulness in selection and placement, but supporting validation for most measures of interest is meagre or lacking. Thus prospective users of an interest measure should inquire into its research basis.

Research suggests that measures of interest are more useful in predicting job stability than in predicting levels of success. Interest apparently determines the "direction of effort," and ability the "level of achievement."

Interest inventories are susceptible of "faking," and special care should be used in their administration. Applicants must be convinced that it is to their interest in the long run to answer all questions honestly.

Measures of Personality

The importance of personality in job success is generally recognized. Most failures are due not to lack of ability, but rather to inadequacies of the person in his relationships with other people, in his attitude toward his work and toward society, in his motivations, and in his attitude toward himself.

Substantial advance have been made in recent years in the development of devices to aid in clinical diagnosis of personality deviations. But progress in development of personality measures for use in selection is still far behind that of aptitude measurement. Because of this, management will be wise to beware of any personnel consultant or test salesman who makes broad claims for his techniques of personality measurement, unless the data can be submitted to serious study and independent test by competent psychologists.

Miscellaneous Tests

A number of tests are available which do not fit neatly into the previous classifications. Among these are single tests for which claims are made by the publishers as to values for selection and/or training. Examples are safety and supervisory tests. Test batteries represent another type of test (or combination of tests) which do not fit strictly into a functional classification.

Reference Checks

Another selection tool used by firms is the reference check. Most application forms ask job applicants to list previous employers, and some ask for the names of other individuals who will provide a recommendation. The degree to which firms rely on reference checks varies. At one end of the spectrum, some firms make no checks at all. At the other extreme, a college professor who was being considered for a visiting professorship elsewhere was required to provide recommendations from five scholars with national reputations.

Several different reference check alternatives are open to the firm, each with a different outcome. Probably the poorest of all are letters sent by personal friends, for they will inevitably provide a favorable view of the job applicant. A second source of background data may be obtained by communicating with the personnel departments of previous employers.

A third strategy is to telephone the candidate's supervisor in the last job. Some times valid data can be obtained by this alternative. Previous supervisors, however, not wanting to ruin a very poorly performing individual's chances for obtaining another job, may often gloss over major deficiencies. Further, applicants who are currently employed may be reluctant to have a prospective employer talk with the current supervisor for fear of retaliation in their present job.

Physical Examinations

Many organizations require physical examinations of all new employees. The objectives of such examinations are twofold. First are humanitarian reasons. No responsible firm would want an individual with a bad back placed in a job requiring lifting, or an executive candidate with a serious ulcer problem placed in a high-stress decision-making position.

Second are economic reasons. If a firm hires someone with a bad back, and the new employee is injured and must leave the job, the firm's selection and training costs will be wasted. In addition, the employee will be eligible for workers' compensation benefits, which in the long run will be costly to the firm, since safety and health experience affects worker's compensation contributions.

SIMULATION OF A PSYCHOLOGICAL DECISION PROCESS IN PERSONNEL SELECTION

A few years ago it would have been physically impossible to gather, record and analyze the mass of data which today seems necessary if management is to procure the best in engineering. Scientific and administrative personnel. The data processing systems for the recruiting of professional personnel handle a tremendous volume of information at a great saving.

Considerable attention in recent years has been given to the computer simulation of human thought processes in problem solving. The computer simulation of the decision processes of a psychologist dealing with the ill-structured problem of analyzing psychological test scores and other data concerning individuals is being considered for various types of clerical and clerical-administrative positions. The computer model was designed to output, as did the psychologist in his decision making, both: (1) numerous interpretive comments about each applicant, and (2) a specific recommendation as to whether the individual should be employed. The methodology and results of this research are described, and the possibility of utilizing computerized models of this type as an aid in personnel selection is suggested.

The interpretation of psychological data often poses a fairly complex decision problem. Such is frequently the case when an organization utilizes a battery of tests, each measuring one or more psychological dimensions, to test applicants for any one of several different jobs, each with different skill and personality requirements. In this type of analysis, many test scores have meaning only when examined in light of: (1) other scores in the battery, and (2) the requirements of a specific job for which the individual is applying. Further, those interpreting these data are often called on not only to recommend whether or not the applicant should be hired, but also to develop a written description of each applicant's psychological characteristics.

In this type of decision-making, the interpreter is faced with an ill-structured problem which is not amenable to solution by algorithmic techniques. In recent years, considerable research has been devoted to developing computerized simulations of the human thought processes involved in dealing with such problems.

In the present study, a computer simulation was developed of the thought processes of a psychologist as he interpreted various data about job applicants being considered for employment. This model was designed to output, as did the psychologist, both: (1) interpretive comments about each applicant, and (2) a recommendation as to whether or not the applicant should be employed. This research was aimed at both developing a descriptive model of the human thought processes involved in this type of analysis, and exploring the possibility of utilizing computerized interpretive simulations as prescriptive models for personnel selection.

The Decision Problem

Selected for study was psychologist employed by a large consulting firm specializing in personnel selection, as he analyzed data regarding certain individuals being considered for jobs with client firms. All applicants being analyzed were females under consideration for clerical and clerical-administrative positions such as billing clerk, statistical clerk, and executive secretary. These individuals had been subjected to initial screening by the client firms prior to being tested.

In making his analysis of each applicant, the psychologist had three basic types of informational inputs at his disposal.

First were nineteen tests scores from the following test battery:

1. The Otis Mental Ability Test
2. The Gordon Personal Profile, which measures four personality characteristics: ascendancy, responsibility, emotional stability, and sociability.
3. The Gordon Personal Inventory, designed to measure the individual's cautiousness, intellectual curiosity, personal relations, and vigor.
4. The Washburne Social Adjustment Inventory, which provides both a measure of seven specific personality characteristics, including truthfulness, and an overall measure of social adjustment.
5. The Short Employment Tests, measuring verbal, numerical and general clerical skills.

Second, the psychologist had information as to the applicant's age and number of years of previous relevant job experience, and whether the individual was: (1) applying for a job with the firm, or (2) a present employee being considered for a promotion.

Finally, the interpreter was provided by the client firm with an indications as to the relative importance of each of six job requirement variables for the specific position for which the individual was being considered. These job variables were: ability to process numerical data, vocabulary and verbal fluency, accuracy, speed, ability to work under time pressure, and all-around administrative ability.

The psychologist's task was to analyze each of the above inputs, and their interrelationships, and to provide the client firm with both: (1) a written description of the applicant's skills, ability and personality characteristics as related to the requirements of the job under consideration, and (2) his recommendation regarding the advisability of hiring (or promoting) the individual. Analysis revealed that the psychologist's recommendations fell into one of four categories: hire (or promote); hire or promote, but only as a fair risk; reject; or check the applicant's background further. The further background check recommendation was made primarily when an applicant's score on the Washburne truthfulness factor was low, giving an indication that the individual may not have been honest in the personality tests in the battery and/or in providing information on the firm's application blank. A schematic diagram summarizing this decision process is provided in Figure 2.

The Research

Three basic steps were involved in conducting the research: (1) data collection; (2) developing and programming the model; and (3) analyzing the results generated by the model. We will now discuss each of these steps.

Data Collection. Data upon which the model was to be built were collected in two ways. First, the decision problem was discussed with members of the consulting firm, and all manuals available relative to the psychological tests utilized were analyzed. Second, the protocol method was utilized as a means of examining the thought processes of the particular psychologist chosen for the study. That is, the psychologist was asked to verbalize his thoughts as he analyzed the selection problem, and these

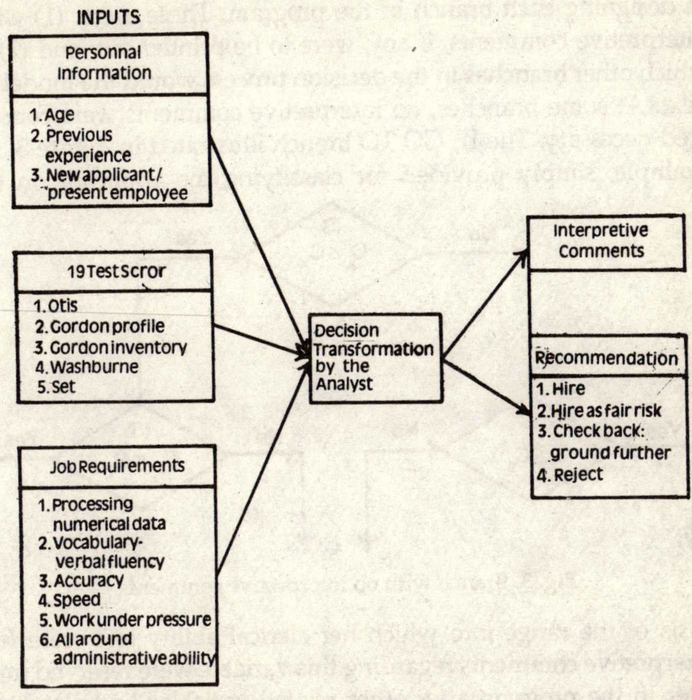

Fig. 2. The decision problem under consideration.

verbalizations were recorded on tape, to be transcribed later into written form for analysis. These verbalizations were examined in two distinct ways. First, the psychologist was asked to discuss each of the numerous input variables and their interrelationships, and to indicate how they influenced both his written interpretations and hiring recommendations. Second, he was asked to analyze sixteen cases from the files of the firm and to verbalize each step in his analysis.

Development of Model. Constructing a model of complex thought processes involves the breaking down of these processes into simple elements. In the construction of our model, a network of simple branching statements was developed, each representing a decision rule employed by the psychologist. Since the output desired from the model was to include interpretive comments as well as a selection recommendation, two decisions had to be made in designing each branch in the program. These were: (1) what interpretive comments, if any, were to be printed out, and (2) to which other branches in the decision process would the model go next. At some branches, no interpretive comments were considered necessary. The IF, GO TO branch illustrated in Figure 3, for example, simply provided for classifying the applicant on the

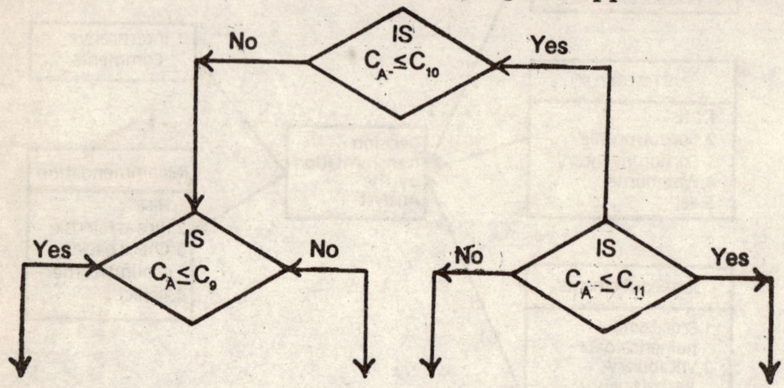

Fig. 3. Branch with no interpretive comments.

basis of the range into which her clerical ability test score fell: interpretive comments regarding this variable were reserved until later in the program after other related variables had also been examined. An example of a case in which interpretive comments were included is the IF, PRINT and GO TO branch illustrated in Figure 4. All applicants channeled up to this branch had failed to score well on "goal orientation," and this branch differentiates applicants simply scoring somewhat below average from those scoring quite poorly on this factor. In its completed form, the model network consisted of approximately 300 IF and GO TO statements and 150 PRINT statements.

Analysis. The final step in the research was that of the measurement and analysis of the output obtained from the simulation model. Some researchers who have developed simulations of thought processes have verified their results by comparing decisions made by the computer with those made humanly, given the same input data. This type of verification indicates the degree to which the model arrives at the same solutions to decision problems as does the human. Since this study was designed to provide not only final selection recommendations, but also numerous

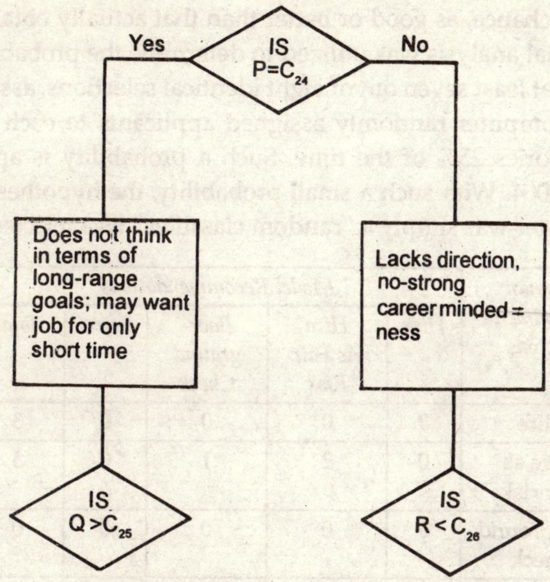

Fig. 4. Branch with interpretive comments.

interpretive comments supporting each recommendation, it was necessary to examine both types of outputs.

As a means of first determining the degree to which the model generated the same selection recommendations as had the analyst, all input data for each of the 16 cases from which the protocol was derived were fed into the model. In all 16 cases, the model provided the same employment recommendation as had the psychologist. Of these, six were to hire; three to hire as a fair risk; one to obtain a further background check; and six to reject. Then, as a more valid test of the model, eight new cases which had been interpreted by the psychologist since the protocol had been obtained, and which had not been used in the development of the model, were presented to the computer. In seven of these eight cases, the model provided the same employment recommendation as that which had been arrived at by the human analyst. The results of this test are illustrated in Figure 5.

These data were then analyzed statistically to answer the following question: "If the model were randomly classifying applicants into each of the four possible categories, what would be the probability of reaching agreement between the model and human, purely by chance, as good or better than that actually obtained?" Multinomial analysis was utilized to determine the probability of obtaining at least seven out of eight identical selections, assuming that the computer randomly assigned applicants to each of the four categories 25% of the time. Such a probability is approximately 0.0004. With such a small probability, the hypothesis that the computer was simply a "random classifier" was rejected.

Human Recommendations	*Model Recommendations*				
	Hire	*Hire As Fair Risk*	*Background Check*	*Reject*	*Total*
Hire	3	0	0	0	3
Hire as fair risk	0	2	1	0	3
Background check	0	0	0	0	0
Reject	0	0	0	2	2
Total	3	2	1	2	8

Fig. 5. Human and model recommendation.

The next step in the analysis of results was that of examining the interpretive comments outputted by the model. Determining the degree to which such model-generated comments were in agreement with the humanly made ones, given the same input data, involved considerably more subjective judgment than had testing for agreement on the selection recommendations. This was because the phraseology of computerized comments was generally somewhat different than the human phraseology; and the semantic question had to be asked: "Was the psychological *meaning* of the words utilized by the model and the human substantially the same or not?"

In attempting to answer this question, the complete computer output from six cases was presented to the psychologist upon whose thought processes the model had been developed, for further analysis. He was asked to compare the computer output with the interpretive comments he had originally made, and to answer the following question:

1. How many of the interpretive comments possessed substantially the same meaning as had his own?
2. How many of the comments were "incorrect" when compared with his own analysis?
3. How many comments which he had included in his own analysis were *omitted* in the computer report?
4. How many psychologically valid comments, if any, were included in the simulated interpretation which *he* had omitted in his own analysis?

The results of this comparative analysis are summarized in Figure 6.

Applicant	*Total Number of Comments in Simulated Report*	*Number of Comments in Simulated Report Included Also in Human Analysis*	*Number of "incorrect" Comments in Simulated Report*	*Number of Comments Omitted in Simulated Report, but Included in Human Analysis*	*Number of Comments Included in Simulated Report, but Included in Human Analysis*
1	27	23	0	1	4
2	29	24	2	1	3
3	30	28	1	1	1
4	23	19	3	1	1
5	36	30	4	0	2
6	28	24	1	1	3
Total	173	148	11	5	14

Fig. 6. Human and model interpretive comments.

As a further means of obtaining a judgment as to the "correctness" of the computer interpretations, another psychologist with the consulting firm, who was quite familiar with the interpretive methods used by the psychologist under study, was asked to examine some of the output data. He was given all input data from the sixteen protocol cases, and the computer interpretations generated for each case; but was not shown the interpretive reports originally made by the protocol analyst. He was then asked to judge whether each interpretive comment was psychologically sound or not. Altogether, the sixteen cases contained a total of 290 interpretive comments, of which 273 were judged sound. These judgments, of course, did not provide any indication of the degree to which the model successfully simulated the protocol analyst's thought processes. The fact that 94% of the comments made by the computer were considered sound, however, does suggest that the simulated interpretations were highly congruent with the psychological thinking of the firm, at least as so perceived by the evaluator.

PERFORMANCE APPRAISAL

Performance Appraisal or Merit Rating is the process of evaluating the performance and qualifications of the employee in terms of the requirements of the job for which he is employed, for purposes of administration, including placement, selection for promotion, providing financial rewards, and other actions which require differential treatment among the members of a group as distinguished from actions affecting all members equally.

In practice, the term *merit rating,* when applied to salary administration, has been used by many companies to cover almost all kinds of salary adjustments, including recognition of length of service, economic adjustments, and even general increases stemming from or preceding union contract negotiations as applied to non-union groups of employees, as well as for recognition of individual meritorious performance. Because of this broad use of the term, many managers prefer to use other terminology, such as *Performance Appraisal* or *Employee Appraisal* for purposes of identifying and recognizing individual differences among employees.

Value of Ratings

By means of a systematic rating procedure, management is enabled to maintain a record of the relative worth of its personnel and thereby be more able to make sound decisions regarding employment, placement, transfers, promotions, dismissals, and individual salary rewards related to worth. Despite their imperfections, appraisal records are relatively objective and provide information that often cannot be obtained in any other way.

Ratings replace subjective, general impressionistic opinions with judgments that are analytical and generally describable in quantitative terms. Based on observation over a period of time, they provide information that is valuable when critical decisions must be made in emergency situations. In general, ratings provide evidence that should serve as the bases for decisions. In addition, ratings, soundly developed and systematically administered, stimulate the person being appraised, especially when he is informed about his standing and has an opportunity to discuss ways and means of improving. They also cause the rater to be more analytical and objective, especially when he knows that he must be able to answer such questions as, "What is the evidence to support your rating of this employee?"

OBJECTIVES OF PERFORMANCE APPRAISAL

Feedback

In modern organizations, performance appraisal data may serve as an input to other personnel functions as well as provide feedback to employees in order to help them improve their performance. These are illustrated in Figure 7, which presents a general schematic model of the whole performance appraisal process. Two sets of terms presented in Figure 7 need definition. First, by *feedback,* as opposed to *no feedback,* we mean information given to individuals in the performance appraisal process specifically geared toward improving their performance. Thus, a supervisor's simply telling subordinated their numbered ranking in the department but providing no information on how the subordinates might improve their performance would not be considered feedback. Second, by *comparative* we mean systems in which an individual's performance is systematically compared with that of other employees; *absolute* systems are those in which an individual's performance is compared with one or more written standards.

Inputs to Other Functions

As may be noted from Figure 7, performance appraisal data, aside from their feedback function, can provide inputs to selection, training, human resource planning, and wage and salary decisions. They may aid in selection decision making in two ways. First, supervisory ratings may be used to validate selection instruments. Second, supervisory appraisals may indicate the need for an organization to modify its current selection policies. For exam-

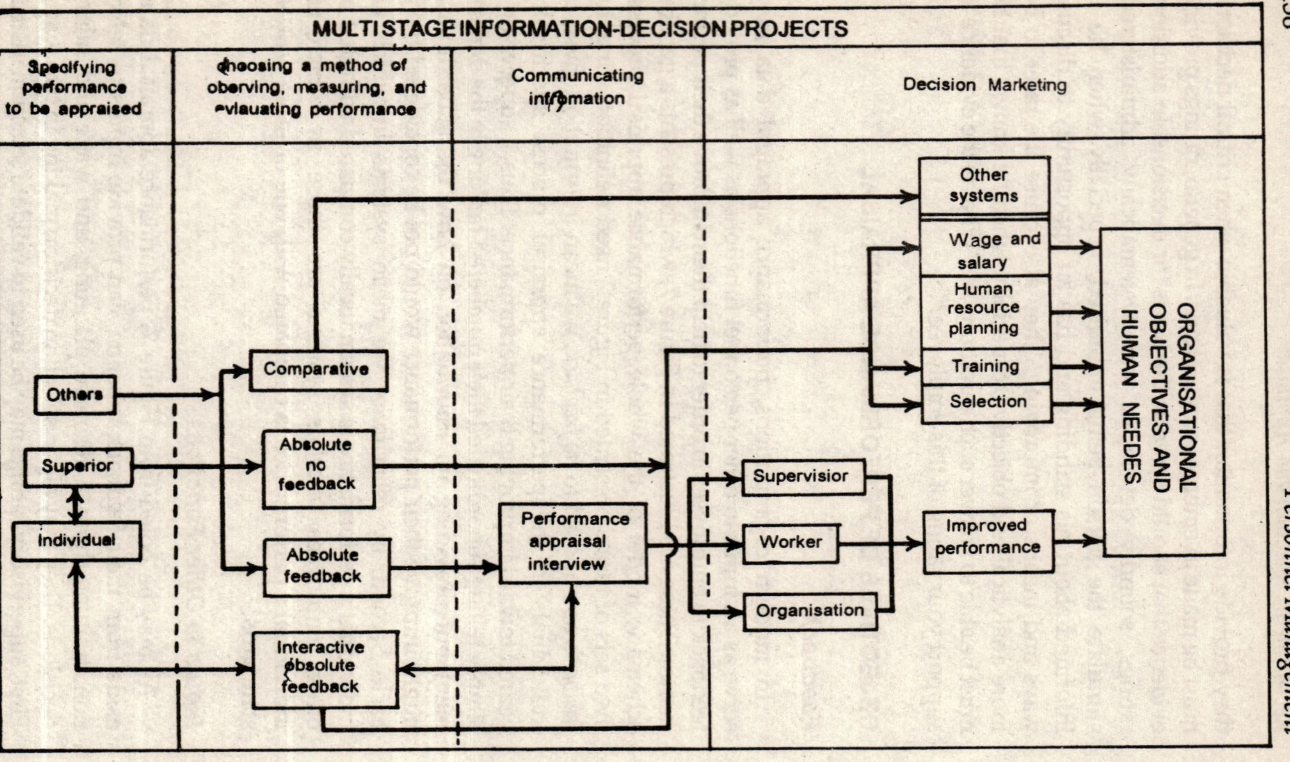

Fig. 7. Performance appraisal process.

ple, a firm may find that the performance of certain blue-collar workers who have graduated from high school is rated significantly higher by first-line supervision than that of employees who have less education. Such a finding might indicate that the firm should require a high school degree for *all* individuals applying for such jobs.

Performance appraisal data may indicate a need for specific types of training and aid in the evaluation of training programs. With respect to training needs, for example, an evaluation of supervisory skills in the Tennessee Department of Public Health spelled out not only what specific kinds of supervisory training were needed but also in which particular divisions and locations in the organization the training was needed most. As an example of performance appraisal data used to evaluate training, one manufacturing concern conducted two two-hour briefing sessions for all first-line supervisors on changes in its contract that had just been negotiated with the union. When the performance of these supervisors was next appraised by their supervisors, analysis of their handling of contract-related problems with their subordinates indicated that the briefing sessions had been fairly effective, although no statistical analysis of the appraisal data was undertaken.

Data obtained from appraisals may aid in making appropriate human resource planning decisions. Performance appraisal data can often help determine whether an individual possesses the necessary skills to be promoted to a higher level or whether current job skills are lacking. If the latter is true and it is determined that training will not help, the organization may consider demoting or firing the employee.

Finally, appraisal data may aid in making wage and salary decisions. In fact, one study found that performance appraisals were primarily used for making compensation decisions. Outstanding performance should be recognized with merit increases in pay. Since salary decisions fall so greatly within domain of wage and salary administration, this will fall in the purview of Chapter 5.

A CRITIQUE

Lamouria and Harrell describe an "operational analysis," employing

> The OR emphasis...[in] a formal model used to combine various quantified factors relevant to the process being examined [to build an objective criterion for research managers]. [They assume] (a) Management evaluation using OR yields a more objective and more accurate measure of performance than traditional clinical rating procedures. (b) The success of a research and development manager can be assessed entirely by measuring the performance of the group acting under his direction.

The writer of this critique agrees with the first assumption, but finds that the model developed by Lamouria and Harrell is neither necessary nor sufficient for their intended purposes. Further, the writer believes that the apparent scientific rigor of their approach is deceiving to the quantitative unsophisticate. The criticism will consist of four points.

1. One class of criticisms rests on the irrelevance of the authors' elaborate weighting procedures to their findings. The "criterion" employed was a ratio of actual to a "predetermined ideal standard" performance. The ratio was then summed in a double-weighting procedure—once for objectives and once for activities—to achieve an overall index. The determination of the standard will be discussed further below. In this first point the weighting procedure will be examined. (a) If the performance ratios are simply summed (unit weights) for each department (and objectives are ignored) the values are 5.95, 1.67, 3.55, and 4.39. This order is identical with that found by the authors in their Tables 5 and 6. (b) Perhaps the procedure in *a* is not fair, since not all of the activities listed for each department were used by the authors; thus the sum could be inflated for a department which had more activities. For this reason, only those activities having more than zero relevance were used for each objective in each department. This time the sums of the unit weighted ratios were divided by the number of activities summed to get a mean value. The resulting ordering by department (with objectives merged) again agrees perfectly with the authors' Tables 5 and 6. When considered separately by objective, the agreement is perfect for Profit and Diversification, and there are minor inversions for

Growth and Welfare. One of these inversions will be accounted for below. (c) The authors' Table 5 shows directly that, using their double-weighting procedure, the rank order of departments *within* each objective is identical and thus breakdown by objectives need not have been used. There is a good reason for this finding. One can argue that the objectives of Diversification and growth are highly correlated or at least performance directed toward the one will also proceed toward the other. Further, both of these objectives are strongly related to Profit, perhaps negatively in the short run and positively in the long run. This interdependence of objectives refutes the justifiability of weighting the objectives to sum to unity, as though they were orthogonal. If we combine the Diversification and Growth scores for an overall mean of these two objectives, the inversion reported previously disappears.

In summary of Paragraph 1, while the assumption of interaction between objectives and activities implied in the double-weighting procedure is a priori plausible, the authors have demonstrated empirically that it does not exist. Not only is the interaction unnecessary, but so are differential weights for objectives, and for activities when compared across objectives. This finding for activities is curious since only four of the eight named activities were common to all four departments.

2. Paragraph 1 has shown that the overall ranking of departments depends directly on the unweighted mean of the performance ratios. Examination of the procedure for computing these ratios shows that the numerator represents objective performance, while the denominator, in contrast, "was based on the subjective judgment of the *department manager* and represents a theoretical goal deemed both desirable and feasible. Note that the OR results were contrasted with the *unit director's* clinical rankings. Thus the discrepancy could be due to differences between unit director and department managers in estimates of an ideal standard for each of the activities. Two hypotheses are implied by the procedure used. First, that the rankings of the departments were sensitive to the aspiration level of their department managers. When aspiration is high, the performance index will tend to be low, and vice versa. Could the poor showing of Department B be attributed to his very high expectation as to what his department will be able to do? This leads to the second hypothesis. If the first hypothesis be true,

could the unit director have rated Department B second on the list (even though it performed poorly) because he recognized the need for such a high level of aspiration, and perhaps shared it? Note that Department B had not been in existence long enough to learn the rate of return on its proposals, so the hypothesis is plausible.

3. In their closing remarks, Lamouria and Harrell consider the influence on an objective index of factors beyond the manager's control. They dismiss these after (a) conjecturing that a manager may be responsible for his group's actions whether or not they are within his control; (b) claiming that the unlucky manager can use the model in his own defense by showing how his superior's acts and stated objectives are inconsistent. The writer believes that external influences cannot be ignored when personnel decisions are to be taken on the basis of the computations. Three factors militate for their inclusion. (a) It is simply not conceivable that subordinate group means with respect to aptitude, training, experience, and personality will be equal in natural setting. The manager with the better subordinates profits by the index. (b) The resources (money, equipment, etc.) available to each manager will seldom be equal, and the one with the best access will earn the best index, other things being equal. Of course, gaining the best access may show managerial ability, but this factor is not being measured directly. (c) Not all R and D problems are of equal difficulty. Progress and hence performance is more likely for easy problems. Lamouria and Harrell have not considered this factor; however we note that differential difficulty expresses itself in the denominator of the performance index. The denominator, as shown previously, is partially self-serving for the department manager and also interacts with the personality of the manager's supervisor to influence his clinical rating.

BASIC CHARACTERISTICS OF APPRAISAL SYSTEMS

The Setting of Standards

The effective functioning of any performance appraisal system depends, first of all, on establishing realistic performance standards for each position in the organization. Jobs have to be analyzed, job descriptions must be developed, and performance standards must be set. Performance standards will be defined differently from one job to another in the organization: "In many industries, the product and the tasks required to make it are easily defined. If it is to be a widget, we can figure out the precise steps required to manufacture a widget." In many other jobs, such as professional ones, it can often be extremely difficult to develop precise job standards.

Once a standard has been set, precise or imprecise, individuals need to be informed about the specific types and levels of performance expected of them. Finally, in the performance appraisal process, (1) individual behavior needs to be monitored, (2) corrective actions need to be planned should desired levels of performance not be met, and (3) future plans for improving already satisfactory performance may be spelled out.

Mutual interaction

It is important to recognize that the effectiveness of any appraisal effort depends upon an appropriate *mutual interaction* among techniques, both the human appraiser and appraisee and organizational objectives. If we utilize an appraisal technique that provides no feedback to a subordinate while our objective is to improve performance, our efforts will fail regardless of how expert the supervisor is in appraising performance. Conversely, suppose that a firm has developed an appraisal technique that is highly appropriate for providing feedback to its members. If managers are inept in and indifferent toward using this technique in dealing with their subordinates, or the appraisees are unable to respond appropriately, no effective appraisals can be expected. In short, effective appraisal requires both an appropriate system in light of its objectives and managers and subordinates who understand how to use the system. We will indicate later how appropriate various appraisal systems in use today are in meeting different organizational objectives.

Duration of Appraisal Interviews

It is not uncommon for performance appraisal interviews to be held at fixed intervals, frequently once a year. This approach, however, ignores individuals' varying needs for feedback and the need to reinforce positive behavior and negate undesired behavior immediately. Further, it fails to recognize that different jobs require different amount of time to complete. Because of these factors, some observers believe that variable-interval appraisals may be more effective than fixed-interval ones. Among the ways that variable-interval appraisals can be structured, the most appropriate one, when feasible, is probably tailoring the timing of the measurement and feedback of performance "to the completion of an assigned or agreed upon project." For example, under the management-by-objectives (MBO) approach to appraisal, which we will cover later, a supervisor and subordinate may agree that it should take 6 months to complete one project and 14 months for another, and the appraisal periods for these projects would be set at 6 and 14 months, respectively. Subobjectives of projects of such duration may be set with earlier time limits, so that more frequent appraisals on these subgoals may be appropriate. Further, if an individual is to maintain and possibly increase proficiency in the organization, much more frequent feedback will usually be necessary. In fact, a manager's day-in and day-out on-the-job coaching and counseling of subordinates is often more important for individual growth and development than either periodic appraisal interviews or participation in off-the-job training and development programs.

Top-Management Support

Effective performance appraisal systems additionally require top-management support. As we will indicate more fully later, conducting appraisals and communicating appraisal data to their subordinates is a difficult task which many supervisors dislike and attempt to avoid. One effective decision strategy utilized by a top-management that wants to see a truly effective appraisal program in operation is to have the president appraise vice presidents on how well they appraise their general managers, who in turn will be evaluated on how well they appraise their middle-level managers, and so on, all the way down the organizational hierarchy. If such continuous reinforcement throughout the organization is not provided, excellent performance appraisal systems, first greeted with enthusiasm, may soon lose their appeal and effectiveness.

From Traits to Behavior

A further development leading to more effective performance appraisal systems in recent decades has been a switch away from assessing personality *traits* and toward appraising actual *behavior.* There are basically two reasons why emphasis on behavior rather than traits is more effective. First, telling a subordinate that he or she is, for instance "not aggressive enough" will often be perceived as a threat and arouse defensive attitudes and behavior. On the other hand, telling him or her about things that are factually based can often lead to mature discussion. Second, indicating to a subordinate that he or she has a trait deficiency (such as the one mentioned above) will in no way help indicate to the individual just how to improve performance. Behaviorally oriented appraisal feedback, on the other hand, will tend to both minimize defensiveness and lead toward constructive suggestions for performance improvement.

Here there is not reference to any possibly defective personality trait. Rather, a specific problem has been focused upon with a specific suggestion as to how performance may be improved.

Separate Discussion of Salary

It is fairly widely agreed today that salary discussions between superiors and subordinates should be conducted *separately* from performance appraisal interviews. A basic reason for this is that the economic issues will typically "dominate the interview to the extent that neither the supervisor nor the employee is in a proper frame of mind" to discuss possibilities for improved subordinate performance. Further, in some organizations pay raises are automatic, not dependent on performance, so that there could be no logical performance appraisal-merit increase linkage.

Common Appraisal Rating Errors

The are certain common appraisal rating errors that should be minimized if an effective appraisal system is to be maintained. Among the more important of these are the following.

Halc. As in selection interviews, some managers let their rating of a subordinate as either good or poor on one factor excessively influence their ratings on all other measures of performance.

Bias. It is only easy to be biased either toward or against another individual, perhaps due considerably to basic differences in personality characteristics. To effectively appraise the performance of subordinates, a manager should attempt to identify and set aside any such biases.

Leniency and Strictness. In colleges and universities, some professors develop reputations as "easy" graders, while others are noted for the few A's and B's they give. The same problem exists in performance appraisal in all organizations. Some managers will tend to be lenient in rating all of their subordinates, while others may be extremely strict. Such differences can create difficult problems for the organization. This might be the case, for example, in comparing the performance of individuals working in different departments for a promotion into a higher-level position that has just opened up.

Central Tendency. Some appraisers are reluctant to rate individuals as either very good or very poor. An appraiser who does not know too much about the behavior of the individuals being rated may consider rating them as average a safe strategy. This problem is sometimes referred to as the *central tendency* error.

Favorable Impressions. Somewhat related to the preceding two errors, some authorities have indicated that with most companies "appraisal ratings cluster around the better-than-average classification." This may occur because superiors want to impress others with their ability to pick and train good subordinates.

Recency. One reason for providing day-to-day performance appraisal feedback is that appraisers tend to remember recent events better than events in the more distant past. Thus, with a six-month or yearly performance appraisal, there may be a tendency for the supervisor to remember more about what subordinates did in the period just prior to the appraisal, which could distort the appraisal.

Approaches and Techniques

Probably the first "scientific" or modern type of rating scale was one developed by Sir Francis Galton and described in his "Inquiry into Human Faculty and Its Development." His scale (in his example he describes the recollection of a break-fast table) presents nine degrees of "mental imagery," with a detailed description of each degree, ranging from *Highest–brilliant*, distinct, never blotchy, and "*First Suboctile*—the image once seen is perfectly clear and bright," through "*Middle most*—fairly clear: brightness probably at least from half to two thirds of the original, one or two objects being much more distinct than others, but the latter comes out clearly if attention be paid to them." to "*Lowest*—my powers are zero, to my consciousness there is almost no association of memory with objective visual impressions, I recollect the table but do not see it."

A somewhat similar scale was developed by K. Pearson and reported in 1906. This describes seven degrees of Mental Ability, as follows:

(1) *Mentally Defective.* Capable of holding in the mind only the simplest facts, and incapable of perceiving or reasoning about relationships between facts.

(2) *Slow Dull.* Capable of perceiving relationship between facts in some few fields with long and continuous effort; but generally not without much assistance.

(3) *Slow.* Very slow in thought generally, but with time understanding is reached.

(4) *Slow Intelligent.* Slow generally, although possibly more rapid in certain fields; quite sure of knowledge when once acquired.

(5) *Fairly Intelligent.* Ready to grasp and capable of perceiving facts in most fields; capable of understanding without much effort.

(6) *Distinctly Capable.* A mind quick in perception and in reasoning rightly about the perceived.

(7) *Very Able.* Quite exceptionally able intellectually, as evidenced either by the person's career or by consensus of opinion of acquaintances, or by school record in case of children.

These scales point the way to the construction of valuable performance scales for use in industry. The basic material is the Position Description, and the performance scale is a series of statements to describe "essentially perfect performance," "intermediate between perfect and standard performance," "standard performance" "marginal performance," and "failing performance." Since such descriptive paragraphs are rather complex, intermediate steps, without description, can be used to indicate "better than a described level, but less than the next higher described level." Thus, given a nine-step scale, descriptions may be written for steps 9, 7, 5, 3, and 1. Steps 8, 6, 4, and 2 provide for the non-described in-between levels of performance.

Such scales are likely to be of more value when applied to incumbents of complicated positions of broad scope, such as managerial and professional, than when simpler, specialized job holders are being rated, but their values for all kinds of positions extend beyond the establishment of a performance index. Properly done they provide bases for analysis and identification of needs for development of the employee for improved performance.

The Order of Merit or *Rank Order* method of rating was developed originally by J. McKeen Cattell in connection with his studies of the prominence of scientists. Each judge was requested to place a list of names of scientists in rank order from "best" to "least." Such a procedure is sometimes used within a relatively small group. It is effective for differentiating the extremes of ability, personal characteristics of other kinds, and performance, but it is not analytic or diagnostic, unless a number of rankings are made, one for each of a number of traits and performance characteristics. Furthermore, the use of such a technique requires that the ratings of people in a group must all be done at the same time.

The Paired Comparison method, when applied under controlled conditions, probably is the soundest and most technically exact for the determination of individual differences. It requires a comparison of each person in the group with each other person and the recording of a judgment of *superior.* (sometimes a judgment of *equal* may also be used.)

The number of *superior* judgments about each person establishes his relative standing in the group. The result may be a rank order, but degrees of difference will have been determined to a greater extent than by simple ranking.

Neither the Rank Order nor the Paired Comparison method is applicable when an appraisal of only one or of a few persons is undertaken at one time. Since many administrative decisions are required throughout a year, these methods cannot yield up-to-date ratings. For example, many companies have salary reviews on anniversary dates of employment, transfer, or promotion.

Accordingly, if ratings are determined through ranking or paired comparison methods, requiring review of a considerable number of persons at the same time, they will not be "current" on most anniversary dates. Therefore, other reference points must be established. Such reference points should be related to job requirements. Thus, if "quantity of production" is a significant item for rating employees, quantitative criteria should be established. Such criteria are not revealed in Ranking or Paired Comparison and related methods of rating, except through statistical determinations of central tendency and variability.

The Army Man-to-Man Rating Scale is of great historical significance, although it has been judged to be too cumbersome for use in industry. This method, stemming directly from the work of the Bureau of Salesmanship Research at Carnegie Institute of Technology, under the leadership of Walter Dill Scott, in 1916, can be briefly described as follows: A five-step scale is constructed in which each step represents a known person. The highest step on the scale for *Leadership*, for example, is represented by that person who, in the opinion of the rater, possesses leadership qualities to the highest degree of any of his acquaintances in the type of activity engaged in by those to be rated. Other persons are selected to represent high level, middle level, low level, and lowest level possession of the trait. Persons to be rated are then slotted into the scale by comparing them in the trait in question with the individuals representing scale levels: hence the name, Man-to-Man Rating Scale.

As used in the Army, officers of a given rank were rated by this technique. In industry, such a method might be applicable to rating all general foremen, or foremen, or superintendents, or salesmen, but since each job even of the foreman type has its own characteristics, many scales, each covering relatively few people, would be needed, except as the ratees are to be judged and rated for their personal characteristics, regardless of their specific work assignments.

Other systems developed for performance appraisal or merit rating since World War I, include the following:

(1) *Graphic Rating Scales*, originally developed by the Scott Company Laboratory (Walter Dill Scott and Associates), provide a series of traits and their definitions, opposit each of which the

rater places a check mark on a line representing the full distance from "highest" to "lowest" rating. This approach, with variations, is one of the most commonly used rating forms in industry today. Variations include "boxes" to represent varying levels of quality or performance, and descriptive phrases under the graphic line or boxes to define degrees.

(2) *Lists* of descriptions of varying degrees of the characteristic or performance, to be checked by the rater.

(3) *Written* descriptions of the ratees' personal traits and performance characteristics, with or without a letter or number index (score) to represent the appraisal in quantitative terms. This method is used more often for appraising managerial personnel rather than clerical or manual personnel.

(4) *Forced-Choice.* The rater selects from each of a number of groupings of generally unrelated "personal characteristics" statements, one that is *most like* and one that is *least like* the ratee. Numerical values are assigned on a statistical basis, and scores obtained. This method appears to improve objectivity and to reduce the effect of such pitfalls as the "halo" tendency, but it lacks face validity.

(5) *"Critical Incident."* The appraiser keeps a running record of activity incidents which were "critical" for successful and unsuccessful performance. This method, used over a period of time, identifies those types of activity which are characteristic of successful and of unsuccessful employees in specific types of jobs, and furnishes the basis for continuing appraisals of subordinates and for day-to-day discussions with them for corrective and development purposes.

(6) *Field Review.* Here a personnel specialist in appraisal and development work meets with supervisors and staff personnel and observes the persons to be appraised. Following discussions with them, he writes out an analytic appraisal and reviews it with the supervisor for certifications. This is an effective method, especially as applied to managerial personnel, when the specialist is properly qualified.

(7) *Performance Standards.* Appraising performance in relation to performance "standards" is not unlike the Graphic Rating Scale method in some respects. It tends to reduce the common tendency of many raters to rate high, because the basic reference point is

"standard," and deviations are in terms of "above" or "better than," or "below" or "less than" standard. (This type of approach to appraising performance is described fully below, with examples of some forms in use in industry.)

(8) *Appraisal by Objectives.* This approach entails the preparation by the subordinate appraisee of written statements covering his understanding of the objectives of (a) his superior's job; (b) his own job; (c) the proper criteria of performance from his viewpoint; (d) the situation, including problems to be overcome; and (e) his plan of action to accomplish the objectives. This report is discussed with the supervisor for purposes of communication, analysis, modification or approval, and appraisal. The subordinate participates throughout and has largely *appraised himself* in the process.

Appraisal by Result

A basic procedure in the performance appraisal of managerial personnel is now being labelled "Appraisal by Results." This involves participational planning of work programs, with objectives, goals, or targets. At regular intervals, depending upon the plans, the employee and his superior review and appraise progress in relation to plan. The time span may vary up to a year and beyond.

Since the plan or plans were developed jointly by the employee and his superior, agreed upon, and made a matter of record, the employee generally will be objective at the time of a progress review. He may, of course, rationalize deficiencies and failures, but the review process furnishes a wealth of evidence for arriving at a judgment of the employee's performance.

Obviously, the critical phases of this approach are the planning phase, the implementation phase, and the "audit" phase. If the planning is unrealistic, the implementation will be disappointing, and the appraisal may then be inadequately descriptive of the employee's qualities. Nevertheless, this approach is not only sound for appraisal purposes, it is or should be a standard operating procedure in fulfilling the management functions of planning, leading, and measuring.

Technical Problems

The preceding discussion of appraisal methods has not included any discourse on various technical problems such as corrections for "leniency tendency" or its opposite; overcoming the "halo" effect; and various statistical methods for determining the reliability and validity of ratings. These are matters for the technician, and text material is available in the literature of psychology and mental measurement, including textbooks on Personnel Administration.

ROLE OF THE PERSONNEL DEPARTMENT

Basic Roles. The personnel department participates in the performance appraisal process in many ways. First, as indicated earlier, personnel aids in developing job descriptions and specifications necessary for the development of standards of performance for jobs. Second, and of key importance, personnel chooses, usually with the approval of top management, the particular type of performance appraisal system or systems that the firm is going to use. Without effective supervisory appraisals, no system can be effective. Hence, a third central role that personnel plays in performance appraisal is that of training supervisors in how to appraise performance and conduct performance appraisal interviews. Other functions of personnel are to (1) train employees in how the system works, (2) take various steps in implementing the system (such as designing, disseminating, and seeing that enough copies of performance appraisal forms are available), and (3) monitor the system by checking to see whether superiors are actually conducting appraisals when and how they should be doing so.

The Training Role. A number of researchers have found that the training role of personnel may be difficult to fulfill. Bernardin and Buckley, for example have pointed out that it is not difficult to train individuals to help overcome their rating errors, such as halo and leniency. To improve *accuracy* of appraisals, however, was found to be much more difficult. These researchers found that using training techniques such as having the raters keep diaries to increase their observation skills led to more accurate appraisals. In a somewhat different vein, it has been suggested that giving managers feedback of the *current* performance of their *former* subordinates to enable them to evaluate how well they had assessed their personnel in the past would help in appraisal training. This approach assumes, of course, that current performance is being rated accurately.

Security. Personnel departments must also provide security to protect the privacy of any performance appraisal information stored in either its manual or computer file Hayden has argued that performance date "must be available to all persons who have a need to know that information in the course of making decisions concerning salary adjustments, transfer and promotion decision, reduction-in-force decisions, etc." He has indicated, however, that data derived for employee development and counseling should not be disseminated, since constructive suggestions for improvement may be interpreted as destructive criticisms were they to become a matter of public record in the employee's personnel folder. Our position is that some constructive suggestions may be quite relevant to such decisions as promotional ones and therefore are needed in the employee's data base. However, it is the responsibility of the personnel department to permit only authorized persons access to these records in order to minimize the possibility of misuse of this information by individuals not responsible for making such decisions.

Computers and Performance Appraisals. With respect to computers, traditionally, as one writer has put it, "Computer systems have not been fully used to compare performance between departments and locations or to provide management information as to which kinds of employees best perform the work for which they have been hired." At the company this writer was discussing (Texas Instruments), however, the computer handled for employees the type of comparisons mentioned above, rank-order performance ratings of each first- line supervisor's workers, and two-and-a-half-year performance reports for them.

With gigantic leaps in computer technology, however, we expect to see more and more use of computers to deal with performance appraisal. Computers could easily maintain records such as data on tardiness, absences, accidents, and violations of company policy. Besides serving as an input for performance appraisal decisions, these data would be of value both for progressive discipline and as providing quantitative data to support the company in any EEO appraisal actions.

The appraisal of an indivudial's performance has always been a difficult problem, involving subjective supervisory judgments' *especially* at the managerial and professional levels in organizations, where many intangible variables are involved. Over the years, a number of different approaches and techniques have been developed in an attemnt to improve the performance appraisal process. Some of these have tended to be more "qualitative" in nature; others have focused greater attention on possible ways to quantity performance data.

In our opinion, effective quantification of performance appraisal data can help in overcoming the manager's problem of dealing with intangible performance variables; and further efforts to develop such approaches should be encouraged. We do not, however, consider that any "quantitative" performance appraisal technique will ever "solve" all of the manager's problems of performance appraisal. For example, suppose a supervisor were to have at his disposal a highly sophisticated operations research model for objectively and quantitatively measuring the performance of each of his subordinates with respect to each of all relevant performance criteria. Even having the data generated by any such model, the supervisor would still need to relate to and communicate effectively with his subordinates in performance appraisal interviews if he wanted to provide feedback to them for self-developmental purposes which—increasingly has become considered a key objective in managerial and professional performance appraisal. Thus, we envision the utilization of any "management science appraisal models" as but one facet of the total performance appraisal process.

THE PERFORMANCE APPRAISAL INTERVIEW

In the performance appraisal process the interview is the central communications medium through which feedback is provided individuals to help them improve their performance. In understanding this medium, which has been both "cussed and discussed"extensively, attention needs to be given to three basic questions: (1) Who is to conduct the interview? (2) What kinds of problems are encountered in traditional interviews? and (3) What different types of decision strategies may the appraiser and appraisee take to improve the performance of the latter?

Who Is to Be the Appraiser

Performance appraisal interviews may be conducted by the employee's supervisor, peers of the supervisor, peers of the employee, or the employee's subordinates. By far the most commonly utilized type of appraisal is one in which the individual's immediate superior is the appraiser. This is a logical approach from the point of view that the organizational hierarchy legitimizes the right of the supervisor to evaluate, help develop, and reward (or punish) subordinates.

Sometimes the superior is joined by other managers in the organization who are at the same hierarchical level or above and are also familiar with the subordinate's work. Although these other managers may observe behavior not apparent to the individual's superior, some evidence indicates that "the immediate supervisor's appraisal is highly related to the average evaluations across several appraisers," and that consequently, this supervisor may "function adequately in the absence of other assessments."

Further, involving other managers in the appraisal process is more time-consuming and costly to the organization. The other rater(s) may simply provide information to the supervisor, who digests it and presents the data to the subordinate; or others may actually join in the interview itself. The latter strategy may make subordinates feel even more defensive than they often do with just their supervisor present. We will discuss the whole problem of feelings of threat and defensiveness in traditional superior-subordinate interviews in the next section.

Peer rather than (or in addition to) supervisory ratings are also sometimes used by organizations. They are appropriate, however, only under certain conditions. For example, a high level of interpersonal trust and knowledge about the person being appraised, as well as a noncompetitive reward system, seems essential for peer appraisals. Peers tend to "rate down" each other if they function in a closed (or zero-sum) system in which only a *specified number of dollars* is available for merit-rating distribution. In such case, the better people can present themselves compared with their peers, the greater would be their rewards.

In a small number of cases, managers will be rated by their subordinates, although the subordinates may not have a performance appraisal interview per se. For example, in one university, the department head developed a simple rating form and gave it to each professor in the department. Then, a three-person committee of subordinate professors analyzed the ratings from each professor, added their own ideas, and presented a summary of results to the department head.

Although subordinate ratings may provide supervisors with valuable feedback, they pose some problems. First, such feedback is potentially stressful to the supervisor. Further, subordinates may fear that their superior may punish them if they make a candid but unfavorable appraisal. This problem was not present in the university cited above because all professors' responses on the department rating form were kept anonymous. Finally, according to Cummings and Schwab, there is some evidence to indicate that subordinates will rate their superiors primarily on how well they have met *their own* needs.

In a growing number of cases, subordinates are being asked to participate more fully in the appraisal interview, both in examining their own previous performance and in helping to set goals for performance improvement. This approach, as we say, is the MBO approach.

Problems with Traditional Interviews

There are a number of problems often encountered with traditional superior-subordinate interviews, Some of the appraisal problems already discussed (leniency, bias, halo, etc.) may easily slip into the appraisal interview. We will now turn to other aspects involved in feeding back appraisal data to subordinates in the interview.

In the performance interview situation, both positive and negative feedback are required if a fair assessment of performance is to be expected. Many supervisors find it difficult to provide tactfully negative feedback, and many individuals find it difficult to accept their limitations as described by their supervisors. Further, even though supervisors may find it pleasant to provide an employee with positive feedback, they are well aware that they may have to give the individual less favorable or outright negative feedback sometime in the future. It is for reasons such as these that supervisors frequently resist holding performance appraisal interviews and find successful interviews often difficult to achieve.

"Playing God"

In a classic articles, Douglas McGregor spelled out in 1957 some of the basic reasons why supervisors find performance appraisals so difficult. McGregor pointed out that supervisors are uncomfortable when they are placed in a position of "playing God" in judging subordinates' performance. One basic reason for this, according to McGregor, is that the inherent respect held for the individual makes it difficult to judge personal worth. He also indicated that with more modern emphasis in management thinking, managers are being called on to help subordinates meet both their own and organizational goals. He and others have emphasized that being put in the position both of helper and judge represents an incongruency. Hayden, for example, has stressed that supervisors cannot assume these conflicting roles simultaneously and that it is this conflict of roles "which probably causes the supervisor the most difficulty in the appraisal process."

One dysfunctional consequence of "playing God" problems is for the supervisor to "fudge" appraisals to make them look more favorable. For example, "A manager may 'fudge' a performance evaluation in order to justify a preconceived salary increase, and then later another manager may use that same appraisal to make a promotion or termination decision." Or a manager may "fudge" comments in order to avoid embarrassment inherent in criticizing subordinates.

Appraisal Interview Strategies

Performance appraisal interviews may be improved by modifying both the method used in communicating information to subordinates and the content of the communications. As far as method is concerned, there is much to be gained in many appraisal interviews if the superior dominates less, listens more to subordinates, and lets them know that he or she understands their viewpoints. Moving more toward the "listening" direction (which Maier has referred to as the "tell and listen" approach), the supervisor permits subordinates to release frustrated feelings, which tends to reduce them.

Further: "The unpleasant aspects of the appraisal interview are reduced when the superior has a method for dealing with defensive responses and when he is in a better position to understand and respect feelings." Moving toward the "tell and listen approach" parallels moving from a more to a less structured selection interview; and it requires considerable skill and patience. Improvement in listening skills is one important facet of management training programs in many companies.

As for content, supervisors in appraisal interviews can help guide subordinates toward *specific* improved performance by focusing attention on behavior rather than traits and involving not only the employees but also themselves and the organization in the efforts to change. This strategy is illustrated in Figure 8. This involvement of worker, supervisor, and organization may be

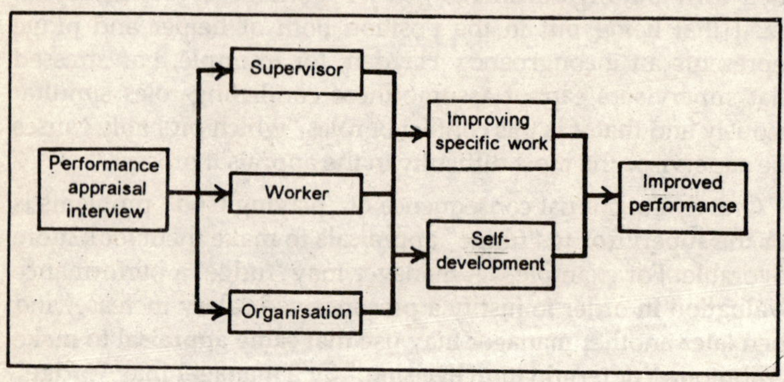

Fig. 8. Feedback-performance improvement strategies.

aimed at improving two dimensions of the subordinate's behavior and skills : (1) specific job performance and (2) self-development. These two categories may overlap to a certain degree, but the following examples should help clarify the differences in these two behavioral dimensions.

Specific Job Performance

Here we refer to improving such specific performance measures as sales dollars, number of rejects, net operating profit, subordinate absenteeism rates, and so forth. In many such cases, performance improvements can be effected to a certain extent by the employee but help may also be needed from the superior and the organization. For example, in a manufacturing plant, the reject rate for items in one department may be 6 percent, and the supervisor would like to reduce it to 4 percent. One possible reason for this problem may be that two new subordinates are not fully aware of correct quality control procedures. In the supervisor's appraisal interview with his or her own superior, the plant manager, the two may agree that the supervisor should spend more time training the two new subordinates in quality control procedures. There may be other problems, as well, however, with respect to quality control. Perhaps the supervisor is not getting reject-rate feedback quickly enough to initiate corrective actions before the system goes out of control. Here, the plant manager may agree and, working with the firm's computer personnel, help get this information to the supervisor more quickly.

Self-Development. As an example of the need for self-development, a young middle manager may have real difficulties in making oral presentations to groups of peers and higher-level managers. His or her supervisor might suggest taking an evening course in public speaking, the manager might agree, and the organization might agree to refund full tuition for the course upon successful completion. The net effect of this effort could well be not only improved communication abilities before groups but also a parallel improvement in the individual's self-esteem.

CASE: KURIAN'S APPRAISALS

My name is Ramachandran Kurian. Graduting in business administration, I post-graduated from Madras with great honors (magna cum laude) about six years ago. I then continued at Madras Business College to receive my M.B.A.

I was fortunate enough to receive a job offer in the personnel department of a multimillion-dollar manufacturing firm. My boss, Ranganathan, the personnel manager, always treated me with dignity. I admired Ranga because he had worked his way up from a production line job to her present one. His control of the English language was also superb in spite of the fact that he had only a high school education. *Every* word that he uttered was the precise word which should have been chosen. And cool! I had chances to observe him in contract negotiations and he never showed any signs of flustering when the union would needle him personally.

And my job—I was a sort of jack-of-all-trades. Some plant interviewing. Some college recruiting trips. Developing and conducting training programs for our supervisors. Interpreting psychological tests.

PERSONNEL COUNSELING

The term "Personnel Counseling" has both a general and a specific usage. In its general sense, the activities designated by the term resemble familiar industrial relations functions. These include such diverse activities as rendering direct assistance to the employee in meeting his problems, reducing turnover and absenteeism, investigating grievances, and improving the two-way flow of information between worker and management. In its specific sense, the term refers to the measures taken by an employer to facilitate the adjustment of the employee to his work situation. These measures are addressed to the mental and emotional state of the employee, his attitudes, feelings, and personal concerns. In its general sense, employee counseling is as old as management itself and designates functions traditionally performed by the employer, manager, supervisor, the industrial relations or medical staff. In its more restricted sense, the functions so designated are usually performed by a specialized staff.

Approaches and Techniques

The methods and techniques used in employee counseling vary with the objectives of the program and the underlying assumptions as to how they may be best achieved. Approaches which depend upon guidance and advice may utilize various diagnostic techniques including interest, aptitude, and personality tests, case study, occupational history, and personal interviews. In the guidance phase, the counselor, through discussion of his findings with the employee, explores attitudes through directive or nondirective methods, seeks to improve self-understanding, impart broader or more objective perspectives, and stimulate motivation for achievement of goals.

In contrast to directive approaches, which focus on the skills of the counselor, nondirective approaches focus on the *interviewee* and stress the importance of the individual's thinking through his or her own situation, identifying sources of difficulty, and deciding upon and carrying through any changes felt to be desirable. Proponents of this approach contend that advice, however well intentioned, rarely accomplishes its objectives, and that ideas or decisions developed by the individual himself or herself are more useful in that they are related to the individual's particular level of development and to his or her total situation in all its complexity. Also, the process of thinking through a problem or situation is believed to encourage self-reliance and to strengthen ability to cope with future situations.

Acceptance

It is difficult to estimate the extent to which the newer concepts of counseling have found their way into industrial application. In an early survey of sixty-one companies or governmental agencies reported by Helen Baker, it was found that in the main the various procedures evolving under the title of counseling were a reassignment, under emergency conditions, of long recognized personnel functions and responsibilities. Yet the results suggested to a limited degree the growth of a new function. A survey made by the Bureau of National Affairs indicated that of the replies received from 136 executives participating in the Forum, 75% engaged in some kind of counseling but that most of the programs were informal. Forty-four percent of the reporting companies used nondirective counseling, 40% used a combination of directive and nondirective methods, and 16% were wholly directive.

Potentials

As to the further prospects of employee counseling, one can only point to current developments as being indicative:

(1) A growing understanding of the importance of the work situation, including job assignment, management climate, and associated social and psychological influences, to the individual's mental and emotional health, and the possible effects of these upon costs in terms of efficiency, absenteeism, turnover, and morale.

(2) A far less general agreement with respect to a company's responsibility for undertaking remedial or preventive measures and the particular form such measures should take.

(3) A continuing interest in general approaches which seek to equip the supervisor with the concepts, methods, and understanding to perform counseling functions as a normal supervisory responsibility.

(4) A continuing interest in and apparently a growing, but by no means general, acceptance of nondirective counseling as a specific approach. One might add here, more referrals to family service agencies, psychiatrists, and psychologists in private practice.

(5) A growing awareness of a company's responsibility to assist those employees whose job skills and knowledge, after many years of productive service, have become obsolete because of economic, social, and technological changes. The transition into new jobs and/or careers is very difficult for many and not possible for some, as it involves leaving the old secure, and familiar and dealing with uncertainties and ambivalences associated with the new job and work conditions.

(6) A growing realization by management that the rapid development and implementation of those technological advances needed to remain competitive and viable may adversely impact on employees' expectations and personal feelings about the work situation—and the possible effects of these on the "bottom line." Counseling can provide employees the opportunity to resolve job conflicts and make appropriate adjustments to become more effective in a continuously changing work situation.

4

HUMAN RESOURCE DEVELOPMENT

HUMAN Resource Development (HRD) has become an evolving concept for building work force performance to meet the needs of an organization. The essential elements of HRD are (1) on-going assessment of work force competency needs, (2) activities to fill those needs—employee education and training, organization development, "quality of work life" programs, or other efforts to serve the needs, and (3) evaluation to determine if the intended purpose has been met.

Developing the competence and productivity of the work force, in reality, is a multi-faceted and direct responsibility of management. The quality of human performance is integral to the quality of organisation success. And while line management must bear a direct responsibility, HRD success is heavily dependent upon effective use of the growing body of available knowhow. The prudent manager would do well, in his or her own interest to get the best available professional HRD support to help build human performance.

HISTORY

Human resource development in the world of work has grown through many stages, beginning thousands of years ago when artisans handed down knowledge and skills of the earliest crafts to younger generations, often through some kind of apprenticeship, which was known as early as 2100 B.C.

Means of developing job competence have progressed through many forms, including major roles played by public and higher education. The need for industrial capacity during World War II was a powerful impetus to the formation of what we have come to know, more recently, as employee training and development, or HRD. The field has seen rapid evolution in the past decade or two with major application of the behavioral sciences, and with a strong emphasis on relating employee development directly to the needs of the organization. Employee training and development has come to encompass broader concerns of developing employee performance so that now the term *Human Resource Development* is commonly accepted as more descriptive of the function.

APPROACH

Basically, the line management responsibility for developing the work force is to ensure that the objectives of the organization are supported with work force competencies which can accomplish those objectives. Strategic organizational plans should be translated into manpower requirements and the manpower requirements translated into work force competency and training needs.

It is essential to recognize the need for a problem-analysis approach. Employee development must be directed to real needs to be effective. Without proper needs assessment, employee development can even be counter-productive. It is not uncommon that management requests (or demands) for a "training program" are inappropriate and misdirected. Reports from highly regarded HRD specialists have shown that as many as 80% of line managers' training requests have turned out not to be training problems at all when thoroughly analyzed.

Need analysis has become so prevalent as an HRD activity that some observers have noted that the HRD department is doing more job definition than the industrial engineers.

IMPLEMENTATION

After the need has been carefully established, the appropriate education or training or development effort must be designed and developed or selected/adapted from existing sources. If the need is broadly generic, the development program might be obtained from the vast array of materials and packages available nowadays from publishers and consultants and other resources that make up a large "training industry." In some instances, educational institutions can be used for employee education and training. Community colleges have often been cited as the educational sector most responsive to employee education needs.

If the need is specific to one company only, the HRD department, or a consultant, usually designs and prepares the developmental activity to meet that need. In most cases, the program can be used time and again with similar groups of employees throughout the organization. Many employers have extensive "catalogs" of employee development activities. The Bell System is reported to have 12,000 employee training courses alone!

It is important to recognize that a major instructional resource for employee development is the organization itself. "In- house" managers and specialists are often the best source of job training knowledge. Getting them involved in formal training has many advantages including realistic carry over from classroom to the job and "ownership" of training results by line personnel.

Once an organization selects and hires individuals who are able to perform jobs or who are trainable, it must integrate those workers into the organization. Failure to do so may result in continuing or increased anxiety by new employees, and permit dysfunctional learning by those individuals as they learn inappropriate patterns of performance and behaviour. Organizations must realize that if they do not explicitly plan to teach employees to behave properly, those employees' may learn these patterns from others.

Company orientation programs are new employees' first exposure to training and development by the organizations. Because of the dramatic impact of orientation programs upon the future success or failure of the worker on the job, we will first consider the purposes, content, and results of such programs. We emphasize this aspect of training, since the simple fact remains, if you don't orient new employees, someone else will!

Although orientation training is an employee's first exposure to training and development, it should be only the beginning of a continuing process of planned development. Organization learning is planned, and as such it is a process of four basic phases depicted in Figure 1. The four basic steps are not as sequential as Figure 1 implies.

ORIENTATION TRAINING

Orientation is concerned with familiarizing new employees with both the general job environment and specific details of tasks to be performed. This process includes not only the socialization of the new employee, but also a recognition of the personal needs the worker brings to the organization which must be met. Consequently, the extent of such orientation will differ depending upon both the individual and the situation.

A totally new employee, for example, will require far more extensive orientation than one who has been transferred, promoted, or demoted. In the latter instances, workers will already know a great deal about the firm, its policies, and employee benefits, and training will focus primarily on the job itself.

In addition, even newly hired workers will differ in the degree of information they have received prior to employment. They may well know something about the company, its history and products, and possibly the job itself as a result of preemployment interviews, plant visits, or previews of the job. The realistic job preview, for instance, alerts new employees to potential problems or difficulties that they might encounter on the job (for example, hazing by fellow employees or rudeness by customers). Such information is provided in order to reduce discouragement during the early period of employment. Even in these instances, however, some learning is necessary for all new position holders.

All employees experience certain levels of anxiety on their first day on a new job. Effective employee orientation seeks to reduce and eliminate many of the questions and fears which contribute to anxiety and which may interfere with future learning. Firms utilize a variety of time spans for orientation, ranging from a few hours to many months. Additionally, a variety of techniques are possible, including mass meetings, individualized briefings, plant tours, personal introductions, employee pamphlets and handouts, and combinations of these procedures.

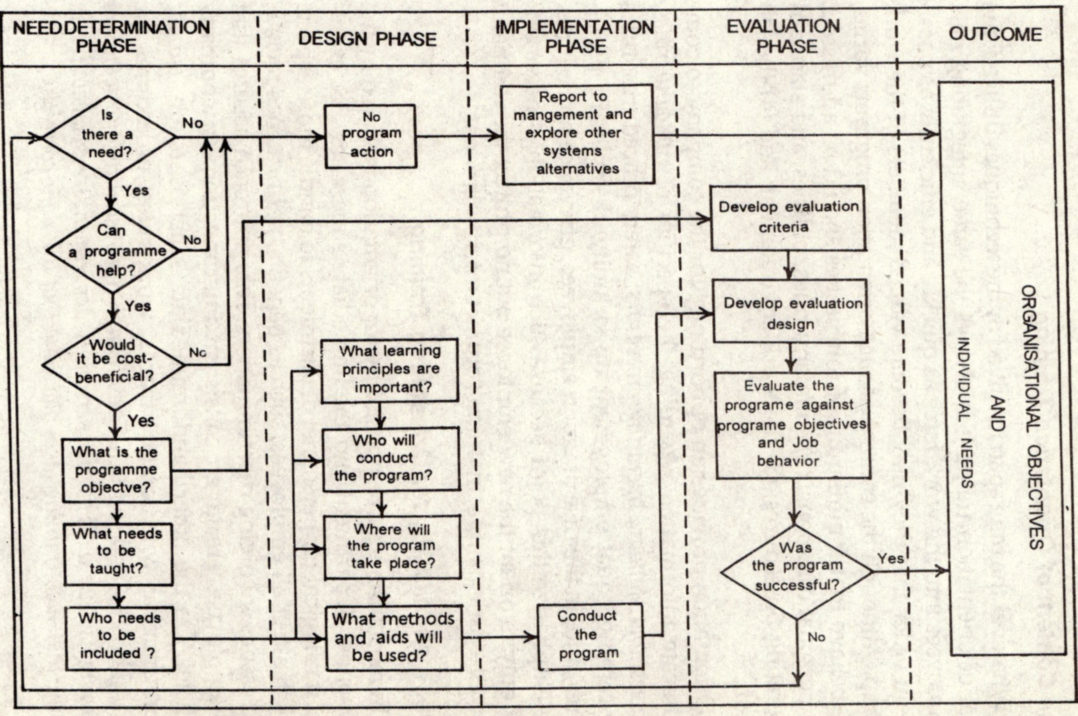

Fig. 1. Planned organizational learning process.

The Content of Orientation Training

Whatever the time span involved or the techniques utilized, the goal of orientation training is always the same: integrating new employees into the work force as quickly and efficiently as possible in order that they may become valued members of the work group. Although the content of such orientation programs varies, we believe that a minimum of four issues should be addressed: (1) personal questions; (2) company rules, policies, and standard operating procedures; (3) the work environment; and (4) the job itself.

Orientation provides an opportunity for the company to communicate information regarding the specifics of *company rules, policies, and standard operating procedures:* safety procedures, rules concerning equal employment opportunity, disciplinary procedures, and, in the case of union employees, grievance procedures. We emphasize this point because such information is necessary not only to orient the new employee but no protect the company as well—for example, in union contract interpretations.

The Responsibility for Orientation Training

In most instances, responsibility for orientation is shared by the personnel department and the immediate supervisor. For example, it is logical for personnel departments to handle those aspects which affect all employees, such as benefits, performance review, and issues involving discrimination. This approach assures that all employees are given consistent interpretations of company policies. On the other hand, immediate supervisors are usually more familiar with safety hazards, work rules, procedures for taking breaks, and so forth. *Even though responsibility for orientation training is shared, it is the personnel department's responsibility to assure that such training takes place and that it is done correctly.*

APPRENTICESHIP PROGRAMS

Apprenticeship as a means of thoroughly learning the intricacies of a trade has been well adapted to modern industry to meet workforce needs. Even with all the innovations in industry, experience has shown that the worker masters a skilled trade only by diligently repeating job operations under capable supervision until they are fully mastered.

Management is recognizing more and more its responsibility to provide the individual worker with the proper training. In many instances, this is a matter of self-preservation for the company if it is to obtain the skilled workers it needs. Trade unions are equally aware that apprenticeship is the lifeblood of their organizations. They strongly urge their members to encourage the establishment of such programs and to take part in them.

It must be emphasized that apprentices are not only students, but *employed workers*. They learn on the job and produce during their learning period. They are paid wages, because what they produce is sold. Apprenticeship, simply defined, is the preparation of youth for those occupations referred to as skilled crafts or trades that require a wide and diverse range of skills and knowledge as well as both maturity and independence of judgment.

In taking a forward look at apprenticeship, the further training of craftworkers to keep them abreast of changing technologies affecting their trades cannot be ignored. Some journeymen did not have the advantage of a complete apprenticeship and need additional training to round out their skills. Other programs are desirable to prepare some journeymen for supervisory positions and to fill vacancies in that category due to deaths and retirements.

ON-THE-JOB TRAINING

Learning by doing is the most widely used method of acquiring operating skill and necessary related knowledge immediately useful on the job. However, its greatest drawback is blind faith in assuming that simply telling, watching, or showing is enough. If the learner has not learned or acquired speed, or continues to make mistakes, it is easy to assume that he is just not suitable for the job, and never would become efficient: the instructor gave him a chance but he couldn't learn.

On-the-job training demonstrates that this is not true. The weakness is usually not in the learner but in the instructor, be he a skilled, experienced worker at the next machine or bench, a group leader, or a supervisor.

Concepts

Over the years, apprenticeship has demonstrated that when jobs are chosen to give experience in progressively more difficult work, versatility, speed, and confidence can be acquired. Related technical knowledge will need to be added to cover what cannot be acquired on the job. On the other hand, upgrading, rotation, introduction of changes in work or processes, and transfers to different work are every-day situations which lean heavily on every-day experience at the job level. But experience is expensive when gained principally through mistakes, rejects, and accidents. It should be emphasized, then that *education* deals with the acquisition of knowledge, whereas *training* is the acquisition of skill. Training may be manual or supervisory. To be most effective and continuously useful coaching must be right on the job where all the factors of actual work situations have to be dealt with.

To improve results of on-the-job training, sound techniques have been developed to pass the know-how along. These avoid having beginners learning in the wrong way. They emphasize the essential key points which must be mastered or the work is unsatisfactory.

Job Instruction Training (J.I.T.). The J.I.T. program as then developed and as still used, was presented to groups of ten supervisors or key men using their own every-day jobs as practice demonstrations. The method was summarized on a pocket-size guide and reference card given to every one of the ten men in the group. On the front were listed points on "How to Get Ready to Instruct"; on the reverse was the four-step formula on "How to Instruct."

From experience in hundreds of plants it was demonstrated that this on-the-job training approach could be organized to contribute to improved every-day work relationships between worker and worker, worker and union representatives, and worker and supervisor.

Job Relations Training (J.R.T). The J.R.T. program used the same "close-to-earth" every day situation approach to helping supervisors in their human relationships. It was also so organized that the four-step formula could be summarized on a pocket size reference card. The card proved to be a valuable reminder as problems came up.

The training is done entirely by solving problems presented by members of a group, and discussion of principles and procedures involved. There are no prepared lectures, no text-books, no illustrative or entertaining pictures. The entire time is spent in practice in the use of principles until there has been some change in habits and attitudes, some more ready recognition of "who has a problem," as well as "what is the problem" and its underlying cause.

Job Methods Training (J.M.T.). The J.M.T. program was an approach to improvement of ways of doing the every-day job by helping supervisors be alert and constructively critical of the way the present job was being done. It was again developed through a four-step method, given on a reference pocket card. A similar problem-solving approach was effective in making better use of equipment, materials, and manpower.

J.M.T. is in no sense a substitute for a major plant engineering approach to introduction of new technical processes, department layouts, or application of new equipment. It is directed to the smaller repetitive operations right on the job. That is where much time and material are wasted. Attention to details at this level has a direct bearing on service, cost, and quality.

Acceptance

Acceptance and use of these simple and practical ways of improving on-the-job training by over 16,000 plants during the war period established them as valuable tools of management in increasing production quickly and reducing costs. This systematic approach replaced costly trials and errors.

Further evidence of the soundness and adaptability of this approach is seen in its acceptance in foreign countries. The basic procedure has been translated into many foreign languages.

EVALUATION

The bottom line question for any HRD effort is to know if it has achieved the desired results. How does management, or the HRD function, know that supervisors are better supervisors after a training program?—that the employees in a job skill training program are better performers after their learning experience? Answering this question is impossible if the objectives for the learning experience have not been specified through careful needs analysis.

Need Determination

The first step in need determination is to ask the question, Is there a problem or potential problem in meeting organizational objectives and/or individual needs? If the answer is No, the organization can spend time on other activities. If, however, the answer more likely is Yes, then the question must be raised, Can training correct the problem?

Even if training can correct the problem, other corrective actions might be more appropriate. For example, an organization may discover that newly hired employees lack necessary skills to a greater extent than anticipated. Rather than undertaking extensive remedial training programs, the firm could decide to raise its selection standards or to alter its pay scales in order to attract personnel with the desired qualifications.

In addition, the type of training necessary may not be readily apparent. For example, a manager may not be performing at an acceptable level, and the firm may believe that a program to update skills is necessary. Closer scrutiny may show that the individual already possesses the necessary skills but simply does not use them. Further investigation may reveal negative attitudes created by interpersonal conflicts with colleagues. In this instance, a frank discussion (a form of training) between the individuals involved may be a more appropriate means to overcome the problem than to send the manager to a two-week course on human relations.

Need Determination: Types of Analysis and Techniques

Three types of analysis must be undertaken in the need determination phase; (1) organizational, (2) task, (3) person. Although we will discuss these three types of analysis separately, it must be emphasized that they are interrelated and overlap in varying degrees.

Organizational Analysis. Organizational analysis includes consideration of overall corporate strategy and must therefore consider the firm's "goals, resources, and the environment in which it exists." Organizational goals and subgoals must be examined if development programs are to meet organizational objectives and members' needs. Utilizing programs that are inconsistent with organizational or individual goals will at best have little impact, and at worst will be dysfunctional. For example, a firm may have no intention of utilizing management science techniques, but may send some employees to a program dealing with these concepts. Upon their return, these newly trained employees may find their ideas rejected by top management, and consequently experience frustration and disillusionment with the firm.

Firms must also examine their physical and human resources in determining development needs. Because a firm must allocate limited resources among competing alternative, budgetary constraints may lead management to a wise decision of purchasing new equipment which can be immediately utilized, while postponing certain developmental efforts. Analysis must also consider current and future human resource needs. This necessitates linking the determination of development needs to future human resource requirements established by effective human resource planning.

Organizational analysis includes evaluation of both internal and external environments in which the firm operates. The external environment consists of social, political, economic, and legal changes which impact upon organization decisions.

The internal environment consists of the philosophies, objectives, policies, leadership styles, and attitudes which create an organizational climate: "The term *organizational climate* refers to a set of measurable properties of the work environment, perceived directly or indirectly by the people who live and work in this environment and assumed to influence their motivation and behaviour." Organizational climate may be the "most important influence affecting the development of an individual in an organization."

The prevailing climate is a contingency with which the personnel department must deal in designing training programs. For example, an organization may encourage employees to complete their formal education, but have no plans to promote or otherwise reward employees who put forth such efforts. In such instances, employees may question the worth of such efforts, or complete their education simply to increase their marketability or mobility. Thus, the prevailing organizational climate may promote development for organizationally dysfunctional purposes.

Task Analysis. Task Analysis involves the undertaking of job analysis in order to develop job descriptions and job specifications: "Just as an organizational analysis is necessary to determine the organizational objectives, a task analysis is necessary to determine objectives related to performance standard for skills, knowledge, and attitudes needed to successfully perform the task". Task analysis, with job descriptions and specifications as outputs, will help to determine what skills, attitudes, and knowledge are necessary for successful job performance.

Loftin and Roter, for example, have identified three levels of complexity for clerical duties from which they identified performance requirements in terms of skills, knowledge, and attitudes. Personnel departments can utilize such analysis in order to identified development needs by worker *level*.

Task analysis, like job analysis, deals with the job, not the individual performing the job.

Person Analysis. Person analysis identifies specific individuals who need development. Three groups must be considered: (1) organization members who are currently performing a job, (2) members who will be performing a job in the future, and (3) non-members who will eventually be performing a job. For example, a personnel department may become aware of development needs for existing employees through performance appraisals which indicate problems with adherence to specific safety rules. As a result, the department may decide to reemphasize training programs in these areas.

Analysis of selection procedures may reveal differences between new employees and current organizational members in skills, knowledge, or attitudes. One retail firm, for example, employed a personnel manager whose experience was in public administration, and the firm recognized the need for special orientation training in the techniques of retailing. This example illustrates the close relationship that exists between person analysis and task analysis. The skills, knowledge, and attitudes required for successful job performance must be examined during both the selection and development process of *specific* employees.

Need Determination Techniques. Personnel departments possess numerous sources for determining organizational training needs, and Kirkpatrick has identified 12 such sources. Since few firms utilize such a comprehensive approach, we have chosen to discuss four primary sources of such information: (1) surveys, (2) statistical data, (3) performance appraisals, and (4) input from managerial and supervisory personnel.

The term *survey* is used in a broad sense to include any attempts by the organization to gain information that is not readily available but is relevant to understanding and meeting organizational needs. Thus, we would consider psychological tests, questionnaires, interviews with employees, and even planned observation as survey instruments.

THE PRINCIPLES OF LEARNING

The design phase involves decisions regarding where training will take place, what methods will be used, and who will conduct the training. Central to all these decisions is an understanding of the *principles of learning* which facilitate efficient and effective learning by individuals. Recent years have witnessed an increased interest in the principles by which learning, transfer, and retention of materials can be accomplished.

Unfortunately, there is no general agreement concerning such principles because of the number of different learning theories. Each theory advances certain principles which may or may not be supported by other learning theories. We cannot cover all of the various learning theories or principles. Rather, we will present those principles which make the most intuitive sense to us, or are supported by adequate empirical research. We have depicted seven principles of learning and their relationship to the learning process in Figure 2.

Individual Differences

Even if all persons in training are highly motivated, trainers need to be aware of individual differences in goals, aptitudes, past experiences, and learning styles. Each of these variables influences learning.

Goals. If trainers can show trainees that learning will result in desirable outcomes, motivation is likely to be increased. However, highly motivated trainees whose goals are at variance with those of the training programs may learn a great deal—but not what is

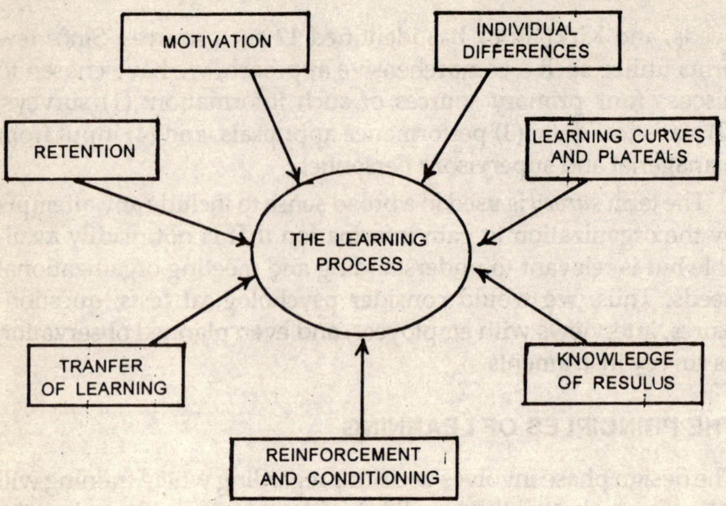

Fig. 2. The principles of learning.

desired by the organization. For example, a supervisor who receives training in performance appraisal techniques may concentrate on using the technique to ensure that a favorite subordinate receives a raise rather than learning how to conduct an honest appraisal.

In a lighter vein, one professor asked a management student, "What do you want out of this course?" to which the student exclaimed, "Me!" A research example of training program goals which conflict with those of trainees has been provided by Chowdhry. He found that many trainees in a university management development program were participating simply to escape job stress and to plan the next phase of career development rather than seeking to meet to goals of the program.

Aptitude. Persons with greater ability to learn will learn more quickly than others. For example, the army found that individuals with higher precourse scores on radiotelegraph operator aptitude tests were able to learn the code more quickly during the training program. The army also found that early differences between high and low aptitude scores actually *increased* as the training progressed. This increase in differences has been found to be more prevalent in highly complex learning situations.

Past Learning Experiences. Past learning experiences of the trainee may also influence the extent to which learning takes place. Individuals who have been successful in prior learning situations will have received positive feedback indicating they can be successful in such situations in the future. This feedback may result in more favorable self-images which will help these individuals become more confident in learning situations in general. Hence, they are more likely to be motivated to learn in specific programs.

Learning Styles. Individuals possess different learning styles which influence how they approach learning. Each style is "uniquely personal" and involves the individual's way of "receiving, perceiving, thinking, problem-solving, and remembering". For example, one classification scheme has identified four basic types of learning styles. We will illustrate two of these styles.

Some people (assimilators) tend to use abstract conceptualization and reflective observation in learning. They use deductive reasoning to create theoretical models. Other individuals (accommodators) take an opposite approach. They tend to use concrete experience and active experimentation is learning, and they utilize intuitive trial and error for problem solving. No particular type of learning style is inherently better or worse than any other. However, if trainers are able to identify a particular style in trainees, they *may* be able to make training more effective.

If, for example, trainers know that particular trainees learn best by thinking in terms of concrete situations, it *may* be possible to gear training in this direction rather than toward highly theoretical concepts. The word *may* has been emphasized twice because some types of training may not lend themselves well to the predominant style of the trainee, and in group sessions there is likely to be a heterogeneous mix of individuals with different learning styles. In this instance, it would not be feasible to develop a particular training strategy that would accommodate all or even most of the group.

Knowledge of Results (Feedback)

For efficient and effective learning to take place, trainees must receive feedback or knowledge of results (KOR) of their performance. KOR gives learners information on how well they are doing and whether or not their responses are correct. If KOR is absent, trainees may learn the wrong skills of knowledge, thus creating a dysfunctional learning situation. For example, a trainee who is learning how to operate a machine but is not told when errors are made is likely to learn incorrect techniques or procedures.

If KOR is not present, trainees may learn, but not in an efficient manner. For example, in one study subjects shot at an unseen moving target. One group was told whether they were shooting in the vicinity of the target, while the other group was not given such feedback. The feedback group outperformed the second group. The nonfeed-back group eventually improved its performance, although it took nearly twice as long as for the feedback group. Thus, although the learning was ultimately somewhat effective, it was extremely inefficient.

KOR may also stimulate intrinsic motivation for individuals who value learning per se, and it can serve as an extrinsic reward by making individuals aware that learning will contribute to other goals. In addition, KOR can make the individual aware of success and contribute to a favorable self-image. But what of individuals who are *not* successful? Locke has suggested that in these instances KOR can be utilized to help trainees modify their goals.

A number of generalizations based upon research on KOR and learning have been presented by Biel:

- ☐ KOR increases both the rate and level of learning.
- ☐ When KOR is removed, the levels of learning and performance generally drop.
- ☐ The more immediate the KOR, the greater the learning.
- ☐ The greater the amount of relevant feedback, the greater the learning.
- ☐ For particular learning situations, some methods of KOR are better than others.
- ☐ KOR has motivational value.

As these generalizations indicate, the timeliness, relevance, and accuracy of the feedback are important variables that influence the relationship between KOR and learning. Timing is important for two reasons. First, the sooner the negative feedback is provided, the more likely is the trainee to see it as relevant and to take corrective action. Second, timing is related to whether the trainee receives the correct amount of feedback. Too much feedback may result in information overload, and too little may be inadequate to assure effective performance. Both conditions are likely to make the trainee feel frustrated and consequently to reduce the amount of learning that takes place.

Reinforcement and Conditioning

The principles of reinforcement and conditioning are closely related to KOR and feedback. For effective learning, desired trainee responses must be rewarded (or positively reinforced) and negative responses ignored (extinguished) or perhaps punished. Although psychologists once argued that positive reinforcement was superior to punishment, they have defined some situations in which using a combination of the two is superior.

Research has generally shown that if a desired response is reinforced 100 percent of the time, behavior will be learned more rapidly. At the same time, however, such behavior will be forgotten (or extinguished) more quickly. Partial reinforcement or reinforcement of desired behaviors only part of the time, although usual resulting in slower learning, will make the behavior learned more resistant to extinction. Many of these observations are related primarily to what is called *operant conditioning*, the nature of which is still debated by psychologists. A simpler type of conditioning, called *classical conditioning*, is less controversial and may also be used to facilitate certain types of learning.

In classical conditioning, subjects are taught to respond to some sort of *stimulus* because the response is reinforced. An association is formed between the stimulus and the response. Then, as the stimulus that created the response is modified, behavior may be changed. The classic work in this area was that of Ivan Pavlov, who observed that dogs would salivate when food (the stimulus) was given to them. He further observed that he could train a dog to salivate when a bell was rung with the food present, making the bell the stimulus. Eventually the dog began to salivate in response to the bell even when food was not present.

What happened in this experiment was that the dog associated the bell with the presence of food. Thus, a natural response (salivation) became associated with what was previously a neutral stimulus. Pavlov also found that if the bell was rung and food was not present, the conditioned response began to diminish. Eventually the conditioned response would be extinguished because the association between the bell and the food would no longer exist.

Classical conditioning can be used by trainers in development programs. For example, paratroopers must be trained to jump from a plane when a signal is given. During training, the jump instructor shouts "Go!" (stimulus) and trainees pretend to jump (response). In actual conditions, however, with the door to the plane open, paratroopers will not be able to hear the command. During training, therefore, when trainers shout "Go!" they also slap trainees on the buttocks. The slap is therefore, when trainers shout "Go."

Eventually the command and the slap are associated, and the verbal command can be omitted. Thus, the previously learned neutral stimulus (slap) becomes a conditioned stimulus that elicits a response (jumping). In a similar fashion, training employees to respond to a bell when an overhead crane is moving through the plant carrying tons of steel is using a stimulus that results in a response in terms of safety.

Transfer of Learning

A basic consideration of off-the-job training is the extent to which such training can be transferred to the job setting. Learning in a training environment may serve no function if it cannot be transferred to the actual work situation.

Two theories have been postulated regarding maximum transfer of learning to the work environment. The first, referred to as the *identical element* theory maintains that for transfer to occur, identical elements must exist in the old and new settings. The more similar the two settings are, the more likely it is that transfer will occur. Advocates of this theory would favor on-the- job training because such training consists of identical elements.

The second theory of transfer is *transfer through principle.* This theory maintains that transfer of learning will occur even if identical elements are not present, as long as principles are learned that can be *generalized* to other situations. The readers of this text should be hoping that transfer through principle can occur. They are learning principles, concepts, and tools that hopefully will have application in an actual work environment in which they will be involved upon graduation. Neither of these two theories can be said to be better than the other. However, having identical elements seems generally to provide the greatest likelihood of transfer.

A number of guidelines on transfer of learning may aid the decision maker in designing development programs. Since maximum transfer of learning results when identical elements are present, trainers should attempt to maximize similarities between the learning situation and the situation in which trainees will actually work. The similarities should include not only the physical equipment used, but similar noise levels and supervisory styles as well.

Transfer of learning appears to be facilitated if trainees are given adequate experience with the task in the training situation. Trainees must be permitted to learn the desired behavior completely before being placed in the actual work environment. Transfer may be enhanced in transfer through principle if the trainee is exposed to a variety of conditions in the training environment. For example, in teaching managers about human relations in small groups, trainers could provide a number of different settings in which managers could apply what they have learned, utilizing role playing with feedback.

Retention

A final consideration in designing development programs is the problem of retention of learning. As with transfer of learning, retention is facilitated if a number of learning principles are applied during training. For example, if the individuals are motivated, they are likely to learn more, which will result in more being retained. Similarly, if the material is meaningful, retention is likely to be greater.

Retention will be facilitated if what has been learned in the training environment is reinforced on the job. If the work environment does not support what has been learned, the individual will be unlikely to retain the learning or to use it on the job. A study by Fleishman reported that human relations training was effective in producing on-the-job behavior changes *only* if the trainees' supervisors supported such behavior. In short, if what the individual has learned is interfered with, retention will diminish.

Criterion Measurement

Top management supports training programs because it expects desired changes to occur. "The purpose of training evaluation, therefore, should be to determine *if* such management-desired changed *did* occur as a *result* of the training."

In order to be successful, evaluation must be considered an integral part of the training program:

> Evaluation must be built into the training program from its very conception. Evaluation cannot be thrown in at the end of training without regard to the goals of the program, knowledge of pretraining performance of the trainees, and the methods used to present the training. A hastily or ill-planned evaluation cannot be expected to give a meaningful appraisal of the effectiveness of the training program.

A widely respected model for looking at training evaluation was suggested by Dr. D.L. Kirkpatrick. He emphasized the need of four levels of employee training evaluation:

Reaction

Reaction refers to asking participants what they thought of the training program. This measurement is essentially subjective in nature and therefore may be biased. In one training program the trainees gave positive reports because they did not want to "get into trouble" with the firm's corporate personnel staff.

A second problem with reaction is that students may rate the instructor rather than the content of the program. As a consequence, trainers may try to create favorable evaluations which have little if anything to do with what should have been learned. In a study by Kelley, for example, students were told that their class would have a substitute. Students were given information about the substitute, with one group being led to believe his personality was "cold," and another group led to believe that it was "warm." Even though both groups were taught by the same person, the group that had been told the instructor's personality was "warm") rated him more favorably than the group that had been told it was "cold".

Learning

The learning level criterion measures the extent to which skills, knowledge, and attitudes covered by the program are understood and acquired by trainees. Measuring learning is much more difficult than measuring reaction to a program. It may involve test development and necessitate quantifying the results of those tests by the trainers. A major problem of measuring learning, however, involves the issue of transfer: "It does not include the on- the-job use of these principles, facts, and skills." For example, someone may readily learn factual material and display mastery of that information on a test, only to discover that the information acquired is totally useless on the job.

Behavior

The behavior level refers to the measurement of actual job performance. The primary concern at this level is with the transfer of learning to the actual job situation. Unfortunately, there is ample evidence that transfer is often low. It is likely that both objective and subjective criteria will be utilized at this level, since some transfer of learning, such as turning out pieces on a machine, may be directly observable, whereas other learning, such as attitude changes, may have to be inferred.

Results

The final level of criteria for evaluation, results, involves relating training objectives to organizational goals. In other words, Does the training pay off for the organization? As Kirkpatrick has noted, "The objectives of most training programs can be stated in terms of results such as reduced turnover, reduced costs, improved efficiency, reduction in grievances, increase in quality and quantity of production, or improved morale..."

Criteria Selection

Criteria selection is not an easy decision. Criteria must be both reliable and valid. To simply use a criterion because it is reaidly available, or because it has been used before, may result in meaningless information. Criteria must be related to the firm's objectives, and vary depending on the level of manager being trained. Criteria must be measurable and specific enough to permit assessment of successful and unsuccessful accomplishment of objectives. If a firm's objective was improved quality control, the criterion would be the percentage of rejects. However, the firm would also have to specify what percentage of rejects was acceptable.

Timing of the administration of the criterion measure is also important. A measurement that occurs immediately after the development program evaluates reaction and learning levels. A later measurement is more likely to evaluate behavior and results levels. In fact, evaluation at the behavior and results levels is best conducted through longitudinal studies which provide sufficient time for desired changes to take place before measurement is undertaken. Such studies are necessary to assess whether learning persists, and even to evaluate whether learning ever took place *if* this can only be assessed on the job.

Experimental Design

In the evaluation of training programs, two design considerations are of major importance: (1) whether or not before and/or after measures will be used, and (2) whether or not control groups will be used. Answers to these questions will indicate what type of experimental design is to be utilized.

After-only-Design. At the end of a training program, participants can be given a measuring device (for example, a test, a questionnaire, an interview) to determine if they have learned the materials. This is an after-only design. Unfortunately, such a design does not tell whether learning will be transferred to the job or whether it will contribute to the achievement of organizational objectives.

Another problem is the uncertainty that *anything* was learned as a result of the training. Since the after-only design provides only a final score for each person, it is not known what skills, knowledge, or attitudes the trainees brought to the learning situation. Individuals who score well on tests used to evaluate training may be demonstrating prior expertise rather than current learning. One simply cannot tell when an after-only design is used.

Before-After Measures Without Control Group. To overcome the problems of the after-only design, a measuring device can be given before the training and again afterwards. Learning can then be assessed by comparing the results of the measure taken prior to training and those after. When using the before-after design, however, one should avoid making the invalid assumption that a better score on the after measure than on the before measure indicates that learning has occurred.

This assumption is invalid for two reasons. First, the use of before measures may sensitize trainees to look for aspects of the training situation which relate to the before measure. Thus learning may occur primarily within the limited range of the before measure rather than the full range of the training program. Second, learning may have resulted from uncontrolled events rather than from the training itself. For example, if a program is conducted for supervisors on how to encourage employee suggestions, and supervisors simultaneously receive a new manual on the subject, how much of an increase in employee suggestions would be due to the training program and how much to the new manual?

To compound the problem, suppose that the firm also decided to change the reward structure for adopted suggestions and publicized this change while the training program was being conducted. Under these circumstances, one must ask. To what extent would an increase in suggestions be due to better-informed supervisors (whether from the training, the manual, or both), or to better-informed subordinates, or to some combination of both? In order to help overcome such problems, control groups may be used in evaluating programs.

A control group consists of individuals who do not receive the training. These individuals should be comparable to members of the trainee group in characteristics that might have an impact on training. Where such comparability is lacking, trainee groups may appear to learn more or less relative to the control group than they really have. For example, if a complex manual skill is taught in a training program, the control group and the trainee group should be comparable in manual dexterity.

After-only Measures with a Control Group. Control groups can be used with both after-only and before-after designs. In the former case, the two groups can be compared on the criteria established to evaluate the development program. If the trainee group performs better than the control group, there is some basis on which to conclude that the program was effective. This assessment must be a qualified one, however. Because no before measure was undertaken, it is not known if the two groups differed in the skills, knowledge, or attitudes being dealt with in the training program.

This design also does not indicate whether any uncontrollable events confounded the results. For example, interaction between the control and trainee groups during the evaluation phase can distort results. In this case, the control group may receive some training through the trainee group, thus distorting differences on the after measure. In longitudinal studies, this problem is intensified because of the time span involved and the impact of other system changes, such a promotion and transfers resulting in contact between members of the two groups.

Before-After Design with a Control Group. The before-after design with a control group provides more accurate information about the effectiveness of the development efforts than the three designs previously discussed. The results of a before measure give some idea of group comparability about the materials to be taught before the program begins. The results of the after measure can be compared to those of the before measure to see if they significantly differ. In addition, the groups' before-measure and after differences can be compared to see which group has changed the most. From an evaluation standpoint, the ideal situation would be for the control group to be comparable to the trainee group prior to the training, and for the training group to show a *major favorable* change. We emphasize *favorable* here because it is possible for the trainees to show no change, or even unfavorable change.

The before-after design with a control group should generally be used because it provides greater information. However, the use of this design may not always be possible. For example, small organizations may not have enough employees to permit the information of a comparable, control group. In addition, the use of control groups represents a cost to the firm, and smaller firms may find it impossible to fund such programs.

Employers must recognize that money-measurable costs are not the only costs associated with control groups. There are psychological and social ones as well. Both trainee and control groups may feel they are being manipulated by management if they know an experiment is being conducted. If an incentive pay system is in effect, the group that has not received initial training may feel it was "cheated" if the trainee group is able to earn incentive pay sooner. In such instances, it is possible that members of the control group may become dissatisfied, with the dysfunctional results of increased absenteeism or lowered productivity.

Given the trade-offs of various costs and the additional information provided by the more complex designs, the decision maker must choose which one to use. Simply because the most complex or "scientific" design cannot be used does not mean that evaluation should not be attempted. Rather, the most satisfactory viable design should be utilized.

Despite the need for evaluation of training, there is evidence that little evaluation is done by firms, and that what is done often tends to be of the reaction type. This lack of evaluation can be attributed to three reasons: (1) design, (2) attitudinal, and (3) cost-benefit. Reasons related to design have already been discussed in the sections on criterion measurement and experimental design. Some firms simply give up on evaluation because they believe it is too difficult to carry out.

Attitudinal reasons for not evaluating training arise because some individuals believe that all training is worthwhile and that evaluation is therefore unnecessary. A second attitudinal reason for not evaluating training may be the personnel department's fear of evaluation: It may be perceived as an attack on what they have done. Frequently this fear arises because personnel fails to see that such evaluations can be beneficial by providing feedback useful in designing future programs. In addition, personnel may be concerned about who conducts the evaluation, or may not understand the methodology utilized. Finally, personnel may rightly perceive that top management does not understand the problems involved in program evaluation and will not support personnel in conducting such efforts.

RANGE

The range of Human Resource Development activities is broad. It can include *entry level education and training* to help with the transition from school to work for youth. Many employers must provide education in basic skills (reading, writing, basic math, etc.) since young people often come into the workforce lacking in these areas. Orientation training and apprenticeships also fall into the entry level.

Probably the largest area of human resource development in the world of work is *job-skill training*—crafts, technical training of all sorts, clerical and data-processing skills, and specialized training for the myriads of jobs we have today. Managers can call upon a wide range of external sources for training in these job areas. Many trade and professional groups can provide good information about training resources in their special fields, and they may also have extensive training materials or programs themselves.

RECENT DEVELOPMENTS

Increasingly, employers are providing more training for their women and minority employees to help integrate them into the work force and to provide them with opportunities for upward mobility as part of *affirmative action* initiatives. In this HRD activity, as with all employee development, managers should make certain that their selections and the developmental experiences offered are nondiscriminatory and can be shown to be job-related.

Organization development is a movement that has gained wide acceptance in the past decade and in simplified terms, is directed to building "team" effectiveness, as distinguished from development directed to individual employees.

More information can be obtained from the Organization Development Division, American Society for Training and Development.

A newer movement that has developed widespread interest and increasing acceptance, as the U.S. productivity growth rate has dropped, is known by the broad term. Quality of work life QWL programs are usually intended to increase job satisfaction for employees through involving the employees in the decision making of their work groups. It may include techniques variously labeled as participative decision making, autonomous work groups, industrial democracy, job redesign, and others. Invariably, an expected outcome of a QWL program is increased productivity. In fact, much of the credit for better productivity and better quality of product in Japan has been attributed to QWL practices such as QC Circles. The ASTD Task Force on QWL has defined QWL as: "a process for a work organization which enables its members at all levels to participate actively in shaping the organization's environment, methods, and outcomes. This people-based process is directed to meeting the twin goals of enhanced effectiveness of the organization and improved quality of work life for employees."

It seems inevitable that HRD will become an even more vital concern for the manager in the future as the cost of labor escalates, as the international marketplace becomes more competitive, as technological change creates demands for new job knowledge and skills, as attitudes and demographicsof the work force change, and as social change impacts the work place. A proficient work force will undoubtedly be a major factor in managerial success.

HUMAN FACTORS ENGINEERING

Human Engineering means engineering for human use. In a more philosophical sense, human engineering could be described as a point of view, an attitude or frame of reference within which the engineer approaches design problems. In describing the activity of the human factors specialist, an analogy commonly made is that of impedance matching between the human operator and the machine system of which he is an element.

Within the past fifteen years the term *Human Engineering* has been expanded to the more inclusive *Human Factors Engineering*, and it may be formally defined as "the application of social, biological, and psychological science or knowledge from other sources to the design, operation, and maintenance of man-machine systems and system components." The System Development Corporation, employing what is probably the largest single group of human factors engineers in this country, lists typical duties as follows. "...the human factors engineer designs and implements scientific experiments and other research methodology" to study human factors areas as they pertain to the operation of man-machine, weapons, and other complex systems and concepts. Evaluates existing or proposed man-machine, systems and sub-systems in terms of human physiological and psychological requirements so that optimum system reliability and durability from a human input standpoint are established. Consults with design engineers and other professionals prior to, during, and after design and development of systems to assure optimum operation in terms of human capabilities, limitations, and variables.

provides the most current state-of-the-art information in his particular field of specialization."

Approaches and Techniques

A human factors engineering group will generally include engineering group will generally include engineering psychologists, mathematicians, several types of engineers, physiologists, anthropologists, radiobiologists, physicians, and specialists from related fields who have worked together as a team long enough to have developed a common technical language and meaningful methods for the solution of man-in-systems problems. Some of the well-known tools and techniques now used in human engineering include the following: experimental design, mathematical modeling, game theory, human linear programming, information theory, decision theory, simulation and testing, field testing statistical sampling, and direct case history studies. The methodology of human factors engineering research and design relates in many ways to associated technical fields such as operations research, industrial engineering, weapons systems analysis, industrial design, life support engineering, and systems development engineering.

Acceptance

The functions and responsibilities of this discipline have continually broadened in scope, and participation by human factors specialists in virtually standard on most government- sponsored system development projects. In numerous other, non- government organizations such as the automobile industry, farm machine industry, and business machine industry, human factors staffs are becoming permanent parts of these organizations. And, of course, considerable industrial human factors effort is sustained through government contract requirements that impose human engineering specifications and standards on the products produced for the government.

Within parent organizations, the position occupied by the various human factors engineering programs ranges from a one- or two-man staff to fairly large groups of 50 or more specialists. Responsibilities vary from management to line organization, making it apparent that organizations are beginning to recognize the broad scope of human factors needs, and the value of applying human factors principles not only to design, but to management procedures and personnel and training.

Potentials

The decade ahead will see a widespread utilization of human factors engineering in the consumer goods and transportation industries, in architecture and civil systems, and some utilization by the agricultural machinery, heavy equipment, and machine tools makers. Until recently, there has been a shortage of trained specialists in the field, some of which has been relieved by entry into human factors of growing numbers of technical specialists from allied fields such as industrial engineering, computer technology, physiology, physics, electronics, reliability maintainability, industrial design, interiors design, and safety engineering.

Nearly 60 institutions of higher learning offer course work in human factors/bio-technology. Numerous universities have outstanding curricula in human factors engineering, many of them offering programs at the graduate level.

TRAINING AND DEVELOPMENT

In today's rapidly changing technological society, organizations are increasingly recognizing the need for training their employees to enable them to keep abreast of new information and to develop new skills. This is especially true at managerial and professional levels, where personnel are often faced with new problems arising from computerization, automation, rapid new product development, etc. In addition to on-the-job training and development, many firms, for example, have run in-company training conference and seminars provided tuition-refund plans to help finance employees taking job-related university courses, and sent managers to outside training programs sponsored by universities and such organizations as Management Associations. The content of today's training and developmental efforts is, of course, extremely diverse, depending on the specific needs of the individuals involved.

Management Development—A Systems View

Before discussing managerial development in systems terms, it will be useful to present a systems view of the manager's role as an organizational member. Central to such a conception are two basic notions. The first of these is that the basic activity performed by the manager in any organization is that of decision making. Developing organizational policies, rules, procedures and methods, handling human problems, organization structuring, communicating information to subordinates—all involve managerial decision making in one way or another.

The second notion of central interest to our discussion is that his managerial decision-making process takes place within an organizational information-decision system. The organization, viewed as such a system, is comprised of six different kinds of systems *elements:* input, transformation, output, feedback, memory and control. Let us now examine briefly the manager's role in the organization in terms of each of these.

What the manager essentially does as a decision maker is to transform information relative to his operations into specified courses of action to be taken by himself and/or other members of the organization. For example, when a first line production supervisor observes one of his men violating the plant's no smoking rule, he may decide to discipline the man. In systems terms, this decision represents the *transformation* of an informational *input* (knowledge of the rule violation) by the supervisor into a performance *output* (the disciplinary action undertaken).

Two further observations are in order concerning the nature of system inputs and outputs. First, many elements of organizational behavior may be considered as representing either inputs or outputs, depending upon the vantage point from which they are viewed. Looking at the events described in the previous illustration from the point of view of the disciplined subordinate, rather than his supervisor, for example:

1. The rule violation would be considered as a performance output, and
2. The supervisor's communication of his disciplinary decision would represent an informational input to the subordinate.

What this observation points up is that the total organizational system is, in effect, comprised of a number of interdependent sub-systems (and sub-sub-systems), with the outputs of some serving as inputs to others. Whether one wishes to consider the individual members of an organization as constituting its subsystems, (as above); to view the organization's departments as sub-systems, and their members as sub-sub-systems; or to focus attention on still other sub-organizational elements, will depend upon the purposes of his analysis.

Second, the input elements of the organizational system (or any of its sub-systems) may assume any one of at least four different forms:

1. A message communicated orally to a member of the organization.
2. A message communicated in written form to a member of the organization,
3. Human behavior observed by an organizational member—e.g., the rule violation in our above example, or
4. A non-human even or process observed by an organizational member, as when a foreman sees that a machine in his department has broken down.

All of these input types represent messages which may help provide the basis for making managerial decision transformations.

The manager's decision transformations also influence and are influenced by the other three types of systems elements indicated previously. In making decision, the manager:

1. Draws on information about previous happenings as stored either (a) in his own human memory, or (b) in some external memory system—e.g., organizational data recorded in files, on punched cards, etc.,
2. Receives *feedback* as to the appropriateness of his behavior aimed at its improvement in the future, as when a manager's performance is appraised by his superior, and
3. Is guided by certain *control* elements within the organizational system. The control elements include those policies, objectives, models, procedures, decision rules, etc., which specify for the manager what shall be done with the input, memory and feedback in order to produce the output required.

In order to provide a basis for an examination of management development in systems terms several observations are now in view. First, a major value of the systems approach is that it permits us to sharpen our analysis of the decision-making process by breaking it down into its basic elements and examining each in relationship to the others rather than simply viewing this process as a gross phenomenon. Second, the ultimate objective of all managerial endeavor, including management development efforts, ought to be, in systems terms, that of improving the quality of the organization's *outputs*—i.e., arriving at more effective courses of action in terms of attaining organizational objectives. Third, the quality of any organizational output is conditioned by the quality of all other relevant systems elements—input, memory, transformation, control and feedback—and, hence if any of these other elements is inadequate, output too, will not be adequate. For example, some courses of action chosen by a manager may be ineffective largely because his *transformational abilities* are weak—i.e., he lacks skill in making decisions. In other cases, however, inadequate output may be generated primarily because the manager is not able to obtain the information needed to make an effective decision, or because the courses of action which he is permitted to choose are circumscribed by poorly programmed control elements—policies, rules, procedures or methods. Fourth, from the above it follows that if managerial development efforts are to be effective in improving the quality of the outputs produced by the manager as a decision maker, they must take into consideration *all* systems elements relevant to his performance within the organization.

Let us now turn into the question: "To what extent have those responsible for managerial training and development taken such a systems view?"

In attempting to answer this question, it will not be possible to give specific consideration to all of the many different kinds of managerial training and development programs being carried out by business (and other) organizations. Rather, the ensuing discussion will center around some observations about one major type of management development approach in wide use today—off-the-job training. Included in this category are in-company conferences, university executive development programs, and institutes and seminars sponsored by professional associations. Although the objectives and content of different programs of this type vary considerably, all are similar in that they take the executive away from the organizational system in which he normally functions, and attempt to induce improvement in his managerial abilities in one way or another—utilizing such approaches as the lecture or discussion methods, case studies, role playing, business gaming, etc.

In terms of our system view, these off-the-job programs generally focus primary attention on further developing either the manager's own *memory element* and/or his *transformational skills,* both in which, of course, are interrelated facets of the same personality system. That is, the manager:

1. May be furnished with information which hopefully will be stored in his mind for future utilization in making decisions—e.g., being familiarized with the company's new contract with its union, or
2. May be provided in the training conference with some form of synthetic experience in actually transforming certain types of inputs into outputs—e.g., assuming the role of a supervisor in a mock performance appraisal interview, or playing a business game.

On the other hand, it would appear that in the design of many off-the-job training programs, inadequate consideration is given to the other systems elements which have an important bearing on the outputs of those managers whom the organization is attempting to develop—i.e., *organizational* memory, input, control and feedback. As a number of observes have noted, certain kinds of human relations problems in the business firm seem to occur more because of the existence of stress situations which are largely a function of organizational design—work flow inputs on the job, types of interaction patterns required, etc.—than because of any major inadequacies in the human skills of the organizational members so involved. For example:

1. Chapple and Sayles in their book. *The Measure of Management* have cited a case in which repeated arguments between a firm's sales manager and credit manager although "interpreted by management as a clash of personalities," were basically due to the fact the flow of certain work in the organization "was divided into separate pieces on the basis of functional similarities."
2. In his "Parable of the Spindle," Elias Porter has indicated how a number of human problems existing in a restaurant operation were largely overcome when through the intro-

duction of a spindle, it was no longer necessary for waitresses to give their orders verbally to the cook.

Yet in designing, and in deciding on which managers are to participate in, many so-called "human relations" courses in industry today, concern is often given only to the modification of the human skills (transformational abilities) of the manager, without consideration of the impact that such other organizational system elements may be having on his performance output.

Further, the question may be raised: "In light of the considerable difficulty usually encountered in attempting to change the individual's basic personality structure once he has reached adulthood, might not it often be easier to improve the manager's output by modifying the organization inputs, feedback and controls which affect his performance, rather than his own memory system and transformational skills?"

One should, of course, not infer from this suggestion that all attempts to develop the manager's transformational skills be abandoned, for within the constraints of his personality structure, these skills may often be improved considerably. Moreover, it is obviously not always possible to restructure the organization's input, feedback memory and control elements to suit the personalities of its members. Rather, the view just described simply suggests that in attempting to improve managerial output, all systems elements be considered with the question in mind: "Which elements may be most easily modified so as to meet organizational objectives?"

Another point that seems to be importance in viewing management development efforts is that in many cases if the manager's transformational skills are to be improved so also must certain other systems elements be modified. Evidence suggests that managers exposed to off-the-job development may fail to apply the knowledge and skills learned in such training when they return to their own jobs largely because the changes which they attempt to make in their own behavior are *not supported* by their own supervisors. For instance, a manager who comes to the conclusion, through exposure to a human relations course, that he ought to be more "permissive" in his leadership style may find that any attempts taken to these ends will be ridiculed by his own boss. Or, in systems terms, he may fail to modify his transformational skills largely because of inappropriate *feedback* from his supervisor rather than because of any major inadequacies in the training program inputs or in his willingness to try out new patterns of behavior.

In recognition of this need to modify the supervisory feedback element as well as the trainees' own memory and transformational and training program input elements, a number of companies have followed the approach of exposing their management groups to various forms of training "from the top down." In one manufacturing plant with which this author is familiar, for example, the plant manager and general foremen were given courses in creative thinking and employment interviewing before these programs were instituted for the first line supervisors. Having been exposed first themselves to the new skills and concepts taught, the general foremen seemed to be more respective to and to give more support to attempts by their subordinates—the supervisors—in trying out new patterns of behavior on the job than when such an approach was not followed.

A Broader Role For The Training Director

Now that a number of observations have been made about off-the-job training programs in systems terms, some concluding observations about the role of the training director with respect to these programs are in order.

In spite of the many millions of dollars being spent each year on off-the-job developmental programs, an uncomfortably large number of these efforts seem not to have been as successful as hoped in effecting significant improvements in managerial output. In some cases, this probably has been due more to the utilization of inappropriate educational methodologies than to anything else—e.g., employing the lecture method to try to improve the manager's interpersonal skills. In many other cases, however, even developmental programs based on sound learning theory have not enjoyed the success which their designers had intended.

A central thesis of this article is that the effectiveness of off-the-job training programs has in many cases been limited because their designers—by conceiving of their role primarily as *educators* interested in improving the manager's memory and transformational abilities—have not given adequate consideration to the impact of other systems elements on performance output. The

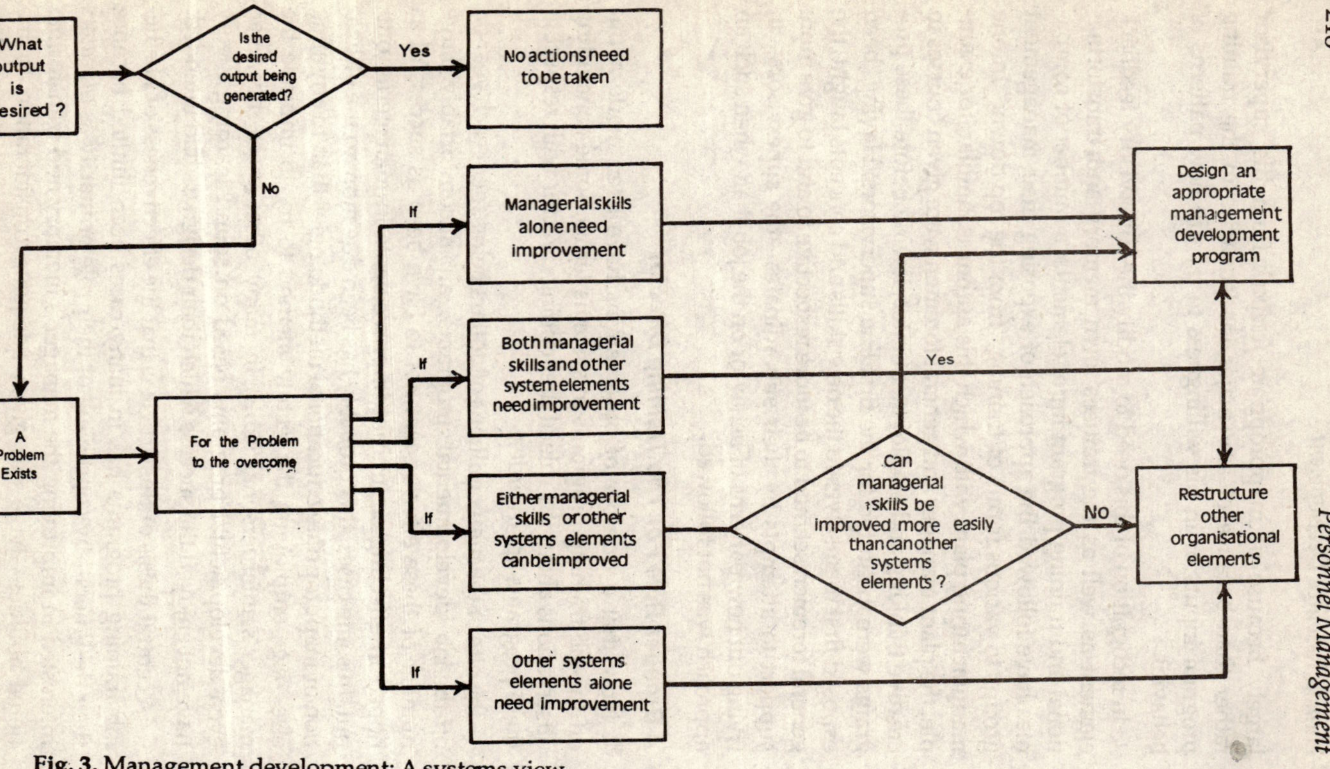

Fig. 3. Management development: A systems view.

systems view suggests that for more effective developmental efforts the training director must conceive of his role more broadly—both as an educator and as a systems analyst. In doing so, he must focus attention on a number of questions such as those indicated in Figure 3, concerning the need and feasibility of improving all types of systems elements relative to managerial performance. Only in this way can those responsible for managerial development contribute significantly to the betterment of organizational output.

TEACHING MACHINES AND COMPUTER-ASSISTED INSTRUCTION

Society is conscious today, as never before, of the importance of education, both in its qualitative and its quantitative aspects. As a consequence, the educational profession finds itself under unprecedented pressure to broaden its responsibility and increase its productivity.

The profession is being asked to train the mass of our young people to higher standards than ever before. It is being pressed to bring an end to conditions which presently permit a great many underachievers to drop out of the process of conventional education. It is being called on to devise and develop institutions and techniques for the re-education of adults whose education is either inadequate or obsolete.

The potential benefit to society of these educational reforms, now being actively formulated, has led to a rapid increase of the funds available to accomplish them. However, non-financial factors may limit progress towards the desired goals; these factors include the limited supply of trained teachers, a shortage of facilities, lack of adequate techniques, and lack of institutions for training those persons who have not received a satisfactory education by normal progress through the conventional educational system.

Teaching-Machines, Programmed Instruction, and Computer-Assisted Instruction (CAI), represent a major stage in the development of teaching and human learning. They combine traditional learning theory, an advancing engineering technology, and an increasing acceptance of man-machine relationships by business and governmental managements. While much of previously known adult learning theory is involved, the introduction of the "non-human instructor," the teaching machine, programmed text, and computer program brought the application of a number of unused principles. Machine instruction is an evolutionary development for the improvement of employee performance on the Job.

Formal Definition

Teaching-machine technology, programmed learning, and *CAI* are techniques of instructing employees without the presence of a human instructor. The teaching machine is a mechanism or apparatus, possibly a computer system, while presents a lesson consisting of information, actions, or objects in a prescribed of information, actions, or objects in a prescribed sequence. The lesson is understood, learned, and retained by an employee completely without the presence of a human instruction. The *criteria* that distinguish this technology are:

1. Instruction is provided for without the presence of a human instructor.
2. The employee learns at his own rate.
3. The employee receives immediate knowledge of his progress through feedback, and this controls his behavior.
4. There is a participative, overt interaction or two-way communication between the learner and the machine or program.
5. The sequence of the lesson is carefully controlled and consistent.
6. Reinforcement is used to strengthen learning.

The valid statement is often made that the mechanism is not of prime significance, but that the "program" or lesson plan which constitutes the step-by-step teaching points is. However as computers are utilized, it may be necessary to add an additional criterion to the list:

7. The teaching machine *software and hardware mix* shapes controls employee behavior.

History

One of the most important out-growths of training experience during World War I was the realization that no train effectively, it was first necessary to determine by a careful *analysis* of the work to be done, the skills and information which the employee must be taught. Charles R. Allen is credited with two extremely significant contributions to training methodology which rank with the history-making efforts to Pressey and Skinner. Both of these techniques form the foundation for what is now called "instructional programming." In 1910, Dr. Allen began to formulate a systematic approach to vocational education and training. It was not until 1917 that, as director of education and training of Emergency Fleet Corporation, he could implement his methods of job analysis and the principles of instruction incorporating preparation, presentation, application, and test. In 1918, Dr. Allen's book, "The Instructor, The Man, and The Job," not only established analysis as a necessary prerequisite to effective instruction, but also stated the principles which, in World War II, became known as the "Four-step Method." Of these steps, "presentation" is most interesting because it was generalized in 1941 as "...instruct slowly, clearly, completely, and patiently, one point at a time...question and repeat...make sure the learner really learns."

The Job Instructor Training Program called for one employee or learner to be instructed step-by-step by one supervisor or instructor. This constituted a "man-man" relationship. Industry soon found that the efficiency of the human instructor's communication could be improved by the use of such familiar curriculum materials as the textbook, workbook, and text-workbook which in the trade areas included the operation sheet, job sheet, information sheet, and assignment sheet. Further improvement resulted from the judicious utilization of audiovisual aids or training devices. They were fundamentally *instructor-centered* in the sense that they were aids to the human instructor's communication.

Beginning in 1920, Dr. Sidney L. Pressey developed what became known as teaching machine technology. In 1926, he described the first teaching machine which he used at Ohio State University.

An influential voice was added to that of Pressey's in favor of the teaching machine, when in 1954 Dr. Burrus F. Skinner published his famous paper. "The Science of Learning and the Art of Teaching". Both Pressey and Skinner visualized teaching machine technology as a *method*, a curriculum method in which the device was important but incidental to the curriculum. One might say that the "what" or subject-matter was the content, the "how" or psychological technique was method, and the "way" or machine was the mechanism. This is a *learner-centered* concept, particularly since there is no human instructor, but more significantly because the curriculum is designed around the learning needs of the learner rather than upon the communication needs of the instructor.

A New Educational Tool

The existence of such problems enhances the potential importance of the new instructional tool, *Computer Assisted Instruction* (CAI), which we wish to discuss. This is a tool which can substantially increase the output of a teacher. Also, it is a tool of unique value for purposes of observing, evaluating, and improving the efficacy of instructional technique.

The instrument for effecting CAI is an electronic communication station controlled by a stored program computer. For practical reasons a number of communication stations will ordinarily be controlled by a single computer. So we will refer to the tool as a *computer-assisted instruction system.*

The Man-Machine Relationship

The fact that a human may learn as the result of exposure to any machine does not attest to the efficacy of a teaching machine environment. A teaching machine is not merely a machine which teaches or communicates—it must operate according to the criteria established for it. Important here is the interaction between man and machine. Overt responses by the learner fall into these modes in the general-purpose teaching machine: (1) multiple-choice (recognition); (2) written-completion (recall); (3) oral-completion (recall). The constructed response in manual form known as the "written-completion" frame or step is a direct outgrowth of Skinner's original work. The constructed response in oral form is referred to as the "oral completion" frame or step and is an outgrowth of early language laboratory experience, coupled with the marriage of the laboratory and the pure teaching machine in 1960 by Silvern.

This entire process is characteristic of the man-machine or better, the learner-teaching machine relationship. Unlike traditional instructor-centered environment, the learner is the only human in the man-machine system, and the system, therefore, is obviously "learner-centered."

A programmed text may be substituted for the machine in the model, and the five steps, with some modification, continue to describe the same fundamental relationship. Because the text format is relatively inexpensive, and publishing houses traditionally have served training and education needs faithfully, a major emphasis was placed on the Crowderian "scrambled book" and various text versions of linear-like Skinnerian programs.

A programmed text may be substituted for the machine in the model, and the five steps, with some modifications, continue to describe the same fundamental relationship. Such a text is organized into a *program* or sequence of carefully written, small, logical steps. Each step give the learner as new piece of information, and may also review instruction given in previous steps. Then it poses a question that calls for a *response* from the learner.

Each step of a programmed text (also called a *frame*), in addition to giving substantive information, asks a question and provides space for the learner to write his response. The step may refer the learner to a page in a supplementary workbook or manual, or to other material, such as film, kit of parts, etc.

Programmed instruction texts conceal the correct answer from the learner until he either turns the page as directed, or slides a masking device with a "window" in it along the page. The window is the size of the step, and, when it moves to a new step, it reveals at the same time the correct response to the question posed by the preceding step. This immediately tells the learner whether he is right or wrong. Success reinforces learning; and if he is wrong, the error can quickly be isolated.

Programmed texts using a masking device which reveals one step after another going down a page are said to be "segment vertical."

Some texts are "segment sequential", and require to mask. Instead, for a given set of pages, the learner proceeds horizontally by reading step No. 1 at the top of Page 1, step No. 2 at the top of page 3, step No. 3 at the top of page 5, and so on for the given number of pages. After this he returns to page 1 again and reads, say step No. 6, which appears second from the top of page 1, then step No. 7, which appears second from the top of page 3, and so on. The advantages claimed for the vertical type is that it is less confusing and, more importantly, that by concealing *everything* else on the page, the masking forces the learner to concentrate on the step without distraction.

A text programmed as above, whether vertical or sequential, is said to be a *linear* program. In a *branching* program, the learner reads a step and answers a question which provides for a multiple-choice response. The next step he reads is determined by his answer. If correct, he moves on to more advanced material, but if incorrect, the next piece of information is designed to clear up his misunderstanding. The branching programs generally have fallen into disfavor as being too simplistic, especially when instructing complex subject matter, and written-completion programs in linear format constitute most of the programmed texts. Laboratory research supports this trend.

Introduction of the tape cassette has liberated the audio tape device and encouraged its utilization in audiovisual programmed instruction. The microprocessor-controlled slide-cassette device has afforded foolproof synchronization of projected image and audio, thus poularizing the AV teaching machine, but the response mechanism remains as multiple choice.

Time-shared computer systems have also contributed by providing languages which the lesson planner or instructional programmer can use with ease. However, the low cost of a printed text and the mobility of such a device make it clear that programmed materials will continue to roll of an offset press or letterpress rather than a video recorder or computer.

Powers of a Computer-Assisted Instruction System

When suitably programmed a *CAI* system can, to a useful extent, do all the following things for a student at one of its terminal stations:

1. Engage in two-way communications with a student by means of natural language messages.
2. Guide the student through a program of tasks, helping him where he has difficulty, and accelerating his progress where he finds little challenge.
3. Observe and record significant details of the student's behavior, including steps, and undertaken in performing

tasks, time taken for particular steps, and values of varying physiological or environmental quantities.

4. Simulate the operation of a physical, mathematical, or social process responding to variation in parameters.
5. Analyse and summarize performance records and other behavioral records of individual students and also groups of students.

Limitations

As we have described a CAI system, it has among its characteristics many of the capabilities of a human teacher's assistant. However for the near future a CAI system will have substantial limitations of technical ability in comparison to a trained human assistant. A fundamental limitation is that it can act only along the lines of a very specific predetermined program. Unlike a human, it cannot devise on-the-spot solutions to problems which have not come up before.

Moreover, its capability for natural language communication is quite limited compared with a human. In "speaking" it is ordinarily limited to the use of pre-recorded messages, or, in the case of written messages, to messages pre-recorded or synthesized according to very simple patterns. In "listening" it can accept only symbolic messages, and with respect to them is largely incapable of dealing with any subtleties of meaning; when "confused", it has very limited ability to "think things through" and understand a "partial meaning."

Help From a CAI System

Despite these limitations a CAI system might be quite valuable in instructing where conventional methods are unable to approach ideal conditions for learning.

Let us characterize an ideal learning situation as one in which every student has:

- ☐ the experience of working on tasks that are meaningful and challenging;
- ☐ is involved in work adjusted to his individual capability so that he can be encouraged with suitable successes; and
- ☐ is continually getting appropriate help for overcoming his own short-comings.

Comparison With Classroom Instruction

In relation to this ideal, classroom instruction is characteristically inefficient in dealing with such subjects is mathematics or a foreign language. In these subjects, a high level of skill is ultimately possible, student ability varies greatly, and students may need considerable individual recitation and drill on partly learned material before they achieve mastery. We may further characterize these subjects as requiring of the student a composite skill, a facility to deal with a hierarchically structured subject, or the ability to bring together disparate elements to solve a problem.

If, in dealing with such a subject, the teacher uses a classroom procedure in which the individual student recites before the class, then because of the spread of ability in the class, what is done at any given time will ordinarily not interest or help every student or even most of the students in the class. On the other hand, if the teacher uses a classroom procedure in which all of the students simultaneously work on problems during class time, the students get little personal attention; and in particular the students who are having the most difficulty do not usually get adequate tutorial aid.

Individualization of Instruction

The *desideratum* lacking in such classroom instruction is often referred to as "individualization of instruction." It has two main components. One is the proper selection of student tasks to provide a suitable level of challenge and to respond to specific deficiencies in student performance. The other is the capability for "individualization of remediation"—a term meaning "providing individual remedies for individual deficiencies."

Both these components are inherent in the structure of a *CAI* system. Even in a routine recitation each student works directly with his own communication station and recites individually in direct relation to the system. The repertoire of exercises in a single computer can span a great range of difficulty. Thus every student can work on material appropriate to his ability. The logical power of the computer permits complex processing of the student response to reveal individual deficiencies, and to determine what assignment should be given next. Thus each student as he works receives immediate individualized feedback whenever he runs into difficulty.

Even though the range of remedial "tutoring" available on a particular problem will often be narrower when provided by a machine tutoring can be valuable and effective. It seems clear that by proper choice of drill and by appropriate design of tasks, the greatest part of routine drill in many courses might be effectively administered by computer.

The ability of the computer to take over a major part of recitation and drill makes the computer an instructional tool of the greatest promise. It offers the hope that a skilled teacher could concentrate his activities in relation to his special students, his very poor learners, and perhaps his very good learners, for whom non-routine assignments may be most important, and he could spread his effective teaching over a larger number of students. So used, the *CAI* system would be cast in a "task upgrading" role, and the human teacher could devote his effort exclusively to the less routine parts.

How to Reach The Potential?

These then are some of the important potentials of *CAI*. What are some of the developments needed to accelerate realization of that potential? There are several. To be broadly useful, *CAI* systems must satisfy stringent cost criteria and at the same time moderately demanding technical requirements in high-speed logical processing.

The only promising approach to this dual goal is to multiplex a fairly large number of student stations to a single central processor. Since very fast response is essential for "conversational mode" operation, time-sharing programming systems written for suitable processor and designed to deal with the special character of *CAI* programs must be developed. While general purpose central processors seem adequate for the job, new terminal stations of moderate cost need to be developed.

Pedagogical Questions

Fundamental pedagogical questions need to be answered in each of the important areas of institution:

- What parts of a subject can be efficiently taught?
- What instructional techniques would be effective and economic?

- ☐ What administrative restructuring of traditional coursework is necessary?

Thus, an art of *CAI* course programming needs to be developed. This will help experts in subject disciplines who want to adapt material from traditional formats into formats appropriate to *CAI*.

In recent years a number of research groups have investigated the usefulness of *CAI* in a variety of subject areas. Some of the subject areas in which computer assistance of some kind has been explored are: computing, mathematics, physics, chemistry, foreign languages, several vocational subjects, ideology, reading, business gaming, economics, medical diagnosis, behavioral gaming, optical system design, and architectural design. In spite of the number of subjects on this list, the state of development of the field is still exploratory and preliminary.

Systems Software

The development of subject programs and of systems software are closely related. The work at *IBM* has been oriented towards mathematical and physical science and language skills. The machine capabilities stressed accordingly have been intended to facilitate recitation of these subjects using natural language for communication. Compilers developed for research purposes and the ready preparation of programs in these areas have contained specialized macros which:

- ☐ Recognize any of a set of fixed-form answers to a given questions and respond appropriately to each.
- ☐ Evaluate moderately complex free-form responses to questions which have essentially simple answers.
- ☐ Construct specific hints based on the nature of a student's error (the author of the course does not have to anticipate the exact form of the response).
- ☐ Recognize responses involving minor errors of spelling or punctuation (the errors did not have to be anticipated).
- ☐ Vary the program tasks on the basis of statistical as well as detailed historical criteria according to general algorithms.

In the course of work at *IBM* and a few other research locations, a number of different *CAI* specialized operating systems for time sharing of particular central computers have been developed. In addition, several prototype programming languages and compiling or assembling programs for course preparation have been developed. A general understanding of both the systems engineering problems and the applications problems is beginning to emerge, although it has not yet been fully articulated.

The Present And The Future

Obviously, much development remains to be done before *CAI* systems will be able to take over a major part of the routine, pedestrian work of the teaching profession. On the other hand, *CAI* should not be regarded as a technique of the far future: we stand today at the threshold of practicability with regard to the technique. At *IMB*, systems performing a broad range of cost-justified instructional tasks have been postulated within the frame of reference of present technology. Features of the systems considered include audio and visual message capability, cathode ray tube displays, touch plate and light pen input, and various systems packages to facilitate use of the *CAI* system by student, author, and researcher.

Our work has convinced us that practical means of working with *CAI* could soon be made available to a much larger community than hitherto. In our opinion the broad adoption of *CAI* need not await hypothetical future major breakthroughs in technology. Instead, the rate of adoption will be primarily determined by the rate at which resources are applied to develop the necessary system methodologies and pedagogical techniques.

TRAINING WITHIN INDUSTRY PROGRAM IN USA

Training is considered to be a crucial part in achieving productivity from the workers. Training helps in producing quality goods and services, meeting production targets through greater efficiency. Training is imparted externally and internally. The government and other agencies which impart training is called as external training and the training imparted to an employee as fresh recruit or under the modernisation programme is known as internal training. Realizing the importance of training to boost productivity the USA Government has desired various training performance, internal and external. A brief report of an internal training programme, known as "Training within industry" (TWI) is not out of place.

The Training Within Industry Program was an activity designed to teach foreman and key men, during the World War II years, how to teach a job or a specific task to totally inexperienced workers. The training was done on the job, and the techniques developed were so effective that the basic approach has become a classic.

History

In 1940, the Federal Government and industry were greatly concerned over production in defense industries. At a meeting of, it was agreed that there was great and growing need for more skilled supervisors and workers in defense plants, and that the solution would have to be a training *within* industry, a "learn by doing" activity.

The resulting Training Within Industry program was authorized in August 1940 by the National Defense Advisory Commission, and was continued under the Office of Production Management and then the War Production Board. By Presidential order on April 18, 1942, TWI functions were made part of the War Manpower Commission.

TWI functioned from 1940 through 1945 on a nationwide basis as a Government service, performing the biggest industrial training job in history. By September 1945, its four national directors had trained 22 regional field representative who had trained 200 TWI institute conductors. Through this multiplier method. 23,000 trainers were trained, who in turn trained 1,750,000 supervisors in 16,500 plants.

The program was terminated a the close of the war. However, it was continued under private auspices through the Training-Within- Industry Foundation.

Supervision and training had previously often been regarded as separate functions. TWI's concept was that they were actually concurrent with management, and its work dealt excluten been regarded as separate function. TWI's concept was that they were actually concurrent with management, and its work dealt exclusively with what management itself could do to train its supervisors.

Throughout the war effort, TWI policy did not change—the real job had to be done *by* industry, *within* industry. Industry's own men collected, standardized, streamlined, and developed techniques for industry itself to use.

The TWI effort was handled from the very start by industrial management personnel and training were chiefly responsible for the program—C.R. Dooley of Socony Vacuum Co., Walter Dietz of Western Electric Co., M. J. Kane of American Telephone and Telegraph Co., and William Conover of U.S. Steel Co. They organized Training-Within-Industry as a clearing house for up-to-the minute methods in improving supervision at the job level. Advisors from both management and labor served throughout the war.

While TWI started out in 1940 as a dollar-a-year organization, paid staff members were added until the paid staff in 1944 reached a peak of over 400, on loan from their companies. At TWI Headquarters in Washington was a small group which reached a peak of forty-five in 1943, with ten additional technical men who were on the Headquarters payroll but who were stationed in the field.

From the beginning TWI operated as a decentralized service. In September 1940, it divided the country into twenty-two geographical districts according to the main industrial areas. In each an informal group was headed by a prominent local production executive or industrial personnel man who gave TWI part-time service as a "dollar-a-year" man.

T.W.I. Program

The demands of war production placed emphasis on products, materials, and methods, many of which were new to industry. It was necessary to discover a way of talking about supervisory needs that would prove useful in outlining what TWI was prepared to do, and making clear the fields in which the plant, itself, would have to develop its own programs. An early statement of TWI proved effective in discussing the special needs of a plant and made "our business is different" concepts clear in relation to basic needs of all supervisors. The statement, which became a standard part of TWI thinking and publications emphasized that every supervisor has five basic needs:

1. *Knowledge of the Work*—materials, tools, processes, operations, products and how they are made and used.

2. *Knowledge of Responsibilities*—policies, agreements, rules, regulations, schedules, interdepartmental relationships.
3. *Skill in Instructing*—increasing production by helping supervisors to develop a well trained work force which will get into production quicker; have less scrap, rework and rejects, fewer accidents, and less tool and equipment damage.
4. *Skill in Improving Methods*—utilizing materials, machines, and man-power more effectively by having supervisors study each operation in order to eliminate, combine, rearrange, and simplify details of the job.
5. *Skill in Leading*—increasing production by helping supervisors to improve their understanding of individuals, their ability to size up situations, and their ways of working with people at the job level.

TWI's job was to get top management to accept the responsibility; to get executives to back their program through the line organization; to help the training director and operating supervisors plan and operate an adequate program; and to coach supervisors in the three skills–instructing, improving methods, and leading. The company job consisted of establishing policy, giving executive backing, operating the program, and making supervisors available for training.

An intensive method of presentation was developed, designed for ten men in five two-hour sessions. These covered scheduling of timetables to meet their own training needs, making job breakdowns, and giving instructions through a standard four-step method.

This presentation evolved out of the initiative and research of Glenn Gardiner, then with Forstmann Woolen Company. Using the original World War I steps of Charles R. Allen, a vocational training pioneer, he proposed a standard ten-hour program on "How to Instruct." The activity adopted as a standard training demonstration was the typing of the Fire Underwriter's knot. This was a dramatic example of something easy to do, *once the learner knew how,* but which could be confusing to the learner unless the four definite training steps were followed. It built confidence in the usefulness of the method when applied to local needs.

Training was done entirely by solving problems by members of a group and discussion of principles and procedures involved.

There were no prepared lectures, no text books, no illustrative or entertaining pictures. The principles were not new. The entire time was spent in practice in the use of principles until there had been some changes in habits and attitudes. The same basic approach was developed in skills in improving *methods of improving jobs* and in doing pioneering work to present the problems of *human relationships* at the job level in a way that gave supervisors confidence in meeting their responsibility in getting results through people. In most cases this was new to them.

Other Uses of TWI

The program spread to the Armed Forces and was used by the Federal Government in various agencies.

During the war, wide use was made of TWI programs outside American industry. Hospitals and many service organizations used the techniques to meet pressing manpower needs.

Training Within Industry Foundation

After the war, proposals were advanced that the TWI activities be carried on as a U.S. Government Service, either in the Department of Labor or the Department of Education. However, many industrial managers felt that if this work was worthwhile, it should not be another Government service but should be carried on within industry and by industrial people. Sufficient financial backing was secured to launch a modest non-profit foundation to carry on under the guidance of the same directors who, were loaned by industry for the wartime effort. The Training Within Industry Foundation was incorporated in 1946.

Since 1946, the staff and associated field men have worked with more than 125 companies and organizations, some at several locations. An increasing number of plants are using TWI techniques, integrated into their own programs. Universities are promoting instruction in the programs.

During the years since the war, under sponsorship of the British Ministry of Labor, TWI programs have gone to more than thirty foreign countries. The International Labour Organization of Geneva has granted fellowships for men from developing countries to come to Britain for intensive coaching. TWI activity has been introduced into Mexico, Italy, Ceylon, India, Trinidad, Nepal, Indonesia, Cyprus, and New Zealand. The job instruction program was widely used in South America by American oil companies. The program has been promoted and carried out under the auspices of consulting engineering firms in Canada, Australia, France, Holland, and Belgium.

Having realized importance of on-the-job and within-industry training the program designer must decide as to (1) *who* will conduct the training, (2) *where* will that training take place, and (3) *what* specific development methods will be used.

We will how describe and evaluate alternatives in these decision areas in terms of their relative advantages and disadvantages. In addition, emphasis will be placed upon the effects of the principles of learning on these decisions. Also, contingencies such as organizational size, the number of individuals involved in training, and the costs entailed in these decisions will be discussed. Finally, alternative development approaches will be compared in order to highlight how decision makers may choose from among them.

WHO SHOULD CONDUCT TRAINING

The responsibility for *conducting* development programs and the responsibility for development itself are two different issues. Because of special staff expertise, the responsibility for planned organizational learning is generally considered to be a function of the personnel department.

The responsibility for actually conducting training, however, presents the decision maker with five alternatives. Programs may be conducted by (1) line managers, (2) non-managerial employees, (3) staff members and (4) outside consultants. In this section our concern is with who should actually conduct various developmental programs. This choice is closely related to where the program will actually take place—on the job or off the job—which we will discuss later.

Line Management

Line managers are frequently the trainers in on-the-job training situations. The selection of line managers is a logical one, *if* they possess the necessary technical expertise, teaching abilities, and time to conduct such training. At times, however, some or all of these conditions may be lacking. For example, first-line supervisors may lack specific technical expertise if their technical training was received on older, obsolete versions of the equipment currently in use.

Even if managers possess the necessary technical expertise, they may be inept at training others to perform the tasks. For example, overfamiliarity with a job can result in expectations that trainees will understand everything immediately, and consequently trainees may not be give opportunities to ask necessary questions. Or supervisors may omit certain "obvious" steps in the procedures or be too hasty in their explanations. Under these circumstances trainees may learn on their own, acquiring both good and bad work habits. Such problems may occur even if other employees attempt to help the trainee with or without the supervisor's permission.

Technically competent supervisors who have the ability to train may not be selected as trainers because they lack the *time*. Managers with large spans of control may experience such time constraints, as may managers with smaller spans of control but with complex work to perform. Finally, line managers may lack time simply because of higher-priority responsibilities.

Nonmanagerial Employees

A great deal of consideration is necessary in selecting nonmanagerial employees as trainers. It is important that any employee selected as a trainer possesses the necessary technical expertise, teaching skills, and time to conduct the required training. In addition, it is important that these trainers have positive work attitudes and habits.

When trainers are selected, there is sometimes a temptation to choose a poor performer in the department in order to allow better workers to continue in their more productive efforts. Such a decision is dysfunctional in the long run, since new employees may acquire poor attitudes or skills and have to be retrained or fired later on.

Selecting a proficient employee, however, does not necessarily mean selecting the *best* one. As previously discussed, technical competency does not necessarily include the ability to teach those skills. The "best" worker may be overfamiliar with the job and therefore rush through steps or skip them entirely. Also, using the most proficient employees as trainers may lead to lower productivity in the short run and a slowdown upon their return to regular duties, since they have "broken rhythm" during the training period.

Care must be taken to choose trainers with favorable work attitudes as well as necessary skills. For example, one experienced quality control clerk was called upon to train new colleagues. Although adept at both quality control work and teaching skills, the trainer possessed a negative attitude toward the supervisor. In training, this negative attitude surfaced and biased the new employees against the department head.

Finally, employees who are not properly rewarded for training others will be unlikely to take such responsibilities seriously. For example, manufacturing operations may reward employees on the basis of incentive systems. In such instances, taking time for training could result in lower productivity and consequently less money for the trainer. To overcome this problem, it is common practice to guarantee the employee-trainer the person's average past incentive rate during the training period.

Staff

Staff may conduct training programs because they have special expertise which line does not possess. In addition, staff may be used when the training is needed in large numbers of organizational units or for all employees in the organization. For example, if the personnel department of a firm has recently computerized personnel records, it may be advisable for members of the computer department to conduct training in the operation of the new system for all members of the personnel department. This illustration also emphasizes the fact that all staff may be periodically involved in training programs.

External Resources

Firms may also utilize external resources, such as outside consultants, to conduct training programs. For example, if a new law is passed by parliament, a firm might hire an attorney to conduct a training program for top executives on the impact of the legislation on the firm. A major factor influencing the decision to use outside resources is whether the program will be repeated.

Location of Development Programs

Development programs are generally classified as (1) on-the-job and (2) off-the-job. On-the-job development occurs when trainees learn the skills, attitudes, and knowledge in the actual work environment. Off-the-job development, on the other hand, exists when trainees learn in settings other than the actual job environment.

On-Location Training

It has been estimated that 90 percent of all industrial training involves on-the-location training. One reason for such a high percentage is that *all* employees receive at least some on- the-location training: "Each employee, whether he is newly hired, transferred, or promoted, must be formally introduced to his specific job environment, to the people with whom he will be working, and to company policies and objectives that concern him."

Another reason is that employees may need training or retraining that can only take place on the job because of either the technology or the environment involved. Unique characteristics of technology (for example, computers) may be too costly to duplicate off the job, or interpersonal skills may be so important for successful job performance that the individual must be trained while working with colleagues. For example, astronauts were trained together for the space shuttle program because of the necessity of close cooperative efforts for the success of the program.

On-the-location training affords advantages to both trainee and the organization: No special facilities are required, and trainees actually do "real work" while learning. Such "real work" for production workers may be useable units of output, while for management trainees it might involve handling complaints about late orders. As a consequence, such training is often more cost-effective and easier to administer than off-the-location training.

There are also a number of disadvantages with on-the-location training. First, trainees utilize existing resources (such as equipment, facilities, and the time of the trainer) that would normally be used for more productive purposes. In production activities, for example, trainees are likely to produce fewer goods at a lower quality than would experienced operators. In addition, risk of accidents or damage to equipment is likely to be greater during training.

Also, managers and professionals trained on the job may make decisions without adequately utilizing available resources. For example, in one college of business a bright and energetic professor who was well liked by both students and faculty was promoted into an administrative position. In addition to many easily learned routine tasks, this new administrator was responsible for directing the M.B.A. program. Unaware of many of the requirements and procedures involved in directing the program, the new administrator had to rely upon the assistance of previous M.B.A. directors. When such guidance was not readily available, the new administrator frequently made errors in judgment owing solely to inexperience. As a result, the time of other professors, students, and fellow administrators was wasted in efforts to correct these avoidable errors.

A second limitation exists when trainees are under pressure to show results quickly, Such pressure may actually increase anxiety which may interfere with learning. In addition, too much emphasis on results may lead to success being evaluated on the basis of immediate results. In turn, trainees may receive feedback on achievement but not enough information "about the reasons for mistakes or failures." A third limitation occurs because trainers are often line employees. As previously discussed, line managers may not do an adequate job of training because they lack technical competence, are not capable of or interested in conducting training, or lack the time. The same problem may exist if a line employee rather than a manager is selected to conduct the training. These problems are even further compounded if the workers who are selected are not proficient or have poor work attitudes.

Finally, such training may be inefficient since only one person can be trained at a time. For example, one trainee may be hired at a specific time in order to meet an existing need, or space may exist on a production line for only one trainee to learn on a particular machine. In both instances, the ratio of trainer to trainee is 1:1. Grouping trainees together under on trainer when possible may be more cost-effective for the organization.

Off-the-Location Training

Off-the-location training is often more efficient because trainers may be able to work with groups rather than simply with individuals. When a number of checkout clerks must be trained for a new supermarket, several clerks may be trained through off-the-location programs. Such training may facilitate learning because of its emphasis on learning rather than on immediate work results, and because it removes the new employee from the pressure of the job.

Off-the-location training may be better planned because trainers are evaluated on the basis of the success of the employee upon return to work. Consequently, trainers themselves may possess greater competencies in their knowledge of the materials, and in the application of learning theory and the principles of learning which facilitate the learning process.

Finally, such training may be particularly beneficial to smaller firms which may be able to offer learning experiences unavailable internally. Such companies may lack the financial or human resources necessary to teach the materials.

The major disadvantage of off-the-location training is transfer of learning to the actual job situation. Too often such training is undertaken with little concern for the effectiveness of learning in other than the training situation itself. For example, trainees taking a university operations research course may learn much as evidenced by test scores and their final course grade. Their new knowledge, however, may be of little practical value and unuseable on the job.

A second disadvantage is lost output during training. This represents a cost to the firm, since it is paying the employee during the training period. The company, however, is hoping that in the long run it will benefit because the future output of the new employee will be greater. In addition, the firm will not be utilizing on-line productive equipment at lower levels necessitated by the training period.

A firm's financial resources will greatly affect the decision of training location. Since on-the-location training is generally less expensive, firms with limited resources might choose this method for production workers. The financial capabilities of the firm are also directly related to the need for more immediate work results, since firms in a poor financial position are more likely to need immediate output.

Finally, it may be appropriate to combine both techniques. For example, trainees may be given classroom instruction, then assigned to a work area to use that training, and later returned to the training environment for additional instruction. One example in which on-the-location and off-the-location training techniques are merged is *apprenticeship training*, which will be discussed later in this chapter.

DEVELOPMENT AND TRAINING TECHNIQUES

Bass and Vaughan have classified on- and off-the-job training techniques. This classification is based upon the location in which such techniques are *generally* used, when, in actuality, some of the techniques may be used in either setting. For example, job instruction training is classified as on-the-job, even though it may be used off the job as well. (See Table)

Objectives, principles of learning, and organizational contingencies will all influence the appropriateness of the techniques selected. Following is a discussion on a number of the techniques, which are utilized primarily for on-the-job and off-the-job training techniques.

On-the-Job Techniques

In this section we will discuss five on-the-job training techniques: (1) job instruction training, (2) apprenticeship training, (3) job rotation, (4) committees and special assignment, and (5) coaching.

Job Instruction Training (JIT). Job instruction training (JIT) was developed during World War II to provide a guide for on-the-job *skill training* of white- and blue-collar employees as well as technicians. Essentially, JIT involves four steps: (1) preparing the trainee, (2) demonstrating the job, (3) having the trainee perform the job, and (4) following up on the employee's performance.

Trainee preparation involves relaxing the new employee through anxiety reduction. Trainers can do this by showing an interest in the new workers, introducing them to co-workers, describing the importance of the trainees' jobs and the objectives of the training,

Table 1

Training Techniques and Priciples of Learning

Alternatives	*Evaluation of Alternativcs in Light of Principlesof Learningand Other Contingencies*				
	Motivation active participation of learner	*Reinforcement feedback of knowledge of results*	*Stimulus meaningful organization of materials*	*Responses Practice and repetition*	*Stimulus-response conditions most favorablefor transfer*
ON-THE-JOB TECHNIQUES					
Job instruction training	Yes	Sometimes	Yes	Yes	Yes
Apprentice training	Yes	Sometimes	?	Sometimes	Yes
Internships and assistantships	Yes	Sometimes	?	Sometimes	Yes
Job rotation	Yes	No	?	Sometimes	Yes
Junior board	Yes	Sometimes	Sometimes	Sometimes	Yes
Coaching	Yes	Yes	Sometimes	Sometimes	Yes
OFF-THE-JOB TECHNIQUES					
Vestibule	Yes	Sometimes	Yes	Yes	Sometimes
Lecture	No	No	Yes	No	No
Special study	Yes	No	Yes	?	No
Films	No	No	Yes	No	No
Television	No	No	Yes	No	No
Conference or discussion	Yes	Sometimes	Sometimes	Sometimes	No
Case study	Yes	Sometimes	Sometimes	Sometimes	Sometimes
Role playing	Yes	Sometimes	No	Sometimes	Sometimes
Simulation	Yes	Sometimes	Sometimes	Sometimes	Sometimes
Programmed instruction	Yes	Yes	Yes	Yes	No
Laboratory Training	Yes	Yes	No	Yes	Sometimes
Programmed group exercise	Yes	Yes	Yes	Sometimes	Sometimes
Computers assisted instruction	Yes	Sometimes	Yes	Yes	Sometimes

and pointing out the responsibilities and duties of the trainees. Formal job descriptions and specifications can help employees know what is expected of them, thereby facilitating the learning process.

In *demonstrating the job,* trainers should also tell trainees how to do the job. Such parallel auditory and visual measures help to foster learning by making use of two sensory organs rather than one. Learning is further facilitated and made easier to follow if the job is broken down into subparts and a step-by-step sequencing followed when appropriate.

Trainees should also be positioned so that they will observe the demonstration from the same perspective they will have when actually performing the task. For example, in demonstrating a word processor, trainees should be positioned directly behind the trainer so they will not see the job performed backwards or upside down. In addition, the JIT technique utilizes the principle of repetition, and *requires even the simplest of jobs to be demonstrated at least twice.*

JIT also requires trainees to perform the job at least twice. During the second performance, the trainees must explain *how* and *why* they are doing each doing each step. This procedure helps trainees conceptualize the task better, and also shows the trainer how well trainees understand the task.

Trainers should point out errors and omissions as trainees are doing the job, and *should not wait until the total task is completed.* This allows immediate feedback (KOR) and an opportunity to correct behaviors before they become incorrectly learned procedures. Another reason for immediate correction of errors is to avoid damage to machinery or products, or injury to the trainee or other employees. Trainers must correct trainees in a non-threatening manner in order not to create too much anxiety which could impede motivation and learning. In addition, positive feedback will help foster proper learning by rewarding desired behaviors.

The final step in JIT is *follow-up on employee performance.* The organization must make certain that the worker is correctly performing the task in order to assess the need for additional training. An important aspect of this step is to let trainees know to whom they may go for help after the formal training period has been completed—for example, their immediate supervisor, fellow employees, or a combination of the two. Follow-up also provides information to trainers and the firm for evaluating and modifying existing training programs. Finally, follow-up lets trainees see that the organization is interested in correct performance, and it provides feedback to the worker as to the effectiveness of that performance.

During World War II, thousands of individuals were trained quickly and effectively using JIT. As recently as 1970, JIT was still the most commonly used technique for industrial training. The reason for JIT's popularity is that it has proven extremely successful as an on-the-job technique. Its success can be accounted for because it incorporates *many* of the principles of learning that were presented in Chapter 8. Analysis of the four steps of JIT will show the use of such principles of learning as motivation, knowledge of results, and positive reinforcement.

Apprenticeship Training. Skilled crafts, such as carpentry, plumbing, ironworking, and airline mechanics, utilize apprenticeship training. These crafts require a diverse range of knowledge, skills, independence of judgment, and maturity.

A broad definition of an apprentice is:

> a person at least 16 years of age who is covered by a written agreement registered with the State Apprenticeship Council providing for not less than 4,000 hours of reasonably continuous employment under an approved schedule of work experience and supplemented by a recommended minimum of 144 hours per year of related class-room instruction.

Each apprentice is assigned to an experienced worker who has already learned the trade, and who is referred to as a *journeyman.* As this discussion indicates, apprenticeship programs are formal and lengthy, frequently involving two or more years, and emphasize combining off-the-job and on-the-job supervision under skilled instructors. There are many trades which use apprentices, and there are a great many workers involved in apprenticeship training. In one survey, one-third of all firms which responded indicated that they conducted apprenticeship training.

Apprenticeship training is widely used when complex skills are involved. When such training is well planned and correctly conducted, it permits the integration of the best features of both on-the-location and on-the-location training. It also provides the apprentice with an opportunity to earn while learning, and thereby increases motivation. The company also receives some benefits from these programs in the form of some productive output.

There are limitations to apprenticeship training as well. Some of these limitations are the same as those discussed for on-the-job training in general. Sometimes apprenticeship programs are unplanned or haphazardly conducted. In addition, production rather than learning may be emphasized. Programs may be too long for some individuals, too short for others, and just about right for others. Because apprenticeship programs have fixed rates which apply to all trainees, differences in individuals' learning curves and learning rates simply cannot be taken into account.

Unions may sometimes fear that management may want to lengthen the time period of apprenticeship programs in order to get skilled but less expensive workers and may therefore oppose apprenticeship training. Finally, apprenticeship programs may become so rigid and inflexible that change becomes difficult. Journeymen may wish to protect their position, which they can do by not changing techniques or work rules even when technology itself changes.

Even though apprenticeship programs are restricted to the skilled crafts, there is no reason why the basic idea of integrating on- the-job and off-the-job training cannot be applied to management development and unskilled-worker training as well. In fact, on- the-job techniques involving job rotation, special assignments, and coaching (which will be discussed next) all have characteristics that are similar to apprenticeship programs, even though they tend to be thought of as management development techniques rather than techniques readily applicable for non-managerial skills as well.

Job Rotation. Job rotation is associated with a number of meanings. It may refer to assigning managerial trainees to different jobs in order to broaden their supervisory skills, knowledge, and experience, and to acquaint them with the functions of various departments in the organization. In some instances, this managerial *training* may be for *experienced* managers who are being groomed for top-level management positions. Even managers who are not likely candidates for promotion can benefit from this procedure, since it provides them with the ability to handle more varied assignments.

Job rotation can also be used for non-managers as a technique to reduce boredom brought on by specialization. For example, production workers can be taught to performs three jobs, and rotated from one to another every month. In addition to reducing boredom, such procedures may allow employees to understand how their jobs relate to other jobs in the company. It also provides the company with a pool of trained resources that can be quickly utilized in the event of sickness, vacation, terminations, or other emergencies.

The following example of a one-year management training program highlights some important aspects of this development technique. During the first half of year, trainees were assigned to the head-office and moved from department to department for periods ranging from four to eight weeks. In addition, for a period of two months trainees were "loaned" to subsidiary firm with whom the main office had extensive dealings.

During the second half of year, trainees were assigned to a field office. This provided the trainees with additional information about the company and its relationships to subordinate units as well as with an opportunity for hands-on managerial experience. Following completion of the training program, participants selected two departments in the main office to which they would like to be assigned. They were then assigned to one of these two choices—a decision based upon both the needs of the organization and the desires of the individual trainee.

This particular program had two primary benefits for both worker and firm. First, trainees were given opportunities to acquire specific skills, knowledge, experience, and information about the work of various functional departments. Such development included an understanding of the relationship of specific departments to the total organization, other departments, and outside customers. It also enabled trainees to personally assess their styles and personalities, and to choose a department where they felt they might best fit in.

The firm also benefited from this program by permitting a number of managers an opportunity to evaluate trainees in a variety of settings. This type of information can be helpful to personnel departments and top management in evaluating trainees' strengths and weaknesses, and in developing career planning for these new entrants into the work force. Although a number of problem areas surfaced during the program, the overall effects proved beneficial from both the organizational and individual sides.

Job rotation may also facilitate cooperation among departments, since those rotated become much more familiar with each other's problems. When trainees are assigned to departments later on a permanent basis, they will have a much better feel for interdepartmental working relationships. Further, management trainees may bring new ideas to the departments to which they are assigned. The procedure also provides a better basis for trainees to choose the department to which they would like to be assigned on a permanent basis.

If properly organized, job rotation programs provide trainees with many of the principles of learning discussed previously: KOR, positive reinforcement, and customized developmental efforts based upon individual differences. For example, unlike apprenticeship training, job rotation can actually take advantage of individual differences by structuring the program to meet the needs of the individual being trained. In the example previously discussed, one trainee spent the entire two years in the main office, since the final assignment for which the trainee had been hired did not involve working with the field offices.

There are also limitations to job rotation. Some programs require movement from one geographical area to another. Such moves may be hard on the individual, but refusal to move could limit chances for promotion within the firm. Frequent movement also tends to reduce loyalty to the firm. Also, for trainees who are practicing managers, such moves result in their focusing primary attention on short-range projects with quick payoffs to make their performance look good.

This short-range focus may lead manager trainees to view their supervisor as the person to please, and to fail to develop good peer relationships or adequately represent their subordinates. The short-range focus is a two-sided problem in that subordinates of frequently rotated managers may not adopt their suggestions because they view those managers as only temporary supervisors. Such subordinates believe that if they change now, they will simply have to change again when another new manager arrives.

Another limitation (related to an emphasis on showing immediate results) is that some capable trainees may adjust slowly, have difficulty showing immediate results, and therefore receive unfavorable evaluations—which may or may not be justified. For example, slow adjustment may appropriately be negatively evaluated if the organization is a dynamic one in which all managers must adapt quickly to rapid change. However, slower adjustment in a stable environment may not represent a problem at all.

Another problem is that training may be uneven from one department to another. As a consequence, trainees may learn a great deal from one assignment but relatively little from others. Finally, job rotation may be difficult in smaller companies because opportunities to move are limited by the small number of available positions and by the fact that individuals cannot be spared to conduct the training efforts.

Thorough planning of job rotation may reduce or eliminate many of these problem areas. To begin with, the personnel department must gain support for the program from the managers of the departments to which trainees are assigned. One way of accomplishing this is to assure that managers know the goals of the program and possess the skills necessary to conduct effective training.

Trainees must be informed of the goals of the program is they are to gain the most from job rotation. In addition, such programs are most effective when they take into account the individual differences between trainees and thus are tailored for each person in order that the specific types of learning needed by each individual are obtained.

Committees and Special Assignments. Many types of special assignments are available for on-the-job training. First, trainees may be give special projects on which to work in order to broaden their experiences. For example, if a trainee is assigned to a project involving data collection or employee turnover, the trainee may learn not only about the reasons for and consequences of turnover but also how to conduct surveys and evaluate their results.

Trainees assigned as as assistants to managers may become prepared to perform the tasks of the manager if necessary. For example, a professional in personnel department who is being groomed as a possible successor to the manager may be taken from a specialized area (for example, testing administration), and assigned to work directly with the manager in handling all functional areas of personnel management.

Individuals may also be given committee assignments in order to broaden their experience. In a unionized plant, for example, a trainee in personnel might be assigned to a committee handling employee grievances. This could provide insight into how the grievance procedure works from both the management and union perspective. Or a junior university faculty member might be assigned to the college grants committee in order to better understand the kinds of research conducted by others as well as the budgetary procedures of the university.

Closely related to committee assignments is the concept of junior boards of directors, or *multiple management* for management development. Under this approach, lower- and middle-level managers "participate formally, along with top management, in the planning and administration of corporate affairs" through what amounts to permanent advisory committees. Such junior boards may investigate specific problems and recommend solutions, or they may actually carry on activities which are representative of those undertaken by the firm's real board of directors.

Coaching. Coaching occurs when a supervisor assists subordinates on a continuous basis by providing them with feedback on how they are doing and what is expected of them. This may take the form of answering questions, guiding individuals in finding answers to problems, having them participate in decision making, and even helping them resolve personality problems.

Coaching is also an important part of performance appraisal in that it helps to stimulate individual growth and development. It is also an important ingredient in *all* on-the-job development techniques. In fact, Bass and Vaughan have suggested that job rotation and some types of special assignments simply represent coaching that has been formalized.

Coaching contributes to learning and improved performance because it is an excellent opportunity to provide KOR to the trainee on an almost continuous basis. However, with respect to performance appraisals, managers need to be careful that they do not overload subordinates with too much information particularly of a negative nature. This same problem exists whenever coaching is used. However, if done properly, coaching includes the better aspects of both on-the-job development and performance appraisal.

OFF-THE-JOB TRAINING PROGRAMS

We will now focus on off-the-job training techniques which are based on the classification of Bernard M. Bass and James A. Vaughan. We will not discuss films and television. These media have many of the same characteristics as lectures, and they are really aids to training that are "used to increase the effectiveness of a training program" rather than techniques for conducting training.

Lectures, Special Studies, and Discussion

The lecture is probably the most commonly used method for both on-the-job and off-the-job training. Its principal advantage is that it can provide *factual information to large numbers of people,* making it a relatively low-cost alternative. Such economy can be false, however, because merely exposing trainees to information does not mean they will acquire knowledge.

A number of limitations of the lecture method are frequently cited. First, in lectures per se, communication is one-way. Trainees are passive, have no opportunity to practice, and receive neither reinforcement nor KOR. In addition, individual differences in learning rates are not taken into account, so some trainees may be hopelessly lost while others are bored. This results because trainers do not receive feedback about whether or not trainees understand the materials presented.

Because of these limitations, much criticism has been voiced against the lecture method. In one study, the lecture method (with questions permitted) was ranked last of nine development techniques evaluated. In this same study, two other techniques (films and television) that also involve one-way communication, passive learning, lack of opportunity for practice, and no feedback were rated seventh and eighth. Thus, the lecture, even with provisions for questions, was ranked lower than two communications media that did not permit any two-way communication.

It appears that such strong criticism of the lecture method is unwarranted. Although this technique is not appropriate for teaching complex skills and may not be appropriate for trying to change attitudes and values, it does appear to be effective for imparting factual information. Given the costs associated with certain training techniques such as television, films, computer-assisted instruction, and programmed instruction, the lecture method does have significant cost advantages when the goal of training is knowledge acquisition.

One way to overcome some of the disadvantages of the lecture method is to assign trainees special materials to study rather than to have them simply sit through a lecture. This allows trainees to proceed at their own rate, to make notes, and to check back on materials read previously. This procedure involves active participation by learners and takes into account individual differences of participants. Practice and reinforcement are still lacking, however, and this technique is most appropriate in the acquisition factual information.

Group discussion of problems, issues, and other materials is sometimes used to overcome the disadvantages of both the lecture and special study methods. The primary advantages of the conference or discussion method are that it permits two-way communication and provides for active participation, feedback, and clarification of materials. For example, colleges and universities frequently utilize seminars in advanced under- graduate and graduate courses as a means of instruction rather than simply relying upon the lecture. In addition, the conference or discussion method appears to be effective for teaching complex materials and some types of problem-solving and decision-making skills, as well as for changing attitudes.

The conference or discussion method has some disadvantages as well. It is restricted to relatively small groups, since active participation by most individuals is less likely to occur in large groups. Further, discussion takes time, and less factual information may be imparted in a given period of time than would be the case in a lecture. Consequently, training costs per person are likely to be higher than with the lecture method. Finally, there may be irrelevant discussion because many participants may simply want to be heard.

It is possible to combine discussion with special studies to facilitate learning. Such would be the technique used in a seminar on personnel management where students would be assigned outside materials and come to class prepared to discuss the content and issues involved. This technique has applicability in business as well. For example, it was reported that the chairman of the board of the Koppers Company met three times a month for three hours in his office with a group of ten young managers for discussion of some previously assigned readings. The goal of the meetings was to provide managers with an opportunity to see how upper-level executives thought. In addition, these meetings gave top-level executives a chance to observe how the younger managers thought and conceptualized materials. It is also possible to combine lectures with discussion.

Programmed Instruction

During the 1950s' programmed instruction (PI) was widely discussed as a revolutionary development technique. Although the revolution never materialized, and PI did not turn out to be the solution to all training problems, this technique has taken its place as an important form of instructional technology.

Programmed instruction involves dividing the materials to be learned into small units or parts called *frames.* These frames may be provided through different media, such as sequential sections of a PI textbook or visual images on the screen of a teaching machine, or by a combination of the two.

Trainees read the first frame, which provides them with certain information. Each subsequent frame provides additional information and builds upon the materials previously presented to the trainee. Typically, trainees are required to respond to specific questions about the materials by filling in a blank or selecting a true-false alternative. Trainees are immediately informed whether their choice is correct or incorrect.

In some instances, when incorrect answers are given, trainees are merely informed of the error and permitted to continue. In other instances, the concept of *branching* is used. Branching means moving trainees to other predetermined questions based on their previous responses. For example, if trainees respond incorrectly, they may be moved back for remedial materials.

In very complex PI programs, *multiple* branching may be used. Trainees who answer a number of questions in a row correctly are moved to more advanced materials. Trainees who miss one question may be moved to remedial materials, and if they miss the first few questions in the remedial section, they are sent to even more basic materials or perhaps even referred to the instructor.

A major advantage of PI is that it utilizes a number of the principles of learning discussed earlier. It is individualized, since trainees proceed through the frames at their own rate. Learning is active, since trainees must respond in some manner to each frame. In addition, KOR is immediate. Reinforcement is immediate also if responses are correct, and even if responses are incorrect, the immediacy of KOR permits trainees to correct errors before incorrect information is learned.

A second advantage of PI is that groups do not have to be assembled at the same time, as would be the case in the lecture method. The resultant flexibility in assigning individual trainees may permit more efficient allocation of organizational resources. For example, Tata Iron and Steel Co. (TISCO) has developed a series of audiovisual tapes on a variety of technical materials. These tapes and learning machines are provided to units of 40 or more workers, and subjects included in this program range from basic accounting to how to manufacture a complex alloy.

A final advantage of PI is that consistent information is transmitted to each trainee since everyone works with precisely the same materials.

Given the extent to which PI appears to utilize the principles of learning, one would expect it to be a very effective development technique. However, a review by Nash, Muczyk, and Vettori of more than 100 research studies dealing with the effectiveness of PI as opposed to conventional techniques (primarily the lecture) in both industrial and academic settings revealed contradictory findings. Comparisons were made in terms of training time, materials learned, and retention of the learning.

In terms of training time, PI appeared to have some clear advantages over conventional methods. The results on immediate learning were less clear, since PI was superior in only nine studies, not significantly different in 20, and less effective in three. In terms of retention, PI was found to be equivalent to conventional techniques.

In addition to the inconclusive nature of the research on its effectiveness, PI possesses other disadvantages. First, it is primarily effective with *factual materials,* especially those which can be presented in a *logical sequence,* such as basic statistics, accounting, or instructions on cleaning and assembling a rifle. Therefore, PI may not be useful for programs dealing with human relations training and attitudinal change.

PI may be very expensive, at least during its initial design and development stages. Therefore, organizational size will influence whether PI is utilized, since unless there is a large enough number of trainees who will use the program, the cost of development may be prohibitive. In addition, even if the number of trainees is large, the cost of PI may be prohibitive if the content is rapidly changing in a dynamic organization, thereby necessitating frequent updating and change.

While these costs can be lowered by purchasing PI materials developed by others, the lack of complete congruence between the purchased program and organizational needs may result in a loss of effectiveness or even of some incorrect learning: "A reasonable conclusion is still that, for appropriate material, PI is faster but probably does not lead to greater proficiency on an immediate post test. Long-term retention remains an open question."

One relatively recent development closely related to PI involves *algorithmic learning.* Tavernier has reported the results of such a program at Morgan Guaranty Trust Company in training individuals in investigating and resolving customer complaints. Prior to the adoption of this new technique, the firm had utilized an on-the-job training program requiring four to six months. The bank "developed a self-instruction manual complete with algorithms (a kind of decision tree) outlining the decision-making process used by experienced...[personnel]."

In studying this particular job, the bank found that approximately 80 percent of customer inquiries could be reduced to three algorithms. In addition, only a 30-minute training session in the use of the algorithmic manual was necessary, after which trainees were able to perform actual work immediately. This process proved so successful that "within two or three weeks, the trainees no longer needed the manual: They could make correct decisions without it."

Algorithmic learning appears to be a promising technique for a variety of training situations. It could be utilized, for example, "to clarify complex administrative and clerical procedures, labor-management agreements, hiring and promotion policies and practices, and to handle warranty claims and training manuals for technical employees."

In addition to its applicability to a broad spectrum of training programs, algorithmic learning proved cost-effective at Morgan Guaranty. It "saved on overtime, hiring costs, and training time; obtained higher output from the trainees at an earlier stage; and reduced the number of mistakes both during and after the training period." In addition, the bank "saved" the time of experienced workers who continued to devote their full time to work during the training period. This pilot program has proven to be so successful that the bank is currently developing additional training programs based on algorithmic learning for use with new employees in other job classification.

Computer-Assisted Instruction

Computer-assisted instruction (CAI) is "the use of the computer for instruction, i.e., as a means of presenting material to, and interacting with, a student." It is primarily useful in teaching the same kinds of factual materials as is PI. As the definition points out, CAI is dependent upon the use of the computer. However, there are a number of different forms of CAI based upon the extent to which the computer is actually utilized. Based upon the degree and complexity of trainee-computer interaction, CAI has been classified as (1) drill and practice, (2) tutorial, and (3) dialogue.

Drill and practice is the simplest and the most common form of CAI. Typically, a trainer presents materials to trainees, after which they go to a computer terminal and check their comprehension of the materials. For example, the trainer in a basic statistics course might present the concept of the mean as an average of a set of numbers, and then have trainees go to terminals in order to check their understanding of how the calculations should be performed.

The problems presented in many CAI programs will differ from time to time since they are randomly generated from among a number of similar ones stored in the computer. The trainee is then given immediate feedback as to the correctness of the response. Although we have presented an example in which the direction of the error (too large or too small) is indicated, this is not done in all CAI programs.

In more sophisticated systems, even more information might be provided. For example, the trainee might be informed that the decimal point appears to be misplaced. In very sophisticated systems, the program might identify the nature of the errors being made (such as the misplaced decimal point) and shift the trainee into additional remedial work. Conversely, trainees answering all questions correctly might be shifted into more advanced work.

Such movement, or branching, may be based not only upon the trainees' recent performance, but also upon prior knowledge of their proficiency if the computer is programmed to keep continuous records on each trainee. Trainees will not be permitted unlimited numbers of attempts to get the right answer. Rather, after some predetermined number of incorrect responses, the correct solution will be given, and a new problem will be generated by the computer.

Finally, some CAI systems are designed so that the computer displays visual materials in addition to typed responses. For example, Bell and Howell has designed a system that "allows learners to teach themselves by responding—with a microcomputer—to simulated job situations displayed on a color TV monitor. These simulated job situations may be pre-recorded on video-tapes, films, or slides, or simply generated by the computer itself."

Vestibule Training

Vestibule training involves learning in a nonwork environment in which conditions and equipment are *virtually identical* to what will be encountered on the job. In fact, the environment and the equipment may be so similar in this technique that vestibule training almost becomes on-the-job training.

For example, in the early 1950s a group of researchers at the RAND Corporation used the vestibule method to train military personnel who were responsible for defending the United States against enemy air attacks. Groups were given a number of simulated tasks to perform, such as monitoring radar screens and, if unknown aircraft were detected, dispatching a simulated interceptor that might open fire on the unknown aircraft.

The researchers could manipulate the task conditions, for example by creating mock attacks and simulating attack conditions to which the trainees had to respond. The researchers found that subjects began to behave as if they were in real-life situations: They became anxious and highly involved, and they learned to perform their tasks, handle information overload, and so forth. One officer, in fact, became so involved in the training that he continued to stay in the simulation even after breaking a leg!

Trainees were also reported to be highly motivated to learn, largely because of the realism of the simulated conditions. In addition, this simulation provided trainees with (1) immediate KOR, which was objective, pertinent, and accurate; and (2) positive reinforcement for defending their areas adequately. Both KOR and positive reinforcement contributed to the motivation of the trainees. In this setting, the learning was total-systems-oriented—that is, both people and physical elements were in mutual interaction. The total-systems orientation and the attempt to replicate very complex real conditions represent major drawbacks to using such sophisticated vestibule training for industrial purposes—it can be extremely costly.

The primary advantage of vestibule training is that, like all forms of off-the-job training, the emphasis is on learning and not on results. Another advantage is that the problem of transfer of learning is minimized since trainees learn under conditions which are similar to actual job conditions. In addition, such training draws upon the principles of learning of both KOR and reinforcement.

Vestibule training is also applicable to teaching human relations skills. In the checkout example above, trainers acting as customers could pretend to become irate because the trainees were proceeding too slowly. If a trainee snapped back at a "customer," the trainer could point out that such behavior would be unacceptable toward actual customers.

Finally, vestibule training tends to use trainers who are specialists in conducting training. Such individuals are more likely to be able to draw on the principles of learning that enhance the training situation, give special attention to individual trainee needs, and utilize training techniques because of their familiarity with them.

Vestibule training also possesses certain inherent disadvantages. A primary disadvantage is cost because of the need to duplicate facilities and equipment for non-productive purposes. However, as illustrated by the example of the checkout counter, such duplication may not always be necessary. Another problem arises when a firm decides to use damaged or obsolete equipment in order to reduce costs. In such instances, training may be slower or may even result in incorrect learning and erroneous transfer of learning. The learning environment may also differ significantly from the actual work environment in terms of rules, relationships, and other aspects of organizational climate. For example, the pressure for production in the work environment may cause anxiety which was not present in the training environment. In sum, vestibule training is most effective when it replicates as closely as possible the actual work situation.

Vestibule training is likely to be justified when the risk of error is high, when such errors are costly, when many people need to be trained at the same time, and when it is impossible to conduct training on the job. If on-the-job training could result in injury, damage to the equipment, waste of raw materials, or other loss of money to the firm, vestibule training may be more appropriate.

Simulation

In a simulation, an attempt is made to replicate the system in which trainees are ultimately expected to perform. The illustrations of vestibule training are also examples of simulation, since they were attempts to replicate actual work environments in training situations. As with these examples, simulations can be used for skills, knowledge, and attitudinal training for individuals, groups, and entire systems. Four development techniques of simulation are of importance. There are: (a) case studies, (b) role-making exercises, (c) in basket exercises, (d) business games.

COMPARISON OF DEVELOPMENT TECHNIQUES

Given the large number of development techniques from which to choose, how can a firm decide which one to use? Ideally, this decision would be based upon extensive research conducted by the firm to assess which techniques work best under what specific conditions. This type of research is often lacking, however, because its costs may be greater than its presumed benefits, or the organization may simply not have the time and resources to conduct such research. In addition, in small companies there may not be enough employees requiring a particular form of training to obtain an adequate sample size on which to base such research.

Individuals in charge of development, however, must decide which techniques to use. Frequently they will rely on the opinions of "experts" or the theories and research of others. This section will present the findings of two studies in which training directors reported on the development techniques they regarded as most frequently used and most effective in helping to meet various objectives. We will also provide some guidelines for making decisions about the techniques to use for meeting different organizational objectives.

Table 2 presents the findings of a survey of 112 firms. Training directors were asked to rank the frequency with which they used the training techniques illustrated in Figure 2. These firms, which varied in size, were engaged in both manufacturing and non-manufacturing activities. The authors of the study reported that there was very little difference between manufacturing and non-manufacturing firms in the reported frequency with which the various techniques were used.

Training directors in manufacturing firms ranked only three of the 18 techniques (JIT, conference or discussion, and apprenticeship) as being used to an "average" degree or above. In non-manufacturing, only two of the techniques (JIT and conference or discussion) were ranked as being used to an "average" degree or above. Interestingly, on-the-job techniques appear to be more frequently used in manufacturing firms, since they occupy four of the five top rankings. The low ranking of both internships and assistantships and junior boards is not surprising since the population with which these techniques is used is small. In sum, these

Table 2

Rank Order of Fequency of Use of 18 Training Techniques by Type of Firm

Training technique	*Type of firm*			
	Manufacturing		*Non-manufacturing*	
	Rank order	*Mean value*	*Rank order*	*Mean value*
1. Job instruction training	1	3.9	1	4.0
2. Conference or discussion	2	3.5	2	3.4
3. Apprentice training	3	3.1	6.5	2.5
4. Job rotation	4	2.8	3	2.8
5. Coaching	5	2.6	6.5	2.5
6. Lecture	6	2.4	5	2.6
7. Special study	7	2.3	4	2.7
8. Case study	8	2.1	10	2.2
9. Films	9	2.0	8.5	2.4
10. Programmed instruction	10	1.9	8.5	2.4
11. Internships and assistantships	11	1.8	11	2.0
12. Simulation	12	1.7	12	1.9
13. Programmed group exercises	13.5	1.6	16.5	1.3
14. role playing	13.5	1.6	13	1.6
15. Laboratory training	15	1.5	16.5	1.3
16. Television	16	1.4	14.5	1.4
17. Vestibule training	17	1.2	14.5	1.4
18. Junior board	18	1.1	18	1.1

Source: Stuart B. Utgaard and Rene V. Dawis, "The Most Frequently Used Training Techniques," *Training and Development Journal* 24 (February 1970):41 Copyright 1970, *Training and Development Journal*, American Society for Training and Development. Reprinted with permission. All rights reserved. The techniques included are those suggested by Bernard M. Bass and James A. Vaughan in *Training in Industry: Management of Learning* (Belmont, Calif.: Wadsworth, 1966).

findings reinforce the earlier view that on-the-job training is used more frequently than off-the-job training.

In Table 3, the findings of a second study are presented. This study obtained the "expert" opinion of training directors, but compared their judgments to the "limited research available" con-

Table 3

Ratings of Training Directors on Effectiveness of Alternative Training Methods for Various Training Objectivts

Training mothod	*Knowledge acquisition*		*Changing attitudes*		*Problem-solving skills*		*Interpersonal skills*		*Participant acceptance*		*Knowledge retention*	
	Mean	*Mean rank*	*Mean*	*Mean rank*	*Mean*	*Mean rank*	*Mean*	*Mean rank*	*Mean*	*Mean rank*	*Mean*	*Mean rank*
Case study	3.56	2	3.43	4	3.69	1	3.02	4	3.80	2	3.48	2
Conference (discussion) method	3.33	3	3.54	3	3.26	4	3.21	3	4.16	1	3.32	5
Lecture (with questions)	2.53	9	2.20	8	2.00	9	1.90	8	2.74	8	2.49	8
Business games	3.00	6	2.73	5	3.58	2	2.50	5	3.78	3	3.26	6
Movie films	3.16	4	2.50	6	2.24	7	2.19	6	3.44	5	2.67	7
Programmed instruction	4.03	1	2.22	7	2.56	6	2.11	7	3.28	7	3.74	1
Role playing	2.93	7	3.56	2	3.27	3	3.68	2	3.56	4	3.37	4
Sensitivity training (T-group)	2.77	8	3.96	1	2.98	5	3.95	1	3.33	6	3.44	3
Television lecture	3.10	5	1.99	9	2.01	8	1.81	9	2.74	9	2.47	9

Source: Stephen J. Carroll, Jr., Frank T. Paine, and John J. Ivancevich, "The Relative Effectiveness of Training Methods–Expert Opinion and Research," *Personnel Psychology* 25 (1972):498.

cerning "adults in the employment situation." The respondents were 117 training directors who "worked for the companies with the largest numbers of employees as indicated in the *Fortune* list of the top 500 corporations." Any inferences, therefore, drawn from this study must recognize the contingency of organization size.

This study compared nine techniques in terms of six training objectives. PI was ranked *most* effective for acquisition of knowledge, and lecture (with questions) *least* effective. Based upon our earlier discussion of PI, we do not feel that the highly favorable evaluation of PI is fully warranted at this time. In addition, the low rating of the lecture method is not supported by a number of other research studies. For example, when compared to the discussion method, the lecture has been found to be superior in some instances. However, in this study, training directors believed that the discussion method was significantly better than lecture in the acquisition of knowledge.

Training directors also saw sensitivity training (which has many of the same characteristics as role playing) as the most effective method for changing attitudes. In addition, role playing, discussion, and case studies were all seen as being superior to business games, films, PI, and lectures for changing attitudes. A number of research studies support these opinions. However, the research on case studies for attitudinal change has been limited, and as we previously noted, business games may be used to change attitudes in some circumstances.

For the teaching of problem-solving skills, the training directors expressed the opinion that case studies, business games, role playing, and discussions were most likely to be effective. The growing body of research comparing case studies and business games is so contradictory that it is impossible to state which is more effective for teaching specific problem solving skills.

It would appear that role-playing and discussion methods would also help to develop problem-solving skills because of active participation. However, these two techniques are more likely to focus on human relations aspects, with case studies and games emphasizing the economic aspects of business operations.

For developing interpersonal skills, these training directors perceived sensitivity training and role playing to be the most effective. Research appears to justify these opinions. However, further research may well show that case studies and business games are also useful in this area. Case studies in which trainees discuss human relations problems might prove useful in further developing interpersonal skills. Business games can be used to teach interpersonal skills when the game involves trainees making decisions as part of a group.

In terms of participant acceptance, the training directors rated discussion, case studies, and business games most favorably, although the other techniques covered, except lectures and television, were also thought acceptable. For retention of knowledge, training directors expressed the view that PI, case studies, sensitivity training, role playing, discussions, and business games were significantly more effective than films, lectures, and television.

There is not a great deal of research in this area, and what does exist does not support the beliefs expressed by the training directors. The research that has been conducted has primarily involved college students and generally has indicated that the lecture and discussion techniques are comparable to one another. Interestingly, the techniques which the training directors believed were most effective in terms of retention all require active participation by trainees, and those rated least effective do not.

Where organizations do not engage in their own evaluation of development techniques, "expert" opinion and research findings may be useful guides in the choice of specific training techniques.

CURRENT PROBLEMS AND ISSUES IN HUMAN DEVELOPMENT

Special Problems Encountered by Women Employees

The composition of the labor force has changed dramatically during the past years. Despite the increased representation of females in the *total* work force, much of this growth has been in the lower-level and lower-paying positions. It was reported in 1980 that women comprise less than 5 percent of middle management and less than 2 percent of top business executives, and a 1978 *Fortune* survey of the top 300 American corporations revealed only 268 females holding positions on boards of directors.

According to Rosabeth Kanter's sociological case study of a corporation. There are three specific issues which confront women in the corporation: (1) proportions, or the relative numbers of females of mid- to top-level executive positions; (2) lack of opportunity; and (3) lack of power, or the capacity to mobilize resources.

We believe that more and more women will enter mid- to top-level positions in the future because of affirmative action programs by business organizations. Further, with their continuing increased representation in the total work force, more women will be available for promotion to managerial, professional, and top-management positions. These two factors will help to reduce the problem of lower proportions of females in managerial ranks.

The lack of power and opportunity experienced by many females has its basis in (1) stereotypes and myths concerning female behaviors, and (2) attitudinal problems concerning the role of the female employee. These two problems are further compounded by the lack of rôle models and mentors for lower- and mid-level female executives to rely upon. We will now discuss each of these issues and suggest some types of developmental activities that may be used to overcome them.

Stereotypes and Myths. One problem facing women entering managerial positions is that various stereotypes and myths have developed concerning their ability and desire to operate at this level. For example, it has been argued that women have higher rates of sickness, absenteeism, and turnover than do men. In reality, however, although some differences do exist between the sexes, those differences have not been shown to be significant.

Turnover rates, for example, have been found to be somewhat higher for women than for men. However, additional analysis of these differences has revealed that the major factors relating to turnover were number of years with the organization (those with fewer years tended to have higher turnover), age of the worker (younger workers tended to have higher turnover rates), and occupational level (higher turnover rates tended to exist in lower positions). Since women have been overrepresented in each of these three areas (that is, less time with the organization, younger, and lower in the organization hierarchy), it is not surprising that they have had higher turnover rates than men.

When men and women in professional positions have been compared, however, turnover rates have been found to be nearly identical. Men in professional positions have tended to take longer periods of sick leave than females in comparable positions. Similarly, other stereotypes such as the following are *not* borne out by research studies: (1) Women are more emotional than men; (2) women lack ability in the mathematical and scientific areas; (3) women are motivated by different factors than are men; and (4) women lack skills related to managerial success, such as objectivity, abstract thinking, and communication.

Individuals conducting development programs in which women are involved must recognize that these stereotypes are incorrect. Otherwise, erroneous development approaches may be used. For example, if a male trainer assumes that women are more emotional than men, he may try to avoid training situations which are emotional in nature (for example, stressful role playing involving disciplinary problems). In this case, the trainer may be neglecting an important area of job-related development for the trainee.

The existence of myths and stereotypes about women would appear to call for training that is informational in nature. Such techniques as the lecture and PI, useful for imparting factual information, appear to be appropriate for providing the facts concerning these myths. However, many of these myths are based more upon emotionally based attitudes than intellectual misinformation, and participative methods such as discussion or role playing may be necessary in addition to purely informational training. It is to some of these attitudinal problems that we now turn.

Attitudinal Problems. Women entering managerial positions face a major attitudinal problem that development programs may help to overcome: the attitudes of many males—whether subordinates, peers, or supervisors—about a woman manager. Through cultural learning, many males have developed attitudes about male-female roles that may lead them to have predetermined role expectations concerning women.

Some males, for example, may react negatively to a woman supervisor because in this role she is violating their cultural values that women should assume positions subordinate to men. Although one might think that younger, more "modern" males would hold such attitudes to a lesser degree than older males, one study found that older, more experienced male employees were more willing to accept a woman as a supervisor than were younger, less experienced ones.

Organizations can conduct development programs to help overcome such attitudinal problems (although changing the attitudes of certain individuals may be difficult if not impossible). Several approaches to such developmental programs can be utilized. Information sessions can be used to provide factual materials to participants. Discussion sessions, involving both men and women, can be used to explore areas of misunderstanding concerning the proper role of women managers. Role playing can also be used to help change attitudes. For example, role reversals in conflict situations may help expose biases on the parts of both males and females. Such programs can help to change male attitudes and thus make the work environment more favorable for women managers.

Changing male attitudes alone, however, will not eliminate the problems women face in managerial positions. Women must modify their own attitudes as well, since they have often accepted as "correct" the traditional behavior patterns and role expectations relative to male-female relationships. As Schwartz and Rago have stated: "Full acceptance of women as professional peers or supervisors requires relearning by both sexes to dispel previously learned male-female expectations."

A number of specific attitudes of some women need to be modified if they are to be successful in managerial positions. There is some evidence, for example, that women in general have lower self-esteem than men. From a socialization standpoint, women in our society are often trained to be more people-oriented, non-aggressive, and dependent than men. Managerial positions, on the other hand, are frequently seen as requiring task orientation, aggressiveness, and independence. *As a consequence, the established modes of behavior of women are often in conflict with managerial role expectations.*

The extent to which females accept this stereotype was indicated by a study in which women and men were asked to rank nine characteristics in terms of their importance for managerial positions. Both sexes agreed that decisiveness, consistency and objectivity, emotional stability, and analytical ability were the most important *and* that men were more likely to have these characteristics than women! Thus, the basic socialization of many women contributes to a self-image that is in conflict with the image of a manager as perceived by members of both sexes.

As a consequence, many women may be reluctant in mixed-sex groups to assume the leadership position. To the extent that women have lower self-esteem, they may be more likely to doubt their own abilities and competence. There is even some evidence that women may fear success in competitive situations with men, and that they may in fact "underachieve in competitive intellectual situations when a male is present."

Some of these attitudinal problems of women entering management positions may be dealt with by means of development programs. For example, a number of off-the-job techniques, such as case studies, in-basket techniques, and role playing may be used to help women managerial trainees gain practice in decision making. Utilizing appropriate positive reinforcement during training may also help to increase the self-esteem of women managerial trainees.

In addition to attitudinal training, women entering managerial positions frequently do need specific skills training which may not be necessary for men. For example, women may need special training in how to deal with conflict situations, since cultural conditioning frequently leads women to hide their hostile or aggressive feelings. In conflict situations, therefore, women managers may seek to smooth things over, whereas their male counterparts may possess other modes of behavior as well, such as direct confrontation.

MULTIPLE DEVELOPMENT TECHNIQUES AND GROUP-ORIENTED APPROACHES

In this section we will discuss two relatively new approaches to development: assessment centers and organization development. These two techniques differ from the development techniques discussed previously in at least two ways. First, many of the techniques presented before can be used for either individual or group training. However, both assessment centers and organizational development by their very design involve groups during at least some phases of training.

Second, both involve more than simply training groups or individuals. For example, assessment centers deal with evaluating as well as training individuals. Organization development, on the other goes beyond focusing attention on only individuals or groups. It emphasizes changing attitudes and behaviors of individuals working together throughout the total organization. Finally, both approaches usually are used with managers rather than with non-managerial employees, although recently they have been adapted to all organizational levels.

Assessment Centers

The assessment center concept had its origins in the selection of officers for the German military during the 1930s. The concept was borrowed during World War II by both the British War Office and the United States Office of Strategic Services. In the 1950s, the assessment center concept was adapted for industrial uses by AT and T's Management Progress Study for the evaluation and selection or promotion of managers.

Recent studies have indicated a marked rise in the use of assessment centers in the past decade. Company-operated assessment centers have increased from slightly over 100 companies to over 2000. In addition, not only business organizations but Central agencies and state governments as well have adopted this technique for use in selecting supervisory personnel.

The basic requirements for an assessment center are presented below. As can be seen, *the assessment center is a process, not a place.* Persons participating in assessment centers are evaluated and the results of the evaluation are generally fed back to them. Participation in assessment centers usually lasts for two or more days. Finally, observers who are doing the evaluating must be trained management consultants and/or organization members who have been trained as observers and who hold positions at two or more organization levels above the persons being evaluated.

To be considered as an assessment center, [a program must meet] the following minimal requirements....:

1. Multiple assessment techniques must be used. At least one of these techniques must be a simulation. A simulation is an exercise or technique designed to elicit behaviors related to dimensions of performance on the job by requiring the participant to respond behaviorally to situational stimuli in the

work situation. Examples of simulations include group exercises, in-basket exercises, and fact finding exercises.

2. Multiple assessors must be used. These assessors must receive training prior to participating in a center.
3. Judgments resulting in an outcome (i.e., recommendation for promotion, specific training or development) must be based on pooling information from assessors and techniques.
4. An overall evaluation of behavior must be made by the assessors at a separate time from observation of behavior.
5. Simulation exercises are used. These exercises are developed to tap a variety of predetermined behaviors and have been tested prior to use to insure that the techniques provide reliable, objective and relevant behavioral information for the organization in question.
6. The dimensions, attributes, characteristics or qualities evaluated by the assessment center are determined by an analysis of relevant job behaviors.
7. The techniques used in the assessment center are designed to provide information which is used in evaluating the dimensions, attributes, or qualities previously determined.

In summary, an assessment center consists of a standardized evaluation of behavior based on multiple inputs. Multiple trained observers and techniques are used. Judgments about behavior are made, in part, from specially developed assessment simulations.

As the definition of an assessment center presented in the box indicates, many of the development techniques previously discussed are used with this approach. For example, in a typical two-day assessment center program described by Byham, the following techniques were used: business gaming, group discussion, case studies, in-basket exercise, leaderless group discussion, and role playing.

On the first day of the typical two-day program, participants first had an orientation meeting. Then, four-person teams played a management game which involved forming different types of conglomerates and bartering with other teams to achieve planned objectives. In addition, four-person groups were called upon to assume the role of management consultants in solving problems presented in four short cases. After discussing the cases, each group was required to present a written analysis and sets of recommendations. Thus, the first day of activities focused on group decision-making problems.

On the second day, participants performed an in-basket exercise involving problems such as scheduling and planning activities, answering questions, and delegating responsibilities. Following the completion of the exercise, each person participated in a one-hour interview with an assessor. Next, a leaderless group discussion was conducted during which each participant played the role of a department head deciding how to allocate money for salary increases.

Participants then played the role of a management consultant seeking to resolve a financial problem. Individual recommendations were developed first, and then groups formed to develop a single set of recommendations. On the two days following the conclusion of the assessment center, assessors met "to share their observations on each participant and to arrive at summary evaluations relative to each dimension sought and overall potential and training needs." This discussion illustrates the overlap between management development programs and assessment centers. In addition, assessment centers have been recognized as having many used beyond the evaluation of managerial potential. Richard Steiner, for example, has suggested the following used of assessment centers.

- ☐ Identifying and determining the immediate management potential, which aids in making selection decisions.
- ☐ Identifying and developing individualized developmental programs.
- ☐ Developing individuals just through participation in the assessment center.
- ☐ Positively influencing employee satisfaction, job expectations, and motivation.
- ☐ Evaluating development programs.

Assessment centers are valid for selection purposes because they often serve as good predictors of success on the job. Where such predictive validity has been established by organizations, assessment centers can be particularly useful in dealing with minorities and women.

Assessment centers are also useful in identifying and helping to decide on individual development programs. In fact, as Byham noted, the primary or highly rated secondary objective of most assessment centers is to help build individual development programs. Because participants are evaluated on a number of specific dimensions, weaknesses can be identified and specific programs developed to deal with those problems.

For example, individuals may be observes as having difficulty with time management during in-basket exercises. These persons may be given special training in establishing priorities and proper utilization of time. The identification of specific weaknesses is facilitated because the assessors (if they are from within the company) hold positions in the organizational hierarchy at two or more levels above the trainee. Thus, they are likely to be familiar with the specific skills the individual will need in future job assignments.

Participation in assessment center may serve as a development exercise in and of itself. For example, by participating in the discussion groups, individuals may learn how well they function and relate to others in group problem solving. Steiner has pointed out that participants in assessment centers believe they have learned through participation because many of the tools used are "tried and true training methodology." Since most centers provide both oral and written feedback concerning performance, participants are operating in a training environment. Even in the absence of special feedback mechanisms, there is evidence that "most participants gain self-insight from participating in assessment exercises and that this insight is fairly accurate."

Assessment centers may also influence such variables as satisfaction, job expectations, and motivation by providing objective feedback on how participants performed in the program and on their future development needs and prospects within the company. Satisfaction and motivation may also be enhanced when participants are able to talk candidly with assessors who hold positions above them in the company. However, when individuals are not selected for promotion or further development, problems can arise.

A final benefit is that assessment centers may serve as development programs for the assessors as well as for those being assessed. For example, assessors who observe groups in discussion sessions may also learn how group norms are formulated. Such information may help them in dealing with their own subordinates on the job. Kraut has even suggested that future managers may be sent to assessment centers as observers rather than as participants to help them "become more astute in behavioral observation, group dynamics, and problem solving."

Assessment centers also possess certain limitations. First, these programs can be costly. Because of the possibility of high costs, cost-benefit analysis should be undertaken to justify the use of the technique. A second problem involves the need for each organization to develop and validate its own assessment center. This is particularly true if the organization requires unique skills or is using the center for positions not previously evaluated through the technique. Haynes has noted the need for each organization to identify its own needs. In this researcher's study, statistical analysis of several assessment center techniques resulted in their elimination since they provided no additional information about participants in the program.

A final problem centers around the contingency of organizational size. Due to the cost of assessment centers and the need to validate them, it is unlikely that smaller firms can afford this approach. Millard and Pinsky have pointed out that validation studies have been done only in "very large organizations and may be inappropriate if applied to smaller businesses."

Organization Development

In this section we will focus attention on organization development—often simply referred to as OD. Organization development is difficult to define because so many different techniques and tactics referred to as OD have been used in various organizations. However, in most cases today:

> Organization development is in effort (1) *planned*, (2) *organization-wide*, and (3) *managed* from the *top* to (4) increase *organization effectiveness* and *health* through (5) *planned interventions* in the organization's "processes," using *behavioral science* knowledge.

The last two points in this definition are important because they reflect the fact that OD efforts are basically oriented toward people and reflect a humanistic bias in which an attempt is made to modify the attitudes, values, and behavior of organizational members. As Miner has noted, these directions include the following:

- A more democratic or participative set of values that is antihierarchy, antiauthoritarian, and antiauthority. The result is a movement in the direction of democracy within the enterprise.
- A greater orientation to a consciousness of the immediate peer and work group, as reflected in team building efforts.
- Less individual competitiveness and less use of power. This has been called power equalization and is reflected in the strong emphasis on collaboration.
- More openness and freer expression of feelings as reflected in the stress on confrontation.

Another important characteristic of OD may be inferred from these dimensions and from the fact that *OD efforts are organization-wide. OD focuses on changing the total organizational system.* In essence, OD represents a systems- oriented approach in which the interactions of various individuals and groups are considered when human-oriented changes are introduced into an organization.

Members of organizations participating in OD efforts are actively involved in organizational change. Further, many of the OD involvement efforts are aimed at having groups within the organization, rather than simply individuals, work together actively to learn how to function better, make decisions, and relate to each other in a manner congruent with the humanistic values of OD. As Luthans has stated, "There is a sociological flavor to much of OD."

With respect to the question concerning who should conduct the training, many OD experts emphasize the need for an outside, third-party *change agent,* or catalyst, to be involved in OD programs. Many business firms and other organizations, however, have developed their own internal training staffs to undertake OD activities.

Although OD focuses on total systems change, its orientation is quite different from the systems-oriented vestibule training method mentioned in Chapter 10. OD attempts to change behavior within the organizational system, whereas the RAND efforts attempted to replicate a real system in order to teach specific knowledge and skills.

OD has often been compared with management development. although both are similar in that they represent development efforts, management development is geared primarily toward improving the performance of managers as individuals. OD, on the other hand, is concerned with improving the performance of systems that make up the total organization—work groups, departments, teams, task forces, and so forth. As such, OD has much broader implications than management development, although management development can be seen as a component of OD. Further, it is possible to view OD as an outgrowth of some of the approaches originally used for management development, such as sensitivity training.

Sensitivity Training. Sensitivity training, often referred to as T-group or laboratory training, was originally devised as a management development technique. It was pioneered in the 1940s by a group known today as the National Training Laboratory Institute for Applied Behavioral Science, or NTL. The basic objective of sensitivity training in its original formulation was to help individuals achieve a variety of behavioral goals that would contribute to both more effective organizational performance and individual need satisfaction.

The specific behavioral goals of sensitivity training have typically included one or more of the following:

- Increasing self-insight to enable participants to better understand why they behave as they do.
- Providing both a better understanding of values and attitudes that may facilitate or hinder group functionin- and an awareness of the interpersonal dynamic- groups.
- Developing skills for di- group settings.

-g has been upon Sensitivity organizational -er of training techniques in order to The ma- goals—role playing, theory sessions on group dynamics, and so forth. The relative emphasis given to any one of these techniques may vary considerably from one sensitivity training session to another. At the heart of all sensitivity training, however, is one special technique—the training group, or T-group. The T-group is a relatively unstructured leaderless group of about 8 to 20 individuals engaged in face-to-face discussion over a one- to two-week period.

These emotional reactions emerging from such a session can be used to help participants focus on how they perceive others in the group and how others perceive them. Such awareness may contribute to self-insight and better understanding of the dynamics within the group. The discussion might reveal that the person who spoke first did so because of discomfort with the silence. Others, however, may have perceived this as an attempt to control the group, and responded by not participating. The persons who withdrew might be surprised that active participants were hostile toward them. After the trainer's intervention, all participants will be encouraged to analyze what is happening in the group *now*.

Throughout the T-group sessions, the trainer may intervene in a non-directive manner to try to get the group to see for itself certain dysfunctional types of behavior exhibited in group behavior. Such awareness, it is hoped, will lead the participants to understand which alternative forms of behavior (for example, active listening) might be more effective in certain circumstances. In some instances, participants may be given opportunities to try out alternative forms of behaviors through case studies or role playing.

Action Research. The second historical thread underlying
[illegible] OD efforts is a strategy referred to as the *action research*
The g[illegible] [illegible]del involves extensive collaboration between the
Two important po[illegible]ternal or internal change agent) and the
at this juncture First, action res[illegible]discussion, and planning."
collecting research data about an ongoing [illegible]icted in Figure 4.
objective, goal, or need of that system; feeding these [illegible]hasized
the system; taking actions by altering selected variables within th[illegible]

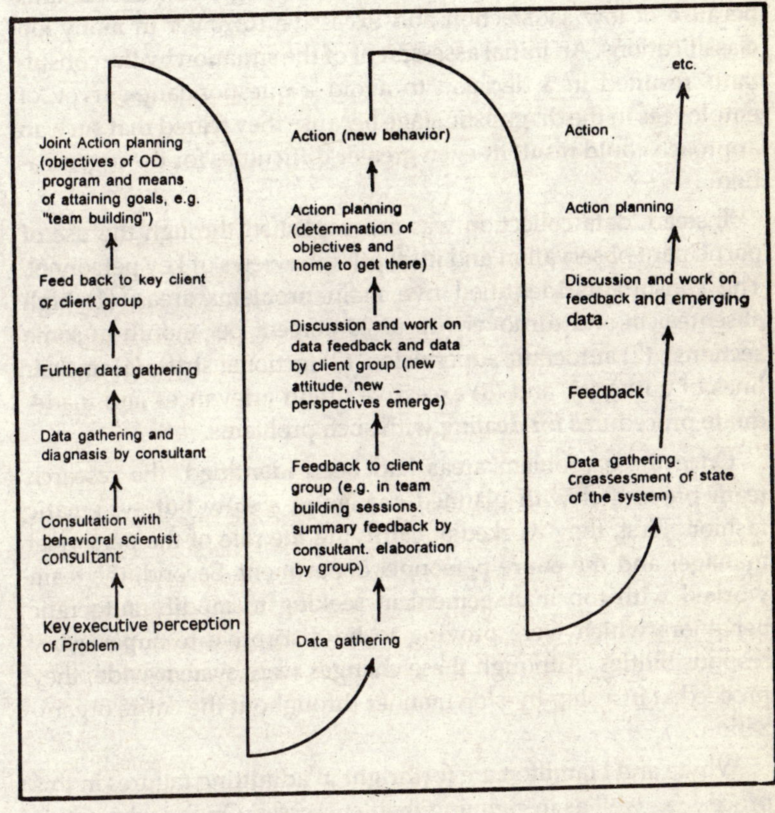

Fig. 4. An action research model for organizational development.

system based on the data and hypotheses; and evaluating the results of actions by collecting more data.

Second, "the sequence [of the action research model] tends to be cyclical, with the focus on new or advanced problems as the client group learns to work more effectively together."

An example of this cyclical process applied to an organizational setting is reported by William F, Whyte and Edith Hamilton in an intervention conducted shortly after World War II at the Tremont Hotel (this early "action research" project would properly be classified as an "OD intervention" today). Tremont management requested the assistance of external management consultants because of low satisfaction and excessive turnover in many job classifications. An initial assessment of the situation by the consultants resulted in a decision to avoid a questionnaire-survey of employees in the diagnostic stage because they feared that such an approach could result in-even greater difficulties for the organization.

Instead, data collection was accomplished through the use of participant observation and in-depth interviews of key personnel. The consultants identified five main problems areas: (1) high absenteeism and turnover (up to 20 percent per month in some sections), (2) autocratic supervision, (3) factional strife, (4) unclear lines of authority, and (5) excessive union grievances and inadequate procedures for dealing with such problems.

Once these problem areas had been identified, the research team proceeded with planned change in a slow but systematic fashion. First, they worked at clarifying the role of the personnel manager and the entire personnel department. Second, the team worked with top management in seeking to modify autocratic behaviors which were proving to be disruptive to supervisory responsibilities. Although these changes were system-wide, they proceeded in a step-by-step manner throughout the entire organization.

Whyte and Hamilton are forthright in admitting failures in this process, as well as in claiming their successes. On the whole, this action research process was a success: Turnover decreased significantly and the productivity of the work force increased. In sum, the total organization underwent significant changes through an ongoing action research process by the team of management consultants.

The action research model is a frequent strategy in current organizational development programs. Its key features are a collaborative, cyclical process which seeks to develop an organization's internal coping mechanisms in order to constructively deal with problems: "While descriptions of this model vary in detail and terminology from author to author, dynamics are essentially the same."

Classifications of OD Interventions. Researchers have categorized what OD consultants actually do in numerous ways. One classification scheme which we have fond to be helpful in understanding what consultants do has been developed by Blake and Mouton in their Diagnosis/Development Matrix. The matrix classifies interventions by five types (ranging from cathartic to the use of models) and the settings within which such changes occur by five types (ranging from the individual person to society at large).

Managerial Grid Development. The managerial grid consists of two parts: (1) a conceptual model to describe managerial behavior, the managerial grid; and (2) a six-phase program for introducing change. The grid uses combinations of two variables to classify managerial styles: (1) concern for production and (2) concern for people. Each variable is scaled from 1 to 9, with 1 indicating low concern and 9 indicating high concern. Thus, a 1,1 managerial style represents a minimal concern for both production and people. The 1,1 manager exerts just enough effort to get the job done.

The 1,9 managerial style indicates a high concern for people and a low concern for production. The manager using this style is primarily interested in a satisfied work group and comfortable, friendly atmosphere. Conversely, the 9,1 managerial style indicates a high concern for production and a low concern for people. The 9,1 manager is interested in getting the task done and does not care very much whether or not subordinates are satisfied.

The 9,9 style indicates a high concern for both production and people. It is regarded as the ideal situation in the grid, since both participatory decision making and team building are emphasized. Finally, Blake and Mouton have described a 5,5 leadership style, representing a moderate concern for both production and people.

The grid concept is used as the basis for a sequential six-phase OD program which can take from three to five years. Phase one involves seminar training in which managers are exposed to the managerial grid concept and are given an opportunity to identify their own style. During this seminar, managers also solve problems that attempt to simulate organizational interpersonal problems.

Phase two is an on-the-job extension of phase one. Now, team development of intact groups takes place "after each work group or department decides on its own 9,9 ground rules and relationships." These first two phases represent management development types of activities, while the next four phases are geared toward organizational development.

In phase three, interdepartmental groups begin to work together to build 9,9 relationships beyond the single work groups. The goal of phase three is to move the groups from common "win-lose" pattern of behavior to joint problem-solving activities, in which groups resolve their problems on a more open and mature basis.

Organizational goal setting occurs during phase four. Problems and goals, such as cost control and safety, are identified by special task groups composed of individuals from different segments and levels of the organization.

Phase five involves goal attainment, in which teams decide how to achieve the goals set in phase four. Specific problems are identified and it is determined how they can be dealt with through organization-wide activities.

Finally, in phase six, the changes introduced during the first five phases are reinforced so that the organization will continue to operate in a 9,9 style. These phases, it must be emphasized, are not only sequential, but also represent movement from a micro to a macro focus.

5

EMPLOYEE COMPENSATION

WAGES AND SALARIES

WAGES refers to compensation given to hourly paid employees, while salary refers to compensation paid on a weekly, biweekly, or monthly basis. Although the distinction between wages and salary seems simple, there are a number of important facets of this distinction. Wage earners, for example, frequently have to punch a time clock, whereas salaried workers do not. Further, salaried workers are often given greater freedom in such matters as arriving late to work, making personal telephone calls on company time, and so forth. Salaried workers are also perceived (sometimes correctly) as being less subject to layoff than wage earners. Thus, there is often a greater status associated with being a salaried worker as opposed to a wage earner. On the other hand, hourly paid employees receive additional compensation in the form of overtime pay, whereas salaried workers usually do not receive such pay.

MONEY, MOTIVATION, AND SATISFACTION

One basic reason for financial compensation, either wages or salary, is that money will somehow motivate individuals to achieve some minimum level of performance or to perform better. The function of money, however, is not clearly understood. As tow researchers have pointed out, "Although it is generally agreed that money is the major mechanism for rewarding and modifying behavior in industry...very little is known about how it works."

Some research, however, has made it possible for us to make generalizations about some of the key contingencies under which money is a motivator. For example, in one study of managers, those who were most highly motivated to perform well expressed two basic attitudes.

1. They indicated that pay was important to them.
2. "They felt that good job performance would lead to higher pay for them."

These two contingencies—importance of pay and pay linked to performance—seem to basic ingredients of any successful compensation system. It should be stressed, however, that the organization may have only a limited impact on influencing how important pay is to the individual. Thus, to the extent possible, the organization should attempt to find out how important financial rewards are to individuals in the selection process. Additionally, the organization can continually demonstrate to individuals through its action that higher financial rewards are linked to better performance. Finally, it should be emphasized that other organizational variables influence the performance-pay link.

Why Money is Important

Our previous discussion raises the questions of why individuals do place value on money and why money is more important to some people than others. Different general models of motivation provide some insights into these questions. We will now discuss briefly four of these models.

A. H. Maslow developed a widely known conceptual framework which postulated the following:

1. All human behavior is geared toward meeting unsatisfied needs.
2. There exists a *hierarchy* of five basic kinds of needs. From lower to higher, these need types are: physiological, safety and security, love and belongingness, recognition and esteem, and self-actualization.

3. The lower-level needs are the most "prepotent" and must be met first. Only then, as these become met, will the higher levels of needs begin to emerge.

Money, in our exchange economy, can obviously serve to meet Maslow's lowest level of needs, physiological (for example, hunger and thirst). Money can also very often meet higher levels of needs, such as esteem and recognition. For example, one can use money to buy a flashy sports car, which will provide esteem and recognition that one has reached a successful status level. Thus, following the Maslow framework, people can have different needs satisfied by money, and to the extent that an unsatisfied need acts as a motivator, people will be motivated by money.

Research done by others has attempted to provide motivational models that are more predictive than Maslow's. For example, Victor Vroom has viewed the individual as decision maker, and his model emphasizes the individual's making choices to achieve certain desired outcomes. This model stresses the importance of the perceived link between individuals' efforts and the probabilities of their achieving their desired outcomes (one of which may be money). Here again, if money is valued highly and the performance-pay link is perceived to be strong, individuals would be predicted to choose to perform well.

Adams and others have developed another theory which may be applied to motivation and money—*equity* theory. This theory is basically concerned with whether or not individuals *perceive* that they are equitably treated in comparison with others. Among other things, equity theory tries to explain "the process by which employees decide that the reward system of the organization is fair." This process "involves making a comparison of pertinent…inputs [what the individual gets] and desired outcomes to some standard—reality, an internal standard, or another person or group" (often referred to as reference groups). As a concrete example, it has been found fairly consistently that underpaid individuals studied who were paid by the hour produced less or poorer-quality work than equitably paid persons, and those underpaid on piece rate tended to produce a large number of low-quality items as compared with equitably paid persons.

Satisfaction

In addition to the relationship between money and motivation, considerable research has been carried out to determine what variables influence the individual's satisfaction with pay. This research has been excellently summarized by others, and we will simply highlight some of its key aspects.

Even if satisfaction with pay had no bearing whatsoever on employee performance, from a humanitarian viewpoint a firm would prefer to have satisfied employees, as long as providing such satisfaction created no negative side effects in the organization (for example, too-high labor costs). Although perhaps not contributing significantly to poor performance, dissatisfaction with pay may lead to two other potentially undesirable and costly organizational outcomes—high absenteeism and turnover rates.

It appears very important that organizational members *perceive* that financial remuneration has been distributed *equitably* among members of the organization. For example, college professors may become extremely upset, and in some cases leave an organization, upon finding out that one of their colleagues with fewer publications is making more money than they are.

Finally, with respect to money and satisfaction (and motivation), some individuals believe that money has no intrinsic meaning by itself. Rather, they perceive of money as serving a symbolic function: "Or, in systems terms, money serves as a perceived input into the individual's open personality system. It will lead to different behavioral and attitudinal outputs, depending both upon how he has learned previously to symbolize the 'value' of money, and his current life situation."

WAGE AND SALARY OBJECTIVES AND DECISIONS

As with many of the other personnel functions, we view wage and salary determination as a multistage decision process aimed at meeting organizational objectives and individual needs. In this area, there are three basic sequential decisions geared toward meeting objectives. These are illustrated graphically in Figure 1.

As may be noted from this figure, working from the macro to the micro level, the organization must first establish its overall wage level, then set up a wage structure to determine the pay for

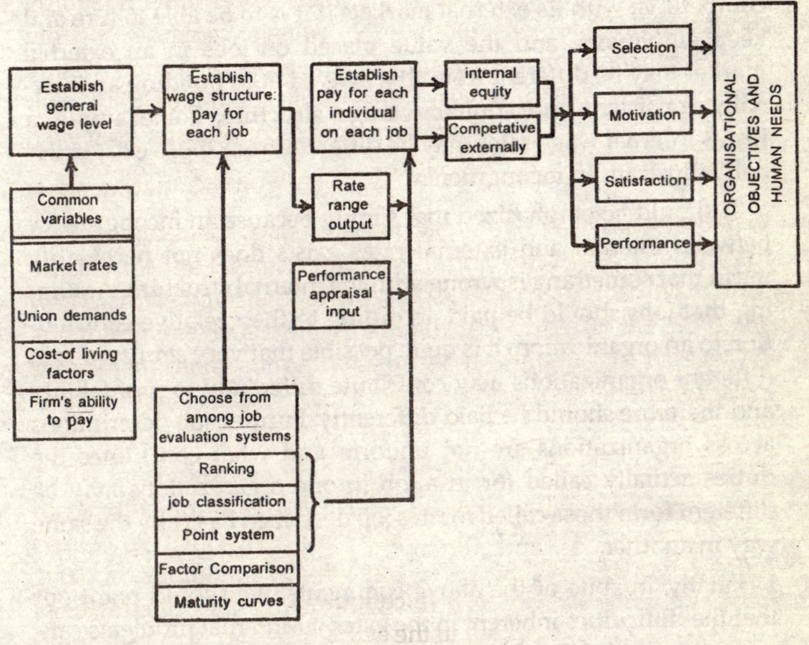

Fig. 1. The wage determination decision process.

each job, and finally decide on how much each individual should be paid on each job. These decisions will hopefully meet two subobjectives—maintaining internal equity and being competitive in its external labor markets. Meeting these goals will help achieve not only the objectives of motivation to perform and pay satisfaction discussed previously, but also the goals of being able to select competent personnel and to retain employees. These four subobjectives, in turn are directed toward meeting the firm's ultimate goals of profitability and the provision of need satisfaction to its employees.

Unfortunately, problems may arise in this decision process, in that internal equity may be incongruent with its companion external competition objective. Based on the criterion of equity, if job A is more difficult than job B, which is in turn more difficult than job

C, then the first should be remunerated more than the second, and this, in turn, more than the third, However, the firm must also be competitive with its external markets if it is to be able to hire and keep employees, and the value placed on jobs in an external market may be different from that arrived at in building an internally consistent and equitable wage structure. For example, a firm's internal wage rates may be different from those exist externally illustrate an incongruency.

It should be emphasized that simply because an incongruency between internal and external rates exists does not necessarily mean that something is wrong with the internal structure. Assuming that jobs should be paid according to their relative contribution to an organization, it is quite possible that very similar jobs in different organizations may contribute differently to profitability and therefore should be paid differently. Further, job descriptions across organizations are not uniform and what constitutes the duties actually called for in a job in one organizations may be different form those called for in a job described basically the same way in another.

Finally, in spite of the above comments. we should point out that the difficulties inherent in the external-internal problems cannot be overstated. For firms that are constantly in the labor market seeking human resources, external wage pressures may well quickly ruin the internal consistency of a wage structure that is not constantly monitored and updated. On the other hand, firms that seldom enter labor markets may soon find themselves internally consistent but hopelessly out of step externally.

ESTABLISHING WAGE AND SALARY LEVELS

The first of the three key managerial decisions illustrated in Figure 1 is establishment of the firm's overall wage and salary levels relative to other firms. If a firm's overall wage and salary level is too low, it will not serve to meet the basic objectives illustrated in Figure 1. If it is too high, on the other hand, the firm's finances will be strained. We will first look at some of the key variables influencing overall wage levels and then focus attention on how information may be obtained and utilized in determining the overall wage and salary structure.

Factors Affecting Wage Levels

A number of key variables affect a firm's overall wage level. Probably the most significant one is the amount paid by competitors for labor in each of the firm's labor markets. Although identifying labor markets sounds easy, in reality it may be difficult to determine precisely what the organization's labor markets are. In addition, a labor market will typically vary, depending upon organizational level. For example, more local markets generally exist for blue-collar workers as opposed to managers and professional. With respect to local labor markets, the time required to get to work seems to be an important determining factor.

Firms may face relatively little competition for prospective employees from other organization under a variety of conditions. For example, if a firm is the only one of any size operating in a geographically isolated "company town" it may face virtually no competition for labor, especially with respect with respect to blue-collar and clerical jobs. In times of depression, with large supplies of human resources available in comparison to demand, wage levels may be set lower than in prosperous times, when there are labor shortages and more competition for qualified employees. Further, some firms make conscious efforts to establish for themselves an image as a good place to work by providing security through few layoffs, excellent pensions, and other employee benefit plans. Firms that have established such images may not have to be as competitive as others in their wage and salary levels.

Firm size, as might be expected, is another contingency that may affect overall wage levels. Larger firms are generally in a position to pay a higher overall level of wages and salaries. This is not always true, however, because an extremely important variable affecting wage and salary decisions is the firm's ability to pay. In one firm with annual turnover of more than Rs. 1000 crores, financial problems became so great that it could not afford to grant any salary increases to its employees, and a salary "moratorium" was put into effect for six months.

FIRM'S WAGE STRUCTURE

A personnel problem facing all organizations is that of developing an effective wage and salary program. Among the basic facets of wage and salary administration are:

1. Job or position evaluation determining the relative worth of each position in an organization. Several methods of job evaluation have been developed, the most common of which is the so-called "point system."
2. Merit rating determining the periodic salary increases for individuals, based on job performance, and other factors.

In designing wage and salary systems, organizations are confronted with two basic problems, the first of which is that attempting to maintain "internal equity." By this we mean developing a wage and salary structure in which employees generally *perceive* wage rates to be internally fair and consistent positions calling for greater skills and responsibility paying more than lower level positions. At the same time, however, organizations must be concerned with the external problem of being competitive, salary wise, in the labor market lest they have difficulties in hiring new employees and keeping present ones.

Once an organization has determined its general wage level, it must determine its wage structure—how different jobs calling for different skills should be rated (and paid) in comparison with each other. While a firm can base its internal structure completely on a wage survey or some other external criterion, such a practice is likely to be inadequate. This is because the relative worth of jobs among firms varies and, since surveys usually only include a sample of all jobs, those jobs not included in the survey would be priced without benefit of knowledge of actual labor market conditions. For such reasons, most firms establish their internal wage and salary structure by engaging in job evaluation, which is a process involving "an orderly, systematic method and procedure of ranking, grading, and weighting of jobs to determine the value of a specific job in relation to other jobs."

Now we will make some observation about job evaluation in general, discuss six different methods of job evaluation, and illustrate how the job structure developed may be translated into wages for specific jobs.

When job evaluations are conducted, separate evaluations are usually carried out for managerial, clerical, and blue-collar employees, because their work is difficult to compare. Similar jobs may also often be grouped into job families. For example, several similar secretarial jobs may be grouped together into one category.

This grouping renders job evaluation simpler to carry out. Further, many authorities believe that the employees themselves should participate in the description and analysis of their jobs. This view assumes that those who participate in helping to develop the system are more likely to accept it. Sometimes extensive person-to-person interviews about jobs may be carried out, but this is costly and time-consuming. In unionized firms, the union may also want to participate. Unions, however, have varied considerably in their attitudes about job evaluation. This is because job evaluation is a difficult process, creating problems unions wish to avoid, and unions have historically believed that job evaluation "tends to limit bargaining and to freeze the wage structure."

In light of the objectives indicated in Figure 1, there should be a real need before a firm revises its wage and salary system. If employees seem basically satisfied with current wage and salary practices, establishing a new system may do nothing but open up a Pandora's box of complaints. This results because, with a new system, some jobs may be rated lower as compared to other jobs than they had been previously, and the holders of these jobs will often perceive the new system as effecting a reduction in their status as far as pay is concerned. If there are serious inequities in the firm's current wage structure, on the other hand, installation of a new system may be mandatory. Periodic review of job evaluations to detect and correct for "creeping changes" in job content will help prevent creeping inequities from occurring.

The Ranking Method

The ranking method is the oldest and simplest job evaluation scheme in existence. It provides for ranking jobs as a whole, without breaking them down into subfactors. The ranking may be simple, alternation, or paired comparisons as in performance appraisal. From a contingency view, ranking is usually carried out in small firms. With large numbers of jobs, ranking is difficult, since no one person would have enough information about them all and the comparisons would become very cumbersome. Simple to understand and easy to install and modify, ranking can be easily used in small firms in which dynamic job situations exist.

On the negative side, the method is crude and highly subjective. Admission of this crudeness, however, avoids the danger of considering numbers as "highly scientific," as may be done with more sophisticated job evaluation programs. As most commonly used, ranking dose not measure the *distances* between jobs. For example, it might rate three jobs as A B C but not account for the fact that job A is considerably more difficult than job B, while the latter is only slightly more difficult than job C.

The Job Classification Method

The job classification method is a second well-known approach to job evaluation. It calls for development of a series of job grades or classifications. In the federal civil service system, where it is used most widely, for example, grades have been set up from GS-1 (highly routine work) to GS-18 (top executive positions). An initial step in this method is to predefine the grades that management intends should form the basic structure of the system. Sometimes grade descriptions are very briefly stated, such as: "Performs routine typing and clerical duties under the close supervision of the person's superior." In other cases, however, the grades may be more fully spelled out. For example, one author, in illustrating the description of chemist positions, first looked at four factors: general characteristics of the job, direction required, typical duties and responsibilities, and responsibility for the direction of others. He then developed a brief description of each for eight classes of chemists. The lowest classification (chemist 1) called for a B.S. degree in chemistry, no experience, working under close supervision, performing a variety of routine tasks, and usually having no responsibility for directing others. The highest (chemist VIII) on the other hand, was described as involving making decisions having a "far-reaching impact on extensive chemical and related activities of the company," receiving only general administrative direction, having considerable supervisory responsibilities and/or being an individual researcher and consultant, and supervising several "subordinate supervisors or team leaders." Once such grades have been established, it is necessary to slot each job in the organization into a grade classification by comparing the job description as developed through job analysis to the classification descriptions.

The job classification approach is more complex than simple ranking and requires judgment both in defining each grade and in placing each position into an appropriate grade. A description of a particular job may be written, for example, in such a way that the job may appear to fit logically into more than one classification. Like ranking, job classification is also nonquantitative and global—traditionally jobs are not broken down into various factors. It is also often considered necessary to have a separate classification system for managerial and professional, office, and factory employees because the nature of their jobs is so different.

Merit Increase

It is axiomatic to progressive salary administration that individual salary increases should be granted on a merit basis. Salary increases, in other words, ought to come neither automatically nor on the basis of some personalized formula but, rather, in recognition of individual work performance. In this connection, we are currently hearing a good deal about "total merit" concepts, plans for getting more mileage out of merit budgets, and a trend away from the blanket or general increase. Some authorities are even suggesting that merit increases should be limited to reward for truly superior performance.

It is widely recognized, too, that the success of a merit program depends upon the accuracy of the company's method of measuring performance and that obtaining a reliable and valid measuring instrument is far from a simple task. But let us assume for the purpose of this discussion that such an instrument can be developed and move on to ask, "What do we really mean by merit in terms of salary increase?"

Perhaps at first blush Webster's definition of merit as "reward deserved" seems to meet the need. Everyone knows that employees ought to be rewarded according to their contribution, difficult to measure though these may be. But is the matter truly this simple, or are there other considerations involved?

Casual reflection discloses a number of related issues that are apt to give us trouble, particularly in firms employing engineers and scientists in research and development activities. Some of these issues are posed in the following questions:

1. Are all salary increases given for "merit"? If not, what other factors contribute to salary growth?
2. How can one determine what constitutes a true merit increase?

3. What bearing do employee and employer attitudes have upon merit increases?

Let us consider each of these questions in turn.

It is well known that wages and salaries have been rising rapidly in recent years. Studies and experience have demonstrated that nearly all companies with a formal program of salary administration make use of wage and salary surveys for the maintenance of their competitive position. In response to the upward trends shown by these surveys, most companies have been in the habit of granting either general increases or larger-than- usual "merit" increases.

Many firms dislike the general-increase approach, especially in contrast to what they like to call a "total merit" approach. The simple truth persists, nevertheless, that most of a firm's personnel are going to have to be given what amounts to a general increase as a matter of sheer necessity—that is, so that the company can keep pace with rising salary levels. In fact, it has sometimes been said that "total merit" programs result in nothing more than unequally distributed general or blanket increases.

Salary increases given in response to an increase in general salary levels cannot, however, be considered true merit increases or can they?

It seems we are back with that troublesome question "What is a merit increase?" If we take the position that not all increases are the result of merit, how do we distinguish the merit portion from the others? As was previously postulated, merit increases should be based on performance, and should serve to differentiate employees in accordance with their differing contributions to the organization's total work effort. "Merit," then, can be only the portion of a salary increase that exceeds the general upward movement of salaries. In other words, increases granted to individuals to keep their salaries in line with rising market conditions do not qualify as merit increases.

This gives us our first proposition: *A merit increase is an increase that is given in recognition of work performance and that exceeds the general upward movement of salaries.*

It follows from this proposition that the general upward movement of salaries must be used as the base on which to build true merit increases. How, then, does one compute this general upward movement? "By conducting periodic salary surveys," the answer might come back, "and analyzing the change in median salaries and rate ranges."

In short, this method shows that salaries have been moving upward by about 4 per cent a year. Roughly the same results could be obtained from a comparison of salary curves based on years since degree or years of ex-perience.

This leads to the statement of our second proposition: *The general upward movement of salaries is best indicated by the percentage change in median salaries for bench-mark jobs or in experience curves from one year in the next.*

Applying these two propositions, we can see that an employee receives a "merit" increase only if his salary is raised by more than 4 per cent. By how much more, however, still remains to be answered. Assuming that the figure of 4 per cent accurately reflects the general upward +movement of salaries, does any amount in excess of 4 per cent indicate merit recognition?

Once noted expert on salaries has stated that merit increases, at least for scientific and professional personnel, should average between 5 and 7 per cent for the year. If these figures are meant to include all salary considerations other than promotion, then he is actually proposing merit increases of from 1 to 3 per cent annually. If, however, these figures are not meant to take account of the general upward movement of salaries, then he is proposing total increases ranging from 9 to 11 per cent. Clearly, these two approaches lead to widely divergent salary programs.

Before we can attempt to evaluate them or choose between them, we must note that merely computing the change in median salary levels of comparable jobs from year to year affords us no information about what is happening to individual salaries. People are constantly being siphoned off to fill more responsible positions, and the change in median salaries is in part a result of this movement. Numerous surveys, particularly in the scientific and professional fields but in others too, have shown that there is a high positive correlation between salaries on the one hand and years of experience, years since degree, and age on the other. The effects of these three variables cannot be readily seen in a classical bench-mark survey, which does not examine maturity indices.

Figure 2 illustrates the typical configuration, showing the relationships between median salaries and the other variables.

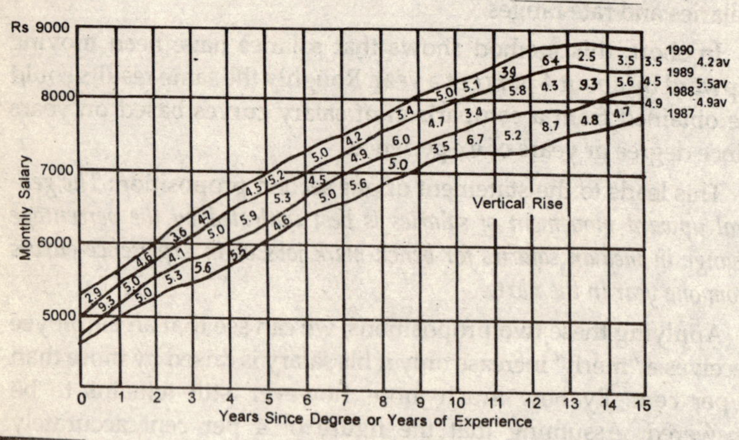

Fig. 2. Percentage change in median salary for a specific experience group from year to year.

Because of this correlation, it is not sufficient to note only the vertical movement of either salary curves or median salaries for specific jobs. As Figure 3 shows, individual salaries rise not only

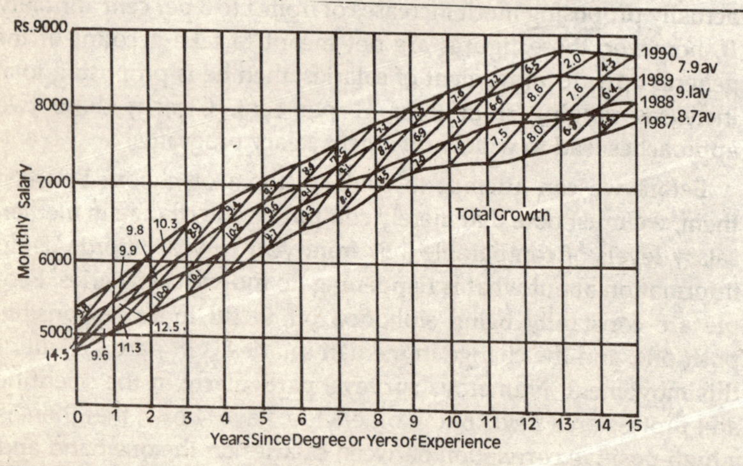

Fig. 3. Percentage change in median salary for a specific experience group from year to year.

with the general upward movement of salaries but also with their own movement along the curve.

The year-to-year salary growth of a median-salaried employee at any given experience level thus constitutes quite a different picture from the year-to-year general rise in salaries. As was pointed out earlier, salary levels in general have been rising by 4 to 5 per cent annually over the past several years. Following a median salaried engineer or scientists along from year to year, however, we find that his salary has been growing at rate averaging 11 per cent a year in the first two to three years of experience and tapering off to 6 to 7 per cent a year at the 14- to 15-year experience levels. This reflects both inflationary growth and experience growth.

Consider what this means for employees who must be properly compensated in relation to their experience and their performance, particularly in the professional and scientific fields. If they are to maintain the same relative salary position among their peers next year as they have now, their current salaries will have to be increased by anywhere from 6 to 11 per cent, depending on their experience.

This, then, suggests an alternative to our second proposition, according to which the general upward movement of salaries is best indicated by the annual percentage change in median salaries or experience curves. The alternative formulation, our third proposition, might be stated as follows: *The general upward movement of salaries is best indicated by the percentage change in median salaries resulting from a vertical salary rise plus the compensation for an additional year of experience.*

Now we are in a position to ask whether an individual salary increase of 6 to 11 per cent for the year includes a "merit" consideration. At this point, obviously, the definition of "merit increase" embodied in our first proposition requires us to choose between the second and third propositions, for it restricts the term to increases exceeding the general upward movement of salaries.

If we couple this definition with the second proposition, then the answer must be *Yes*, since increase of 6 to 11 per cent do of course exceed the average 4 per cent general lifting of salaries.

If, on the other hand, we couple it with the third proposition, on the grounds that this latter formulation is the more representative of the general upward salary trend, then the answer must be *No.* We could make this position even more cogent by qualifying out definition of "merit increase" to include only reward for superior performance. For with the salaries of most engineers and scientists actually growing at the rate of 6 to 11 per cent a year, an individual increase of this magnitude cannot be regarded as a reward for exceptional performance.

By way of recapitulation, let us consider what has been covered to this point:

1. Salary increases should be granted on the basis of "merit" or performance.
2. Defining what is meant by a merit increase is not so simple as it might first appear in view of the following:
   (a) Salaries in general have been rising by an average of 4 to 5 per cent annually.
   (b) Median salaries for individual engineers and scientists have been rising at rates ranging from 11 per cent at the start of their careers to 6 to 7 per cent in the later years.
   (c) Companies have been responding to these pressures by granting general increases or liberalized "merit" increases.
3. Isolating either the "merit" or the inflationary portion of these rising salary trends is a very difficult enterprise.

Where does this discussion leave us with regard to determining appropriate merit-increase percentages? Probably somewhere between the position of the authority who says that "merit" increases should average 5 to 7 per cent annually and that of the engineer who suggests a range of 5 to 7 per cent on the top of an inflationary factor.

Much more important than the particular percentage given for meritorious performance, however, is the context in which it is given. No matter what the amount of the increase, the recipient must perceive it in the right perspective if it is to foster the desired results. In other words, implicit in a "merit" increase program if the need to communicate to the recipients just what level of performance is being recognized by any given sum. If an employee is to be given an increase for performing in an average fashion, it is important that he understand that the amount he is given implies only average performance.

Assuming that there is some substance to the argument that has so far been set forth, it seems clear that there are no "magic" dollar figures or percentages that will universally convey the massage of reward for average, below-average, or above-average performance. What kind of salary-increase program. then, can we follow in order to achieve the "merit" objectives?

The importance of internal salary. We must start from a different tack altogether specifically, from the recognition that salary relationships within the company have a much greater effect upon employee attitudes than do those outside the company. As wage and salary administrators have long maintained, employees will tolerate salary inequities in relation to the external market for many more reasons than they will any discrepancy within their own firm's salary structure: This being true, the effectiveness of any merit-increase program is contingent in large part upon how the employees see two important factors.

First, the majority of the employees must perceive a favorable relation between complexity of job assignment and salary paid, i.e., they must see that, by and large, personnel with the more responsible assignments receive the higher compensation.

Second, employees must perceive a relatively high positive correlation between the size of the "merit" increases granted and on-the-job performance. This means, of course, that they must have some knowledge of which amounts represent average, above-average, and superior recognition within their firm's environment. No matter how lavish the percentage or dollar formulas a company may employ, its "merit" increase program will not achieve its aims unless the employees know what constitutes a "good" increase. Needless to say, it is equally essential that they perceive that, for the most part, the personnel putting out the greatest effort and making the largest work contributions receive the greatest recognition in terms of salary increases.

Looking back over the preceding discussion, we can now draw three conclusions that should be helpful in the conceptualization and administration of merit increases:

First, "merit" increase formulas stated in terms of 5 to 7 or 5 to 10 per cent ranges for the year constitute an oversimplification of the problem. Each particular set of figures presupposes a certain way of defining "merit" and measuring the general upward movement of salaries; thus none of them can claim to be definitive. At least from one perspective, the upward trend has been proceeding at a faster rate than these figures would suggest.

Second, because national salary movements are the product of a complex interplay of many variables, it is difficult, if not impossible, to segregate their inflationary portion from their pure "merit" portion. It is for this reason that some firms prefer the designation "individual increase" program to "merit increase" program.

Finally, every company should give top priority to making a particular increase mean something within its own environment. In the final analysis, salary increases are given for the purpose of motivation people to stay with the company and to maintain high levels of performance. If this aim is to be accomplished, the people receiving increases must know how to interpret them. Though a firm cannot afford to give salary increases that are consistently and markedly out of line with those given by its competitors, still less can it afford to let its increases become meaningless within their own environment.

Maturity Curves

In some scientific and engineering positions, the work is of such an organic nature that the use of traditional wage and salary approaches may pose problems. As one author has pointed out, "Formal position analysis, preparation of position descriptions, and position evaluation were techniques which did not readily lend themselves to application in highly technical areas, particularly where jobs had ill-defined limits and the technology was very new or rapidly changing." Such was the case in many research laboratories following World War II, especially in southern California. To cope with this lack of structure, *maturity* or *career curves* were developed as either an alternative or a supplemental approach to traditional wage and salary systems.

The curve approach is based on the assumption that salary growth should be related to the number of years a person has worked in a profession since receiving a college degree. By means of salary surveys, firms obtain data for various types of scientific positions. These data are used to form wage curves based upon salaries paid by years of experience coupled with performance. A family of such curves is illustrated in Figure 4.

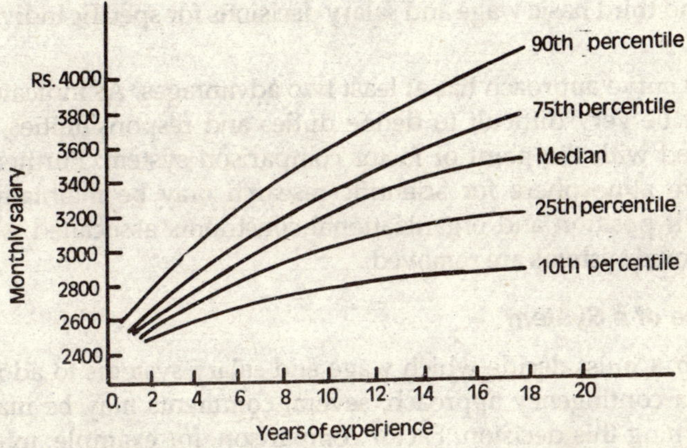

Fig. 4. Hypothetical set of maturity curves.

Such curve data can serve several functions. They help to plan the firm's overall wage level (as with wage surveys). They may help a firm compare its own internal wage structure with the surveys obtained outside the firm. This provides the firm with a control to make sure its salaries are not too high. Finally, the data may guide salary determinations for specific individuals. To meet this objective, for example, a scientist with four years of experience in the ninetieth percentile performance-wise might be given a salary of Rs.3000/month, as shown in Figure 4.

Typically, the curve approach has been utilized more to develop overall salary increase budgets than to determine specific raises for individuals. When the latter is done, however, effective performance appraisal is critical. This is because nowhere in the curve approach itself are direct references made to job descriptions or positions—its basic assumption is simply that people, as resources, become more valuable with more experience. When performance appraisal is undertaken, management will find it necessary to look at how well individuals assume responsibilities on work projects and other endeavors they have been assigned. It should also be noted that from one year to the next, a particular individual, although being evaluated on the basis of one more year's performance, may be moved up or down into a different percentile curve, depending on that person's performance. Thus, the curve approach, unlike the five traditional job evaluation methods discussed earlier, may involve the making of both the first and third basic wage and salary decisions for specific individuals.

The curve approach has at least two advantages. As indicated, it may be very difficult to define duties and responsibilities, as required with the point or factor comparison system. Further, a creative atmosphere for scientific research may be maintained better if position and organizational constraints associated with traditional systems are removed.

Choice of a System

A firm must decide which wage and salary systems to adopt. From a contingency approach, several comments may be made concerning this decision. Factor comparison, for example, might be appropriate in large firms having many blue-collar jobs which are highly programmed and precisely defined. However, in small firms a sample size large enough to utilize this system might not be available. For fluid, dynamic professional situations the maturity curve approach may be useful for reasons given earlier. Further, one observer has indicated that the more certain the task and technology, the more precisely defined jobs should be if workers are to gain a sense of competence from successful performance. Regardless of technology it has been postulated that "professional and managerial jobs change quite rapidly in a dynamic economy and do not provide a stable base for factor comparison evaluation."

Finally, with respect to contingencies, we find size of firm, degree of change facing the organization, and level in the organization (managerial and professional as opposed to nonmanagerial) important with respect to wage and salary administration as was also found with other personnel systems. Further, regardless of the numerical complexity of any wage and salary system, one must not become "hypnotized" by the numbers. Factor comparison wage rates and job points, for example, are no better outputs than the subjective judgmental inputs of those who designed the system.

ESTABLISHING THE INDIVIDUAL'S PAY ON EACH JOB

A basic question that must be decided by a firm is the extent to which performance appraisal data is to be used in giving merit increases within the rate range established for an individual's job. In using such data, management may want to consider past, present, and future performance to varying degrees. Past performance may be considered as a payment for continuing membership in the organization. Future performance, on the other hand, might be considered when "an employee who is ready to be promoted to a job for which there is no opening will receive a raise designed to prevent him from leaving before an opening occurs."

In many situations, organizations have not tied wages or salary to performance appraisal. For example, one study of the Fortune 500 list of firms showed that "a majority of them do not, in fact, relate wage and salary advancement to job performance" for nonsupervisory employees. More recently, at the top executive level, a lack of correlation was found between pay and financial performance in companies with one dominant business, while in firms comprised of a number of businesses, changes in top-level compensation were linked more closely to financial measures, such as profits and earnings per share.

In many organizations that do not related merit increases to performance, periodic wage and salary increases are based on *automatic progression.* Under this system there are a number of salary steps for each job, and individuals' compensation moves ahead, step-by-step, at predefined times and levels as long as their performance is satisfactory.

It is possible to develop a combined plan—starting an employee on an automatic raise basis up to the range midpoint, and then giving raises based on merit. In the inflationary economy that has often characterized the United States since World War II, organizations have often given *cost-of living* wage and salary raises in addition to merit ones. Additionally, some firms give one annual or semiannual raise that includes both cost-of-living and merit components. The whole question of what part of *any* raise is for merit and what part for cost of living is a very difficult one, as is the whole question of how much should be given an individual as a raise.

Several other points are in order concerning merit pay. First, with rewards for hard work an important part of the national ethic, a great number of people in our society accept the merit principle as a cultural belief. As one observer has phrased it, "Managers may like to believe that theirs is a merit company—like motherhood, apple pie, and ice cream, who can be against the merit principle."

Second, there continue to be differing opinions as to the values and limitations of the merit principle and merit systems. Emerging from this discussion of contempory value are the following points:

- □ In times of high inflation, many firms cannot give their employees merit raises high enough each year to even maintain their purchasing power, to say nothing of increasing it, meritorious performance or not.
- □ The weakest internal link in the merit pay for meritorious service chain is in firms' performance appraisal systems. As Lawler has pointed out, "at many companies, merit pay is a fiasco because the crucial link between higher pay and superior performance is missing."
- □ Now any merit pay decisions may have to be looked at even more carefully in light of possible challenges on EEO grounds which could reach the courts and be quite costly. There is special vulnerability here because meritorious (or nonmeritorious) performance is so often derived from subjective and unvalidated performance appraisals.

Various approaches have been suggested as alternatives to straight pay. One author has suggested a step progression up to the midpoint of the rate range and then periodic bonuses to distinguish performance, with satisfactory performers receiving no bonuses. This approach is still, it should be observed, open to EEO court challenges because it is based on subjective performance appraisal data.

Lawler has taken the position that bonuses have been underutilized in wage and salary system, especially group or plant-wide bonuses like Scanlon plans and the Lincoln Electric plan. The assumption here is that group performance is easier to measure than individual performance.

When all is said and done, a firm can probably contribute most to a merit pay system by developing a sound performance appraisal system as discussed in Chapter 3. In organizations where the performance on most jobs is not measurable, the best strategy is probably not to have an individual merit system.

WORKERS' COMPENSATION IN USA

Workers' compensation is the statutory system under which an employer is made liable regardless of fault, for medical care and definite monetary benefits to employees injured in its employment to compensate for loss of wages or earning capacity. It embodies the concept, now generally accepted, that economic loss due to such injury is part of the cost of production and should be incorporated in the price structure. In exchange for this definite liability, for which management can make provision through the purchase of insurance or through self-insurance, the employer is relieved of liability at law with no limit on the amount of damages that may be recovered for such injuries which may be caused by the company's negligence or that of its agents.

History

Prior to the enactment of workers' compensation laws, the employer was faced with extensive and expensive litigation if an employee were injured at work. On the other hand, the employee was faced with a slow and uncertain remedy and with the necessity of paying medical bills and living expenses in the meantime. While one injured employee might eventually obtain a substantial judgment, another might be unable to obtain any recovery at all. Even if a judgment were obtained, it might not be possible to collect it. The uncertainty of the result was increased by the existence of certain common law defenses which the employer could assert: assumption of risk, contributory negligence, and the negligence of a fellow servant. However, even before the enactment of workers' compensation laws, courts and legislatures had begun to limit the application of such defenses.

Dissatisfaction with this situation, by both employers and employees, caused a search for a better remedy. This was found in workers' compensation which provided prompt payment of definite benefits regardless of the question of negligence. The first valid state workers' compensation law was enacted in 1911. Ten states enacted workers' compensation laws in that year. The Federal Government had previously enacted a law covering Government employees engaged in hazardous operations in 1908. A few crude attempts to provide compensation, very limited in scope, were enacted by one or two states about the same time, but most of them were held invalid.

In those days the concept of making an employer liable for an injury where he was not at fault was controversial, and the constitutionality of such laws was often attacked. A law enacted in New York in 1910 providing for compulsory compensation in certain hazardous employment, Chapter 674 Laws of 1910, was held unconstitutional in the case of *Ives v. South Buffalo Railroad Company,* 201 N.Y. 271. Some states adopted constitutional amendments to make certain of the validity of compensation acts. Others adopted elective statutes. Now such laws have gained general acceptance both by employers and labor, and have usually been upheld by the courts. Most of the early workers' compensation acts in this country were patterned somewhat after the British Compensation Act enacted in 1987.

Today there are workers' compensation laws in every state, the District of Columbia, and Puerto Rico, and in some form in most of the countries in the world.

Development of these laws in this country was somewhat curtailed by economic conditions prevailing during the Great Depression of the 1930s, followed by World War II. With the removal of wartime wage and price controls, a sharp escalation of wages and prices occurred. However, workers compensation benefits, dependent on legislative action, did not keep pace with the wage-price spiral, and Congressional concern developed.

In 1971, president Richard Nixon, pursuant to act of the Congress, appointed a national Commission on State Workmen's Compensation laws, on which the undersigned had the privilege to serve. The Commission's report aroused a great deal of interest among legislators, administrators, and business and labor groups. Benefit and coverage improvements were recommended, but these were conditioned on other recommendations relating to administration.

Great legislative activity followed submission of the report, directed primarily at benefit and coverage aspects of the problem. Recommendations covering improvements in the operations of the system remained largely unimplemented. At the same time, the courts, as they have in other areas of liability during this period, greatly broadened the concepts of what injuries, illnesses and disabilities were compensable under those laws. The effect of these developments has had a substantial cost impact. Benefit payments increased from some what over $ 3.5 billion dollars in 1971 to over and 10 billion in 1979. The cost of workers' compensation is presently (1980) causing some concern.

Compulsory or Elective

As indicated above, a number of state laws were at one time elective. Today, the laws in all but three states are compulsory. In these states, employers and employees subject to the Act must comply with its provisions. In two additional states, for constitutional reasons, employees but not employers may elect not to be covered. Because of the generally accepted view that coverage under workers' compensation laws is desirable, the right of election is seldom it ever exercised.

Scope and Coverage. It has been estimated that about 88% of employees today are covered by compensation laws. Two large classes of employees that are not fully covered are agricultural employees engaged in interstate commerce are covered by the Federal Employers' Liability Act. In some states, specific employment. e.g., recipients of charitable aid, professional athletes, executive officers, etc., are excluded. The present trend is to bring practically all employments under the acts. Fourteen states still have numerical exemptions, but in seven, only companies with two or less employees are excluded. The highest exemption is five, in Missouri. Thirty-nine jurisdictions have no numerical exemption provisions for covered employments. In nearly all states an employer can elect voluntarily to bring exempted employments under the act.

Security

Nearly all laws require that an employer subject to the Act must insure or otherwise secure his liability to his employees. This can usually be done through the purchase of insurance from a company authorized to do business in the state. Most states also will permit large employers, who are of sufficient financial stability, to "self-insure" upon making a substantial deposit of money, security, or bonds and assuming the obligation to pay all compensation claims directly. In some states, a form of reciprocal co-insurance known as "group self-insurance" is permitted. In six states and Puerto Rico insurance must be obtained from a monopolistic state compensation fund. These funds were created in the early days of compensation, before the advantages of competitive insurance became apparent. The last of such funds was created 1919. In twelve other states, there are state funds which operate in competition with insurance companies. Most employers obtain coverage from insurance companies rather than from a state fund.

Rate for workers' compensation insurance are scientifically calculated and subject to regulation by the various state insurance commissioners under rate regulatory laws. Early in the operation of workers' compensation laws, it was recognized that the pooling of experience would be of great value in the determination of proper rates. At the request of the National Association of Insurance Commissioners, a national rate making organization, the National Council on Compensation Insurance (One Penn Plaza, New York, N.Y. 10119), was organized in 1922. In some states, however, there are individual state rating bureaus. Presently (1980), increasing attention is being given to the feasibility of allowing greater interplay of competition under such laws, while maintaining the necessary data base.

Rating plans and methods are constantly being reviewed and improved to give the insured the benefit of improved experience. These are designed to give an employer an incentive to maintain effective safety programs. Insurance companies have been among the leaders in the field of safety. They are in a position to assist employers in making such programs effective, to their joint advantage. As a result of cooperative efforts among employers, employees, government, and insurance companies, countrywide, the frequency rate of industrial injuries was reduced between 1926 and 1972 by 68% and severity rate by 73%. There was a further improvement of 14% between 1972 and 1977 in the new rate of recordable injuries under the system instituted under OSHA (occupational Safety and Health Act).

Even though many factors have increased workers' compensation costs, overall premiums for workers' compensation amount to only about 2% of payroll, largely because of effective safety work. The security features are a vital part of the compensation system because they assure that the employee will receive all benefits due him or her in the event an injury occurs, and at the same time enable the employer to know or accurately estimate in advance the cost of this protection.

Injuries Covered

Worker's compensation laws of all states cover accidental injuries arising out of and in the course of employment. This has been liberally construed to apply to injuries resulting from a variety of situations related to employment activity. In some states the reference to "accidents" is omitted. In addition, in all states, there is broad coverage of occupational diseases. Formerly, in some states only specifically listed occupational diseases were covered.

The tendency has been constantly to broaden coverage of injuries in workers' compensation laws. This subject is presently (1980) receiving increased attention. Industry is concerned that it may be held liable for conditions which are not causally related to the employment. Others contend that employees are not receiving compensation for disabilities due to exposures which have not been recognized and may be long past. Current laws provide broad coverage for present exposures. Equitable solutions for the effects of long-past exposures which antedate current laws may be more difficult to achieve. This has been attempted in the Federal Black Lung Benefits Act for coal miners under which financing and other problems have developed with costs to the Federal Government, now being transferred in part to private industry, exceeding one billion dollars a year.

Medical Benefits. In all states the employer is obliged to provide unlimited medical benefits. (At one time a number of states had limitations on such benefits.)

The emphasis in workers' compensation today is on rehabilitation rather than indemnity. It is obviously far preferable to restore the injured employee, if possible, to useful employment than to compensate for any wage loss. The quality of medical and physical care plays a very important part in reaching these results. In most states it is the obligation of the employer and the insurance carrier to supply such care, but in a number of states the employee can obtain such care at the expense of the employer. In actual practice it has been found that some guidance in obtaining the best medical care available is beneficial to the employee.

Indemnity Benefits

Monetary benefits, usually referred to as "compensation," are payable under workers' compensation laws for the following disabilities:

Temporary Total Disability. This is the most frequent type of disability. It covers cases where an employee is unable to engage in employment for a limited period of time because of a work-connected injury. Compensation in such case is usually payable at the rate of 66 2/3% of the employee's average weekly wages, subject to a specified weekly maximum and minimum.

In many states, the maximum for injuries occurring in a particular year is adjusted annually to reflect changes in the average state wage. In 30 states, such maximum must equal 100% or more of the state average weekly wage. In some states, the weekly benefit, once established, is adjusted in the future to reflect changes in wage levels or the cost of living in long-term disability and death cases. The maximum applicable in the different states ranges from $650 a week in Alaska to $98 a week in Mississippi. As of July 1, 1980, in forty-two state jurisdictions, the weekly maximum amounted to $150 or more and the average countrywide was $219.82. In some states the weekly maximum is increased if there are dependents.

Permanent Total Disability. This is intended to cover cases where the injury is so severe that the employee is permanently unable to return to employment. Fortunately, these cases are infrequent. In some states, certain disabilities such as blindness or loss of two major members are presumed to constitute permanent total disability either conclusively or rebutably. Through remarkable advances in rehabilitation, persons who previously would have been disabled for life are today increasingly returning to useful employment, or at least, they become able to take care of their personal needs without assistance.

Concepts of what constitutes disability are constantly being broadened. Factors other than physical ability to perform work are taken into consideration. In some states, compensation must be paid without a formal finding of permanent total disability where the employee has a considerable degree of earning capacity.

Compensation for permanent total disability is usually payable at the same rate as temporary total disability, but in some states the weekly amount of such compensation is reduced after a certain period of time. As of January 1, 1980, in 45 jurisdictions such benefits were payable for life. In others, there is a monetary overall limit ranging from $42,000 to $120,624.

Temporary Partial Disability. This covers cases where an employee temporarily suffers partial wage loss as a result of an injury. This may be due to inability for a time to perform full- time work, or temporarily having to perform lighter duties at a reduced rate. Usually compensation in such cases is payable on the basis of a percentage of the loss in earning capacity subject again to a specified weekly maximum. In one state (Massachusetts), compensation is payable for the full difference in earnings subject to a maximum of $45,000. In a few states a minimum as well as a maximum is specified, but this sometimes causes inequitable results where the difference in earnings happens to be less than the minimum specified.

Permanent Partial Disability. This category covers cases where the injury results in a permanent condition which is partially disabling. In most cases, compensation for such conditions is payable for a period specified in a schedule listing such disabilities. These usually refer either to complete or to partial loss or loss of use of specified members. The weekly amount of compensation is usually subject to the maximum and minimum applicable to cases of temporary total disability. The scheduled payments are intended to compensate for possible future loss of earning capacity even though no loss of earnings may be suffered after the healing period. Usually the amount of payment under such a schedule constitutes the full remedy for such injuries, but in a few states additional compensation is payable if there is actual wage loss. In a few states, benefits for permanent partial disability are based primarily on wage loss.

naturally, it is not possible to list all permanent partial disabilities in this schedule. Many laws, therefore, provide that in "other cases" compensation is payable on a basis of percentage of loss of earning capacity, subject again to a specified maximum. In some states compensation is payable in such cases on the basis of a percentage of a person as a whole.

Waiting Period

In all states a waiting period of a few days is provided before compensation is payable. In 23 states it is three days, in 22, one week. This is intended to eliminate cases involving very minor injuries for which a very limited amount of compensation would be payable. The loss of wages for this period presents no serious hardship and the administrative cost of providing such benefits would outweigh the benefits which the employee would receive. In all states, if disability extends beyond a specified time (in many states two weeks), benefits become payable from the first day of disability.

Death Benefits

In the event of death due to an injury, payment of funeral expenses and compensation for dependents of the worker are provided in all states. Benefits to children are usually paid until they reach eighteen years of age, or over that age if they are physically incapacitated. In a number of states, the age limit is somewhat extended while a child is a full-time student. Compensation to the widow is usually paid during widowhood. In some states a lump-sum payment is made upon remarriage. Usually, death benefits, subject to a weekly maximum, are based on a percentage of the employees earnings. Subject to this maximum, provisions is usually made for payments to other dependents such as brothers or sisters or parents.

In fourteen states an overall maximum is provided as to either time or amount.

Third Party Actions

Most workers' compensation laws provide for a right of subrogation (i.e., some method of reimbursement for compensation and medical benefits) to the employer and his insurer against the employee's tight of action again a third party who may have caused a compensable injury. In the past, these presented no serious problem, being applicable usually to motor vehicle accidents and the like. Under the broadened rules of liability established by the courts with respect to products in recent years, there has been increased litigation involving either machinery or other products used in the employment where the rights of the different parties are more difficult to determine.

Administration

Workers' compensation laws are usually administered by a board or commission or by an individual administrator. In five states such laws are administered by the courts. However, since this is a specialized field, administration by persons who devote full time to this work is generally deemed preferable.

Payment is made in about nine out of ten of the cases without controversy. The relatively simple remedy and the avoidance of litigation are an important feature of the workers' compensation system.

Information on the operation of the law in a particular state may be obtained from the appropriate administrative agency.

Role of the Personnel Department

If any wage and salary plane is to be effective, the personnel department must develop effective working relationships with line management, employees, and unions. As with other personnel activities, top-management support is critical. Further, one function of the personnel department is that of training line managers in wage and salary administration, Zollitsch and Langsner have expressed the belief that this is especially true for first-line supervisors. They have indicated that these supervisors "carry the burden of most administrative activities involved in maintaining and equitable wage and salary plan." Employees look to their superiors for answers about how their pay plan works, and the supervisor must be knowledgeable in this area.

Both establishing and updating wage and salary plans are important. In general, with larger companies, the personnel department will conduct the wage and salary surveys (or obtain such data elsewhere), and submit these data to top-level management for final approval of the firm's first basic decision—determination of the firm's overall wage level. Further, such data must be updated annually.

With respect to the second major wage and salary decision—establishing the wage structure for each job—personnel will often find it most desirable to gain input from line managers, employees themselves, and sometimes unions. For example, in one company, individual employees filled out job summary questionnaires, then the supervisors reviewed and modified the questionnaires (if necessary) and returned them to the personnel department, job evaluations for each job were carried out by the personnel department, and salary evaluation results were presented to top divisional management for final approval. From a contingency point of view, updating job evaluations and descriptions will be especially important in firms which are dynamic and in which the content of specific jobs changes frequently. In such cases, employees and their supervisors may tend to bring the change to the attention of the personnel department if the work content if upgraded and a higher rate range is called for, but they tend not to report changes that downgrade jobs. Further, with respect to the third basic decision area—establishing pay for individuals on a job—some supervisors may tend to push for high salary increases for their personnel.

For these two reasons, an effective wage and salary system needs to establish some effective control mechanism. In larger organizations, a committee of wage and salary personnel specialists, line managers, and employees often may be established to review job evaluations and salary increases on some sort of periodic basis. One of the primary values of committees so structured is to gain employee acceptance of any necessary updating changes (as well as to introduce the plan initially).

Finally, one specific control technique had been developed for monitoring job description data. This is the so-called *compa- ratio*. The compa-ratio is defined as

$$\frac{\text{Average of all salaries within any grade}}{\text{Midpoint of the salary range}}$$

The compa-ratio can help pinpoint wage and salary administration problems for control purposes if (1) salary ranges exist and (2) the midpoint of the range represents a "good competitive level which need not, on the average, be exceeded."

Two points of broader significance emerge from this discussion of compa-ratios. First, with ratio analysis, in general, one must look behind the actual numbers and ask why, as may be seen with the different possible interpretations of the above compa-ratios. Second, following the concept of personnel departments assuming the control function, we recommend that the personnel department generally show any possible wage and salary problem to the line manager first. Then, if discussions indicate that there are problems and the manager involved refuses to deal with them, personnel may have to go over the manager's head to higher-level management.

EXECUTIVE COMPENSATION

Some time ago, it was quite acceptable—and even considered good from—to pay an individual only a salary. Gradually, however, pay began to take on added dimensions, to become a package rather than a single entity. In today's complex business world, we find this trend most marked in the way executives—a company's upper-middle and top managers—are paid. The elements which collectively comprise the Executive Compensation package of these individuals include: base salary, incentives for short-term performance, incentives for longer-term performance, perquisites, and fringe benefits.

The salary an executive receives is influenced by at least seven major factors:

1. **Type of Responsibilities.** Here are considered the skills and experience necessary to do the job, and the types of output desired.

2. **Level Within the Organization.** The less the number of intervening management levels between the executive and the CEO, the higher is likely to be the salary.

3. **Scope of Responsibilities.** Two company CEOs may have the same type of responsibilities, and both occupy the same level within the organization. But the one with the greater sales volume to manage is apt to receive the higher salary. Sales volume, profits, assets, number of employees and other similar factors measure the scope of the executive's job. Many correlation studies show that

about 40% to 50% of the variance in executive salary levels can be accounted for by differences in position scope.

4. **Type of Industry.** Differences in pay among various industries, while once pronounced, are gradually eroding as talented executives from one industry move to another. It is more often the case today that pay differences cut across industry lines, being associated more with company performance, management challenge, and governmental regulation. Thus, high-performing companies in two different industries may pay more like each other than high-performing and low-performing companies in the same industry. And running a highly diversified, multinational company generally involves more challenge than running a company engaged in a single industry servicing only United States customers. Finally, heavy government regulation has a dampening effect on executive pay, as witnessed by the pay levels in most power utilities.

5. **Presence of Incentives.** Companies with executives bonus plans tend to pay lower base salaries than those without such plans, but the combination of base salary and bonus in the bonus-paying companies almost always exceeds the lone salary paid by the other companies.

6. **Supply/Demand Factors.** In many ways, the "career executive" is becoming a contradiction in terms. Executive talent is essentially a free market commodity, and its price therefore varies according to the classic laws of supply and demand. For example, marketing executives were typically paid more than production and financial executives during the Depression, since an ability to move goods in a ravaged economy was highly prized. During World War II and the early 50s, however, it was the production man who was the highest paid, reflecting the fact that a company could sell virtually anything if it could only make it. Today, we see the financial man emerging as the compensation "star," owing to the stress being placed on capable asset management, and in controlling diversified, decentralized global enterprises.

7. **Performance.** The outstanding executive is apt to receive more than the mediocre one, but this is not always the case, since base salaries go up but hardly ever down, and therefore most

managements see that they don't go up very fast. It is hard to reward performance properly when the compensation device being utilized contains a good deal of inertia.

INCENTIVES FOR SHORT-TERM PERFORMANCE

Because of the problem mentioned in connection with performance, the great majority of companies offer their executive personnel an opportunity to earn extra money based on the performance of the company, the unit in which the executive is employed, his personal performance—or all three factors.

Eligibility and Size of Awards

Eligibility for participation in executive bonus plans is typically limited to about the top 1% to 2% of total employment, depending on company size and type of industry. Awards range from Zero all the way up to 300% of salary, although it is more common to "cap" bonuses at 100% of the base salary. There is a distinct tendency for bonuses, expressed as a percentage of salary, to rise as the salary level rises. Thus, the average bonus for an individual earning Rs. 50,000 per year is around 20% of salary, but the comparable figure for one earning Rs. 150,000 per year is about 50% of salary.

There are two reasons for this trend, but one is no longer markedly valid. The first involves risk vs. reward. By discounting a senior executive's total cash compensation opportunity by a higher percentage than is utilized for a less senior executive, the former ends up with a lower base salary in relation to his/her total case compensation opportunity than the latter. Hence, if the company performs poorly, the senior executive will experience relatively more pain than the less senior one. But fair is fair: if the company performs brilliantly, the former will also experience more joy.

The second reason involves taxes. When a tax structure is steeply progressive, it is necessary to give a more senior executive a larger bonus percentage if his/her *after-tax* total compensation is to exhibit the same percentage increase as is the case for a less senior executive. Today, however, tax structure is not very "progressive." Maximum marginal tax rates on salaries and bonuses, which once ranged as high as 91%, have remained at 50% for about the past ten years. Given inflation, this means that almost anyone worthy of being called an executive will be at the same marginal tax rate as the CEO. Hence, the tax argument for differential bonus percentages is now moot. But since the risk vs. reward argument is not, the pattern of accelerating bonus percentages will likely continue.

Funding Formula

The funds required for bonus purposes are sometimes voted by the board of directors on an *ad hoc* basis, but more often, they are generated by a specially designed formula which is applied to the company's income statement and balance sheet. Although numerous formulas are used, a typical one would be as follows:

> 5% of pre-tax profits which are in excess of an amount equal to a 14% return on stockholders' equity but are less than a 21% return; plus 10% of pre-tax profits which are in excess of an amount equal to a 21% return on stockholders' equity.

This formula has several major features:

Performance Parameter. It rewards, not for raw profits per se, but for an increasing return on the stockholders' investment. Thus, it "incents" the company's executives to give the stockholders a better return than they could receive from alternative sources.

Elimination of Tax Effect. It is based on pretax, rather than after-tax, earnings, since changes in Federal income tax rates are essentially beyond the control of the company's executives.

As of 1980, a number of companies were beginning to have second thoughts regarding the non-controllability of income taxes. First, an executive faced with the need to build a new plant or other facility can elect to switch operations to another state with a lower tax rate, as even to another country. Second, the U.S. Government is itself in the incentive compensation business. Among other things, it offers companies a tax credit for making new investments. Finally, even though an executive may not be able to counter the effects of a tax increase, he/she can adopt other strategies (raising prices, cutting costs) to deliver the same bottom-line result to the shareholders. Because of these factors, the majority of newly adopted bonus plans are geared to rewarding after-tax, not pre- tax, profits.

Deductible. It reserves all of the first portion of company profits for the stockholders. In our example, incentive funds are created only when the return on stockholders' equity is at least 14%.

Accelerator. It recognizes that it is harder to move from above average to outstanding performance than it is from mediocre to average performance. Thus, the executives get 5% of the middle slice of corporate profits. But 10% of the top slice.

Allocating the Bonus Fund

Having created an over-all incentive fund, the company must then decide how it should be apportioned among the executive group. Here, several methods are available. If the company is divisionalized, chunks of the over-all fund may be distributed to each division based on its particular performance achievements for the year. That approach may certainly motivate individual division performance, but it may also unwittingly create a certain divisiveness among the various division managers—especially when it comes to allocating scarce capital resources and to transferring good people. As a result, many companies will distribute most, but not all, of the fund based on divisional performance, and will distribute the remainder based on over-all corporate performance. In this manner, division general managers are given an incentive, admittedly often symbolic, to play ball on the corporate team to the extent required.

In distributing its own fund, a division in turn may employ one of three methods. It may apportion all awards pro rata to salary, it may distribute awards based solely on individual executive performance, or it may utilize a combination of these approaches. The first method obviously encourages a maximum degree of teamwork, but it certainly gives no incentive for individual excellence. The second method does that, but it may possibly squire a group of "prima donnas" as well. The combination approach, on the other hand, seeks to achieve the best of both worlds: some team work and a large amount of individual initiative.

Payment Methods and Media

Awards, once decided upon, are typically paid in cash and in a lump-sum shortly after the close of the fiscal year on which they are predicated. Sometimes negotiable company stock is used, or a combination of cash and stock, with perhaps enough cash to pay the taxes on the entire award. Other companies employ forcible deferrals, where, for example, the award is paid out in five annual installments, with the individual forfeiting any subsequent installments if he voluntarily resigns.

This approach is supposedly justified on the grounds that it will hold down the executive's tax payment and will also help to retain good executives. In fact, it is likely to do neither. With lower marginal income tax rates and an income-averaging provision built into the tax law, there is little advantage in spreading bonus payments over a series of years. And from a motivational standpoint, forced deferrals—derisively called the "golden handcuffs" approach by many executives—are uniformly resented. If they hold anyone, they are likely to hold a company's mediocrity, since the best performers can be bought off by a competitor.

Still other companies offer optional, as opposed to forced, deferrals. The executive can take his award in cash, or he can defer any part or all of it. He can choose the length of the deferral period, the number of years over which the award will be paid, the types of securities in which it will be invested and even the disposition of dividends and interest. Although there is relatively little tax advantage in deferred compensation payments, there is some motivational appeal in giving each executive what he wants, when he wants it.

INCENTIVES FOR LONGER-TERM PERFORMANCE

Not too long ago, the results of most executive decisions were realized in the very same year in which the decisions were made. Now however, technological complexity has created a situation where the results of major decisions are often not known for many years. To illustrate, an oil company may decide to build a giant petrochemical facility, whose cost will be $500 million. Just designing the plant may take one or two years; three or four years more may be required for it to be built. And perhaps a one- or two-year period is needed to break in the plant and bring it up to peak efficiency.

All told, five to eight years will thus have elapsed between the time the decision to build the petrochemical complex was made and the time that the profit results of that decision could be judged. Meanwhile, the company incurred significant cost for engineering talent, interest charges on $ 500 million of debt, and so on. During that period, its profits would have been increased had it not decided to build the facility. And if its profits had been increased the incentive bonuses payable to its executives for short-term performance would also have increased. Yet not to build the facility might have meant parlous times for the company five years later.

Thus, incentives to maximize the current years' profits, although satisfactory as far as they go, do not go far enough in motivating optimum business behavior. What are needed are *additional* incentives for performance, not in a single year, but over the longer term. Once monolithic in their design (all companies used to employ the qualified stock option, a device that has now been killed by Congress), long-term incentives today fall into a number of categories, as indicated below.

Plans Based on Increasing the Market Price of the Stock

The plan of choice in this category is the *non-qualified stock option.* Although the plan designer can call for any option price he/she likes and any length of exercise period, it is almost always the case that the option price will be equal to 100% of the fair market value (FMV) of the stock on the date of the grant, and that the option will have a term of ten years. The underlying theory here is that if the company does well over a series of years, its performance will be reflected in a higher stock price, thereby creating a "spread" between the option price and the FMV at exercise. From a tax standpoint, the executive incurs no tax until exercise takes place, and then the "spread" is taxed at personal service income rates (maximum of 50%).

Should the executive hold the stock past exercise, any further gain or loss between the date of exercise and the date of eventual sale is treated as a capital gain or loss. For its part, the company is granted a tax deduction in the year of exercise and for an amount equal to the option "spread." What more, if the company follows the plan design discussed above, it need not charge its earnings with the option "spread." However, this dose not mean there is no cost to an option, as some believe. Rather, the cost is buried in the balance sheet and is not so visible as would be the cost of a comparable amount of cash.

Options create problems for corporate officers, however. Being subject to the "insider trading" provisions of the Securities Exchange Act, these executives are effectively barred from selling their option stock for six months. As a result, they are saddled with interest costs to carry stock purchase loans and, worse, should the stock decline during the six-month holding period, they can end up receiving no gain but still paying the taxes attributable to the gain on exercise.

Because of these problems, many companies have added so-called *stock appreciation rights* (SARs) to their option arrangements. Under current SEC rules, a company can, under certain circumstances, permit the executive to receive a cash payment equal to his/her option "spread" in lieu of exercising the option itself. This cash payment would not be considered to be in violation of SEC "buy-sell" provisions. But it would have to be charged to earnings, which is why SARs are typically extended only to the most senior executives (Assuming the option shares are registered and that there is no formal or informal pressure applied to hold shares past exercise, a non-insider can create his/her own "do-it-yourself SAR" simply by selling the shares as soon as they are exercised. The individual gains the same cash payment as the insider, but the company is not forced to take a charge to its earnings.)

Plans Based on Internal Performance Measurements

While one cannot deny the validity of the argument that excellent corporate performance will, sooner or later, be validated by an increasing FMV (else the stock would eventually sell for less than its earnings per share!), the stock market, at least at this writing, seems bent on proving the proposition that the FMV will rise later, and never sooner.

The fact is that one major component of the FMV—the price/earnings multiple—is simply outside the control of any executive. To be sure, a well-aimed PR campaign might have some effect on the P/E multiple, but the effect will be transitory. It is sad but true that the Chairman of the Federal Reserve and, indeed, the Chairman of the Soviet Union can have more effect on the P/E multiple of a given company's stock that that company's own chairman. Because of this, some companies have eliminated the FMV incentive in their long-term incentive programs and have instead geared payouts to *long-term corporate performance achieve-*

ments. Thus, one company might offer its executive a large bonus opportunity for achieving, say, a 15% compounded annual increase in earnings per share (EPS) over a five-year period. Or another company might offer the same payout for delivering, say, a 20% average return on equity over the same period. In either event, the executive is being rewarded for performance that is truly in the shareholders' interest and that is more under his/her control. Plans for this type are generally called "performance unit" plans.

Combination Plans

Although few companies have seen fit to remove entirely the FMV component in their long-term incentive plans, and to move to pure performance unit plans, a large and growing number of companies have decided to adopt a *combination plan,* whereby an executive receives a lesser number of option shares than was the case in the past, together with a number of performance units. In this manner, the executive is being simultaneously "incented" to deliver excellent long-term internal performance and to do what he/she can to raise the FMV.

Other Plans

In a few companies, the executive is granted the same number of option shares as he or she would be granted were the company to employ only options. Then the executive is also granted the same number of performance units as would be granted were the company to employ only performance units. At the end of the performance period, usually four or five years, the executive is then permitted to take whichever of the incentive devices—the options or the units—has the most economic benefit. The device not chosen is then cancelled.

Under such a plan, the executive really ends up with the best of both worlds. If the company performs brilliantly, but the P/E multiple has sagged, the executive ends up with the same economic benefit as he/she would have received from a company offering only performance units. And if the company performs in only a mediocre manner but the P/E multiple unaccountably rises, the executive ends up with the same economic benefit as he or she would have received from a company offering only stock options. Small wonder that executives love this sort of plan. Equally small wonder that informed shareholders do not.

In some other companies, although happily not too many, the executive is given free shares of stock. The shares carry restrictions such that they cannot be sold for, say, five year. During the five-year period, the executive receives dividends and may vote the shares. However, if he or she quits before the restrictions lapse, the shares are forfeited back to the company.

To gain an economic benefit under a performance unit plan, the executive must deliver solid, long-term performance achievements. To gain an economic benefit under an option plan, the FMV of the stock must rise. But to gain an economic benefit under the plan we are now discussing, the executive need only breathe in and out approximately seventeen times a minute for five years and exhibit a positive pupil reflex. After all, if the executive remains with the company, the only way he or she can gain nothing under the plan is if the FMV plummets to zero—an event that makes any long-term incentive plan an academic matter.

Eligibility

If there are few people in an organization who have a significant impact on annual operating results, there are even fewer who impact long-term results. Hence, eligibility for long-term incentive plans is typically more restrictive than that for annual bonus plans. However, companies employing stock options tend to be more liberal than those employing performance unit plans. The reason, of course, lies in the earlier discussed fact that most stock option plans do not carry a charge to the earnings.

Frequency of Awards

Most companies follow the practice of making annual long-term incentive grants. Thus, in 1981, an executive will receive a contingent grant based on performance to be delivered during 1982 through 1985. And in 1982, he or she will receive another contingent grant based on performance to be delivered during 1983 through 1986.

Size of Awards

Perhaps reflecting the necessity to look more to the long-term than the short-term, many companies now offer their senior executives more in the way of long-term incentive opportunity than they do in annual bonus opportunity. Among the larger companies, it is not at all uncommon to find that the annualized value of long-term incentive opportunities significantly exceeds 100% of the base salary. Thus, if the company's performance is excellent over a series of years, the executive will receive more of his total compensation through long-term incentive payments than through any other medium.

PERQUISITES

Lastly, we come to a rather shadowy group of compensation elements, which, taken together, are called perquisites. These include such things as: lavishly furnished offices; company cars; chauffeured limousines; luncheon club memberships; country club memberships; corporate jets; extra medical insurance coverage; extra life insurance coverage; enhanced pensions; and personal financial counseling. Perquisites, such as these, are typically offered for one or both of the following reasons:

Status

Any item, whether of high value or virtually no value, that is given to those generally perceived to be high-ranking and that is not given to those generally perceived to be of lesser rank carries instant status implications. Increasingly, companies are discovering, as armies have known for millenia, that the need for status is never dead, no matter how ostensibly democratic is the society. Executives are often apt to denigrate the value of status symbols ("It's what's in the little old paycheck that counts"), but if actions speak louder than words, they crave them deeply.

Tax Considerations

Many perquisites can be offered to the executive on a wholly or at least partially tax-free basis. This is one reason why perquisites are rampant in countries such as England, where the maximum marginal tax rates border on the confiscatory. It should be noted, however, that the Internal Revenue Service is taking an increasingly stringent view towards perquisites, and most are therefore short-lived from the standpoint of producing any significant tax advantage. And in any event, perquisites constitute a very small fraction of the executives's total compensation package.

CASE : THE CURVE APPROACH TO THE COMPENSATION OF SCIENTISTS

During the years following World War II, new approach to the compensation of scientists emerged in such organizations as the University of California's Los Alamos Scientific laboratory, Hughes Aircraft company, and Space Technology laboratories. The new technique—which reputedly had its genesis at the Bell Telephone Laboratories in the 1930's—has been variously identified by such names as "the maturity curve," "the career curve," "the octile system," and "the individual contributor approach."

Regardless of designation, the several curve programs have in common a philosophy and related methodology that represent a significant departure from the familiar classification systems. Traditionally, classification systems employ classical position analysis and evaluation techniques. The curve approach, on the other hand, relates salary to the variables of educational attainment, maturity or experience, and relative job performance, making no direct reference to actual position responsibilities.

It should be emphasized that this description is of the curve system in its raw form and that there is a great deal of variation in the practical from and application of the curve approach. This variation ranges from the use of a curve merely as a descriptive market reference to its use as a mechanism for arriving at individual salary determinations. Some compensation managers will claim that the maturity factor has absolutely no bearing in their curve system and that salary apportionment is at management discretion through such control devices as the salary increase budget. On the other hand, many compensation managers will attempt to somehow integrate position evaluation and job criteria with their curve programs. Such differences from one curve approach to another will subsequently be discussed in some detail, but for the moment it is sufficient merely to indicate the range of this variation. It is more important to appreciate the major shift in emphasis that that the curve system has brought to formal salary determination processes.

The Postwar Experience

The historical origins of the curve approach are not entirely clear, but one gains the impression that its early use occurred somewhat independently and in varying forms at several organizations. This being the case, it is difficult to pinpoint without some speculation the basic forces behind the evolution and development of curve programs. However, based on the historical facts that are known, as well as an analysis of current problems in scientific compensation, it is possible to make some pertinent observations and deductions.

First, the curve approach is basically a phenomenon of the period after World War II and accompanied the growth of scientific research and development. The increase of defense contracts and the concomitant surge in demand for large numbers of engineers and scientists also encouraged the use of the technique. Shortly after the close of the war, the Los Alamos Scientific Laboratory, an Atomic Energy Commission contractor, put into use a curve system for compensating its scientific personnel. In doing so, the Los Alamos management wished to create an environment compatible with scientific research and emulating, to an extent, the academic environment of top-flight universities. It was, apparently, also believed that application of the classical salary techniques would not be entirely consistent with this aim.

Throughout the late 1940's and early 1950's more organizations adopted the curve approach for compensating their scientific staffs. For the most part, these organizations could be characterized as being small- to medium-sized laboratories. A number of them were nonprofit organizations doing work related to the national interest. But there were, in addition, other users of this new compensation technique. Major industrial firms such as Hughes Aircraft Company and General Electric had also developed curve systems for compensating their scientific personnel.

Undoubtedly, the initial motivation for the adoption of some form of the curve approach was the goal of maintaining a creative atmosphere conducive to scientific research. This was based on the contention that removal of position and organization restraints associated with classification systems would promote self-actualization and creativity in the scientist. However, other factors also played a part in encouraging the spread of curve systems. One of these was the ever increasing shortage of engineers and scientists. The inadequate number of qualified personnel created a number of problems from the salary administration point of view. For example, many organizations instituted college recruiting practices in an effort to stockpile graduates. Students frequently were hired directly off the campus many months before their graduation and with no specific job in mind. This practice is no longer as common as it once was. However, the main point is that a condition precedent to classical position analysis and evaluation is a well-defined set of duties and responsibilities. When no such condition existed, and in the absence of other scales of reference, the best an employer could do was to evaluate job potential based on observations of relevant individual qualifications. This set of circumstances and practices was not limited to the new graduate. It applied to senior scientists and engineers as well.

Even when an employer could offer a position with specific duties, quite frequently he found that the salary range established by the classical methods had to give way to the upward pressure on salaries in the scientific and engineering labor markets. Again, this conflict between salaries established in the labor market and those established by internal hob evaluation plans applied not only to the new college graduate level but to all scientific and engineering levels. Evaluation points assigned to technical positions often would not result in a salary high enough to meet labor market demands. On the other hand, internal administrative problems arose if such positions were given the same evaluation as other positions in a company but were paid a higher salary as a result of the market pressures.

This conflict, however, generally could be resolved by the simple expedient of establishing a separate salary structure for the scientific and engineering positions. Even then, extremely difficult mechanical problems occurred in applying the classical salary methods to scientists and engineers. Formal position analysis, preparation of position descriptions, and position evaluation were techniques which did not readily lend themselves to application in highly technical areas, particularly where jobs had ill-defined limits and the technology was very new or rapidly changing.

Perhaps it would not have been impossible to use the classical techniques in these areas, but the staff work required was so extensive—especially in organizations where the scientists and engineers were hired in mass numbers—that the anticipated costs were frequently prohibitive. Therefore, a turn toward a technique such as the curve approach, which on the face of it seemed simpler and far less expensive to administer, was a natural outgrowth of this situation. Furthermore, the curve approach had considerable flexibility of application when it involved such internal processes as personnel transfer or reassignment.

In addition to the problem areas discussed, there were other consideration that militated against the use of classical methods. Certainly there was some lack of acceptance, both by scientists and scientific management, of the validity of existing evaluation techniques. In the same vein, there was some lack of confidence in a nonscientific job analyst's understanding and judgment insofar as scientific jobs were concerned. More implicit than expressed was a feeling that the engineer or scientist, as a professional, should be viewed in light of his personal qualification rather than his job duties. Such status implications in certain organizational environments have been a significant barrier to the use of evaluation plans.

It was probably just such problems which led Los Alamos and other organizations to a curve approach. All of these difficulties, in greater or lesser degree, continue to exist in the contemporary setting, and though many firms have tried and rejected the curve system, it appears that this technique—in one or another of its forms—has been gaining in favor as a tool to cope with these problems.

Curve Derivation and Applications

The curve approach, in the usual case, is based on the premise that salary growth is related to educational attainment, job performance, and maturity factors—that is, years of applicable experience, age, or years since receipt of the bachelor's degree. Typically, the curves themselves are depicted in a fashion similar to that shown in Figure 5.

The actual derivation process is normally based upon labor market surveys. These may be quite general or quite specific regarding such things as field of specialization, degree level, and the like. However, for the purpose of developing the curves, the degree of specificity makes no difference, for the mechanical procedure remains the same. The process simply consists of collecting the individual salaries reported by the survey participants, arranging them in a frequency distribution according to experi-

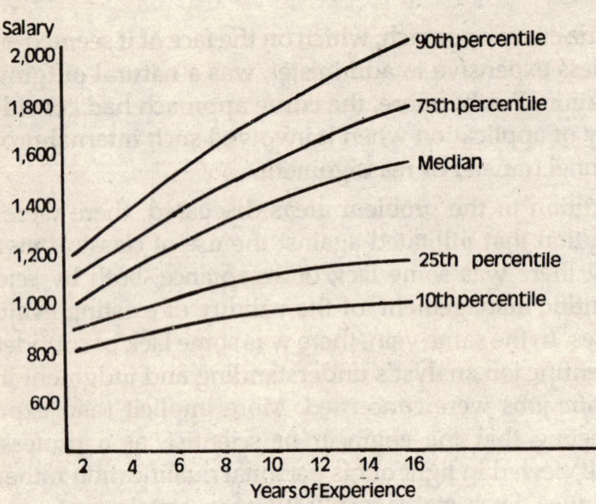

Fig. 5. Hypothetical Curves

ence or some other measure of maturity, and then smoothing the raw data into a family of curves by applying the least-squares statistical technique to obtain paths of best fit.

Clearly, the mechanical procedure is a simple one. However, there are numerous judgmental and policy considerations attending the use of the curve approach that are quite complex. For one thing, conducting a reliable, comprehensive survey is time consuming and expensive. As a result, existing surveys tend to be limited either to major fields, such as engineering, or to the general scientific population, as is the case with the Los Alamos and M.I.T. surveys. This, of course, creates a problem for companies with scientific personnel in more specialized areas such as the human factors field or operations research. Or perhaps a survey is available for a special branch of the scientific workforce, but it does not apply to a particular firm's competitive industry and environment.

Therefore, quite early in the process, a decision has to be made as to whether an organization will use an existing survey or conduct one of its own. This decision cannot be separated from the consideration that is unquestionably most important of all—namely, how the organization intends to use the curve approach in its compensation program. The discussion that follows illustrates this point and is descriptive of some curve applications.

Basically, there are two general uses that can be made of salary curves. One is as a mechanism to guide salary determinations for the individual scientist. The other is as a reference for assessing the firm's salary position in the labor market. In the first case, the curve tend to act as a control device in much the same manner as salary-grade rate ranges do in a classification system. For any given scientific population, there is a range of salaries for each unit of maturity. Referring once again to Figure 1, it may be seen that the range of salaries is described by the 10th and 90th percentiles at the extremes; the median, 25th, and 75th percentiles represent intermediate check points. There is no consistent practice among firm as to the number of curves derived. It may be 7, 8, 10, or even 100, depending of the degree of specificity that the firm wishes to attain.

It should be made eminently clear that, at this juncture, the curves are descriptive rather than prescriptive. The only way in which the curves can become useful guides for the individual salary determination process is through the introduction of some type of quality-rating system. Whether this system is a performance rank, reverse-layoff list, or a ranking of combined factors such as performance, potential, and overall qualifications, it is the highest importance to the curve approach. It is the main variable in determining what the individual's salary level and relative growth rate are to be in relation to other personnel in the same discipline and at the same maturity level.

Thus far, then, it can be seen that individual salary determinations are a function of both descriptive market curves and a quality-rating system. But the matter is not really as simple as this appears to be. For instance, decisions have to be made as to whether there will be a family of curves for each degree level or whether there will only be one family of curves for all degrees combined. Likewise, it must be decided whether to derive a set of curves for each discipline area or to have a combined set of curves for all scientific disciplines in the company. These considerations are in turn related to the previously mentioned question of whether an organization is to use an existing salary survey or conduct one of its own.

In the typical organization, the curve approach is probably less influential in the individual salary determination process than it is in the companywide process. Many firms depend heavily on the curves in order to arrive at their salary increase budgets or to evaluate their position in the relevant labor market. In the compilation of merit budgets, the procedure is essentially a mechanical one. Firms usually measure the year-to-year growth resulting from an added year of experience on the curve plus the upward movement of curves due to economic and inflationary factors, average this movement, statistically weight it by the company's scientific population for each level of maturity, and thereby arrive at a salary increase budget for the coming year. Naturally, if the organization feels that its market position is either too high or too low in certain areas, it will bring such considerations to bear in arriving at a final figure.

In addition to their use in the derivation of annual salary increase budgets, the curves may be effectively employed to define an organization's labor market position. For example, a company may develop internal maturity curves for its own scientific personnel and superimpose these on the survey curves—and thereby determine with relative accuracy the organization's competitive position. In facts, overall medians can be computed and direct comparisons made between the survey and corporate averages. In cases where the problem of small samples precludes the development of company curves, a scatter of actual salaries in the firm can be plotted against the survey curves. Based on such comparisons, adjustments to the firm's competitive position can readily be made.

It is possible to refine this technique so that the salary positions of individual departments within a firm can also be related to the external labor market. A company may decide, for example, that the average salaries of its research engineers should coincide with the 75th percentile of the survey, while those of its other engineers should fall at the 50th percentile. These policy decisions can then be implemented through direct comparisons with the appropriate set of survey curves.

Not only are the curves helpful in comparing central tendency, but they are also useful for making assessments of what the despersion of salaries in an organization should be. To illustrate, a company might decide that the distribution of salaries paid to engineers throughout the firm should approximate the distribution of salaries paid in the external labor market. This can be achieved by providing that 10 per cent of the salaries paid by the firm will be below the 10th percentile of the survey, 15 per cent between the 10th and 25th percentiles, 25 per cent between the 25th and 50 percentiles, and so on—paralleling the external labor market at each selected juncture. Such a plan is dependent on an organization's having a relatively large and homogeneous sample of scientists. Otherwise the exercise becomes rather meaningless. Again, the same technique can be applied to individual departments within a company. For instance, management might decide that the research unit should have 50 per cent of its salaries above the 75th percentile of the survey, while other scientific operations could have only 25 per cent above this point.

Merit budgets, median-curve comparisons, and distributional controls in the curve approach have the same intent and effect as rate ranges, "comparatios," and midpoint controls have in the classification system. Stated simply, there are controls and guides in the curve system just as there are in the classification approach. The forms of the constraints and the philosophy behind them are somewhat different in the curve approach, but it should not be hastily assumed that the new system is deficient in the control devices which can be used.

This discussion of curve applications has, of necessity, been fairly general. There are many refinements which can be introduced, and the main intent here has been to develop a frame of reference and to outline the basic techniques and philosophy of the curve approach.

Problems of The Curve Approach

The curve approach to compensation of scientists is a controversial one. Many compensation managers damn it; many others have high praise for it. As is usually the case, this technique is probably deserving of neither extreme; there should be, however, some discussion of the principal draw-backs and difficulties associated with this system and an evaluation of its effectiveness.

The curve approach has a number of problems that are common to the entire compensation field. Take, for example, difficulties that are encountered in the conduct of surveys: the complexities of survey design and construction, the problems of small samples, inaccurate reporting of survey data, and similar hazards. Taken together, the accumulated error introduced by such factors undoubtedly reduces the reliability of the survey. Likewise, a meaningful performance-rating system is critical to the effective functioning of the curve system as well as the classification system. This of course, is a whole problem area in itself.

Beyond such difficulties of a general nature there are, in addition, those which are unique to the curve approach. Consider, first, the maturity factor to be selected and used. Obviously an employer does not require maturity for its own sake but, rather, for what it represents in terms of an employee's ability to handle the employer's problems and meet his work requirements. Maturity is nothing more than a convenient and tangible measure of ability. But which is the best measure? Chronological age is quite easily calculated, but is probably least meaningful from the point of view of "employee worth." Years since receipt of B.S. degree is more specific but makes no allowance for experience received before the bachelor's degree, time periods since graduation when experience was nonprofessional in nature (military service, for instance), and experience gained by those few individuals who have become professional scientists without having obtained a degree. Some firms attempt to take these factors into account and develop a theoretical degree date or "equivalent B.S" for purposes of calculating years since B.S. degree. The factor that is most relevant and at the same time most difficult to calculate and apply is professional experience. For example, a set of criteria, which inevitably is controversial, has to be developed in order to evaluate professional experience. Further, it must be determined whether the evaluation is to include all professional experience or just experience that is directly applicable to the scientist's activities. if it is to be the latter, additional salary difficulties develop when the man moves from one field of specialization to another. A typical problem case is the senior engineer who goes into operations research work. His operations research experience starts from zero, and quite frequently this would put his salary for that maturity level in stratospheric reaches.

An entirely different area of difficulty has to do with curve forecasting. If an organization is reviewing salaries in October and the survey curves are as of the previous January, there is obviously a need to project the curves forward in order to stay current with the labor market. This extrapolation is generally based on the curve growth rate shown in the most recent survey. But in Figure 6—a set of median curves taken from a national survey of

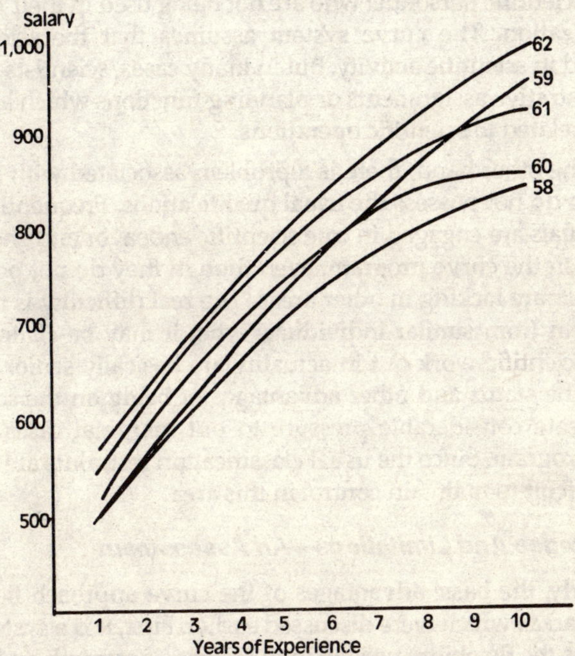

Fig. 6. Median Salary Curves: 1958-62.

one scientific field—we can see what would have occurred of the 1960 curve had been forecast on the basis of the 1958-59 growth. The 1960 extrapolation would have been considerably different than the actual result. Obviously, part of this problem stems from factors unrelated to the labor market, such as sampling changes and perturbations resulting from the statistical technique.

A corollary problem even larger than forecasting is the administration of a salary program when the curve behavior is as shown in Figure 6. For example, strict adherence to the curves in 1960 theoretically would have meant a salary decrease for individuals with seven years' or more experience. In such instances, alternative solutions to annual curve administration have to be sought. These usually take the form of a moving- average growth rate. To illustrate, the 1963 curve might be calculated by averaging the growth rates for illustrate, the 1958-62 curves, the 1964 curve would be derived from the 1959-63 curves, and so on.

A further difficulty in the curve approach is that it provides no logical solution to the problem of establishing compensation levels for scientific personnel who are not being used in their fields of specialization. The curve system assumes that the scientist is engaged in scientific activity. But in many cases, scientists take on administrative assignments or planning functions which are actually unrelated to scientific operations.

On the other hand, there is a problem associated with personnel who do not possess the usual qualifications. Frequently, these individuals are engaged in true scientific endeavor and should be placed on the curve program, even though they do not possess a degree or are lacking in other areas. The real difficulty is to separate them from similar individuals who, it may be claimed, are doing scientific work but in actuality are basically senior technicians. The status and other advantages of being on the scientific staff create considerable pressure to put marginal cases on the curve program. Since the usual classification restraints are absent, it is difficult to maintain control in this area.

Advantages And Limitations—An Assessment

Clearly, the basic advantages of the curve approach lie in the several areas which were discussed earlier. First, it is a system that provides the flexibility needed in the scientific research and development milieu. It does not impose predetermined or artificial job constraints on the scientist but, rather, allows him to expand his activities within the limits of his own creative ability. Therefore, salary administration by the curve method is results-oriented, and it rewards contribution. In a related connection, the curve approach is more acceptable to the scientist as a professional person. Further, from the viewpoint of management and the salary administrator, the curve system is less expensive and easier to administer than the classification technique. Finally, this approach recognizes the shortage in the scientific labor market and the disrupting effect that such shortages have on evaluation plans. Economic studies have shown that internal job evaluation systems cannot operate effectively when they conflict with rates established in the labor market.

However, these advantages of the curve approach do not become operative automatically. For example, a decision has to be made as to which scientific labor market to survey. Even though the theoretical economic model assumes, for analytical purposes, that a single rate clears the market, in actual practice it is not that precise and in the everyday market situation there is actually a range of rates. This range of rates broadens with various factors, but most particularly with the type of industry. The point that needs to be emphasized is that company management often have much more latitude than they choose to exercise with regard to scientific labor market salaries.

Beyond this consideration, there are the previously discussed problems of a procedural nature that attend the application of the curve approach. Furthermore, the particular history and environment of the individual organization cannot be ignored. A salary structure has a real existence outside of the compensation manual. It has both sociological and psychological significance and, as a result, it is generally quite difficult to change a firm's historical salary relationships and differentials. In older organizations, which have had classification systems for a long while, this factor has a distinct influence when the curve approach is introduced into the organization.

Finally, and most important, the underlying assumption of the curve approach is that the individual scientist is a productive resource. The term "maturity curve" is unfortunate because it gives the wrong connotation. Obviously the curve approach, within certain limits, relies on maturity per sent to play a part in both individual and companywide salary determination processed. But in the final analysis, the individuals contribution is the most important than the classical method.

This being the case, it becomes apparent that the curve system is really dependent on effective personnel utilization and, as a corollary, some type of meaningful quality-rating system. Given these, the inherent benefits of the curve approach can be taken advantage of and its limitations minimized. But if these elements are lacking, the curve technique will leave much to be desired.

6

INCENTIVE SYSTEMS

THE typical industrial employee on unmeasured day work is generally found to produce no more than 50% to 70% of what measurement would show to be a fair day's work. This low level of performance has provided management with a strong stimulus to establish Incentive Systems to increase productivity. As a result, a wide variety of systems and plans have been developed with the basic objective of increasing worker effectiveness and reducing unit labour costs. All of these plans can be classified into two major categories: (1) *non-financial plans;* and (2) *financial plans.*

Non-financial incentives are generally of a nature that appeal to an individual's emotions rather than his pocketbook. They include such things as pride in workmanship; recognition of achievement; patriotism; feeling of inclusion; gratitude; shame of poor performance; pride in superior performance; spirit of competition; and a host of other factors which tend to stimulate good performance. Certain of these motivating factors are inherently present in most industrial situations. By themselves, they cannot begin to create the strong pull of a financial incentive. However, they can help to make financial incentives more effective and palatable.

Financial incentive plans, in turn, may also be of two types—*indirect* or *direct.*

Indirect incentives include such things as equitable pay structures, merit increases, pension and profit-sharing plans, hospitalization programs, and other factors generally referred to as "fringe benefits." These indirect incentive benefits are definitely financial in nature. Unlike direct incentives, however, they apply on a company-wide basis and are not directly dependent upon the contribution of an individual or group.

Direct financial incentive plans provide an opportunity for higher pay through increased productivity or effectiveness. They are based upon the concept of plus pay for plus performance.

Background

Piece rates constitute one of the oldest forms of direct financial incentives. This type of wage payment has been in existence for thousands of years and is still very commonly used today—particularly in the needle trades, foundries, and other specific industries. The modern concept of wage incentives, however, is closely associated with Frederick W. Taylor and his efforts in the late 1800s to develop a way of measuring "a fair day's work." While the principle of plus pay for plus performance is simplicity itself, the problem of measuring "normal performance" is extremely complex.

There is little question that direct financial incentive plans do provide a very strong incentive for increased productivity. A study made by the War Production Board during World War II showed that increases in productivity averaged about 60% when incentives were based upon engineered standards, and were applied on an individual basis. Since many of theses plans were installed somewhat hurriedly under the press of wartime production demands, it is likely that they underestimated the full increases to be obtained from incentives. It is not at all uncommon to find that productivity doubles when going from a straight hourly basis of payment to a soundly designed incentive plan.

The greatest single problem in the development of any wage incentive system is the determination of what constitutes a fair day's work. Up until late 1940s, the most commonly accepted means of establishing engineered time standards was the use of stop watch time study techniques. Other less objective methods include supervisory estimates and standards based on past performance. Since the early 1950s, the use of predetermined motion times and standard data based upon these systems has become quite general. Although predetermined time standards were almost unheard of prior to 1948, they were being used as a basis for work measurement by 72% of 302 companies surveyed by *Factory* magazine in 1959.

Application

Because of the difficulties encountered in developing fair and accurate time standards, most wage incentive plans were initially limited to the highly repetitive direct labor operations. As soon as some direct workers began to earn incentive bonuses, however, other direct workers on less repetitive jobs and indirect workers began to demand the opportunity to work on incentives as well. Unfortunately, a number of attempts were made by unqualified people to meet this strong demand for incentives on these types of activities. The loose standards and controls associated with these installations soon resulted in run-away earnings and this, in turn, led many managements arbitrarily to cut the rates. This, in turn, created many industrial relations problems. This was the era of the so-called "efficiency expert"—an era that industrial engineers are still trying to live down.

Business organizations have been utilizing work measurement techniques for many years to aid in meeting numerous objectives. "Work measurement," as often defined, encompasses two basic facets:

1. Motion study, which involves analyzing jobs with the aim of determining more efficient methods by which workers may perform these jobs, and
2. Time study, which is based on motion study, establishes work standards by means of time or other measurement techniques, defining the amount of work which can be turned out by an ("average") employee in any given time period. Such work standards are also commonly referred to as time standards; and we will utilize these two terms synonymously in the following discussion.

Taken together, motion and time study can serve objectives aimed at increasing the overall efficiency of the organizational system by: making available to management better information for both product costing and manpower planning; and providing a basis for establishing monetary incentive plans for its employees.

In many companies, the industrial engineering (or systems analysis) department—rather than personnel is given prime responsibility for the task of work measurement. At the same time, personnel managers very frequently become involved in the area of work measurement in one way or another—e.g., helping develop and administer training programs based upon the work methods which have been established; dealing with worker and union complaints that certain work standards have been set so high that it is not possible to attain adequate monetary incentives, etc.

Work measurement techniques are most commonly applied in developing time standards for production jobs in manufacturing firms. Sometimes, however, they are applied to certain other non-managerial positions, such as clerical and janitorial (as we will see later); but rarely are they applied to managerial and professional jobs, where so many "subjective" performance variables are involved.

Over the years, many different techniques have been developed for determining time standards, such as traditional time study, standard data, micro-measurement methods (such as Methods-Time-Measurement), and work sampling.

As work measurement techniques improved, however, along with improved incentive plans and wage administration practices, it became possible to extend the use of incentives to more and more of the jobbing types of operations and to a wide variety of indirect labor activities as well. In fact, incentives are now being applied to clerical drafting, laboratory, and many other operations formerly thought to be too complex to measure with any degree of accuracy. Indeed, the decade starting in 1950 was characterized by a definite trend towards the application of incentives to all types of indirect labor activities.

Initial attempts to set up incentive plans for indirect labor frequently made use of indirect time standards for these activities. Material handlers, for example, were simply related to the number of production workers they served. Their incentive earnings were then tied to the incentive earnings of the production workers. In other cases, maintenance workers have received incentive bonuses based upon a minimum of equipment downtime. In actual fact, the maintenance men were busiest when the equipment was down and had little to do when everything was working smoothly. Paradoxes such as this, coupled with technical advances in work measurement techniques, have tended to result in indirect incentives based on the direct measurement of the work involved rather than the use of the ratios.

Types of Plans

There is a wide variety of incentive plans from which to choose. In the early days of wage incentive development, it was popular for individuals and consultants to develop unique incentive plans and then to associate their name with the plan. Some of the more widely known plans of this sort include the *Gantt* Task and Bonus, *Halsey* 50-50 Gain Sharing, *Rowan* Plan, *Bedaux* Plan, *Taylor* Differential Piece Rate Plan, and the like. The *Factory* survey previously referred to indicated, however, that by the beginning of the decade of the 1960s most of these unique plans had gradually passed out of the picture. Today, probably 80% of the employees covered by incentives are covered by one of two types—*piecework* plans or *standard minute* (*standard hour*) plans. The standard minute (hour) is by far the most popular. It covers 55% of all employees in the plants surveyed. Straight piece-work plans cover 25% of all employees. Of the remaining 20%, 16% are covered by a plan that pays the worker less than one per cent bonus for each one per cent increase in production. The other 4% are covered by a variety of other plans.

In all of the early incentive plans, there was no provision for a minimum, guaranteed hourly rate of pay. The individual was simply paid whatever he earned. Today, however, all incentive plans make some provision for a minimum, guaranteed rate of pay.

1. **Piecework Plans.** A piece rate is usually expressed in dollars and cents per piece produced. Its great virtue is that it is easy to understand. By multiplying the number of pieces produced by the piece rate, the employee immediately knows how much he (she) has earned. Initially, rates were frequently set on the basis of estimates and past performancne. As a result, the rates were set without regard to standard time as such. But, in fact, a piece rate is

actually made up of two separate and independent factors. One is the *time* required to produce a unit of work—the other is the *base rate of pay.* When these two factors are multiplied together, a piece rate is obtained. Thus, two jobs that take exactly the same time to perform will have a different piece rate if one job is performed by a higher-rates class of labor and the other by a lower labor grade. Since every piece rate changes whenever a general wage increase is granted, this introduces and administrative problem.

2. **Standard Minute Plans.** In order to get away from these problems but still retain the simplicity of the piece- rate plan, a standard minute plan was developed. (Standard hour plans are also commonly used. The only difference between the two plans is the unit of measure—the use of hours in one and the use of minutes in the other). Basically, a standard minute rate is a piece rate expressed in terms of time rather than in dollars and cents. The bonus earnings of an individual working under either plan are exactly the same. In both cases, they are directly proportional to output. By having the rates expressed in terms of minutes, it is possible to make better use of the standards for other purposes such as planning and scheduling the work and the like. A standard minute plan also helps to draw a clear distinction between the base rates of pay and the time standard for a job. Further, the rates are not affected in any way by wage rate increases or adjustments.

3. **The Halsey Plan.** This plan is typical of incentive plans that pay the worker something less than a one per cent increase in pay for a one per cent increase in production. A common version of the Halsey Plan paid the worker one half of one per cent for each additional one per cent increase in production over one hundred per cent. This plan was designed in the late 1800s when time standards were frequently established by estimates or past performance. Since estimating usually results in more liberal time standards, this plan tended to compensate for the looseness in the time standards. In addition, management also reasoned that when production was increased, the wear and tear on the equipment was increased. It was felt, therefore, that by sharing the increase in productivity, management would be compensated for the greater depreciation on the facilities.

4. Measured Day Work. This plan had long been used in the automotive industry and gradually attracted more attention from other industries. As the name implies, the workers under this plan work at a day rate or hourly rate of pay. The work they produce, however, is carefully measured and controlled. Individual or group performance indexes are determined in much of the same manner as they are under an incentive program. The basic difference, however is that the workers are paid a fixed rate for the day, regardless of whether their performance is above or below one hundred per cent.

A variation of the measured day work plan does provide for changes in the base rate of pay for a given job based upon the performance index of the worker. For example, workers performing at a rate below 90% may receive the lowest base rate for the job. Workers performing between 90% and 100% receive the next highest rate; those between 100% and 110%, the third highest rate; and so on. The number of steps in the base rate usually varies from three to five. The performance index is calculated monthly or quarterly, and the base rates are changed whenever there is a change in the performance range. Used in this way, the plan definitely provides a financial incentive.

A more common application of the plan, however, does not provide for differential base rates keyed to performance. Under this version of the plan, the worker has no financial incentive to produce at a rate higher than 100%. However, since satisfactory performance is usually one of the conditions of employment, the worker has an incentive to maintain production at a satisfactory level to insure continuance of employment. In many cases where this plan is used, there is no strict definition of "satisfactory performance." In other cases, satisfactory performance is clearly defined as 100% of standard plus or minus 5%. In other words, the minimum acceptable performance is 95% of the established standard.

This type of plan appears to be best suited to progressive assembly line operations where the speed of the line is mechanically controlled. The line is then manned with the proper number of operators and each individual must keep up with the line or be replaced. This is one reason why the plan had such wide acceptance in the automotive industry. The plan has also had wide application to a variety of industries, however, and is not by any means limited to paced or controlled operations. The chief virtue of the plan is that it does provide management with a measure and control over the standard hours of work produced without tying this control to an incentive wage payment plan. In this way, management can obtain the advantages of work measurement and control without the disadvantages of wage inequities which incentive plans frequently produce.

Individual and Group Plans

Most early applications of wage incentives were made on an individual basis. An individual was paid in direct proportion to what he produced. He was, in effect, placed in business for himself. There is no question but that this form of incentive provides the greatest stimulus to production. There are, however, many cases where a job cannot be performed by a single individual but must be performed by a team. In other cases, team work is to be encouraged rather than individual performance. For these reasons, group systems of incentive payment have been developed.

A wage incentive group is made up of a number of workers who pool their production. The method of computing and distributing the earnings of the group is known as the group system of incentive payment. The group system is not another type of incentive plan like the Halsey Plan, for example. Rather, it is a concept of incentive payment that can be used in conjunction with any of the common incentive plans.

The group system is most applicable under either one of the following conditions:

(1) There is a community of interest among the members of the group.

(2) The work is such that it is impossible to measure the contribution of the individual member accurately.

The most common example of community of interest is the assembly line. In this case, the work has been broken down into a number of equal and specialized tasks. By performing a particular part of the work well, each individual on the line permits the other members of the group to do their work well and the output of the group as a whole rises. In this case, individual incentives are impossible to apply since any one worker cannot proceed at a rate of production different from any other member of the group. They *must* work as a group.

In other cases, such as shipping and receiving operations, plan maintenance operations and the like, it is difficult to measure the output of individuals separately since they work essentially as a team. The only practical method of incentive payment in these cases is a group basis. Following are some of the major advantages claimed for the group system of payment:

(1) Better cooperation between individual workers is achieved.

(2) Need for supervision is reduced.

(3) Operator training time is reduced.

(4) Indirect labor may be included and controlled by the group.

(5) Timekeeping is simplified.

(6) Quality of product is improved.

(7) Wages are fairly distributed.

The major disadvantages of the group are:

(1) Exceptional ability is penalized.

(2) It is difficult to handle jobs that are still incomplete by the end of the pay period.

(3) No check on individual performance is provided.

(4) No check on time standards for individual jobs is provided.

(5) It is difficult to find the right man for group leader.

Individual incentives have varied considerably in their effectiveness. In some cases, they have served well in meeting organizational objectives and individual needs. On the other hand, many have created so many problems that they have been dropped. Thus, before establishing any particular incentive plan, management should ask the question, Would such a plan really help meet organizational objectives and individual needs? Although such a question may be difficult to answer, there are many situations in which management can gain cues as to the need for incentive plans. For example, if the firm's production workers are considered to be producing at reasonable rate, and absenteeism and turnover are low, establishing a direct wage incentive may be unnecessary. Also it might even be dysfunctional, in that it may disrupt existing wages to the point that a number of employees perceive the new incentive rates as being inequitable. On the other hand, a firm may consider it essential to establish some form of deferred compensation if it is to recruit and keep its top executives, simply because most other comparable firms provide such incentives.

If an organization decides to adopt any individual incentive system it must make three subsequent decisions. It must determine (1) which individuals are to be eligible for inclusion in the plan, (2) what the criterion (or criteria) for providing a reward will be, and (3) what the reward will be if any specific criterion has been met.

WAGE INCENTIVES

In establishing wage incentives, management must decide how the jobs included in the plan are to be performed, what standards of performance must be met if an incentive is to be earned, and how much incentive pay the worker is to receive at different levels of performance.

Traditionally, jobs eligible for direct wage incentives have been characterized by an easily measurable output. The majority of these jobs have been in production and related work. We use the word *related* here to encompass such jobs as those of warehouse workers who are paid on an incentive basis for the number of boxes they sort or stack during a particular time period.

In numerous companies wage incentive system have been designed for indirect labor in production operations. These include workers who assist machine operators by providing the materials they need or helping them in other ways. For example, in one department at the Indian Organics Ltd., wage incentives were established for a number of types of indirect workers such as die-setters, crane operators, lift truck operators, and electric truckers. Here, every indirect wage incentive was related to direct labor output. Any increase in production by direct labor forced the indirect workers to increase their pace. Further, if either group slowed down, incentive earnings decreased for both groups.

In traditional production systems, standards of units of output can be defined, with worker effort leading to production above a standard rewarded with incentive pay. In the last few decades, however, more and more firms have turned to various degrees of automation. In automated and semiautomated situations in which there is a high degree of machine pacing it is not possible for the worker to exert more effort and thereby produce more output. This is because the machine primarily determines the rate of production. In such situations traditional incentives based on output are not appropriate.

With incentives, workers may:

1. Work completely independently of each other. In such cases, the incentive reward can be directly related to each individual's performance.
2. Work in interdependent crews. Here the output rate of all workers in any groups will be the same so that everyone must receive the same percentage incentive for any particular period of time. For example, all workers might receive 120 percent of their base rates of pay in a given pay period.

The basic difference between these group and individual incentives is that the level of incentives for the group will be held down to the level of performance of its slowest worker. For this reason, workers may apply pressures to anyone who is "going off," since this behavior would mean less incentive pay for them as well. These crew wage incentives function like individual incentives in all other respects.

Setting Standards

Some knowledge of how the development of work standards on which wage incentives are to be based is accomplished is necessary for a full understanding of how these incentives function. Setting standards involves two steps. First, a methods study is performed that attempts to spell out the best way to perform each job. This may involve a motion study if the volume to be produced is high. Second, one of several available methods geared to determining how much time it should take workers to perform the job is utilized. We should emphasize that both motion and time analyses can have many advantages to the firm other than simply establishing a base for incentive systems. For example, they may provide better control over labor costs and increase profitability as a result of improved methods design.

Motion Study. Modern motion study, a part of the "scientific management" movement, goes back to the early days of this century. Its basic objective is to find the best way of performing a job.

Over the years, scholars and practitioners in this field have developed a number of principles aimed at combining, simplifying, and eliminating work elements in jobs. For example, smooth simultaneous motions with both hands are much more efficient than nonsimultaneous jerky motions. This is illustrated in Figure 1, where the solid arrows represent the motions of the two hands reaching for two parts, which will be taken by an operator and fastened together.

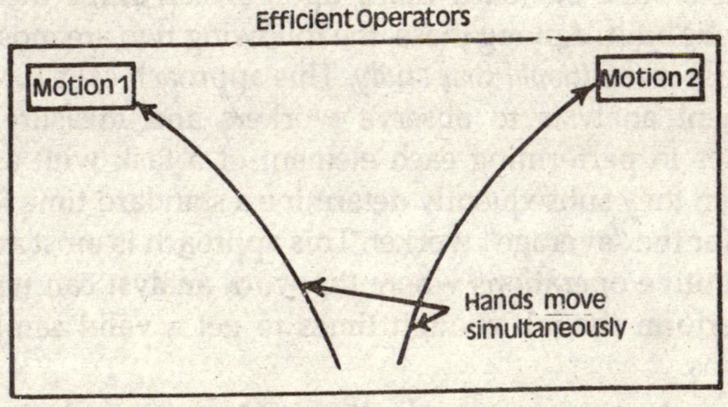

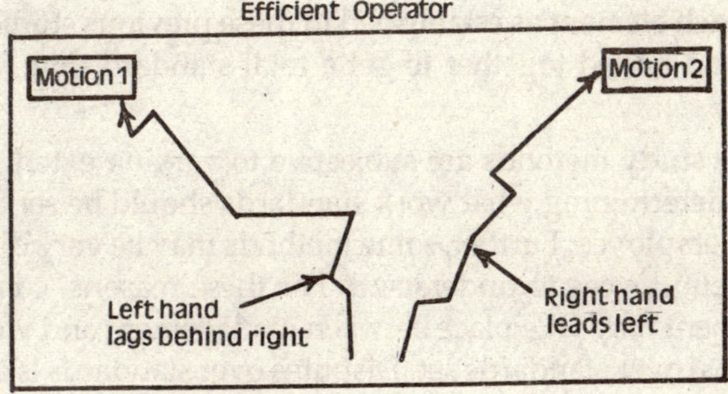

Fig. 1. Efficient versus inefficient motions.

Without question, many significant improvements in the way work has been done have been achieved through the appropriate utilization of motion study. There are, however, two limitations in prescribing the so-called best way of performing a job. First, although some motions are obviously superior to others, in some cases different people may be able to perform the same task most effectively with different motions. Second, it may be more "efficient" for operators to perform a job in one way rather than another. However, if they have to perform it over and over again using the same motions every time, it may become sufficiently more monotonous that overall production may be higher if the individual is allowed some deviation, making the job somewhat more interesting.

Time Study. Over the years, several basic methods have been used to determine standard times upon which wage incentive plans may be built. Among these, the following two are most well known. First is *traditional time study.* This approach calls for work measurement analysts to observe workers and measure their actual times in performing each element of a task with a stopwatch. Then they subsequently determine a standard time for the total task for the "average" worker. This approach is most amenable to repetitive operations where the work analyst can watch a worker perform the job enough times to get a valid sample of observations.

The second method is *standard data.* Here, if all elements of work for a new job are ones that have been previously studies, the times for each element as established in these previous studies can be taken and added together to get a total standard time for the new job.

All time study methods are subjective to varying extents with respect to determining what work standards should be set for the "average" employee. Further, some methods may be very difficult for many employees to understand. For these reasons, considerable argument may take place between management and workers (and unions) over standards set. Disputes over standards is a basic reason for our previous observation that the adoption of a wage incentive plan is unnecessary if operations in the firm are going well without incentives.

Determining Time Standards Through Linear Programming

There are many types of industrial jobs, individual or group, in which the definable work-elements of each job are nearly the same except that the jobs vary in the quantity of each type of work-element used. These types of jobs can be found in the construction industry, maintenance industry, fabrication industry and so forth.

For example, in the electric utility industry, line construction consists of definable work-elements such as, "set a pole," "install a cross-arm," and so on. The number of poles set, cross-arms installed, however, varies from job to job. In this article, a fairly accurate method, which does not require direct elemental time measurement or standard data, will be presented for determining time standards for the work-elements of these types of jobs. This method uses a novel linear programming approach.

In order to apply linear programming effectively, it will be necessary that good methods be used to accomplish the work and accurate data be available for a large number (statistically) of jobs for which the quantity of each work-element and the total time for each job are known. For those companies which do not have the necessary data available, a work sampling study could be used to supply the data.

A work-element should be defined so that components which always go together will be included in one work-element. For example, if a guy-wire always has a guy-guard, do not list the installation of these components as separate work-elements; rather list the installation of the pair as one work-element. The importance of proper classification will be demonstrated in the example used later in this article.

For this application, it is recommended that more jobs be used in the analysis than there are different work-elements. For example, if 100 different work-elements have been defined, 150 to 500 jobs may be required to obtain the desired accuracy for the work-element times. The number of jobs required depends on the variability among jobs and will have to be determined empirically. If data are available on an extremely large number of jobs, it may be desirable to use a sample. A random sample would be drawn if the work-element times were to reflect the average conditions as they existed. Selective sampling would be used if it were desired that only those jobs be chosen which have actual total times that follow some accepted notion of average or expected time for completion.

In setting standards on jobs that are worked on by a group, it will be necessary to set different standards for different group sizes. In addition, for group or individual jobs, it will be necessary to establish different standards for different working conditions. As an example, for outside jobs, a "good" weather standard and a "bad" weather standard may be required. For an electric line construction crew, different time standards may be required for working on "energized" lines versus "dead" lines and for assembly work on the ground versus assembly work in the air. The standards for each different condition can be determined by separate application of the linear programming technique to those jobs which were done under the respective conditions.

The total time for each job may or may not include set-up time, personal time, delays, and so on, depending on the method used to record the data. On group jobs, it is difficult to keep track of personal and delay time of individuals. For a set of jobs in which the set-up and personal delay times have been measured, the allowances for these times can be determined by analysis of the distribution of these measured times or by traditional time study analysis. For those jobs in which the set-up and personal-delay times are confounded with the total time, it will be necessary to determine whether set-up times and personal-delay times are to be prorated to the work-element times or are to be solved for separately. How these last two alternatives can be handled will be discussed in the example problem to follow.

To illustrate how linear programming can be used to determine work-element time standards, consider the following simplified problem. An electric power company wants to set standards for its line construction crews in order to schedule construction more efficiently and to evaluate performance better. In line construction, as stated previously, the jobs differ mainly in the number of poles, cross-arms, feet of wire, insulators, and so forth, installed.

For each job, a record has been kept of the quantity of each component installed and the total time to complete the job. The total time for each job includes the set-up time and personal-delay time. The crew size is constant. Only one standard will be determined for each work-element. For ease of presentation, a sample of 15 jobs which have six possible work-elements will be used. The data for these 15 jobs appear in Table 1.

Method. Linear programming can be used to find the time for each work- element which minimizes the sum, over-all jobs, of the absolute deviation between the actual total time for a job and the total time that would be calculated by summing the determined work-element times for the job. The objective in here is somewhat

Table 1

Job No.	*No. of Poles*	*Wire (100 Feet)*	*No. of Cross-Arms*	*No. of Insulators*	*No. of Guy-Wires*	*No. of Guy-Guards*	*Total Time*
1	1	4	1	2	1	1	8.0
2	2	10	2	4	0	0	14.0
3	3	6	3	6	1	1	17.5
4	1	2.5	2	3	0	0	7.0
5	2	10	4	6	0	0	16.0
6	4	24	8	12	2	2	37.3
7	4	33	7	11	1	1	39.5
8	1	3	2	4	2	2	10.5
9	0	5	3	3	0	0	5.0
10	2	8	4	8	8	1	1
11	3	12	6	12	0	0	23.5
12	2	12	2	4	1	1	16.5
13	3	18	3	6	0	0	22.0
14	1	5	2	3	0	0	8.5
15	4	12	8	12	0	0	28.5

like the objective of the least squares method of regression analysis, except that the sum of the absolute deviations are to be minimized rather than the sum of the squared deviations. This objective is expressed below in linear programming form the problem presented earlier.

Minimize

$$f(S) = S_1 + S_2 + S_3 + \ldots + S_{30}$$

Restriction Equations

$$1P + 4.0W + 1C + 2I + 1G + 1Q + S_1 - S_2 = 0.8$$
$$2P + 10.0W + 2C + 4I + S_3 - S_4 = 14.0$$
$$3P + 6.0W + 3C + 6I + 1G + 1Q + S_5 - S_6 = 17.5$$
$$1P + 2.5W + 2C + 3I + S_7 - S_8 = 7.0$$
$$2P + 10.0W + 4C + 6I + S_9 - S_{10} = 16.0$$
$$4P + 24.0W + 8C + 12I + 2G + 2Q + S_{11} - S_{12} = 37.5$$
$$4P + 33.0W + 7C + 11I + 1G + 1Q + S_{13} - S_{14} = 39.5$$
$$1P + 3.0W + 2C + 4I + 2G + 2Q + S_{15} - S_{16} = 10.5$$
$$5.0W + 3C + 3I + S_{17} - S_{18} = 5.0$$

$$
\begin{aligned}
2P + 8.0W + 4C + 8I + 1G + 1Q + S_{19} - S_{20} &= 17.0 \\
3P + 12.0W + 6C + 12I + S_{21} - S_{22} &= 23.5 \\
2P + 12.0W + 2C + 4I + 1G + 1Q + S_{23} - S_{24} &= 16.5 \\
3P + 18.0W + 3C + 6I + S_{25} - S_{26} &= 22.0 \\
1P + 5.0W + 2C + 3I + S_{27} - S_{28} &= 8.5 \\
4P + 12.0W + 8C + 12I + S_{29} - S_{30} &= 28.5
\end{aligned}
$$

where

P = time to install a pole

W = time to install 100 feet of wire

C = time to install a cross–arm

I = time to install an insulator

G = time to install a guy–wire

Q = time to install a guy–guard

The restriction equations are formed from the total time relationship for each job. Both a positive and negative slack variable, S_1 are used in each restriction equation. This is necessary because the deviation of the actual total time from the calculated total time may be either positive or negative. The objective function is formed by summing the deviations without regard to sign (sum of the absolute deviations). The Simplex Method, used to solve linear programming problems, will insure that at least one of the slack variables in each equation will be zero.

As can be seen in the example problem formulated above, the set- up and personal-delay times were not included as separate variables for each job. Since the total time for each hob includes the set-up and personal-delay times, these times will be prorated to each of the work-element times. Another approach to handling set-up and personal-delay times would be to use a separate variable for each of the two times for every combination of work-elements. This approach would be rather cumbersome; however, a smaller number of combinations could be selected. For example, suppose set-up time is adjusted to be mainly a function of the number of poles installed. Then to each of the job restriction equations which have only pole could be added the variable T_1 and to each of the job restriction equations which have two poles could be added the variable T_2 and so forth, where *Tsubs*1 represents the set-up time for the pole group. The work-elements, using this approach, would not contain prorated set-up times. This same approach also could be used to solve the personal-delay times separately.

The Simplex solution to the example problem yields the following results:

$P = 3.17$	$S_6 = .50$	$S_{18} = .88$
$W = .50$	$S_7 = .12$	$S_{20} = .17$
$C = .92$	$S_{10} = .25$	$S_{26} = .50$
$I = .21$	$S_{13} = .13$	$S_{27} = .37$
$G = 1.50$	$S_{15} = .17$	
$Q = 0$		

minimum $f(S) = 3.08$.

From the solution above, it is noted that $Q = 0$, which implied that a guy-guard takes no time to install. The reason for this obvious discrepancy is that, for this example, every guy-wire has a guy-guard; hence the variables are not independent. This example emphasizes the importance of proper classification of work-elements; that is, those components of work which are always used together, or in the same ratio, on all jobs should be classified as one work-element. In this example, had the guy-wire and guy-guard installation been combined into one work-element, guy-assembly (GA), then the solution would have yielded $GA = 150$ which is the correct interpretation of the solution above. This classification is not limiting since the main concern is not with the work-element times alone but in using these times to predict the total time for a job. After the work-element times have been determined, the total time for a job can be estimated by multiplying the quantity of each work-element by the respective work-element time and summing these products. For the example above, estimated travel time for a job would have to be added to the calculated job time to obtain the "portal to portal" job time.

As was mentioned previously, selective sampling can be used to give some assurance that the work-element times will be average or normal times. Linear programming can effectively exercise the same control over a random sample. This can be accomplished by assigning a coefficient larger than one to the slack variables in the objective functions for those jobs in the random sample which can be adjusted to have average or expected total times. The larger the coefficients assigned, the more assurance that these jobs will influence the work-element times.

It may be found that the linear program has more than one solution. This has its advantages in that it allows the analyst to choose that alternative which best fits reality in accordance with his experience. Of course, any solution will require testing to determine its value as a scheduling and evaluation tool.

Linear programming can be used to determine standard times for those types of jobs in which the discrete work-elements are essentially the same for all jobs except that the quantity of each type of work-element used may vary among jobs. To be able to determine time standards using this technique, it is necessary that, for a large number of jobs, data be available which give the quantity of each work element and the total time for each job.

By using proper statistical sampling techniques and by categorizing the work into logical work-elements, the average or normal work-element times can be determined fairly accurately. It should be noted, however, that this method should be used as a substitute for the more accurate classical time study methods only when qualified time study personnel are not available or time and money are not available for a more detailed study.

Incentive Standards: A Systems View

The introduction and updating incentive standards may be viewed in systems terms, because so many interdependent needs, objectives, and forces are in mutual interaction in these processes. With traditional time study, for example, workers often try to make the job look more difficult than it is by working at a pace slower than normal, thereby misleading the time study engineer into setting easy (or loose) standards for a job. Time study engineers try not be fooled by workers in such a manner, and good engineers do succeed.

In general, regardless of which time standard approach is used, workers will want relatively loose standards. However, they will not want them to be loose enough to arouse management's suspicion that the standards were improperly set and thereby cause the job to be restudied. Management, in general, will want to have standards that are rigorous enough to permit competitive wage costs. On the other hand, management will want to avoid inequities in incentive standards such as very loose and very tight standards in the same plant. This could create serious human relations problems. Interestingly enough, the union (although it may generally want to obtain relatively loose standards) will want to avoid serious inequity problems as much as management. Unions are heterogeneous political entities, representing many different interests. For them to support one department is getting easier rates may open the door to dissatisfaction in other departments on the grounds that their rates, too, should be made easier.

The first-line supervisors will often prefer reasonably loose standards for their workers for two reasons. First, their employees will be less likely to get upset than would be the case if the standards were too tight. Second, if their workers can perform at a higher percentage of standards than workers reporting to other first-line supervisors, if may make them look good by comparison.

Effectiveness of Wage Incentives

The effectiveness of wage incentives has been controversial for many years. It has been argued that incentives contribute to higher labor costs, which in some cases have been led to plant closings. On the other hand, "numerous case studies are available of companies which claim to have cut their costs by 25 to 73 percent through incentive systems, while increasing employee earnings by 10 to 70 percent."

To what extent any increases in productivity are due to incentives *per se*, however, is an interesting question. Nash and Carroll have indicated that part of productivity increases associated with the introduction of an incentive plan may also be attributable to the concurrent improvement in work methods and the establishment of specific work goals in terms of standards.

The success of any wage incentive plan also depends on a number of contingencies. As we indicated earlier, the work must be measurable, and a relatively stable system where job methods are not constantly changing is most conducive to the establishment of incentives. Also, there must be (1) a perceived relationship between effort and output, (2) carefully set incentive standards so that the system will not lead to serious inequities, and (3) a setting of standards so that potential incentives are high enough to be worthwhile to workers.

In many cases, employees will not resist incentives outright but will engage in some output restrictions. That is, they will produce above standard but not work as hard as they might. There are at least four reasons for such behavior. First, with incentive where physical effort is important, employees may not work as hard as they might because of simple fatigue.

Second, there is a belief in our culture that more experienced individuals should be paid more than less experience ones. In many professions, this assumption is valid up to a point. Doctors, for example, gain more knowledge and experience as they practice longer. In jobs in which heavy physical effort is required, however, it may not be possible for many experienced and older workers to keep up with the less experienced but younger workers doing the same kind of work. In such cases, work groups may apply pressures on their less experienced members not to produce to much that they will make the lower production of more experienced workers look bad.

A third problem is that workers may be afraid that if they produce too much they will work themselves out of a job. This fear may be real or imagined, for in some companies all additional output induced by wage incentives may be sold, while in others increased output will result in layoffs occurring. Also, workers may fear that their standards may be made tighter if they produce too much. Finally, if a standard has unintentionally been set extremely loosely, management may have no other alternative than to restudy the job. This is because such loose rates may well create inequities and protests from other workers with tighter standards.

Now-a-days, more and more firms have developed operations characterized by machine pacing and automation—operations not conducive to incentives. In consequence the trend is away from incentives to straight time (or hourly) pay. For example, as reported in 1982 in one study, during the period 1973-1980 the median proportion of manufacturing workers on hourly time was 82 percent, up from 75 percent for 1961-1968. An exception reported was from basic iron and steel, where (in 1973-1980) 80 percent of its 345,000 production workers were on incentives. Probably a good part of this phenomenon has been due to considerable usage of equipment utilization incentives in automated operations in this industry. These incentives, which are beyond the scope of our discussion, basically take into account maximum machine speed, human factors (fatigue), and mechanical delays that can normally be expected to obtain a "practical" measure of maximum possible production.

Suggestion Systems

Essentially, a suggestion system represents a contract on the part of management to buy ideas from employees. A suggestion system provides the three essentials of a legal contract: (1) an offer (publicized) by management, (2) an acceptance when an employee submits a suggestion, and (3) a consideration represented by the award given for an accepted idea.

The available statistics indicate that from the company's point of view suggestion systems may contribute substantially to profits. With regard to the individual, the monetary awards received may serve to meet many needs. The opportunity for individuals to be rewarded for being creative may contribute to their self- actualization needs, and the recognition given to successful suggestion (especially when the award is large) may help satisfy esteem needs.

Eligibility. The basic notion behind suggestions is to reward creativity above and beyond the responsibilities of the employee's job. For this reason, cash awards are usually given only to non-management employees. It is considered to be the job of managers (and professionals) to be creative, and they will be rewarded for creativity by salary increases.

Criteria. Two types of suggestions are acceptable under practically all systems: those which result in the firm realizing tangible savings and those which are accepted but provide to tangible savings. As an example of the latter, cement posts 3 to 4 feet high were used in one firm's parking lot to separate parking areas. At dusk, they were very difficult to see, and several employees damaged car doors or fenders by scraping against the posts. One employee suggested that the posts be painted bright orange for better visibility, and the company accepted the idea as a good one even though it received no net savings from the idea. The employee was given a nominal award for this suggestion.

Awards. Three aspects of awards are often included in suggestion systems. First, to foster good employee-management relations, many firms given minimum awards for intangible savings ideas as above and, in some cases, for ideas resulting in small tangible savings. Second, many firms establish a maximum award that they will pay for any one suggestion (for example, Rs. 10,000) in order to limit their liability. Probably most critical is the award formula for suggestions falling within these two limits. Most frequently, firms agree to pay some specified percentage for each suggestion ranging from 10 to 20 percent of the net savings realized from it for the first year. By net savings, we mean those realized after any necessary investments have to be made. Materials and equipment purchased to implement an idea "should be prorated in the award calculation at the same amortization rate used by the accounting department on the company books.

Effectiveness of Suggestion Systems.

We will now turn to some of the more important conditions that contribute to the effectiveness of suggestion systems.

1. **Firm's Size and Stability.** Neither organizational size nor stability appears to affect the success of suggestion systems in the way they have with many of the other formalized systems discussed so far. Suggestion systems do not require huge expenditures to develop and maintain, and hence can be made effective with the more limited resources of smaller firms.

With respect to stability, the very essence of suggestion systems is to foster change—by developing new creative solutions for problems that will modify organizational behavior and methods to more fully meet the firm's objectives. Thus, suggestion systems might be viewed more positively in dynamic organizations, where there is a constant need to change, than in stable organizations, where change may be less necessary for effective performance.

2. **Managerial Contribution.** As with all personnel programs, suggestion systems need top management support. The support of lower-level managers is also required to encourage employees to make suggestions. Unfortunately, many first-line supervisors have not perceived suggestions from their subordinates as positive input but rather as a threat to themselves, so they have discouraged employee suggestions. Underlying this perceived threat

is the motion that if their subordinates come up with ideas that they have not thought of themselves, others may think that they are not performing well.

3. **Administration of Suggestion Systems.** Another important factor for the effectiveness of suggestion systems is that they be administered well. We can view administration as encompassing two basic functions: promoting the plan and handling suggestions received from employees. In the following section, we shall talk in terms of a manufacturing plant large enough to have a suggestion administrator (usually in the personnel department).

Promotion of Suggestion Systems. Many different practices can be followed to effectively promote a suggestion system. Upon initiation of any system, it is necessary to spell out to employees all the rules of the plan with respect to eligibility and award structure. Further, continued promotion of the plan rather than periodic bursts is considered essential for its effectiveness. In some cases, periodic contests or other types of special promotions have been shown to increase the number of suggestions. For example, IBM held a year-long celebration of the fiftieth anniversary of its suggestion system and received three times the number of suggestions in that year than it had in any single preceding year. In spite of the effectiveness of campaigns, there is a tendency for employees to return to their normal suggestion behavior after the campaign has ended. Aside from such campaigns, of considerable importance is publicity for suggestion awards that have been made, especially substantial ones.

Suggestions. Processing employee suggestions is a multistage decision process, the highlights of which are illustrated in Figure 2. Once an employee has an idea and has decided to submit it for consideration, it is transmitted (via a suggestion box, personally, or in-company mail) to the suggestion administrator. The administrator

1. Has the suggestion immediately dated so that if another identical suggestion is made, the employee who submitted it first would be the person eligible for an award.
2. Acknowledges, with a thank-you letter, receipt of the suggestion.

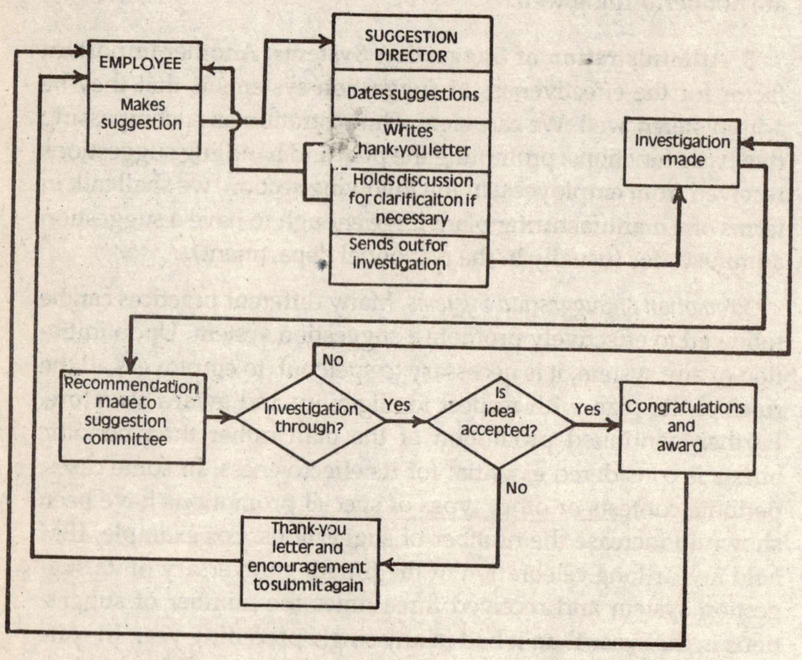

Fig. 2. Administration of Suggestion systems.

3. May go to the suggester and try to clarify the idea, if the suggestion is not written clearly.
4. Transmits the suggestion to those who would have the greatest expertise to investigate its merits. For example, an engineer and the supervisor of the department in which the suggestion was made may be given the responsibility for its evaluation.

Those investigating various suggestions will submit them with recommendations to the suggestion committee, which meets periodically (once every week or two). The suggestion committee may send recommendations back to the investigator if it believes a suggestion has not been thoroughly analyzed. Otherwise, it will make the final decision as to whether to accept or reject the suggestion, and the employee who submitted the idea will be appropriately notified. If the idea is rejected, a thank-you letter, explaining explicitly the reasons why the suggestion was not adopted, and an encouragement to continue submitting suggestions are in order. If the idea is accepted, a thank-you and congratulatory letter along with a check for the award is transmitted to the employee. As indicated previously, publicizing an award is an effective means for promoting the system. To cite the old saying, "Success breeds success."

One other point is in order concerning suggestion committees. In suggestion systems founded more recently, there has been a trend not to have a suggestion committee, particularly if the organization is relatively small. In its place is the suggestion administrator, and the supervisor of the department which would be charged with the implementation of the suggestion acts as the principal evaluator. The right of appeal from negative decisions by the single administrator would then rest with someone higher in the organisation. The reason for such an arrangement is simple economics; suggestion committee members are usually rather highly placed in the organization, command a respectable salary, and cannot be spared en masse for a weekly or biweekly suggestion committee meeting.

Other Variables. Other variables may affect the success of suggestion plans. In some cases, if the firm's demand is inelastic, suggesters may suggest themselves out of a job by coming up with ideas that call for the replacement of manual effort by machines. The usual practice, however, is to follow a more or less unwritten rule that a person will not lose his or her job because of a suggestion he or she made. Rather the person may have to be moved to another work area. Unions, it should be emphasized, simply will not support a suggestion system that allows workers to be phased out because of adopted suggestions. Second, the success of a suggestion system may depend on the kinds of people working for an organization. Some research has shown, for example, that certain personal factors such as "creativity" contribute to an individual's innovativeness in a suggestion system, and that certain structural variables in the work situation such as the job the person does neither "constrain nor sustain" this innovativeness.

EXECUTIVE INCENTIVES

Special incentives for top executives and other upper-level managers and professionals have been used successfully for many years. The well-known industrial and former president of General Motors, Alfred P. Sloan, Jr., believed that his firm's bonus plan was a very important ingredient in its growth and success.

We will how discuss some executive incentive plans from each of two basic types—those providing a cash reward and those providing an equity-based reward. In the cash reward group, we will cover current and deferred bonuses and executive perquisites (commonly referred to as *perks*) which are simply a privilege or gain incidental to one's regular salary. In the equity-based category we will consider stock options—qualified, nonqualified, and incentive stock options (or ISOs)—which provide recipients with some degree of ownership in the firm.

Under the section of cash and equity-based rewards, we will consider different types of incentives, which have varied in favorability to executives at different times as priorities have changed. We will use the terms *executive* and *upper- level manager* synonymously to refer to company president, chairmen, vice chairmen, presidents, Managing Directors, division heads, and other managers or professionals in organizations who are actively involved in decision-making process.

We indicated earlier that the success of any type of compensation depends to a considerable extent on the existence of a clear connection between performance and reward. The manner in which any type of executive incentive functions also has an important impact on this connection. Further, some authorities believe that certain industries are more suitable for executive incentive than others. Patton, for example, has contended that performance to which executive rewards may be connected most easily prevails to the greatest degree where the following conditions exist:

1. Many short-run executive decisions affect profit, such as in the 12-month automobile model cycle.
2. Decentralization is typical and individual managers have "full profit responsibility" for different divisions of the firm.

3. Quantitative tools for judging executive performances are available (for example, market-share data and economic analysis.)

Typical of industries with these characteristics are the following: automobile, retail chains, department stores, pharmaceuticals, and chemicals.

The discussion of both cash and equity incentives together with respect to the first two basic managerial decisions concerning incentives eligibility and criterion for reward is now in order. We will then consider separately the reward given for each specific type of executive incentive.

Eligibility. Some firms have extended bonuses, perks, and stock options down to lower-level managers, but generally (with the exception of perks) these incentives are reserved for upper-level managers. Further, it has been argued that if "more than 1% of a company's total employment is included in an incentive program, the credibility of individual performance evaluations tends to suffer." This is because there is more likely to be a week visible link between lower-level manager's decisions and company success (such as good profit levels).

Criteria. Once a firm decides which executives are to be included in either a cash- or equity-based incentive plan, the criteria upon which the reward will be based must be determined. In developing executive incentives, many different criteria have been utilized. The most widely used criteria for executive bonus plans are overall corporate profits and individual performance, which is generally based on a judgmental performance appraisal. With stock options, the criteria may vary widely—constituting a form of bonus, being related to the executive's base salary, or simply being included as a part of the firm's employment contract with the individual. Perks are generally given to varying classes of individuals depending on the specific perk under consideration.

Reward Systems for Executives

Current Bonus. Current bonuses for executives generally are a function of both individual performance and corporate profits. The basis for determining how much of corporate profits in any given year should be allotted to executive bonuses is usually a formula, which may be the same each year or modified from year to year. Two basic kinds of formulas involve relating the incentives to a straight percentage of profits or basing them on a percentage of profit in excess of a specified return on the stockholder's investment.

How effective are executive bonuses in stimulating higher levels of performance? First, the bonus must be large enough to be significant. It has been argued "that a bonus that amounts to less than 15 percent of salary is hardly worth the bother." One can question this argument, however, as many individuals might be very happy with a 5 or 10 percent bonus.

Deferred Bonuses and Retirement Benefits. In some companies, provisions have been made to pay bonuses to executives not when they earn them, but later, usually after they have retired. Top executives, for example, may be given a Rs. x bonus to be deferred, so that they receive Rs. $x/5$ of it in each of the five years following their retirement. One basic objective for providing such deferred compensation is to decrease individuals' tax burden by postponing the receipt of some compensation until after retirement when they no longer receive a large salary from the firm.

It is difficult to make any broad generalizations as to the effectiveness of deferred compensation. This is because from the executive's viewpoint, the "exact benefit of deferred compensation depends upon a combination of factors: years to retirement, years to separation from the firm, current salary and tax bracket, anticipated income at time of retirement or separation from the firm, and present and anticipated interest rates." From the firm's point of view, it can invest and earn a return on executives' current earnings which do not have to be paid out at present under a deferred program and can then deduct any deferred compensation as a business expense in the year it is paid out. Further, the deferred compensation does not have to be guaranteed by the company.

One can question the effectiveness of any deferred plans since, even though there may be a link between performance and reward, the link is weakened by a time lag. The reward may be provided so many years in the future that the link is barely appreciable by the employee. Further, as is also true of other deferred plans, deferred compensation may induce executives to stay with the company until retirement. This may be dysfunctional, because in some cases, mediocre executives who would have greater difficulties finding a position with another organization may be the ones motivated to stay with the firm.

Perquisites (Perks). Perks—as privileges or gains in addition to one's regular salary—may vary considerably from top executives to employees at lower levels in the organization. Tax-free benefits, of course, represent more to those individuals in higher income tax brackets, and it is not unusual to see the chief executive officer of a major company driving "a company car to the airport where the company jet is waiting to take him to hereby resort for a get-away weekend at the company's midtown hotel suite. On his return he spends the afternoon at the country club whose membership comes with his title. All that without paying a rupee in personal income tax."

Besides the obvious tax benefits of such perks, perquisites "serve to reinforce the idea of status as a reflection of worth due to their observability." Most perks are highly visible signs of status: "Their allocation often defines the hierarchical nature of an organization more pointedly than direct money rewards." In India such perks are taxable by correcting these into money value and adding them back to the income of the executive.

Many perks have been criticized at times as patently disguised compensation that escapes taxation and amendments have been introduced in parliament to control perks. The basic question is what perks should be taxable. Thus, it would seem to be the top-level executive perks which are subject to the most attack.

Equity Participation. A equity participation is a financial arrangement in which executives are rewarded by being given the option to buy company equity at a later date at a price established when the option is granted. The value of the equity will presumably appreciate so that the executive can realize financial gains on the equity at a later time. A basic notion behind the equity participation is that owning company equity will induce executives to look at not only short-term profits but also the firm's performance in the long run.

CAFETERIA COMPENSATION

Since the 1960s individuals have advocated that employees be given some choice in the form of compensation they are to receive. Such an approach has been referred to as *flexible, cafeteria, supermarket,* or *smorgasbord* compensation. Actually, many companies provided some choice situations before this time. For example, in the late 1950s one

large retailing chain gave its employees the voluntary option of purchasing very extensive medical insurance plan coverage to supplement the basic insurance package provided at no cost to all employees. What is being advocated today is extending choice situations from letting employees choose from among a few insurance benefits to letting them choose much of their total compensation package.

The need for such incentive plans lies in the fact that so many changes took place in the 1970s. For example, changes in lifestyles, civil rights, spiraling inflation (including spiraling health costs), and taxation—and interrelationship among them—had not been adequately taken into account. These interacting factors "made it unlikely that a simple, single benefit plan for all employees would accommodate widely differing needs or produce effective use of benefits."

Eligibility, Criterion, and Reward

Eligibility. The laws of each country contain provisions to ensure that cafeteria plans encourage wide participation and do not discriminate against any employees. However, a gist of such laws is presented below.

1. A cafeteria plan must not discriminate in favour of highly compensated individuals with respect to both employer benefits or contributions.
2. A plan will not be discriminatory under an agreement which the Secretary of the Treasury finds to be a collective bargaining agreement between employee representatives and one or more employers.
3. A plan will not be considered discriminatory if it provides health benefits, the contributions to which on behalf of each participant includes an amount which:

(a) equals 100 percent of the cost of the health plan for the majority of the highly compensated individuals in the plan, or

(b) equals or exceeds 75 percent of the cost of the health coverage of the participant having the highest-cost health benefit coverage under the plan.

4. No employee is required to complete more than three years of service with the employer as a condition of participating in the plan.

Criterion and Reward. Cafeteria plans are not strictly incentives in the sense that some production standard, the adoptions of ideas submitted, or a profit goal is involved. Rather, employees obtain a reward by simply choosing the form of compensation benefits they want from among those made available. The company may pay the whole cost of a benefit or the employee may be required to pay for all or part of certain desired benefits. The rewards in cafeteria compensation are simply the "desirable" benefits chosen from among available multiple forms of compensation.

Setting Up and Managing a Plan

There are a number of steps involved in setting up and administering a flexible benefits plan. First, the cafeteria plan must be designed and costed out. Then, many firms will want to test market their proposed plan by trying it out on a sample of their employees: "The plan is... taken to a sampling of employees—a demographic cross section. If the idea is not well received by the sampling of employees, it goes no further." If the sampling indicates that employees want the cafeteria plan, the details of the plan are heavily communicated to the firm's employees who are to be included in the plan.

After a plan has communicated to employees, numerous aspects of plan administration come into play. A mechanism for employee selections to be properly recorded is needed, as is the whole process of handling employee claims. many individuals believe that for medium to large-size firms, a computer is essential for the proper administration of cafeteria plans. Others, however, believe that flexible benefits are feasible in small companies of 8 to 12 members in which case no computerization would be required.

Advantage of Cafeteria Plans

Several advantages of flexible benefits plans have been put forth. Cafeteria plans seem to elicit particular understanding of the company's benefits. As one employee of a large American Corporation puts it: "I can't really say I understood the benefits I was entitled to under our old system. But now you really have to understand the ones you choose, to assess whether or not they are practical for you."

It was found that the employee's whole family often became involved in the individual's choices: "Benefits were hardly discussed at home before. ... Now the wife wants to know what the husband is taking or giving up and what this means for herself and the children."

Cafeteria plans may additionally help attract and retain employees. At TELCO, for example, "many applicants have heard about the program and raise the subject at interviews." Further, surveys which were carried out six months after the plan started indicated that over 90 percent of the enrolled employees liked the plan. In spite of this liking, however, there is little if any evidence that participation in cafeteria plans increases either employee satisfaction or motivation. This seems logical because the all-important performance-reward link is missing from cafeteria plans.

Apprehensions About Cafeteria Plans

We have already implied two of the major concerns about cafeteria plans i.e. high start-up and administrative costs and the lack of the performance-reward link. Three more concerns directly related to the specific characteristics of flexible benefit plans cannot be ignored.

First, managements have always been concerned that benefits payments will be high owing to "adverse selection." This means that people will choose from the cafeteria the benefits that they need most—for example, individuals with bad teeth will pick as much dental insurance as they can, or someone facing a lawsuit will pick as much legal insurance as possible. Generally, those who have dealt with flexible compensation have not found this problem of great concern, for at least two reasons: (1) With larger plans—for example, 10,000 participants—a sufficient sample exists to negate the adverse selection problem; and (2) devices can be built into cafeteria plans to help overcome the problem.

Second, companies are often concerned that employees may make poor benefits choices and consequently get a poor picture of the plan (and company). Thus for, opinion seems to be that this is not a problem of any magnitude.

The third concern is that the employer may be put in a position to be sued by an employee who has made a bad selection of benefits. Without going into all of the legal aspects in detail, essentially employers may be held liable for damages if they initiate *benefit selection counseling.* Thus, if a company proceeds with a cafeteria plan, this type of action should definitely be avoided.

SYSTEM INCENTIVES

In earlier sections we have discussed four basic types of individual incentives. We will now focus our attention to four widely recognized types of incentives referred to as *group, plant-wide, company-wide,* or *system* incentives. (1) profit sharing plans, (2) Scanlon plans, (3) the highly systems-oriented incentive plan in effect at the Lincoln Electric Company, and (4) stock ownership plans.

Overview of System Incentives

The distinction between individual incentives discussed before and the system incentives of this chapter is somewhat blurred. For example, part of the Lincoln systems approach calls for individual piecework incentives of exactly the same type. Generally, however, the system incentives that we will discuss here are considered to foster more cooperative and collaborative behavior among organizational members as opposed to traditional piecework.

Some of the three sequential decisions (eligibility, criterion and reward) require no more than a sentence to describe. For example, management at the Lincoln Electric Company simple decided that all members of the organization would be eligible for participation in the yearly bonus plan except the company's chairman of the board of directors and president. On the other hand, some of the managerial decisions involve quite complex factors. Federal income taxes levied on the reward paid to individuals eligible for lump-sum distributions is deferred profit sharing plans upon retirement provide such an example.

It should emphasized that firms are not restricted to the use of only one type of system (or individual) incentive plan. In many cases firms may have a Scanlon plan and a deferred profit sharing plan, designed to work together to provide an attractive overall financial package for the organization. Further, sometimes system incentives are designed to supplement employee benefit plans, which follow in the next chapter of this volume, Employee Benefits.

Perhaps the most classic example of this decision strategy is the use of deferred profit sharing plans along with pension benefits to provide employees with considerable financial security upon retirement. We will now turn to the most widely used of the four system plans—profit sharing plans.

PROFIT SHARING PLANS

Profit sharing may be defined as a financial arrangement by which a firm establishes some predetermined formula for sharing a portion of its profits with its employees. This idea of sharing profits is not new, nor is interest in profit sharing limited to one nation. The growth of profit sharing plans was slow until recent decades.

Although it is difficult to ascertain the exact number of such plans opearative in the country today, albiet a rough estimate suggests that there are approximately 5,00,000 current profit sharing plans are in operation as of the end of 1990. We have estimated that the total assets of qualified deferred profit-sharing funds that have been set aside for later payment to employees were about 200 crore as of the end of 1990.

There are three basic types of profit sharing plans: current, deferred, and a combination of the two. Under each of these arrangements an employee's share of profits is determined by two factors. The individual's pay is a factor, with persons earning more receiving larger distributions up to certain limits. The profits of the firm are a factor, since employee shares are directly related to profits, and larger sums will be available as profit-sharing distributions as the firm's profits are higher.

Under current plans, "profits are paid directly to employees in cash, check, or stock as soon as profits are determined" (for example, monthly, quarterly, semiannually, or annually). Deferred plans, on the other hand, call for the accumulation of profit sharing contributions over the years into trusts to be distributed as annuities, installments, or lump-sum distributions to the employee upon retirement age or upon leaving the firm prior to retirement. Employee's benefits would be handled according to their beneficiary designation, should they die before becoming eligible under these conditions. Managerial decisions with respect to such deferred plans are constrained in more ways by laws in force than are current plans. In many cases, trusts with huge assets have been set up to invest the funds over the years prior to distribution to employees.

Another type of profit sharing plan is the combination plan, in which some current cash benefits are provided employees and other portions of the employee's profit share are deferred. The deferred plans are far more complex than current plans because of their large assets and because they are subject to more provisions of the law. Combination plans can, of course, become complicated because they encompass both the complex aspects of deferred profit sharing and the comparatively simple mechanics of current plans. We will focus attention almost exclusively on the deferred plans because they are more complex. We do this on the assumption that familiarity with their basic aspects will enable the reader to also understand both the combined and current plans.

One point with respect to current trends in profit sharing plan development, however, does involve combination plans. With such factors as inflation and increased social security payroll deductions, many individuals have wanted more immediately available cash than previously. In consequence, a trend toward more combination plans, which provide both cash and long-term security, has been reported. Further, in a number of these plans, employees have been given some choice as to how much of their profit sharing allocation will be in immediate cash and how much will constitute deferred distribution.

Eligibility

Several considerations are important with regard to eligibility in deferred plans. First, it has been a common practice to require employees to wait one year after they have been hired by a firm before they become eligible for participation in the plan. Second, to become an eligible member in a number of deferred plans, employees must contribute a portion of their earnings to the plan. In some cases it is mandatory that organization employees contribute, in many other cases it is voluntary. Numerous arguments have been raised concerning the advantages of contributory as opposed to noncontributory plans. For example, it has been argued that a plan with a mandatory contributory feature can have the effect of forcing habits of thrift on individuals. Further, it has been claimed that the return on profit sharing contributions is generally greater than if employees had saved money themselves, since deferred profit sharing trusts are managed by professional investors. On the other hand, being required to contribute a sum in addition to social security deductions, federal withholding taxes, and perhaps state and local taxes as well may put the individual in a tight financial position. It is for these reasons that fewer deferred plans have mandatory contributory features today and more have voluntary features.

One additional concept is important relative to deferred profit sharing plans—that of vesting. Vesting has been defined as the *acquisition by the employee of a right (a non-forfeitable claim), according to a definite formula, to all or part of the amount in his account or in his accrued benefits, at date of severance* [from the organization].

The Criterion

The criterion for reward under current, deferred, and combination profit-sharing plans varies widely de£pending in no small part on the size of the company and its profits.

The Rewards

In a sense, we have already indicated what the basic rewards are under profit sharing systems—some share of the firm's profits above a certain minimum. With current plans, companies simply pay out these profits shares and deduct these payments at the corporate income tax rate, and individuals are taxed on the reward by the federal government in the year they receive it as regular income with the 50 percent maximum marginal rate. With qualified deferred plans, on the other hand:

1. The company obtains a tax deduction immediately, to the extent that it contributes to the plan.

2. These funds are taken (along with individual contributions in contributions in contributory plans) and invested professionally in the hope that the funds will appreciate significantly over the years.
3. This appreciation may be furthered by *forfeitures,* which are assets that are left in the fund by those individuals who leave the firm before employer contributions to their accounts are fully vested. (These employees would receive profit sharing distributions to the extent that their accounts are vested.)
4. The reward is paid out to people who do remain with the company when they retire or during the years after retirement when their incomes are at lower federal income tax rates which tend to be favorable.

Thus, two basic functions that deferred plans can provide are (1) tax advantages to the individual on substantial funds paid out beyond normal compensation, and (2) security above and beyond any pension plan the firm may have.

We will now outline various alternative means by which individuals may be rewarded by deferred profit sharing plans if they stay with the firm until retirement. There are basically three different methods of paying out profit sharing rewards. A firm may provide its employees with the option of choosing a combination of these. First, employees can be given an annuity from their accumulated profit sharing account. In such cases, they pay income taxes on the annuity minus any of their contributions over the years since they have already paid income taxes on the earnings earmarked for these contributions.

Second, employees can be given their reward as a series of installments over 10 or 15 years, for example, or over a duration equivalent to their actuarial life expectancy (or the joint life expectancies of the individual and his or her spouse). Income taxes on these installments are treated the same as with annuities.

Finally, they may receive their reward in a lump-sum distribution when they retire. Here again, all prior contributions by the employee are substracted for tax purposes. Realising a large lump-sum distribution all in one year as one retires may be better or worse for an individual than an annuity, since the person may only live six months after age 65 and receive very little money from the annuity. On the other hand, persons may live many years, so the total sum of their annuity payments would exceed any lump-sum distribution at age 65 drawn from the same amount of money in their profit sharing account.

Profit Sharing: A Critical Assessment

Evaluation. As indicated earlier, profit sharing plans have enjoyed wide usage, and many individuals have believed them to be effective system rewards. We will now evaluate some of the major implications of profit sharing plans.

First, evaluating the effectiveness of profit sharing plans is difficult. Aside from being influenced by its employees' efforts, a firm's profits will also be affected by such factors as the business cycle or competitor strategies. Further, the vagaries of the stock market may have an important effect on the value of deferred profit sharing trust funds. As we will indicate later, however, external variables will also affect Scanlon plan rewards (as they will most system incentive rewards).

Recognizing these difficult research limitations, some studies have shown a positive relationship between having a profit sharing plan and company success. The Profit Sharing Research Foundation, for example, compared the financial performance of several department store chains with profit sharing against a similar group without it for the period 1952-1969. On all measures studies (sales, earnings per common share, dividends per common share, and market price per share), based on growth since 1952, those firms with profit sharing outperformed those without this system incentive. The sample size in this study was small (14), however, and a question must raised: Could it be possible that the chains which performed most successfully did so simply because they had more progressive and superior managements, that happened, among other things, to have decided to have profit sharing plans? The authors of this study raised this precise question and answered it as follows:

> If "more competent management" is assigned as the "cause" of the superior performance (and this may well be the major factor), then one must ask himself the next logical question. "Why did 'more competent management' see fit to initiate, continue, and expand their respective profit sharing programs unless

they firmly believed that profit sharing served both organizational goals and individual needs?"

One tangible benefit that may be derived from profit sharing plans is that they may enhance the firm's recruiting efforts. It can, however, be argued that this is less true today than 25 years ago, for as we saw earlier, so many firms now do have qualified deferred plans as compared to then.

It has also been argued that deferred profit sharing reduces turnover. Although, as indicated previously, deferred plans have often been vested more liberally than law requires, full and immediate vesting after one year is still not common, and the individual may gain substantially larger profit sharing sums by remaining longer with the company. This is not only because of becoming eligible for an increased amount of vesting, but also because of appreciation of assets accruing from wise fund investments and forfeitures.

One final question must be raised with respect to profit sharing and turnover: Is it the firm's better or poorer employees who may be induced to remain with the organization because of the forfeiture of profit sharing and other types of employee benefits? Some people argue that it is often the poorer employees who cannot find a comparable job elsewhere who remain with firms, while highly capable people may be very "marketable."

One decided benefit for those individuals who belong to deferred profit sharing plans is that the benefits derived from them upon retirement may serve to meet their security needs. In some cases, deferred profit sharing plans are used as substitutes for pension plans. This is comparatively advantageous to the firm, since it only needs to make payments in profitable years, whereas contributions must be made to pension funds each year, regardless of profitability. Conversely, the fixed commitments of pension plans may provide more security to the employee than deferred profit sharing.

Two other points with respect to the evaluation of deferred profit sharing plans are frequently cited in discussions on the subject. First, contributory plans encourage thrift but may impose a cash strain on employees at certain times. Second, employees reaping the full benefits of qualified deferred plans often receive large sums of money that are taxed favorably.

Finally, do such plans really motivate employees to higher levels of performance? In following our notion that motivation is highly correlated with the existence of a direct link between effort and reward, some current plans in small companies may provide a fairly perceptible link to employees. With deferred profit sharing rewards often time-lagged by many years and with large numbers of employees scattered over hundreds of locations in certain plans, on the other hand, we would not expect to find such a link. However, the existence of such system-oriented rewards may provide more employee satisfaction with the organization and a beneficial psychological effect, legitimate ends in themselves. Such an evaluation has been phrased aptly by Katz and Kahn: "System rewards to little to motivate performance beyond the line of duty, with two possible exceptions. As people develop a liking for the attractions of the organization, they may be more likely to engage in cooperative relations with their fellows toward organizational goals. Further, they may describe their company "as a good place to work" contributing "to a favorable climate of opinion for the system in the external environment," which may enhance recruiting efforts as described earlier.

In sum, there are a number of valid reasons for firms to adopt profit sharing plans. Such plans, however, will tend to be more successful under certain contingencies. We will now examine some of these.

Contingencies

A basic contingency for successful profit sharing plans is that there be profits to share, at least in most years. We hypothesize that this is more important in current plans than deferred ones. This is because in the latter, owing to forfeitures and investment appreciation, an employee's profit sharing account may increase even in years in which there have been no profits to share. Further, for profit sharing to be perceived positively, there is probably a certain minimum percentage of the employee's per that must be realized on the average through the plan. A somewhat related point, which has been used as an argument against the values of profit sharing, is that employees will take their profit sharing payments for granted in good years and become dissatisfied in years in which there are few or not profits to share. This factor may be partially overcome if relevant facts about the firm's business and profits are given to employees through periodic progress reports. Such communications and the design of plans which are understandable by employees will aid in their being viewed favorably.

Two final points concerning profit sharing plans need to be made. First, unlike many personnel programs, size or stability of the company does not appear to be a contingency influencing profit sharing plans as it would be with traditional individual incentive systems. Even if the firm is changing rapidly in a dynamic environment, profit sharing plans will not need the constant updating as would changing the tasks involved in jobs.

Second, as we have indicated with respect to other personnel programs, profit sharing will be more effective if employee- management relations are good. As one author has phrased it, "If the organization's employee relations program is perceived as generally rational, non-manipulative and relevant to the workers' situation, considerable credibility is likely to be given to the incentive plan proposal."

SCANLON PLANS

The evolution and approach of Scanlon plans may be traced back to Joseph N. Scanlon. Scanlon first developed and implemented his ideas while a union worker in the 1930s during the depression. He successfully convinced his company's management to develop a collaborative approach to help solve its economic problems. These efforts attracted the attention of numerous other companies and leading academic scholars. Scanlon ultimately joined the staff of the Industrial Relations Section at M.I.T. in 1946, where he remained until his death ten years later. We refer to Scanlon plans rather than *the* Scanlon plan, since there have been numerous variations among firms in the mechanics utilized in implementing this system incentive.

Scanlon plans represent a philosophy regarding the individual and human relations and a mechanism by which this philosophy can be put into effect in organizations. The Scanlon philosophy is one that takes a very positive view of the capabilities of the human being. It stresses that individuals can and want to meet higher-level needs by participating in decision making. Our own view is that this philosophy is an overly optimistic one since we do not believe that *all* people want to assume more responsibility, participate in making decisions concerning their work environment, and express creative ideas. In fact, even among the strongest supporters of Scanlon plans, it has been pointed out that many employees, "because of their cultural and environmental situations," have learned *not* to behave in this way, and with "competent leadership and supportive guidance...must be helped to unlearn the negative response." *Basic* behavioral dispositions are difficult to modify once individuals have reached adulthood, and in line with this face, the unlearning referred to here may be very difficult, if not impossible, in some cases. Some firms have used the plan with success, however, in overcoming a wide range of problems. For example, Scanlon plans have effectively substituted for traditional wage incentive plans which were functioning very poorly, and in some firms they have mobilized strong support from virtually all workers in reducing production and other costs in order to literally save the firm from bankruptcy.

Recognizing that the Scanlon philosophy may be overly optimistic about human capabilities but that when properly implemented may provide a successful participative decision-making incentive, we will now turn to the three management decisions regarding Scanlon plans: eligibility, criteria, and reward. Then we will specify several key contingencies for the effective utilization of such plans. Finally, we will evaluate and comment briefly on future directions with respect to Scanlon plans.

Eligibility

Only two comments need to be made with respect to employee eligibility in Scanlon plans. First, a basic notion of the Scanlon philosophy is that all employees participate and hopefully reap the benefits of the plan, although sometimes the president of a Scanlon plan firm will be excluded. Second, some firms require a one-, two-, or three month waiting period after an employee begins working before the individual is eligible for the bonuses paid under Scanlon plans.

Criteria

Employees will be rewarded financially under Scanlon plans if cost savings, most commonly computed on a monthly basis, are realized by the firm. These savings may come from two sources.

One means of savings you accrue from more effort on the part of employees. The other means of effecting cost savings is through the generation of employee ideas. Scanlon plans include an elaborate participate decision-making mechanism to foster this goal. There are two different types of committees set up under the Scanlon plan—committees in each department and a plant-wide screening committee.

Production Committees. The production committees, which are usually made up of the departmental supervisor and elected employee delegates, meet every two to four weeks. One of their basic functions is to screen and evaluate employee ideas that fall within the jurisdiction of the department and do not require capital investments. Ideas applying to work in more than one department or those requiring capital investments fall within the jurisdiction of the screening committee.

The second basic function of each committee is to encourage actively employees in its department to submit suggestions. In their meetings, these committees try to identify problems and make these problems known to the employees to guide creativity. This planned proaction represents one major distinction between Scanlon plans and traditional suggestion systems. Further, employees participating in Scanlon plans are not paid directly if their ideas are accepted. Even so, the Scanlon planned proaction appears to result in more suggestions being submitted than in traditional suggestion systems from reports in numerous case studies of plans in different companies. Certain other aspects of traditional suggestion systems, on the other hand, are equally applicable to Scanlon suggestions, for example, prompt decisions on idea acceptance and letting employees know why any unusable suggestions have been rejected.

The Screening Committee. The screening committee is composed of the firm's or plant's chief executive officer, heads of major functional department such as finance, and an "equal or greater number" of elected, nonmanagerial employees.

Reward

The second component of the Scanlon philosophy is the provision of a reward, usually monthly, to all employees if a cost-savings norm is exceeded. This is referred to as the Scanlon bonus. It

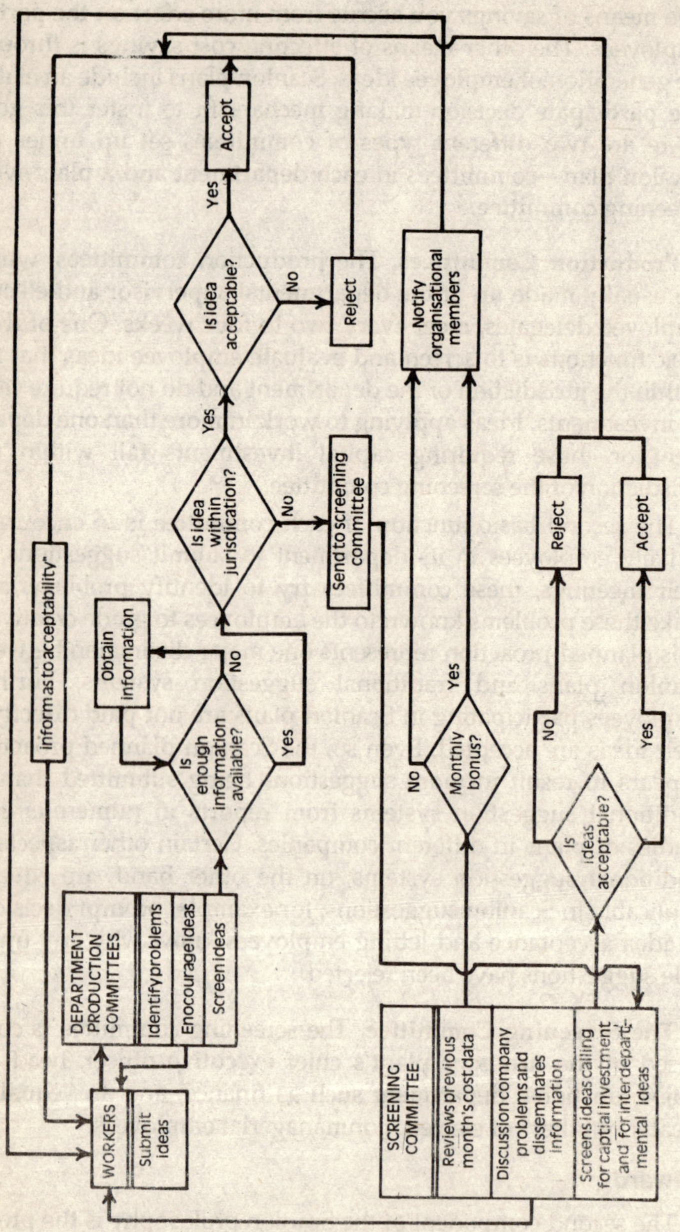

Fig. 3. Committees based on Scanlon plans.

is shared in proportion to the regular rate of pay so that those employees who hold more responsible positions in the organization will receive a larger bonus than those persons with lesser skills. For this reason, it is extremely important that wages and salaries be equitable, since if they are not, neither can the Scanlon bonus be fair.

The Scanlon norm is usually developed by analyzing total labor costs in relation to the value of the firm's output over a representative historical period (for example, the previous two to five years). The norm is developed cooperatively by management and its employees (or their union). In its simplest form, the norm equals:

$$\frac{\text{Total labor costs}}{\text{Total value of production}}$$

If, in any given month, total labor costs are less than would be expected under the norm, the workers and company usually share in these "savings." An example of a typical Scanlon bonus month for a hypothetical firm is given in Table 2.

Table 2

Typical Scanlon Bonus Month Calculations

(a)	Scalon ratio $\frac{\text{total labor costs}}{\text{total value of production}}$	0.40/1.00
(b)	Value of production (Rs.)	200,000
(c)	Expected "norm" labor costs ($a \times b$) (Rs.)	80,000
(d)	Actual total labor costs (Rs.)	60,000
(e)	Bonus "pool" ($c - d$) (Rs.)	20,000
(f)	Share to company—25 per cent ($e \times 0.25$) (Rs.)	5,000
(g)	Share to employees—75 per cent ($e \times 0.75$) (Rs.)	15,000
(h)	Reserve for future deficits (25 per cent $\times g$) (Rs.)	3,750
(i)	Pool for monthly distribution ($g - h$) (Rs.)	11,250
(j)	Bonus for each employee as a percentage of pay for the month ($i \div d$) (%)	18.75

PAY EXAMPLE FOR TYPICAL EMPLOYEE

Monthly pay	*Bonus*	*Bonus pay*	*Total pay*
Rs. 1000	18.75%	Rs. 187.50	Rs. 1187.50

References to this table will allow further discussion of the mechanics of the Scanlon bonus. First, the reserve for future deficits is included to cover those months in which total labor costs exceed the standard. In these months, no pay is actually taken away from any employee, but a "deficit" is recorded. At the end of each year, if these reserves are greater than any deficit months, they are added to the pool and shared on the basis of regular pay as with the monthly bonuses. If the reserves set aside for the year are inadequate to cover deficit months (that is, those in which total labor costs exceed the norm), the company usually writes the deficit amount off at a loss. Hence, employees have an opportunity to "start over again" in the year. A typical reserve figure is 25 percent, but firms in which there are wider monthly fluctuations in demand patterns will usually want to provide for a higher reserve than those organizations with a relatively stable of operation.

Second, the percentage share given to the company is frequently 25 percent, but this will vary depending upon the company's financial position. In an extremely financially strained company, for example, management and its employees may agree on a larger share for the firm. The converse is also true.

Third, the Scanlon factor (or ratio) must be updated from time to time as the cost structure changes, or else the bonus will be inequitable to either management or employees. A question has been raised as to the administrative complexity and feasibility of such updatings, particularly if they are frequent. The only evidence that we have been able to uncover on this point is in a letter written by Frederick Lesieur (1975), which indicated that "in the inflationary spirals of 1972-1974, as material costs outstripped wage increases, Scanlon ratios had to undergo frequent changes. Those involved in managing Scanlon plans found, however, that these changes were made with minimal difficulty." Our own view is that firms, through the use of computers, can probably modify the ratio, as well as handle all aspects of the Scanlon bonus to the point of actually calculating employee paychecks. This assumes, of course, that management and the employees could agree on the changes.

Contingencies

Several conditions seem to be extremely important to the effective functioning of Scanlon plans. One key variable—technology—which might be expected to be important does not appear so. One of what we consider to be the two most important contingencies is that the firm's management will have to commit itself to a tremendous change in the firm's power structure. With the production and screening committees, "The total effect is to move downward in the organization many decisions relating to its specific operations; moreover, this delegation or downward movement of authority and decision-making is carried out by means of formal changes in the organizational structure."

As we saw earlier, the production committee members must have access to cost information that many managements would hesitate to provide workers. Further, the whole suggestion mechanism can provide a threat to supervisors and managers for the same reason discussed with traditional suggestion systems. This can occur even more so because of the organized, structured, and proactive nature of the suggestion process. In short, success of Scanlon plans seems to be very high contingent on the willingness of management to actively display a democratic leadership and be willing to adhere to organic-oriented attitudes in actual practice.

Second, there must be the possibility of being able to obtain bonuses over a period of time for the Scanlon plan to be effective. Without this financial reward, much of the motivation built into the plan is lost. It is far from clear, however, in which types of industries such bonuses will be forthcoming, which brings us to the contingency of technology.

As indicated, Scanlon plans are based on a highly organic philosophy. There appears to be no evidence, however, that they are not effective in technologies where more certainty is present along the lines discussed in Chapter 1. Lesieur and Puckett have shown Scanlon plans to be effective both at the mass-production-oriented Parker Pen Company (theoretically a fairly "certain" technology amendable to mechanistic management practices) and in the highly job-shop-oriented and hence less certain environment of the Pfaudler Company. Katz and Kahn have questioned whether Scanlon plans can survive in highly automated operations because of the sharp decline in labor costs, while Bennis has reported on the adoption of a Scanlon plan at a continuous-manufacturing-oriented oil refinery. With respect to technology, in fact, we know of only one study indicating that this variable has an impact on Scanlon plans, and the technology factors examined were so related to the particular conditions of one firm that we cannot generalize from them.

Elasticity of demand, on the other hand, may well be an important Scanlon success contingency, although there is disagreement on this issue. Puckett studied ten Scanlon plan firms, of which five represented situations in which it appeared that "price reduction based on increased efficiency could result in a significant improvement in sales," and five in which elasticity did not seem to be significant. Among these firms, he found no relationship between elasticity and Scanlon plan success. Strauss and Sayles, on the other hand, have indicated that a company must be able to increase sales to the extent of any increases in production if Scanlon plans are to succeed. We agree that the latter interpretation based on theory and the fact that Puckett's sample size was small and his estimation of elasticity was an extremely subjective one.

Many firms that have adopted Scanlon plans have been relatively small ones with a few hundred or few thousand employees. Puckett's research indicates that large as well as small firms have had successful Scanlon experiences. From a theoretical point of view, however, employees in smaller operations may well be in a better position to perceive the effort-reward link than those in huge manufacturing plants. Further, it has been argued that the "plan may be unwieldy to administer in large companies where time consumed in operating the plan may be disproportionate to the savings gained in labor costs or where firm bigness stifles two-way communications." More recently research has indicated, however, that up to 600 employees, size does not seem to be a factor in determining success.

Finally, as is true with most personnel systems, effective administration is a basic contingency. As an almost unbelievable example of poor Scanlon administration, one firm reportedly dropped the Scanlon plan in favor of a profit sharing plan, even though it was prospering considerably. In spite of this financial prosperity, Scanlon bonus payments were negligible in this case, due to the fact that the ratio had not been updated appropriately "because the accountant felt that the book keeping work would have been too difficult."

A Critical Assessment

Evaluation. Scanlon plans have worked very successfully in some companies, but have been abandoned in others, sometimes because of poor implementation. Implemented properly, and in light of the contingencies indicated here, Scanlon plans may serve to meet the full range of Maslow's needs hierarchy. The Scanlon bonus, if adequate, contributes to meeting many needs, including security. Participation in production or screening committees provides opportunities to meet higher-level needs such as esteem and self-actualization. Simply participating in a Scanlon plan firm to the extent of suggesting ideas can, of course, also help meet self-actualization needs as can be done under traditional suggestion systems.

Supporters of Scanlon plans have also argued that the plans provide a mechanism whereby good bonuses will come about only as a result of hard work. The bonuses are related directly to production savings, not to extra profits because of a competitor's poor marketing decision or other external factors. As one book has phrased it, "There are no Santa Claus gifts or autocratic benefactor's bonuses. There are disciplined team members who are being intelligently coached to win the game." Further, these efforts are system efforts, for the bonuses "reward not the efficiency of the individual or the group, but the gains in overall efficiency of the company as a procurement-production-marketing system. It should be noted, however, that changes in Scanlon bonuses may be influenced by variables other than the combined efforts of individuals in the organizational system. Factors not completely under control of a firm such as general business conditions or competitor actions may influence the firm's sales volume, product mix, or other company characteristics. Changes in these characteristics, in turn, may affect Scanlon bonuses."

Future Directions. The future directions of Scanlon plans encompass two aspects. First, there is the question of whether the number of such plans will grow. As just indicated, these plans do have many merits and may become even more popular in the future. In spite of the use of some important human judgments in some types of automated operations, it remains to be seen, however, whether further automation in our postindustrial society will hamper Scanlon opportunities.

There is also more attention being given to the study of Scanlon plans so as to better understand their properties and contingencies. Most of the earlier writings on Scanlon plans were in the form of case studies, and little, if any, rigorous research was carried out on the plans. More recently, however, there seems to be a renewed and more scholarly interest in Scanlon plans.

LINCOLN INCENTIVE MANAGEMENT PLAN

The Lincoln Incentive Management Plan, instituted in 1934 by James F. Lincoln at the Lincoln Electric Company, Cleveland (welding equipment and supplies), is a combination profit-sharing and incentive plan. It has received wide publicity, not only because of the size of the extra payments made to workers, but also because of the way in which worker- management identification is achieved, resulting in continuing suggestions for method improvements, which in turn lower costs and prices while at the same time returning increased take-home pay. End-of-year bonuses attainable by employees are in the order of magnitude of 60% to 150% of basic pay, while at the same time basic wages and salaries are comparable to those of comparable jobs in the Cleveland area. Everyone but the president and the chairman of the board shares in these incentives.

Performance standards are set by the usual time-study techniques. However, the system differs from time-study-based incentives in the determination of the individual bonus, which is based on an over-all judgment of the worker's performance and attitude, and in the continuing simulation of improvement ideas on the part of the entire organization. Management constantly hammers home the theme that there must be a continuing reduction in the price of Lincoln products, so that not only the management and employees share in the increased productivity, but the customers as well. In Lincoln's own words:

> The man is rewarded for all the things he does that are of help, and penalized if he does not do as well as others in all these same ways. He is a member of the team and is rewarded or

> penalized depending on what he can do in all opportunities to win the game.
>
> The man is rated by all those who have accurate knowledge of some phase of his work...This program runs parallel to the write-ups following the playing of a game or the selecting of an all-American team. The best man gets the praise and the standing he warrants and craves.
>
> Each man is advanced or retarded in his standing by his current record. He is rated two times per year. The sum of these ratings determines his share in the bonus and advancement.
>
> At the time of giving each man his rating, any question he may want to ask as to why the rating is as it is and how it can be improved is answered in complete detail by the executives responsible.
>
> The progress in new methods and techniques flows naturally from the desire of the worker to find...progressive ideas. It is obvious that lower cost will be the outcome.

Size of Bonus is determined as follows: At the end of the year, a fair return is paid to the stockholders as a dividend, which the workers are made to see as "the wages of capital." After the dividend is provided for, the company sets aside what it terms "seed money" for the future. The amount is determined by the directors on the basis of current operations. After these deductions from profits, all of the balance is divided as a bonus among the workers and management on the basis described, i.e. on the basis of the contribution of each person to the success of the company for the year. The size of the individual's bonus depends on three factors: his merit rating, his base salary, and the size of the total bonus pool. The actual bonus is computed by multiplying the base wage or salary times merit rating times the bonus factor. The bonus factor is obtained by dividing the dollars of total bonus pool by the dollars of total company payroll. It can be seen that for this system to work out, each department head must see that the merit ratings in his department average out at 100. Thus for each 120 that a supervisor awards, he must give out an 80, or perhaps two 90s.

Merit Appraisal of the individual worker is made in detailed fashion jointly by his immediate superior and others who are in a position to know what he has done. Appraisal occurs three times a year.

Results

As on 1980, Lincoln stated that the bonus distribution has slightly exceeded wages during the last 45 years. From management's point of view, one major criterion of the program's success is the company's productivity which has attained Rs. 150,0000 annual sales per employee. This compares favorably with the average for all manufacturing. Another success indicator is employee stability. The company has a turnover rate of less than 1% per month. These results were accompanies by highly competitive prices for all Lincoln products.

That industry has not adopted the Lincoln plan in widespread fashion, despite the spectacular success achieved with it by its originator, perhaps testifies to the personal dedication of Mr. Lincoln himself to the furtherance of constructive employee motivation in industry. His philosophy may be summed up in the opening sentence of his pamphlet, "Intelligent Selfishness and Manufacturing." "Great as American industry is, it leaves largely untapped its greatest resources, the productive power, initiative, and intelligence talent in every person."

Reasons for Success

One basic reason for the Lincoln plan's success is that it has implemented a sound philosophy with a total-system approach to motivating individuals to develop themselves and produce, present ideas, and contribute in other ways to organizational goals at very high levels. The Lincoln plan is not just a profit sharing plan. It does not just provide individual piecework incentives. It is not just a plan emphasizing opportunities for advancement by promotion-from-within policies. Rather, it is all of these aspects of personnel management interwoven into a success mosaic.

The size of the firm may be another reason that has contributed to the plan's success. Lincoln Electric is small enough so that many of the interrelated effort-reward links (which we have indicated so often are important to effective incentives) are fairly easily perceptible by most organizational members.

Another contributing factor to the effectiveness of the plan may be that it was installed and initially guided by a charismatic leader. *Charisma* is a quality that has not been well researched, but generally has been used to describe political figures "who have achieved very strong power positions primarily because of the extraordinary nature of their personalities alone." Abraham Lincoln (on the positive side) and Adolf Hitler (on the negative side) would be examples of extremely charismatic leaders. At a much less grandiose level, two noted social scientists, Katz and Kahn, have questioned whether some charisma may need to exist in the initiation of Scanlon plans for them to be successful. This raises the question that perhaps both the personality of Joseph Scanlon (and his followers such as Frederick Lesieur) and that of James Lincoln were so dynamic as to attract organizational members to their philosophies and the implementation of these philosophies.

The Lincoln plan seems to incorporate a wide spectrum of Maslow's five classes of needs. For example, the monetary rewards may meet many needs (from physiological to esteem); the guaranteed workweek helps meet security needs; and election to the advisory board may serve to stimulate self- actualization. The same can also be said for those workers given a great deal of autonomy in performing their work.

Two final comments are in order concerning the Lincoln plan. First, it appears to constitute a unique open system—one which may well be irreproducible elsewhere. Second, the technology of the firm raises some questions about which organizational types are most suitable for organic and mechanistic management systems. In Lincoln's production of both electric motors and arc welding equipment, there are certain tasks conducive to organic management. Special products are manufactured that take a great deal of democratic management where the workers are given latitude in decision making.

With both electric motor and are welding equipment production, however, there is a great deal of large-batch or mass production technology, and many jobs are time studied and highly standardized. Such operations are characterized by a considerable degree of certainty and are therefore theoretically conducive to mechanistic management. In all respects, however, both the Lincoln philosophy and incentive implementation mechanisms are highly organic in orientation. How Lincoln Electric has been able to foster democratic, organic-oriented management practices and the assumption of individual responsibility in production areas conducive theoretically to both organic and mechanistic approaches has been explained by Richard S. Sabo of Lincoln Electric as follows:

> Even in our high [large-batch and mass] production areas, we expect everyone to produce a high quality product and the responsibility for quality falls on the individual, not an inspection department or foreman.
>
> I would have to summarize by saying that one of the keys to our success is that we have been able to incorporate highly-motivated people who take a great deal of pride in their work whether it be on an organic or mechanistic management task.

7

EMPLOYEE BENEFITS

IN recent years there has been a sharp increase in the number of *employee benefits* provided organization members. We will consider as benefits such items as non-incentive-oriented *supplemental compensation, nonwage and nonsalary types of income,* and *indirect payments* to employees. It is expected that such benefits will continue to increase. For example, it was estimated in 1982 that benefits "account for at least 35 percent of the total compensation cost for each employee, and possibly in the next decade they will reach 50 percent."

The two basic trends in benefits have been the introduction of new benefits and the provision of more extensive coverage of existing benefits to employees at a lesser cost to them. A notable exception to lower-cost benefits are those provided by social security, which should continue to cost both employers and employees more and more.

The number of different types of employee benefits in existence or proposed seems almost limitless. Two authors, for example, listed 197 such benefits, ranging from free beer to vaccination shots. In classifying these benefits for purposes of discussion, we find Henderson's three basic categories most useful:

1. *Employee services,* which include merchandise purchasing plans, social and recreational activities, counseling, and legal services.

2. *Time not worked,* which includes vacations, holidays, personal excused absences, and sabbaticals for social services.
3. *Employee security and health benefits,* which include life, health, and disability insurance, pension plans, social security, unemployment compensation, and guaranteed annual incomes or supplemental unemployment benefits.

In this chapter, we well first indicate some of the basic reasons why employee benefits are increasing and some of the more important implications for management decision making. Then we will briefly discuss employee services and time without pay, including changes in traditional workweek hours. Finally, we will discuss in some detail the rapidly growing, extremely costly, and generally legally established or regulated employee security and health benefits. In discussion these benefits we will focus attention on the following key benefits: (1) social security, (2) other forms of income security, and (3) medical insurance.

NEED FOR INCREASED EMPLOYEE BENEFITS

There are a number of reasons for the growth of employee benefits. These reasons can be both external and internal to the firm in nature. For purposes of simplification we will group the external forces that have exerted pressure on organizations to increase employee benefits into the following four categories: (1) economic, (2) governmental, (3) technological, and (4) union. Internal forces consist of management decisions that voluntarily provide employees with benefits deemed necessary for their welfare. Such voluntarily provided benefits are based on the firm's humanitarian objectives. We will now examine these two sets of forces along with some of their major interdependencies.

Background

Great Depression of the 1930s probably provided the earliest powerful force for increased employee benefits. With unemployment rates well over 20 percent, there was a strong perceived need for economic security. Under the New Deal administration of President Franklin D. Roosevelt, the Social Security Act was passed in 1935. This act (both as originally enacted and later amended) provided for old age, disability, and survivors benefits; health benefits; and a basis for a federal-state unemployment compensation program. The passage of the Social Security Act also "gave private pension plans a shot in the arm. Many companies, which previously couldn't afford such plans now could use...[this act] ...as the cornerstone on which to build a private plan."

As the nation emerged from the depression and entered World War II in 1941, government actions and union pressures combined to further stimulate the growth of employee benefits. In the pension plan area, for example, numerous forces combined in the following manner. During World War II the government froze wages and salaries. However, pensions were exempt from the freeze. Therefore, a number of companies began to provide pensions so that by 1945, 5.6 million workers were covered. Pressure to provide benefits resulted from labor shortages and strong union demands. Firms also were encouraged to provide pension benefits because of federal income tax laws. Such benefits had long been recognized as legitimate business expenses for tax purposes. Then, during the war, very high marginal corporate income taxes were put into effect. Many firms were earning high corporate profits, and taxes in the highest bracket were 93 percent. Thus, tax-deductible pensions cost such firms only "7-cent dollars."

Once this pension door had opened, an even greater union push for such plans came after World War II. Four years after the end of the war, a major postwar impetus to pension growth occurred in the Inland Steel case, in 1949, in which it was ruled that pensions could be considered a bargainable issue between unions and management.

After World War II, many wartime scientific innovations were transformed into peacetime technological improvements, which increased the nation's overall productive efficiency. Coupled with union pressures for better wages, increased productivity contributed toward increasing the purchasing power of many Americans (in spite of inflation). At the same time, many jobs, especially in certain mass production industries, although well-paying, were repetitive, monotonous, routine, and boring to many workers. Workers who performed such jobs began to look to off-the-job activities, such as civic activities and hobbies, to meet their self-actualization needs. In consequence, unions pressed for and obtained shorter workweeks. more vacation time, and more paid holidays.

Technology, union pressures, government intervention, and economic conditions combined in still another way to exert pressures for greater employee benefits. This technology has been *medical* technology. In recent decades, numerous new, lifesaving forms of medical technology have been developed. In many cases they have been both very sophisticated and *costly.* In addition, inflation, such as in the 1970s, helped push up the costs of quality medical care. These forces, together with union demands, have combined to exert pressures for organizational medical insurance employee benefits to provide both broader and higher-cost coverage and for governmental intervention in the health area, which we will discuss later in this chapter.

Another factor that has made the growth of many employee benefits attractive is their favorable position in terms of cost. Employer contributions to life and medical insurance programs, as well as pension plans, are deductible as business expenses, and employees are not taxed on them. Further, employer plans, since they insure a number of employees, can take advantage of group insurance rates that are lower than those applicable to an individual. In short, with group insurance plans, we have a combination of government regulations (tax deductibility) and the economies of scale by larger purchases of insurance operating to produce a favorable cost situation.

Finally, we have the humanitarian or social responsibility objectives of managements contributing to employee benefits. Perhaps one of the outstanding examples of this phenomenon is Lincoln Electric's program, discussed in Chapter 6, to voluntarily guarantee annual work.

EMPLOYEE BENEFIT PLANS

Employer-granted compensation to employees which are not directly a part of salary payments are generally classified as employee benefits, and they can run a wide range from vacations with pay to subsidy of the plant softball team. However in its most widely used sense, employee benefit plans relate to programs insuring against the expenses of old age, death, accident, illness, and loss of wages.

Retirement plans, group life insurance and group health insurance, and workmen's, compensation plans are the four major elements providing protection against these expenses.

Retirement plans in industry had their beginning in the latter part of the nineteenth century, and in the early decades of the current century formal program were installed in several large industries. Group life insurance was first introduced in 1911, and the third major factor in employee benefits, group health plans, first appeared in the thirties, but their growth is almost entirely a product of the post World War II era.

The World War II economic climate fostered the beginning of the phenomenal growth achieved in all three areas of employee benefit planning over the ensuing 40 years. At that time, Government regulation of wages as an anti-inflation measure so restricted wage increases that other methods of compensation were necessary to attract and keep competent civilian workers during a period when manpower was at a premium. To most employers and employees, family security programs seemed the most attractive means of benefit compensation.

The depression years of the 1930s and the introduction of the Social Security program in 1935 had already resulted in a growing national emphasis on personal security and protection programs. Therefore, the introduction of retirement programs and group insurance at places of employment was well received. Employers credited these programs with increasing efficiency and employee morale. Employers also were allowed Federal tax deduction for contributions to "qualified" pension and group insurance programs.

In 1949, the U.S Supreme Court upheld the decision of the National Labor Relations Board in the Inland Steel Case, ruling employee benefit plans subject to collective bargaining, further strengthening the position of employee benefit plans. Such plans were ruled to come within the meaning of "wages" and "conditions of employment" as defined under the Wagner Act, and became almost as important an issue in collective bargaining as wages, hours, and other conditions of work.

In the ensuing years there has been a marked development of employee benefit plans in all industries and business, and among government workers. Nearly one-half of all workers in commerce and industry in the United States and three-fourths of all government civilian personnel are now enrolled in retirement plans other than Social Security. This compares with fewer than one-fifty of employees in commerce and industry and fewer than one-half of government workers in 1940. Group life insurance, protecting the family should the worker die, also covers more than three-quarters of the work force as compared to about one-third in 1950 and less than one-tenth in 1930.

Even faster growth in employee benefit planning has been experienced in the health insurance area. About three quarters of all earners now have some form of group health insurance protection for themselves and their families. These plans include insured, self-insured, and Blue Cross-Blue Shield coverages. Over 169 million people under age 65 are protected against hospital expenses, mostly through group health plans. Nearly 145 million of these individuals are also protected against major medical expenses, primarily through insurance company coverage. Protection against the temporary loss of wages due to illness or injury is afforded more than 84 million workers.

Recent innovations in the health insurance area of employee benefit planning have been such added services as dental and vision care.

The impact of employee benefit plans on the national economy can be judged from the following comparisons. Private pension plans, which include both insurance company plans and non-insurance company plans, had Rs. 362.6 billion in assets and reserves at the start of 1980, compared with Rs. 52.0 billion in 1960. The flow of retirement benefit payments under private pension plans amounted to Rs. 14.9 billion, going out to 7.1 million retired persons in 1975. Comparable statistics for 1960 were Rs. 1.7 billion in pension benefits paid to 1.8 million persons.

Immediately following World War II, 11.5 million group life insurance certificates were issued under 31,000 master group life insurance policies, representing nearly Rs. 22.2 billion of life insurance in force in the United States. This averages about Rs. 1,930 of life insurance per certificate. The group certificate is an employee's evidence of guaranteed insurance. At the start of 1980, group life insurance protection was provided under 114.9 million certificates by 559,000 master group life insurance contracts, for total coverage of Rs. 1.4 trillion. Average ownership per certificate increased to about Rs. 12,350.

The cost of employee benefit plans continues to grow. Through the years benefits have become more comprehensive, with the result that the cost of providing these programs has risen faster than wages in the past decade.

For the employer, administration of these plans has become an important budget factor. Administrative services can be sizable and costly, and in larger business organizations especially, technically competent staffs are necessary to provide these services for employees.

In past, employers and employees generally shared the costs of insurance and pension benefits. In recent years there has been a gradual shifting to the point where a considerable number of plans are now entirely paid for by the employer. Full contributions by employers enable them to have greater flexibility in determining the future course of the employee benefit programs.

The end results of this vast planning for economic security are the benefits realized in the time of need. A majority of American families are now receiving protection against that economic losses death, disability, retirement, and unemployment through plans originating at their places of employment.

Progressive management today accepts employee benefit plans as a corporate responsibility whereby the uncertain and unknown economic burdens of our working population are assisted ably through the private sector of our economy.

Three particular factors are often considered by management in the development of employee benefit plans. They are: (1) the social trend; (2) the area of industry practice relating to benefit programs; (3) the general economic climate.

These factors blend into the basic and long-range objectives of management in furthering its own performance through a more satisfied and secure work force.

EMPLOYEE PRIVACY

Ever-increasing information needs of business and government, combined with the miracles of computer and telecommunications technology, are having a profound impact on all of us as citizens of a relatively free society. In a sense, all citizens have become victims of a data dominated environment. What schools they go to...what jobs they are offered...what promotions they are given...what mortgage loans they are granted...what insurance policies are issued to them...even what apartments they can rent or homes they are permitted to buy—all is covered in information contained in their files—information which is now being stored in computer data banks, perhaps never to be destroyed, and retrievable in a few seconds. And the opportunities the world holds for them for the rest of their lives may be based on this information.

The single source holding more personal information of this sort than does any other is the corporate employer. Not only does the employer have the basic data furnished on the original employment application forms, together with the results of various employment-related actions and interviews, but the company files also contain the findings of consumer credit-reporting bureaus, information furnished by reference sources, and reports of supervisors, among others.

The U.S. Privacy Protection Commission, created by Congress during the Ford Administration, presented its report to President Carter and the Congress in July 1977, urging legislation on individual privacy in the areas of banking, insurance, consumer credit, investigative reporting, Internal Revenue Service, and education, among others. However, in the area of Employee Privacy as regards employment records, the Commission, at the urging of business leaders, recommended that industry be given a reasonable opportunity to adopt appropriate privacy safeguards voluntarily. In April 1979, President Carter formally endorsed the substance of the Commission's recommendations.

Guidelines for Action

Following are guidelines which the Commission determined to be necessary if the privacy rights of employees are to be protected:

(1) An employee should have a right to see, copy, and correct if necessary, the record an employer has about him or her.

(2) An employer should not transfer information about an employee to another without the employee's permission, or at least without his or her knowledge.

(3) An employer should not maintain secret records about an employee. (An employer might find it necessary to maintain a confidential record for security purposes, but the employee should know that such a record exists.)

(4) Information about an employee should not be obtained under false pretenses, or through pretext interviews.

(5) An employer should only obtain personal information about an employee or applicant which is relevant for proper administration or decision making.

(6) An employer or prospective employer should use individually identifiable employee data only for the purpose for which it was collected.

Current Practice

The Commission recommended that if voluntary employer action was not forthcoming after a reasonable period, appropriate legislation be enacted. Two years was suggested as a "reasonable time."

Two years after the submission of the report to the President, a research study by the University of Illinois, under the direction of the present writer who had served as chairman of the U.S. privacy Protection Commission, was undertaken to determine the degree to which industry had followed through on the Commission's recommendations—at least for the 20 million persons employed by the largest industrial corporations in the country—the Fortune 500 companies.

With reference to giving the employee a right to see, copy, and correct if necessary his (her) record, it was found that although about three-fourths of the companies allowed the individual to have access to his or her personnel record, less than half gave the employee the right to copy the record. Some 79% of the companies permitted employees to place corrections in the record, but three out of four companies did not forward these corrections to anyone who had received the incorrect information from them.

Most employees still are not being told much about their own records. Over two-thirds of the companies do not inform their personnel of the types of records maintained on them, how they are used, what they have access to, and what the company's routine disclosure practices are. Apparently secret records continue to exist.

Over two-thirds (69%) of the corporations surveyed did not inform the individuals that they gave personal information to credit grantors; 85% of the companies disclosed such information to credit grantors without subpoena, as compared to 49% to landlords and 22% to charitable organizations.

Three out of four companies used medical information in their files for making employment-related decisions; yet 83% of the organizations did not allow their personnel to see it.

Two out of five companies did not have a policy concerning which records are routinely disclosed to government agencies.

It would seem that the research findings do not indicate widespread voluntary adoption of privacy safeguards in the employment systems of the country's largest corporations. This, in spite of the fact that almost four out of five companies indicated that they had appointed an executive-level individual to be responsible for maintaining privacy safeguards in employment records.

Continued exposure to possible abuse of an individual's privacy rights chips away at the personal freedoms of workers and executives alike, with the hazard of further weakening our democratic free-enterprise way of life.

EMPLOYMENT AGENCIES: A CASE OF UNITED STATES

Over 10,000 Employment Agencies in the United States—not counting about 2,500 state employment offices operated as part of the U.S. Employment Service—provide recruiting services covering every class of industrial and commercial employment: skilled and unskilled workers, technical and professional specialists, executives and administrators. The services are by no means confined to rank-and-file help, and the placements of personnel in the Rs. 25,000-and-over salary range are not uncommon.

Many large corporations make use of employment agencies regularly, finding them more effective in time and money spent per hire and in caliber of placements than their own personnel departments in advertising and initial screening. Such companies find the services especially advantageous when they are actively engaged in programs of expansion, diversification, plant relocation, and the like.

Operations

Some of the private employment agencies are small, perhaps two- or three-man operations. On the other hand, some are heavily staffed organizations with offices in many cities. In addition, there are networks of franchised offices or associated agencies, which can make available to a using company the facilities of all locations at no extra cost. However, it should be noted that a large agency may be recruiting largely for clerical or routine jobs, while a small office may represent a specialized firm handling only highly technical or executive personnel. Some agencies, also, may specialize in particular industries or crafts.

In practically all states, as well as Puerto Rico and the District of Columbia, there are laws regulating employment agencies. However, these laws vary widely, running the gamut from mere prohibition of misleading advertising, to licensing and strict regulation, to specifying maximum permissible fees and the kind of references required for certain classes of positions.

Some firms perform retainer-search, but most work on a contingency basis, in which case a placements fee is charged only if a job is actually obtained. This may be paid by the employee, with the employer sometimes reimbursing all or part after a probationary period.

In recent years, however, there has been a trend to "fee-paid" jobs, with the employer paying. The National Association of Personnel Consultants, Washington, D.C., numbering some 2,200 agencies, has published a code of Ethics covering service charges and collections, relations with applicants and employers, advertising, etc. It publishes an annual Membership Directory which includes a listing of the special services of each office.

Selection

The following pointers are recommended to a company selecting an employment agency: Does the agency's advertising indicate that it is active in the company's field? An agency cannot screen effectively if it does not understand or have a "feel" for the types of jobs involved. Does the agency have specialists for the kinds of jobs to be filled, and affiliates who can help fill the company's needs in other locations? Experiences of other users should be checked. Size in terms of numbers of offices operated or numbers of franchised or associated offices may not be meaningful in an area dominated by a powerful independent, or an area where there is an agency geared to the company's special needs.

EMPLOYEE BENEFITS AND MANAGERIAL DECISION MAKING

Numerous objectives may be met by providing employee benefits. In light of the central theme of this text—that managers make decisions to meet objectives—we will now examine certain key aspects of decision making with respect to employee benefits.

First, as discussed earlier, employee benefits may meet a number of employee needs. Second, an attractive employee benefits package may improve the company's competitive position in recruiting new employees. Many large firms, however, have fairly similar benefits packages, so they have no strong recruiting advantage over their most direct competitors. The large firm may have a relative advantage over the small one, however, because it may be more difficult for small employers to provide large benefit packages. Thus, firm size may be a contingency of some importance in the employee benefits area. Good benefit programs may also help retain employees and reduce turnover. However, we must raise the same question as we did in discussion profit sharing: Which employees will be the ones to leave, the most desirable or those who are marginal ones?

Another supposed reason for providing employee benefits is to prevent unionization from occurring. Two questions must be asked with respect to this objective. First, to what extent can good benefits per se keep unions from organizing? Unless the total organizations is perceived to be a favorable one (as with the Lincoln Electric Company), it is unlikely that benefits alone can keep a union out. Second, unions may bring positive values to a firm, and it may be desirable to have unionization. As we indicated, unions may help facilitate collaborative employer-employee relationships as under Scanlon-type plans.

It is also often assumed that benefits serve the objective of motivating employees to work harder to achieve organization goals. Following the reasoning presented in previous chapters, it appears unlikely that there is generally any direct link between effort and benefits. All organization members receive benefits, regardless of how hard they work, although they may receive more benefits as their pay increases. This is because benefits (such as pensions) are often related to pay levels. With this lack of a direct effort-reward link, one important problem with employee benefits is that they may be taken for granted by employees, and that their often high costs may not even be appreciated by employees.

Management must make a number of decisions in the employee benefits area. Management must decide what benefits to provide. To a great extent this decision depends on the firm's financial condition and size and on what comparable firms are doing. Also, with respect to decision making, management in some cases *must* provide certain benefits in order to comply with federal and state laws. A firm covered by social security has no choice but to pay the required taxes to the government if it is to stay in business.

Management also needs to decide how much information it should provide to employees about their benefits. This decision is important because it influences the employee benefits–motivation link as well as the perceived equitability of benefits. One of the basic reasons employees take benefits for granted is that management fails to describe adequately the benefits to which they are entitled and the costs of these benefits.

The provision of information does not guarantee that the employee will work harder or fell equitably treated, since the information may be ignored or forgotten. It this is so, why bother? One basic reason is that certain benefits are not perceived as important, even if the employee is aware of them. Some employee benefits may only meet some employee needs at certain times in their lives. For example, why should a healthy, single 25-year-old person really be concerned with the extensive coverage of a medical plan designed primarily to protect individuals (especially families) against medical catastrophes?

Another type of communication problem exists because, conversely, some individuals may assume that their plan covers more than it does. In some cases, for example, older employees who are married, have families, and do know that they have extensive medical insurance may remember somewhat resentfully that they had to pay Rs. 2000 in medical costs themselves for a major illness, while not paying too much attention to the fact that the company plan paid Rs. 10,000 for them. In short, a benefit in the eyes of management may not be a benefit in the eyes of the receiver.

This fact raises such basic questions as the following: How far should management go in providing benefits to the extent that it does have a choice? Can social responsibilities be carried too far? Are we discouraging responsibility? Are not employees mature enough to take care of at least some of their benefit needs, rather than depending on someone else—their employer—to do it for them? With some benefits, such as medical plans, we would support catastrophe coverage, since many individuals would be financially ruined by a Rs. 20,000 medical bill in one year, for instance. To what extent the employer should provide one of the other benefits briefly mentioned earlier—free beer—we consider another question. Somewhere in between these two benefits, one may debate seriously the question of whether free company legal services are necessary, or whether it should be the responsibility of employees as mature adults to handle their own legal affairs. Having employees participate in choosing from among available benefits, as in cafeteria compensation, seems to provide one means of both making individuals aware of the benefits available to them and encouraging their assumption of responsibility. In discussing responsibility, however, we must not overlook the cost advantages of employer-financed benefits as mentioned earlier. However, since it costs companies money to provide employees with information about benefits, management must consider the costs and benefits associated with providing such information.

Another important decision pertaining to benefits is whether the employee should contribute to the purchase of the benefits or the employer should pay for them completely. The former is referred to as a *contributory* plan and the latter as *non-contributory.* Arguments have been raised to support both contributory and non-contributory plans. One argument for contributory plans is that employees will become more aware of the cost of their benefits, learn more about them, and appreciate them more if they are required to partially finance them. On the other hand, workers may perceive their being required to contribute as an inequitable arrangement. Even with full understanding, and a perceived need for a benefit, individuals may not believe that they should have to contribute toward the financing. For example, managers who have to contribute to their firm's pension plan while many other similar-sized firms in the same industry have non-contributory plans may perceive their situation to be less equitable.

RETIREMENT PLANS

An important personnel problem is posed by older employees whose physical and mental capabilities have begun to decline. It is inefficient to keep them on in their present capacity. It is bad for employee morale and public relations to dismiss them arbitrarily, and it is usually not satisfactory to transfer them to less responsible positions. A better solution is to encourage or require them to leave active employment, with the employer undertaking to provide them with an income for the rest of their lives.

Corporate management has very generally adopted the last of the above approaches. Instead of attempting to judge the time at which the individual employee has passed the peak of usefulness, employment is generally terminated upon fulfilment of a set of conditions, one of which is almost without exception the attainment of a specified age. The Age Discrimination in Employment Act (ADEA) amendments of 1978, however, make it illegal to terminate an individual's employment prior to age 55 *solely* on account of the individual's age, even if such termination is pursuant to the terms of a bona fide plan or arrangement. The body of rules governing the termination of employment and the payment of a specified income to superannuated employees is referred to as a retirement plan or a pension plan.

The earliest plans were informal, with the amount and continuance of a retirement benefit dependent upon the promise (often oral) of one person to another. However, this type has now given way to the formal plan, with the terms and conditions contained in a written document. From 1875, when the American Express Company adopted the first formal retirement plan in this country, the number of formal plans has increased, slowly at first, rapidly in recent years. At the end of 1975, an estimated 45 million persons were covered by private formal retirement plans–15 million persons under insured plans, and 30 million under non-insured plans. In addition, there are public plans covering employees of various Federal, state, and local governmental units.

The principal reasons for a formal plan are (1) the plan is easier to administer if it is written down and can be referred to by interested parties; (2) employees will have greater confidence in the permanence of benefits provided by a written plan which has been adopted by the corporate directors; (3) employees can count on definite benefits at retirement as a matter of right (subject to the ability of the corporation to pay for them); and (4) employees are assured more uniform treatment than if the plan were informal. Furthermore, there are important tax advantages to a plan which qualifies under Section 401 of the Internal Revenue Code of 1954. One requirement for qualification is that the plan be contained in a written document.

Essential Features

The establishment of a retirement plan (insured or trust fund) requires the services of an actuary and an attorney. The actuary designs a benefit formula, makes cost calculations, and consults with the attorney on technical details. The attorney drafts the plan or contract, advises of the applicable laws, and takes care of qualifying the plan with the Internal Revenue Service (IRS). Actual provisions may vary, but certain essential features may be recognized:

(1) The plan should have an official title so that it may be readily identified.

(2) Eligibility requirements should be clearly stated.

(3) The normal retirement date, that is the date on which retirement benefits begin, should be stated. This is generally the first of the month coincident with or next following the 65th birthday. Provision may also be made for early or late retirements, if desired.

(4) The formula for calculating normal retirement benefits should be unequivocably set forth.

(5) Provision should be made for financing the plan. Often, regular periodic contributions of an amount within the minimum and maximum limits prescribed by Regulations of the IRS are specified. Frequently, too, especially in plans covering salaried employees, the corporation simply promises to

maintain the fund in a sound actuarial condition. Contributions by the employees may or may not be required.

(6) The right to terminate the plan should be reserved, and provision should be made for the disposition of the assets of the plan in the event of termination.

(7) The responsibility for carrying out the terms of the plan should be fixed. This duty is generally assigned to a committee, almost invariably composed of executives with or without employee representatives.

Benefits

The purpose of a retirement plan is to provide a stated regular income, usually for life, to an employee who has retired, though disability benefits and incidental death benefits may also be provided. The stated regular income must be calculated by a definite formula. While space does not permit a detailed discussion of the various formulas found in practice, certain general types may be recognized:

1. **Formula Based on Final Average Earnings and Years of Service.** "Final average earnings" means average compensation over a period of years (often five) just prior to retirement. This type is often used in plans covering executives and other salaried personnel where final salaries are usually much higher then starting salaries. From the employee's point of view, this type has definite advantages. The transition from final earnings to retirement benefits is smoother if the two are connected by a percentage relationship than if benefits are independent (or partially independent) of final salary. Inflation is taken into consideration to a greater extent than in other formulas.

The benefit is often computed by a formula which applies one accrual rate to that portion of earnings up to a stated amount, or "bend point," and a higher accrual rate to earnings in excess of the bend point. If a single accrual rate is used, total benefits, including Social Security, will be a smaller percentage of earnings for higher-paid personnel than for the lower-paid. A higher accrual rate above the bend point is designed to mitigate this situation.

As an example, the annual benefit might be years of service times a benefit unit composed of 1% of the first Rs. 10,000 of final average earnings, and 1¾% of earnings in excess of Rs. 10,000.

Higher bend points may be expected in the future because of recent substantial increases in the Social Security tax base. In fact, bend points which move up automatically with increases in the Social Security tax base are common.

Another type of formula which takes Social Security benefits into account is the "offset" type, the benefit from the plan being defined in terms of an accrual rate less a portion of the "primary insurance amount." One such formula, for example, might provide an annual benefit equal to years of service times a benefit unit composed of 2% of final average earnings less 2% of the primary insurance amount in effect at termination of actual service.

When a "bent" or "offset" formula is used particular care must be taken to see that the benefits "integrate" with Social Security benefits if the plan is to qualify for favorable tax treatment. Briefly, this means that total benefits, including Social Security benefits, must not enable higher-paid personnel to receive a higher percentage of final average earnings than lower-paid personnel. One requirement for a "bent" formula is satisfied if the bend point is not in excess of the "average maximum taxable earnings" for Social Security benefits. Integration requirements are not limited to final average formulas, but apply to other formulas for basic income benefits and for certain other benefits such as disability and early retirement.

2. **Formulas Based on Career Average Earnings.** The benefit formula is applied to each year's earnings separately, the pension being the total of the units which have accrued each year. Benefits for service prior to the effective date may be based on earnings at the effective date and years of prior service rather than on historical year-by-year earnings. It is typical to "update" benefits periodically under career average plans, in order to base benefits for service prior to the effective date of the update on pay just prior to such effective date.

3. **Money Purchase Formulas.** A fixed percentage of salary or other stated sum is set aside each year to purchase a deferred annuity beginning at retirement. The benefit at retirement is the sum of the separate units purchased.

4. **Flat Amounts.** The formula may provide a fixed dollar amount for each year of service; for example, Rs. 500 per month

per year of service, or simply a flat amount, such as Rs. 20,000 per month on retirement, this latter often subject to a minimum service requirement.

5. Combinations of two or more of the four previous types.

In addition to the basic income benefit, other benefits may be provided. Certain examples may be cited:

1. **Benefit on Total and Permanent Disability.** Although IRS regulations rule out temporary disability benefits, they permit permanent disability benefits, they permit permanent disability benefits. This is logical. A person permanently incapacitated to the extent that he can no longer perform the duties of his occupation presents a management problem–often more acute than a person who qualifies for normal retirement by normal age and service. Most plans, therefore, provide that after some minimum period of service (usually ten years) and attainment of a minimum age (though the age requirement is disappearing, probably because of the influence of the Social Security disability benefit), an employee who is totally and permanently disabled may retire on pension. The latter is usually the normal pension accrued to date of disability if integration rules permit. Disability pensions are payable until normal retirement date, when the regular benefit becomes payable.

The typical disability benefit in a pension plan provides rather small benefits unless disability occurs after relatively long service, and it often provides no benefit at all for disability occurring before ten years of service. Furthermore, disability must be total and permanent. This leaves many disabilities uncovered or covered inadequately. In recent years, "long term disability" (LTD) plans, separate from the pension plan, have been developed to meet these needs. A long term disability plan will generally provide a benefit which, with Social Security benefits, will be equal to a stated percentage (e.g., 60%) of salary at disability for incapacity which prevents the employee from performing the duties of his occupation. If the incapacity has continued for two years (or in some plans, one year) benefits may continue if the employee is unable to perform the duties of any occupation for which he may be fitted by reason of education or training.

Where long term disability plans are in effect, care should be taken to avoid duplication with disability benefits from the retirement plan. One approach is to remove disability benefits from the retirement plan, leaving disabilities before normal retirement date to be covered by the long term disability plan. Credit for service with the employer is often given for the period during which long term disability benefits are paid. At normal retirement date, the regular retirement benefit becomes payable.

2. **Early Retirement.** Many plans provide that the employee may elect to retire early, usually at any time within ten years of his normal retirement date. The benefit payable is the normal pension accrued to date of early retirement, reduced actuarially because it begins at an age younger than the normal retirement age.

More recently, there has been a trend away from actuarial reduction. Some plans now provide full benefits at age 62 with 30 years of service, or at the point where age and service total 85, or some other specified number. Other plans, especially plans covering executives, deliberately encourage early retirement by subsidizing early retirement benefits, especially after age 55. Any departure from exact actuarial reduction adds to the theoretical cost of the plan, but may be rationalized on the ground that the extra cost may be less than that of keeping an inefficient employee until normal retirement date.

3. **Vesting.** Although one purpose of a retirement plan is to hold employees, there has been a growing feeling that they should not be chained to the job, and that it they wish to change employers, they should not lose accrued retirement benefits. Accordingly, most plans now provide for some form of "vesting." Typically, after a specified period of service, such as ten years, any accrued retirement pension will be payable at age 65. The law requires all plans to have a vesting provision at least as liberal as one of three alternatives specified in the law, all of which require full 100% vesting after no more than fifteen years of service.

4. **Death Benefits.** The IRS regulations permit the payment of "incidental" death benefits "through insurance or otherwise." Although the meaning of "incidental" is not too clear in the event a plan provides a lump-sum benefit of the type described in (5), (6), and (7) below are permitted without question. While many

corporations prefer to have a group life insurance program separate from the retirement plan, an increasing number provide substantial death benefits as part of the plan.

5. **Joint and Survivor Benefits.** Many plans now provide that an employee may elect, in advance of retirement, that his benefit will be paid during the joint existence of himself and his wife and will continue to the death of the survivor. The amount of the monthly benefit will be reduced from that payable during his lifetime only. ERISA requires all plans to provide that married employees are assumed to elect a joint and survivor benefit, unless they specifically choose some other form of payment.

6. **Annuity–Payable for a Period Certain and Life Thereafter.** An option found in many plans is an annuity payable for a definite period of years (such as ten) immediately after retirement and so long thereafter as the pensioner may live. The amount is somewhat less than if the provision for the period certain were not included.

7. **Surviving Spouse Pension.** Law also requires that all plans provide a pension payable to the surviving spouse of an employee who dies while eligible to retire, but before actual retirement. This benefit can either be provided to the employee at no cost, or the employee can be required to pay for this protection by means of a percentage reduction in his or her pension when retirement does take place, which reflects the cost of the employee's having been provided this protection.

Typically, the benefit provided is a specified percentage of the benefit which the employee has accrued up to date of death, or it may be the benefit the employee's spouse would have received if the employee had retired first and then died.

8. **Lump-Sum Option.** Although defeating the primary purpose of a retirement plan, which is to provide an income for life to the retiring employee, a number of plans pay the lump-sum equivalent of the future benefit payments at the election of the employee. Under present statutes, the portion of the lump-sum attributable to employer conditions made prior to 1974 subject to capital gains tax, and the portion resulting from employer contri-

butions made in 1974 and later is taxed as regular income, subject to special 10-year averaging.

9. **Medical Benefits.** Under Section 401(h) of the Internal Revenue Code, medical benefits for retired persons may be provided and funded in advance. Benefits must be subordinate to retirement benefits and contributions must be reasonable and ascertainable and made to an account other than the fund from which retirement benefits will be paid.

10. **Miscellaneous.** There are other benefits besides those mentioned, and new types are constantly being developed, limited only by the imagination of the corporate executive or the union bargaining team and the ability of the Corporation to finance them. However, it must be remembered that each new benefit adds something to the cost of the plan. In recent years, there has been a great interest in a benefit which would compensate for inflation. One attempt to meet the problem is the "variable annuity" under which part of the pension assets is invested in equities, with payments adjusted as the value of the equities varies.

EMPLOYEES BENEFITS AND FINANCIAL PLANNING

The objective of employees are generally to maximise their benefits. The cost of the company is monetary one. The company can maximise benefits to employees only when the corporate objective is in harmony with their interest. The benefits to the employees are either statutory or as per customs of company. This study is concerned with the financial aspects of employees benefit. We discuss first the nature of statutory and customary benefits and the related financial aspects in the following paragraphs.

NATURE OF BENEFITS IN INDIA

Statutory Benefits

Law has made it obligatory upon the company to provide certain basic financial social security to all its employees ignoring the category, status and the class to which they belong. The following are the statutory benefits which in ordinary course of the corporate operations fall within the nature of regular costs, observing proper allocation of funds and financial arrangements.

Statutory benefits which accrue to an employee in corporate sector have been provided in the following statues:

1. Employees' Provident Funds and Family Pension Fund Act, 1952, and Employees' Family Pension Scheme, 1971.
2. Employees' State Isurance Act, 1948.
3. Facilities under the Factories Act, 1948.
4. Payment of Bonus Act, 1965.
5. Payment of Gratuity Act, 1972.
6. The Maternity Benefits Act, 1961.

Employees' Provident Fund. An important consideration here is to ensure that enough provision is made by the unit to meet the commitment of contribution under the Employees' Provident Fund Scheme framed under the Employees' Provident Funds and Miscellaneous Provisions act, 1952. The contribution payable by the employer under the Scheme is normally 8-1/3 per cent of the basic wage, dearness allowance (including any cash value of any food concession) and retaining allowance, if any, actually drawn during the whole months. In certain specified industries employing 50 or more persons the contribution payable by the employer is 10 per cent. In both cases, a matching contribution is to be paid by the employee. It is the responsibility of the employer to pay both the contribution payable by him and also in respect of the employees employed by him or through a contractor. The employer shall not be entitled to deduct the employee's contribution from the wage of a member or otherwise to recover it from him. The employer has the duty to deduct the employees contribution from his wages before paying the employee his wages and shall, together with his own contribution as well as an administrative charge of such percentage of pay for the time being payable to the employees other than an excluded employee, pay within fifteen days of the close of every month by separate Bank drafts or cheques to the fund. The employer is also duty bound to furnish to the Commissioner of Provident Fund within twenty days of the close of the month, a monthly consolidated statement showing recoveries made from the wages of each employee and the amount contributed by the employer is respect of each such employee.

Final Withdrawal. Full accumulations with interest thereon are refunded in the event of death, permanent disability, superanuation, retrenchment or migration from India for permanent settlement abroad/taking employment abroad, voluntary retirement etc. full accumulations with interest thereon are refunded in following cases also:

(*i*) Where a factory or other establishment is closed but certain employees who are not retrenched are transferred by the employer to other factory or establishment not covered under the Act;

(*ii*) Where a member is discharged and is given retrenchment compensation under the Industrial Disputes Act, (14 of 1947);

Table 3

Period of membership of the Fund	*Percentage of Employers' Contribution and interest thereon refundable*
Less than 3 years	25%
3 years or more but less than 5 years	50%
5 years or more but less than 10 years	75%
10 years or more	100%

Note: Now, with effect from 1.4.1990 full withdrawal of Employer's contribution is allowed in all above cases.

(*iii*) The Government of India have also directed that the Provident Fund accounts, should be settled immediately by payment of both the employee's and employer's share of contribution in full in respect of those members who cease to subscribe to the Fund as a result of an establishment going out of the purview of the Act under Section 16(1)(a) thereof. In other cases, the member's own share of contribution together with interest thereon is refunded along with the employer's contribution with interest thereon depending upon the length of membership as indicated below:

The Employees' Family Pension Scheme. In exercise of the powers converted by Section 6A of the Employees' Provident Funds and Miscellaneous Provisions Act, 1952, the Central Government has framed a Family Pension Scheme and brought it in operation with effect from the Ist March, 1971. No separate contribution are payable under the scheme by the employers' and the employees. However, out of the Provident Fund contributions a sum representing 1-1/6% of the employees' pay along with an equivalent amount of 1-1/6% is to be remitted by the employer by a separate Bank draft or cheque for credit into the Family Pension Fund. The cost of the remittance if any is to be borne by the employer. The Central Government also contributes @ 1-1/6% of the pay of the members of the Family Pension Fund. The term pay includes the basic wage, dearness allowance (including the cash value of any food concession) and retaining allowance, if any. All the moneys belonging to or standing to the credit of the Family Pension Fund account are kept in deposit with the Central Government in the Public Account (on which the Central Government allows interest).

Rate of family Pension is prescribed in paragraph 28 of the Employees' Family Pension Scheme, 1971 comprising the following ground rules:

(1) In the case of member who being a member of the Family Fund dies during the period of reckonable service before attaining the age of 60 years, family pension shall be paid at the rates specified in the Table 4 subject to the condition that he has contributed to the Family Pension Fund for a period of not less than 3 months.

Table 4

Pay of the member on which contribution to the family Pension Fund is payable	*Monthly rate of Family Pension*
Up to Rs. 300	Rs. 225 (Fixed)
Exceeding Rs. 300 but not exceeding Rs. 650	Rs. 275 (Fixed)
Exceeding Rs. 650 but not exceeding Rs. 1200	40 per cent of pay subject to a minimum of Rs. 300 and a maximum of Rs. 450
Exceeding Rs. 1200 but not exceeding Rs. 1600	35 per cent of pay subject to a minimum of Rs. 450 and a maximum of Rs. 510.

Pay of the member on which contribution to the family Pension Fund is payable	*Monthly rate of Family Pension*
Exceeding Rs. 1600	30 per cent of pay subject to a minimum of Rs. 510 and maximum of Rs. 750.

Note: The minimum services for entitlement for family pension and lump sum payment of death of employee under Employees Family Pension Scheme, 1971, has been reduced from 1 year to 3 months. Further, the lump sum payment has been increased from Rs. 2,000 to 5,000. The notification shall be deemed to have come into force with effect from 1st April, 1988.

If at the time of death during the period for which contribution to the Family Pension Fund was received of reckonable service a member was not in receipt of full pay, the rate of full pay last drawn by him during that period shall be taken into account for the assessment.

In the case of part-time employee who was a member of the Family Pension Fund while serving in more than one establishment covered under the Act, the rate of Family Pension shall be determined with reference to the aggregate of the full pay last drawn by him in such establishments on which contribution to the Family Pension Fund were recovered.

In the case of a piece-rated or a daily rated employee, who was a member of the Family Pension Fund, the rate of full pay last drawn by him during the period for which the contribution to the Family Pension Fund was recovered, shall be determined by taking into account his average earning in the twelve months preceding that in which he dies.

(2) Where an employee who has been a member of the Family Pension Fund for a period not less than 7 years dies during the period of reckonable service, the above rate of family pension shall be subject to the following modifications:

(*a*) for a period of 7 years from the date of death or, till the date on which the member of the Family Pension Fund would have reached the age of 60 years had he remained alive, whichever period is shorter, the family pension payable shall be at the rate specified in the table plus 20% of pay of the member as determined for the purpose of sub-paragraph (*i*) subject to a maximum of twice the family pension mentioned in the Table 4;

(*b*) the family pension payable atter the expiry of the period referred to in clause (*a*) shall be the same as in the Table 4.

Ad hoc relief to those drawing family pension is given from time to time in terms of notifications issued by the Central Government. Thus, the amount mentioned in the Table is not static, it keeps on increasing so as to maintain the real value of the pension.

Other benefits under the Employees' Family Pension Scheme are:

Life Assurance Benefit. Where a member who has contributed to the Family Pension fund for a period not less than 3 months while in reckonable service, a lump sum of Rs. 500 is payable to him/her family as Life Assuance benefit.

Retirement-cum-withdrawal Benefit. The retirement-cum-withdrawal benefit becomes payable to the member either on attaining the age of 60 years or on cessation of membership from the Family Pension fund before attaining the age of 60 years for reasons other than death provided that the member has contributed to the fund for a period of not less than three months.

The retirement-cum-withdrawal benefit rates are as under:

Last Pay	*Benefit available*
Pay upto Rs. 690	Rs. 110 (for one years' membership) to Rs. 9,000 (for 40 years' membership).
Pay from Rs. 691 to Rs. 1130	Minimum Rs. 112 to Rs. 181 (for one years' membership) Maximum Rs. 9,000 (for 40 years membership)
Pay from Rs. 1131 to Rs. 2500	Minimum Rs. 182 to Rs. 400 (for one years' membership) Maximum Rs. 9,040 to Rs. 19,835 (for 40 years membership).

Besides *ad hoc* relief is also given to family pensioners from time to time.

Employees Deposit Linked Insurance Scheme. This scheme was introduced in 1976 by the Government through Amendment in act in order to provide life insurance benefit to employees of any establishment or class of establishment to which this act applies. Under this scheme, on the death of an employee while in service, who is a member of the Employees Provident Fund or of the exempted Provident fund, the person(s) entitled to receive the provident fund accumulations, is paid an additional amount, equal to average balance in the provident fund account of the deceased during the preceding three years or during the period of his membership, whichever is less if the average balance was not below Rs. 1000 during the said period. The maximum amount of benefit payable under this scheme is Rs. 10,000.

Employees' State Insurance. Employees State Insurance Act, 1948, applies mainly to factories in the notified areas/centres. The provisions of the Acts can however be applied by the appropriate Government to any other establishments or class of establishment, industrial, commercial, agricultural or otherwise.

The benefits available, under the provisions of the Act, to the insured persons or their dependents are noted as under:

(*a*) *Sickness benefit*: Whereby insured person is entitled to a periodical payment in case of his sickness.

(*b*) *Maternity benefit*: An insured women employee in case of confinement or miscarriage or sickness arising out of pregnancy, confinement, premature birth of child or miscarriage is entitled to such periodical payments.

(*c*) *Disablement benefit*: An insured person who suffer disablement as a result of an employment injury is entitled to a periodical payment is called disablement benefit.

(*d*) *Dependants' benefit*: If an insured person dies as a result of an employment injury his dependants are entitled to periodical payments known as the dependents, benefit.

(*e*) *Medical benefit*: Medical Benefits are made available for treatment from sickness for the insured persons. This benefit has since been extended also to the family members of insured persons.

(*f*) *Funeral expenses*: A lump sum payment specified by the government. time to time is admissible to the eldest surviving member of the family of an insured person towards the expenditure on the funeral of the deceased insured person.

In the event of the deceased insured person leaving no family behind him, such payment is made to the person who actually incurs the expenditure on the funeral.

The responsibility for the payment of contributions to the ESI corporation rests upon the employer. He has to deposit his contribution as well as the employees' contribution which he can deduct from wages. The contribution payable by the employer is 5% of wages whereas that payable by the employee is 2.25% of his wages. No contribution is payable by an employee drawing less than Rs. 6 per day.

Benefits under Factories Act. Apart from the provisions for providing facilities for the health, safety and welfare of the employees who work in the factory, the employer has to pay in monetary terms by way of annual leave with wages admissible to the employees under Chapter VIII of the Factories Act, 1948. The Act safeguards any right to which a worker may be entitled under any other law or under the terms of any award agreement, including settlement or contract of service. Provided if such award, agreement including settlement, or contract of service provides for a longer annual leave with wages than provided in the above chapter, the quantum of leave which the worker shall be entitled shall be in accordance with such award, agreement or contract of service but in relation to matters not provided for in such award, agreement, or contract of service or matters which are provided for less favourably therein than, the provisions relating to (1) annual leave with wages; (2) wages during leave period; (3) payment in advance of wages in certain cases; and (4) mode of recovery of unpaid wages becomes applicable.

Benefit of Bonus. Bonus is payable to the employees of an establishment employing 20 or more persons and falling within the purview of the payment of Bonus Act, 1965. Bonus payment is made out of the allocable surplus, computed, under the Act. In case of Non-banks, it is 67% of the available surplus in an accounting period. In other case, 60% of the available surplus is the allocable surplus. Available surplus is the total sum that remains out of gross profits after deduction of the following items:

(i) any amount by way of depreciation is admissible in accordance with the provisions of Sub-section (1) of Section 32 of the Income-tax Act or in accordance with the provisions of the Agricultural Income-tax as the case may be;

However, where an employer has been paying bonus to his employees under a settlement or an award or agreement made before 29th May, 1965, and subsisting on that date after deducting from the gross profits notional normal depreciation, then, the amount of depreciation to be deducted under this clause shall, at the option of the employer continue to be such notional normal depreciation.

(ii) any amount by way of development rebate or development allowance which the employer is entitled to deduct from his income under the Income-tax Act;

(iii) any direct tax, subject to the provisions of Section 7 of the Payment of Bonus Act, which the employer is liable to pay for the accounting year in respect of his income, profit and gains during that year;

(iv) such further sum as are specified in respect of the employer in the Third Schedule. In the case of a company the further sum to be deducted are specified as under:

  (a) The dividends payable on its preference share capital for the accounting year calculated at the actual rate at which such dividend are payable;

  (b) 8.5% of its paid-up equity share capital as at the commencement of the accounting year;

  (c) 6% of its reserves shown in its balance sheet as at the commencement of the accounting year including any profits carried forward from the previous accounting year.

In case, the employer is a foreign company under the Companies Act, 1956 (Section 591 thereof), the total amount to be deducted under this item shall be 8.5% on the aggregate of the value of the net fixed assets and the current assets of the company in India after deducting the amount of its current liabilities (other than any amount shown as payable by the company to its Head Office whether towards any advance made by the head office or otherwise or any interest paid by the company to its head office) in India.

Thus taking into consideration the above aspects, the available surplus in respect of the accounting year shall be the aggregate of (A) the gross profits for that accounting year after deducting therefrom the sums as referred to above at item (i) to (iv); and (B) an amount equal to the difference between—(i) the direct tax,calculated in accordance with the provisions of Section 7, in respect of an amount equal to the gross profits of the employer for the immediately preceding accounting year; and

(ii) the direct tax, calculated in accordance with the provisions of Section 7, in respect of an amount equal to the gross profits of the employer for such preceding accounting year after deducting there from the amount of bonus which the employer has paid or is liable to pay to his employees in accordance with the provisions of this Act for that year.

Section 7 of the Payment of Bonus Act, 1965 is reproduced below:

Calculation of direct tax payable by the employer

Any direct tax payable by the employer for any accounting year shall, subject to the following provisions, be calculated at the rates applicable it the income of the employer for that year, namely;

(a) in calculating such tax no account shall be taken of—

(i) any loss incurred by the employer in respect of any previous accounting year and carried forward under any law for the time being in force relating to direct taxes;

(ii) any arrears of depreciation which the employer is entitled to add to the amount of the allowance for any following account year or years under Sub-section (2) of Section 32 of the Income-tax Act;

(iii) any exemption conferred on the employer under Section 84 of the Income-tax Act or of any deduction to which he is entitled under Sub-section (1) of Section 101 of that Act, as in force immediately before the commencement of the Finance Act, 1965 (10 of 1965);

(b) where, the employer is a religious or a charitable institution to which the provisions of Section 32 do not apply and the whole or any part of its income is exempt from tax under the Income-tax Act, then, with respect to the income so exempted, such institution shall be treated as if it were a company in which the public are substantially interested within the meaning of that Act;

(c) where the employer is an individual or a Hindu undivided family, the tax payable by such employer under Income- tax Act shall be calculated on the basis that the income derived by him from the establishment is his only income;

(d) where the income of any employer includes any profits and gains derived from the export of any goods or merchandise out of India and any rebate on such income is allowed under any law for the time being in force relating to direct taxes, then, no account shall be taken of such rebate;

(e) no account shall be taken of any rebate other than development rebate or investment allowance or development allowance or credit or relief or deduction (not herein before mentioned in this section) in the payment of any direct tax allowed under any law for the time being in force relating to direct taxes or under the relevant annual Finance Act, for the development of any industry.

If the allocable surplus in any accounting year exceeds the amount of maximum bonus payable to the employees in the establishment under Section 11 then, the excess shall, subject to a limit of 20% of the total salary or wages of the employee employed in the establishment in that accounting year be carried forward for being set on in the succeeding accounting year and so on upto and inclusive of the fourth accounting year to be utilised for the purpose of payment of bonus, in the manner illustrated in the Fourth Schedule of the Act.

In case where for any accounting year, there is no allocable surplus or the allocable surplus in that year falls short of the amount of minimum bonus payable to the employees in the establishment under Section 10, and there is no amount or sufficient amount carried forward and set on under Sub-section (1) which could be utilised for the purpose of payment of minimum bonus, then, such minimum amount or the deficiency as the case may be shall be carried forward for being set-off in the succeeding accounting year and so on upto and inclusive of the fourth accounting year, in the manner illustrated in the fourth Schedule. The Fourth Schedule is reproduced below.

The Fourth Schedule
(See Sections 15 and 16)

In this Schedule, the total amount of bonus equal to 8.33 per cent of the annual salary or wage payable to all the employees is assumed to be Rs. 1,04,167. Accordingly, the maximum bonus to which all the employees are entitled to be paid (Twenty per cent of the annual salary or wage of all the employees) would be Rs. 2,50,000.

Year	*Amount equal to sixty per cent or sixty-seven per cent, as the case may be, of available surplus allocable as bonus*	*Amount payable as bonus*	*Set on on set off of the year carried forward*	*Total set on or set off carried forward*	
	Rs.	Rs.	Rs.	Rs. of (year)	
1.	1,04,167	1,04,167**	Nil	Nil	
2.	6,35,000	2,50,000*	Set on 2,50,000*	Set on 2,50,000	(2)
3.	2,20,000	2,50,000* (inclusive of 30,000 from year 2)	Nil	Set on 2,20,000	(2)
4.	3,75,000	2.50,000*	Set on 1,25,000	Set on 2,20,000	(2)
				1,25,000	(4)
5.	1,40,000	2,50,000* (inclusive of 1,10,000 from year 2)	Nil	Set on 1,10,000	(2)
				1,25,000	(4)
6.	3,10,000	2,50,000*	Set on 60,000	Set on Nil	(2)
				1,25,000	(4)
				60,000	(6)

7. 1,000,000	2,50,000* (inclusive of 1,25,000 from year 4) and 25,000 from year 6)	Nil	Set on 35,000	(6)
8. Nil (due to loss)	1,04,167** (inclusive of 35,000 from year 6)	Set off 69,167	Set off 69,167	(7)
9. 10,000	1,04,167*	Set off 94,167	Set off 69,167	(8)
			94,167	(9)
10. 2,15,000	1,04,167* (after setting off 69,167 from year 8 and 41,666 from year 9)	Nil	Set off 52,501	(9)

Notes: * Maximum

** Minimum

! The balance of Rs. 1,10,000 set on from year 2 lapses.

According to the Payment of Bonus Act, 1965, a minimum bonus which shall not be less than 8.33% of the salary or wage earned by the employee during the accounting year or 100 rupees (60 rupees in the case where the employee is below 15 years of age whichever is higher) is payable to every employee in respect of each accounting year, whether there is allocable surplus or not. In case the allocable surplus exceeds the said amount of minimum bonus payable to the employees, an amount in proportion to the subject to a maximum of 20% of such salary or wage. Adjustment of customary or interim bonus paid to the employees is allowed against the bonus payable under the Act. Further, the employer is entitled to deduction of certain amounts from bonus payable under the Act from the employees who is found guilty of misconduct causing financial loss to the employer.

The payment of bonus is not compulsory for the period of first five years of a new establishment. But if in any accounting year even before the expiry of the above limit of five years it makes profit, it is required to pay bonus for that particular year.

Payment of Gratuity. Gratuity is a retrial benefit given as a lump sum amount to an employee by his employer on the termination of the employment. To be eligible to receive gratuity under the Payment of Gratuity Act, 1972, an employee should have rendered continuous service for not less than five years on superannuation or retirement or resignation. When termination is due to death or disablement due to accident or disease, the completion of continuous service of five years is not necessary.

In the case of death of an employee, the gratuity is payable to his nominee or his heirs/as the case may be. The amount of gratuity payable to an employee should not exceed twenty months wages. For every completed year of service or part thereof in excess of six months, the employer shall pay gratuity to an employee at the rate of fifteen days' wages based on the rate of wage last drawn by the employee concerned. The maximum amount of gratuity shall not exceed Rs. 50,000. In case of piece rated employee, daily wages shall be computed on the average of the total wages received by him for a period of 3 months immediately preceding the termination of his employment, and, for this purpose, the wages paid for any overtime work shall not be taken into consideration. In seasonal establishments, gratuity is payable to the seasonal employees at the rate of seven days' wages for each season. To other employees, the usual rate of 15 days wages for every completed year of service applies. The gratuity can be fully forfeited in the following circumstances:

(i) riotious or disorderly behaviour;

(ii) dismissal; and

(iii) moral turpitude.

The gratuity of an employee can also be partially forfeited to the extent of damage of employer's property after giving a reasonable opportunity to the concerned persons.

The Maternity Benefit. The Maternity Benefit Act, 1961, regulates the employment of women in certain establishments for certain periods before and after child birth. The Act also provide maternity and certain other benefits. According to the Act maternity benefit, is payable to a female worker for 12 weeks i.e. six weeks up to and including the day of her delivery and six weeks immediately following that day. Minimum period of service required to be put in employment is 160 days in the twelve months immediately preceding the date of her expected delivery with the employer from whom the woman may claim the above benefit. In the event of death of a woman employee, the maternity benefit shall be payable only for the days upto and including the day of her death. In case the child survives the women employee who dies after giving birth within the six weeks period following the date of delivery, the employer shall be liable for the maternity benefits, for the entire period of six weeks post to delivery of child. In case such child also dies during the said period then the benefit will be given only for the days to and including the day of the death of the child. The Maternity Benefits Act, 1961 does not affect the continuance of payment of maternity benefit where the Employees' State Insurance Act, 1948 is applicable.

Payment of medical bonus: Every woman entitled a maternity benefit under the Maternity Benefit Act shall also be entitled to receive from her employer a medical bonus of Rs. 25 if no prenatal confinement and post-natal care is provided for by the employer free of charge.

Customary Benefits

Besides the above statutory benefits the employer also provide certain benefits to its employees which may be adopted as per customs prevalent in the industry or the social environment. These benefits are generally provided by a corporate unit to build its image in the industrial or commercial world depending upon its earning capacity, profitability and management attitude towards employees welfare. These benefits are listed below:

(1) **Leave Fare Concessions or Leave Travel Grants**: This benefit is admissible in certain corporate sectors of standing to its employees where by the employees are encouraged to take annual leave once in two years or so and spend the leave period at leisure at some hill station or visit those places carrying commercial or historical importance, or visit their home towns or religious places as they like to visit with the members of family and dependents. The employer company allows reimbursement of travel expenses

depending upon the admissibility of class of travel or mode of transport to the category of employment one belongs.

(2) **Encashment of Leave Salary**: Sometimes the employees are given the benefit of encashment of their earned leave who do not want to avail it and want to put more time in work. Generally this benefit is linked with Leave Fare Concession to enable an employee to enjoy fully his part leave with the encashed amount of leave by meeting his other expenditure in addition to the travelling expenses granted by the employer. The benefit is made available as one months leave may be allowed to be encashed in one year or two years period depending upon the facility allowed in a particular company.

(3) **Holiday Home**: Companies establish holiday home at different places of interest where the employees would like to spend their holidays while availing of the leave fare concessions and encashment of part of their leave. These holiday homes provide comfortable place to stay with kitchen facilities to the employees and the members of their family. Hotel accommodation is costlier and holiday home provide the substitute accommodation for a stay. Thus the facility provides monetary benefit to the employee in terms of saving the money which they are likely to spend on hotel accommodation or other stay arrangements while in transit to spend their paid holidays.

(4) **Medical Reimbursement Benefit**: Monthly lump sum is paid to employees to meet the medical expenses of the self and/or family members or dependent parents. In addition to, employees are paid ex-gratia in the circumstances when they have to meet heavy medical expenses to save their own life or the life of their family members. These facilities may be provided in addition to the free medical aid provided by the company to its employees by paid medical consultants during or after office hours.

(5) **Subsidised Accommodation Benefit**: Companies provide subsidised accommodation to their employees in the cities where rented accommodation is costly and beyond the reach of the employees at the nominal deduction from their salary towards the rent for such accommodation.

(6) **Conveyance Allowance:** Companies do provide to their employees either free transport by bus or car from their residence to the place of work and back or award a lump sum monthly allowance differing according to the status and position and category of employment for maintaining their own conveyance being utilised for office purpose. Their benefit is in addition to the salary an employee gets per month. Some employers provide this facility of conveyance maintenance allowance or direct reimbursement of actual conveyance expenses incurred by the employees.

(7) **Subsidised Canteen Facilities:** Subsidised canten and retail purchasing facilities are also provided by the employers for the employees which are to benefit the employees to take their balanced meals in the office premises at minimum expenses and purchase essential items of their daily consumption at lesser prices. Retail shops of the mills sometimes allow concessions to the employee on purchases of the mill manufactured goods.

(8) **Children Education Allowance:** This benefit is also made available by the employers to the employees for one or two children to keep their norms of family planning fully realised and to ensure that the employees with their short families maintain their efficiency and health properly.

PROVIDENT FUNDS AND PROVISIONS OF THE COMPANIES ACT, 1956

According to Section 418 of the Companies Act, 1956 all moneys contributed to provident fund constituted for its employees or the money received or accruing by way of interest or otherwise to such funds shall be deposited within fifteen days from the date of contribution, receipt or accrued in the following manner:

1. in the post office savings bank account or
2. in a special account to be opened by the company for this purpose in the State Bank of India or in a scheduled bank;
3. where the company itself is a scheduled bank, in a special account to be opened by the company for the purpose either in itself or in the State Bank of India or in any scheduled bank; or be invested in the securities mentioned or referred to in clauses (a) to (e) of Section 20 of the Indian Trust Act.

With regard to payment of interest on the above deposits sub-section (2) of Section 418 specifies that notwithstanding anything to the contrary in the rules of any provident fund to which Sub-section (1) applies or in any contract between a company and its employees no employee shall be entitled to receive, in respect of such portion of the amount to his credit in such funds as is invested in accordance with the provisions of Sub-section (1), interest at a rate exceeding the rate of interest yielded by such investment.

Further, under Sub-section (3) it has also been provided that an employee will continue to the right under the rules of a provident fund to obtain advance from or to withdraw money standing to his credit in the fund, where the fund is a recognised provident fund within the relevant provisions of the Income-tax Act, 1961.

In case where a trust has been created by a company with respect to any provident fund referred to in Sub-section (1), the company shall be bound to collect the contributions of the employees concerned and pay such contributions as well as its own contributions, if any, to the trustees (within the fifteen days from the date of collection) but in other respects, the obligations laid on the company by this section shall devolve on the trustees and shall be discharged by them instead of by the company.

It has been held in *Desikachari v. Pirrie* (AIR 1940 Mad. 184) that where the amount of the provident fund lying in deposit in a bank to the credit on the company has not been invested in the authorised securities as provided in this section, the company is guilty of a breach of trust and the bank with the knowledge of this must be held to have participated in the breach of trust.

The employee whose contributions have been so deposited in the Bank is entitled under Section 419 on request made in this behalf to the company, or to the trustees referred to in Sub-section (4) of Section 418 as the case may be, to see the banks receipt for any money or security such as is referred to in Sections 417 and 418 of the Act.

Penalty for contravention of Sections 417, 418 and 419 has been stipulated under section 420 of the Act which may be inflicted on any officer of a company or any such trustees of a provident fund as is referred to in Sub-section (4) of Section 418 who knowingly, contravenes, or authorises or permits the contravention of, the provisions of Sections 417, 418 and 419 of the Act. Such persons shall be punishable with imprisonment for a term which may extend to six months or with fine which may extend to one thousand rupees.

RETIREMENT BENEFITS AND FINANCIAL IMPLICATIONS

Need for Pre-retirement Education

In India, every year a number of employees in public sector, State and Central Government Services, municipalities and other local bodies, army services and private sector organisations retire. Majority of these retired persons, post retirement, face work-free or idle future, i.e. they have no plans to work for economic gains and also no happy past time. No counselling is done by the employers before a person retires to enable him to utilise his retired life in terms of time, energy and money resources in a planned way. In USA, UK and other West European countries proper education and training is imparted to persons retiring from jobs as a systematic and planned retirement package programme as a routine course of retirement planning followed in majority of the business organisations and other institutions. All possible information and knowledge is passed on to the employees seeking pre-mature retirement or retiring after superannuation. In companies where such guidance is not available within the organisation, external experts are engaged who have specialisation in counselling on financial planning for the retired persons, planning for substitute work either as second career placement in another job or taking up personal pursuits.

Education in the area of retirement planning prepares a person with confidence to face change involving shift in work situation, change in rewarding pattern for the work and much more than these is psychological adaptation to aging. If a person has a necessary plan to engage himself in work on retirement from active job situation he has a role to play in the society and while busy in the role playing he can avoid aging. The sad part of the retirement life is the aging factor which makes the retired persons subject to emotional stress which is normally reflected in "irritable behaviour, mean temper, rigid forgetfulness, suffering anxiety, depression and uninvited grief". These ailments occur during the period of post transition from adulthood to old-age and are unavoidable and inevitable natural phenomenon. But careful retirement planning may induce a person to be psychologically more prepared to face the problems of old age. This transition makes a person sad, passive, inactive, and repulsive with acute negative outlook towards life as if he has nothing more to accomplish in life but to wait for death. Education of retirement planning makes him a positive thinker with self-identification and a definite role to play in changed circumstances and environment.

The benefits of pre-retirement education are many. A retired person with pre-retirement education musters self-confidence and enforces his inner strength to maintain will-power. With the growing age, old persons experience diminishing strength, distaste for learning, repletion in memory and gross reduction in capacities of making judgments and perception. Proper guidance given to old people from time to time unable them to dispel these negative forces and provide avenues where they could utilise their competence of interactive capacities which definitely grow with aging. Education of retired way of life definitely makes a man more active than to his age, a person may be bald or wrinkled faced but may feel more smart and active in personal and interactive life. There are some people who do not need any pre-retirement education for a happy and active post retirement life but their background is entirely different as they are not normal persons, they have different outlook towards life and self-interest.

For example, a person may feel young with his active interest in social life, family life of his own or his children or grand- children, community activities, and personal financial independence. Personal financial independence is a matter of concern to all particularly those who have no retirement pension benefits or sources of income to cater their living requirements. Specially for such persons retirement planning is a necessary course of life which should be taught through a well guided process of education means. All retired persons irrespective of their rank or status in active life can attain the state of happiness through creative life if they are well exposed to pre-retirement education phased out in a systematic way.

In this direction, India may learn from the experiences of the some of the well advanced nations. To cite instances below from the experiences and efforts being made in U.K. and U.S.A. in the direction of pre-retirement planning and education in public and private organisations as a routine part of service conditions of the employees.

In U.K., Government have taken steps to foster 'Pre-retirement Education' (PRE), on sound footings having learnt lessons from the experiences of the private agencies like Pre-retirement Association (PRA) and other bodies who have been active in the field and nurtured the retirement planning ideas and ideals for past twenty years. Department of Education and Science (as reported by Gecil Kellehar, who runs regular retirement planning courses for ICL and Norfolk Education Department, in Administrator—January, 1984 p. 29) is providing a grant of £ 75,000 p.a. for three years to PRA enable it to set up an Educational Development Group. The main objectives of the Educational Development Group are: "(i) to stimulate the development and improvement of pre-retirement education and increase awareness of its value and purpose; (ii) to give guidance and support to provides of PRE (employers, adult educators and voluntary organisations); (iii) to identify and disseminate appropriate teaching materials and examples of goods practices; (iv) to promote greater general awareness of the needs of people in middle and later life and encourage the development of better ways of meeting them".

The experience of USA in the area of imparting pre-retirement education are little different than those of UK as discussed above. A survey conducted in 1976 by Prentice-Hall and American Society for Personnel Administration revealed that in USA mostly retirement preparation assistance is in the shape of financial assistance and basic health insurance information. This survey also revealed that 75% of the responding 269 companies have pre-retirement planning programmes. More than half offer individualised counselling, 1/3 conduct group counselling sessions and the remainder have both types programme by 1980. Some of these companies are IBM, Zenith Radio Corporation, Chemical Bank, Amplex Corpn., Sears, Roebuck, Dow Chemicals, Texas Power & Light, Koppers, Polaroid, United Airlines, American Airlines, Eastern Kodak, Lever Bros., General Electric, Lockhead, etc. Evidence is available that earlier to above survey the Equitable Life Associates conducted a survey in 1950, Hewitt and Associates conducted similar survey in 1952. It was reported that 13 of the 355 companies had pre-retirement planning programmes in 1950 of one kind or other. Hewitt had reported that only 2.7% of the Companies out of 657 companies with workforce of 2.5 million had offered educational or lecture programme regarding retirement. At University level, research started on the subject of formal retirement preparation programme at Michigan and Chicago. By 1970, American Association of Retired Persons (AARP) published a series of book-lets on subjects like health, income, financial planning, use of time, housing and location, legal affairs etc. for information on continuous basis to retired persons for their rehabilitation. Besides there are private organisation like Retired Advisers Inc. (RAI) and Retired Services Inc. (RSI) that provide written material for retires and prospective retirees. James W. Walker & Marriet L. Laxer in their book "The End of Mandatory Retirement" (John Willey & Sons, 1978) have revealed that in 1974 out of 800 responding companies 704 offered retirement education programmes viz. 371 offered financial information, 170 basic information on supplementary benefits under companies and health and insurance plans, 103 provide general counselling 60 supplies written materials and counseling on personal basis.

In India, education on retirement or pre-retirement education or retirement planning are the subjects not considered important either at the government level or in the private organisation. There is not even a single scheme which may be cited as a beginning of the era of retirement planning in India. The only exception is the defence services where some systematic programme for the exposure of retirement defence personnel whereby guidance is given to them in the direction of their rehabilitation.

Based on the experience of the developed nations of world, retirement planning or pre-retirement educational programmes should be adopted in India by governments of the States and the government of the Centre besides the private limited companies and the public corporations. Retirement education could become one of the prominent activity of the Adult Education Centres and the educational institutions particularly those devoted to advance management education and training. Part-time course could be commenced in these centres for the guidance of the senior executives of the limited companies and corporations who should be guided to take up In-Company or Out-of-Company programmes for educating and informing those employees who seek premature retirement or for the superannuated retirees. Educational programme should cover and if literature for publicity and educating the retirees is published should comprise of the following areas:

(1) *Financial planning*: establishing the need for finance for retirees, their sources of income, items on which to spend money, budget for income and expenditure, etc. This is the urgent need in Indian circumstances for such planning as majority of retirees lack social security measures adequate to their retirement needs. Particularly in the private sector organisation where no retirement pension is provided, immediate action is required for looking after the retirees. Even public sector undertakings who have been given the importance of a pace-setter for the private sector has lagged behind in this area of social benevolence. How to save money, protect the savings and invest them in less risky high return bearing occupations.

(2) Augmenting sources of income for the retired person on retirement is most important requirement for the survival of the retirees and their dependent and cultural programmes, family and other matters.

(3) Meaningful use of time in leisure and in social activities, in self development and cultural programmes, family and other matters.

(4) Setting house and location or the place where retiree may spend his time, climate considerations, cost of living, amusements and recreation for happy pass-time etc.

(5) Health care and safety: It is the health that faces the challenges of retirement and aging. Medical checkup at periodic intervals is essential, light exercises and walking etc.

(6) Legal affairs retirement places time at retiree's disposal but demands of aging and old age fatigues do not allow him to move into litigations. Help of lawyers to look after his income resources, taxations, property protections and other related matters is essential.

Like-wise there may be other fields which should be covered under the pre-retirement education plan as may be revealed on the basis of experiences. But in the above areas literature could be created to solve the problems of the retirees.

With a view to make a start of pre-retirement education in India, it may be worth consideration that the Associations of employers in private sector, banking industry and financial institutions and investment bodies should take similar steps with a view to expedite the establishment of machinery which could plan, evaluate and assist the retired people in the setting up of activity of commercial or industrial nature as may be permitted keeping in view the experience and expertise of such retirees.

Plea for Retirement Benefits

In the wake of strong support to computer technology expressed by the government in recent years, rethinking is required to be done on the aspects of employees' retirement benefits particularly in the organisations and enterprises where computer technology can be adopted for public convenience, safety and economy. It is in this context that the employment policy as well as the retirement policy throughout the country will have to be reviewed for making adjustments for adoption of computer technology because in these situations it is likely that the work force whether managerial, administrative or in ranks with blue or white collars has got to be reduced and human labour or human skill saving devices, i.e. the computers will replace them in sizeable number. For example, in financial institutions, banking, insurance companies, and other alike institutions computer technology can be adopted without much delay for better, accurate, quick results. People manning positions in these organisations will have to be induced to acquire new skills matching to the computer technology adaptation and those who are constrained to improve may be motivated to vacate the positions voluntarily to give way to the youths with modern knowledge matching with the change.

The issue of this change over is not simple in the present circumstances particularly when there exist already a heavy back log of unemployment of both educated and technically qualified youths besides the skilled and the unskilled labour. Many new issues emerge in such a situation. Trade Union have their own say before any change at any organisational level is contemplated. This situation was faced in the banking industry recently when the Indian Banking Association had to decide upon the computer based clearing system. If the Trade Union leaders are convinced of the wider public interest and adequate compensation for the affected members resulting from the change over, the problem meets a ready solution. But the question of the general change over involving the entire economy, the whole industrial and commercial setup, present a different problem. The main clash exists between the old and new blood. This clash has been experienced in the developed nations like USA and UK and is, at the advent of adoption of new technology is discernible in India also. Experience of the developed nations if has to serve as a guide then reconsideration will have to be given to incentive plan for the early retirement. The most favourably thinking goes to hold the solution to the problem of transition into technological era lies in managing the change with the induction of new blood which is always easy, possible, and successful. The old become adamant to change and cannot deliver the desired results even fresh training in the requisite area of technology despite the fact that such training is expensive and scarce. The best policy is suggested by the experts is the review of incentives for early retirement which serves two ends viz. "old timer working population will go to production activity by engaging themselves in promotion and management of new units; and new trained persons will man their jobs more efficiently and better equipped and modern knowledge of know-how and work process"

Technological transition is a continuous process and if such steps are not taken India will remain many generations behind the new world due to educational lag, technological transition lag, and for want of trained people and modern equipments. This is the first stage of technological transition and is bound to continue with advancement of science and technology and so is the process of retiring the old and replacing them by youths will continue. This is how in USA and other developed nations of West Europe the technological transition is taking place. In American private organisations the practice exists under which attractive premature retirement benefits to their employees along with the intensive guidance to take up production activities is provided. Guidance covers introduction to special agencies which provide money, guidance for promotion of industry, technological help, marketing facilities and managerial know how and entrepreneurial training and advance refresher courses.

Retirement benefits available in India are not much encouraging as compared to the other nations of the world. A review of existing retirement benefits is necessary to carry the discussion further for evolving a plan for premature retirement incentives.

In India, Central Government Civil Service Rules particularly the pension schemes launched in 1950 and 1964 are the main guidelines deserving reconsideration and setting example for the public sector undertakings, banks, financial institutions, as well as the private sector organisations particularly the corporate sector.

Under the existing government rules, the retirement has been stipulated on completion of 30 years qualifying service. This is known as compulsory retirement. There is also provision for voluntary retirement permitted on completion of 20 years qualifying service. In the latter case of retiree is given five years benefit for calculating pension which is reckoned on the basis of qualifying service and the over all benefit does not extend beyond 30 years service period. The benefit which an employee normally gets on retirement from government service are the pension, service gratuity and death-cum-retirement gratuity where admissible. Pension includes gratuity except when the term pension is used in contradistinction to gratuity. The Central Government Pension rules apply to government servants who retire or retired or discharged or allowed to resign from service or dies including civilian government servants in the Defence Services. State Government and Railways have their own pension rules as such Central Government rules do not apply to them. Besides there are also certain classes of persons who are also not governed under the said pension rules viz. (a) pensions in casual and daily rated employment; (b) pensions paid from contingencies; (c) persons entitled to the contributory Provided Fund; (d) members of all-India services; (e) persons locally recruited for services in diplomatic consular or other Indian establishments in foreign countries; (f) persons employed on contracts except when the contract provides otherwise; and (g) persons whose terms and conditions of service are regulated by or under the provisions of the constitution or any other law for the time being in force.

There are various types of pension schemes viz. (1) Superannuation Pension: admissible to one who retires on attaining age of compulsory retirement; (2) Retiring pension: admissible to those who retire or retired in advance of the age of compulsory retirement or who is declared surplus opts for voluntary retirement as per existing provisions; (3) Invalid pension: admissible to those who retire from service on account of any bodily or mental infirmity which permanently incapacitates him for service on medical ground; (4) Compensation pension: this is the type of pension which is allowed to a person who is discharged on abolition of permanent post. It is an alternative option in the form of pension. (5) Compulsory retirement pension: it is admissible in the event when retirement is inflicted as a penalty i.e. pension or gratuity or both at a rate not less than 2/3 and not more than full compensation or gratuity or both is admissible to such person on the date of his compulsory retirement; (6) Besides, compassionate allowance equal to 2/3 of pension or gratuity or both which would have been admissible on retirement. Compensation pension is admissible to that government servant who is dismissed from service whose gratuity or pension is forefieted. Provision of commutation of pension is available to a government servant for a lump sum payment not exceeding 1/3 of his pension. However, commutation or pension is not allowed to the government servant under departmental or judicial proceedings instituted before or after the date of his retirement during tendency of such proceedings. On death of the government servant, the committed value is payable to his/her heir. Extra- ordinary pension benefits are also provided to government servant where death or injury is sustained attributable to service or aggravated by service other than a industrial worker or members of armed forces. Option is available for a civil servant in government either for a pensionary scheme or contributory provident fund benefits. Government of India has made available pensionary benefits to industrial employees since 1960 with option either to retain existing contributory provident fund benefits.

With the availability of pension for a person while in government service there are number of restrictions which have been placed in the matter of re-employment of such persons. These restrictions may be analysed from the angle of disincentives to take up economic activity on retirement. Precisely these restrictions are discussed below:

(1) Restriction on commercial re-employment after retirement: Previous permission/sanction of the government is required

before a person accept commercial appointment within two years of his retirement. By commercial appointment/employment it is understood such employment in any capacity including that of an agent,under a company, cooperative society, firm or individual engaged in trading, commercial, industrial, financial or professional business and includes also a directorship of such company and partnership of such firm, but does not include employment under a body corporate, wholly or substantially owned or controlled by the government or setting up practice either independently or as a partner of a firm, as adviser or consultant in matters in respect of which the pensioner has no professional qualification or the matters in respect of which the practice is to setup or is carried on are relatable to his official knowledge or experience or the pensioner has professional qualifications but the matters in respect of which such as are likely to give his client an unfair advantage by reason of his previus official position or the pensioner has to undertake work involving liaison or contract with the offices or officers of the government. For example, a government servant belonging to Indian Revenue Service or had been member of any other Central Service Group A, retired from a post under the Department of Revene and Insurance in Ministry of Finance, cannot set up practice before two years from the date of such retirement. However, this restriction is not available for employment in University as the same is not a commercial employment.

(2) Another restriction is in the form of disentitlement of a person who is a government servant for two pensions in the same service or post at the same time or by the same continuous service. A government servant on re-employment cannot have a separate pension or gratuity for the period of his re-employment.

(3) Besides, pension is also subject to future good conduct of the pensioner and can be withdrawn by serving requisite notice.

(4) Pension can be withheld for serious crime or offence committed by the pensioner under Official Secret Act, 1923 for grave misconduct which includes the communication or disclosure of any secret official code or pass word or any sketch, plan article, model, note, document or information such as mentioned in Section 5 thereof prejudicing the interest of general public or the security of the country.

(5) Permission of the government is required for a pensioner belonging to Central Service Group A to take-up any employment outside India in any local authority, corporation or other institution which function under the supervision and control of a government outside India or an employment under an international organisation of which government of India is not a member.

The above restrictions are of objective nature and could be relaxed in suitable cases where the government policy towards encouragement of pre-mature retirement is reviewed with the sole objective of solving the unemployment problem linked with the initiation of new economic activity taken up by the pre-maturedly retired persons.

Gratuity is not pre retirement benefit equally important as pension and is admissible to the government servant as per rules. Gratuity is of two types viz. Terminal Gratuity which is allowed to a person who retires on superannuation or is discharged from service or is declared invalid for further service provided that he rendered satisfactory service. For unsatisfactory service the amount of gratuity could be reduced. The government of India has enhanced the amount of Gratuity could be reduced. The government of India has enhanced the amount of Gratuity from Rs. 30,000 to Rs. 50,000 for the total tenure of service depending upon the entitlement of a person. Another form is Death Gratuity which is available to the family of a temporary or quasi-permanent government servant who dies in service. It is admissible as per prescribed rates.

Many public sector corporations, banks, financial institution and investment bodies follow the government plan of gratuity and contributory provident fund instead of pension. Nevertheless there is hardly any provision in these organisation for voluntary retirement benefits.

Nor withstanding the above, even the pensionery benefits provided by the central government or state government are not much inducive to persons thinking in terms of premature retirement for taking up any industrial or commercial activity as revealed under the foregone discussion. In the circumstances the entire matter relating to the policy framework of retirement or the benefit accruing on retirement or on early/premature retirement, deserve a passionate review and reconsideration with a view to create more attractive incentives for the aspirant retirees. Even in private organisation need exist if the options for pensions are created for the general welfare of the retired pensioners. In the connection, experiences of developed nations will pave a way for the guidance in this direction.

The example of USA's firms is more glaring. Private pension plans exist as non-contributory but solely financed by employers as well as those contributory by both employer and the; employee. William C. Greenough and Francis P. King in "Pension Plans & Public Policy". Columbia University Press, New York, have stated that in 1970 in USA, 79% were non-contributory pensions and 21% contributory pensions plans which existed in the private sector firms. These pensions are available after full retirement age of 65 years of age. A study of Corporate Pension Plan prepared by Banker Trust Company, USA in 1975 had reported that 77% employees were of more than 10 years service after full years of retirement age. A substantial number of plans require 30 years service for entitlement of full pensions. Earlier retirement provision do appear in the multi-employer plans. Monthly Labour Review in July, 1970 issue had reported that 6% of the employee preferred earlier retirement at the age of 55–59; 3% preferred at the age of 60–61 years, 8% at the age of 62–63 years, and 69% at the age of 65 years. The pension plans are mostly provided by large private employers i.e. 54% of all members of pension plans were with employers of more than 10,000 employees, 82% were with employees of more than, 1,000 employees. However, Pension Reforms Act, 1974 imposed a limit that pension benefits should not provide income which exceeds 100% of final pay together with social security.

For self-employed persons incentives are given by US government. For example, pre-tax funds can be created for later years and all gains can accumulate tax-free, Keogh Act, 1962 was passed in USA to cause incentives to self-employed persons to set aside a minimum of US $ 2,500 p.a. as a tax deductible contribution to a retirement plan from business income. Under 1981 Tax Act, the maximum deductible amount has been raised to $ 15,000 p.a. plus $ 2,000 as voluntary contributions as deductible. Accumulations, thus, grow and no tax is paid. On retirement of the individual, tax is paid when he withdraws the money so accumulated. At this moment, he has a lower tax bracket because of reduced total income and is thus benefited to a maximum extent. Roll-over is possible of this accumulated sum to a qualified retirement plan or a corporation or individual retirement account (IRA). Besides Keogh Plan, there is individual Retirement Account another plan that allows an individual who is not covered by any other plan to set up his own tax exempt retirement account. Any wage earner can now set aside $ 2,000 p.a. or 1% of income, whichever is less, for retirement investments. In the case of spouse working, upto $ 4,000 can be set aside. It carries same advantage of tax deductibility as Keogh Plan.

In Canada, Provincial Pension Benefits Act and Federal Pension Benefits Act, 1967 apply to Government units and private units. It is not compulsory for an employer to establish or maintain a pension plan. However, if an employer does so, is required to meet funding standards and certain Rules on the vesting of pensions, investments and related matters. Entitlement for pension is at the age of 45 years provided the person has had 10 years continuous service with the employer or has completed 10 years of membership in the Plan whichever occurs first. An employee who has worked for less than 10 years for his employer but has worked for at least 10 years for several employers under a Multi-employer Plan, is entitled to a vested benefit.

In France, private pension are growing social security measures regulated under Ordinance of Oct. 4, 1945. At the age of 55 years a person becomes entitled to a pension in private enterprise. There are different kinds of pension plans obtained in France viz. the cadres plan (Confederation General des cadres) CGC is important others are AGIRC (Association General des Institutions de Retraites de cadres), UNIRS (Union National des Institutions de Retraites des salaries), ARRCO (Assocation des Regimesole Retraites Complimentaires). All these plans cover 8 million employees of more than 6,00,000 employers.

In West Germany, private pension system is voluntarily promoted with the difference that not only large employers but 2/3 of the firms having 50 employees have pension plans and 1/3 of the small firms do have pension plans.

In Netherland, Dutch workers participate in private pension plans. 2.3 million employees out of 3.9 million workers participate in 85 industry-wide multi-employer pension funds.

In Sweden and other European nations private pension plans exist. Amongst all the advanced nations in the world the old age benefits provided by social security are maximum in Italy amounting to 80% of pay regardless of income; in Spain, the retirement benefits range from 80–100% of pay upto a fairly high ceiling. In Luxembourg, Portgal, Belgium, Substantial old age benefits are provided as reported in the 1978 Report from the Conference Board's Division of Management Research, "Rethinking Employees' Benefits Assumption."

In Japan, in 1970, 3.4 million workers out of 20 million workers were covered under private pension plans. Benefits are paid with minimum 20-25 years of participation. The large Japanese companies having private pension plans have more generous schemes than the State-run plans. As in Europe, private Japanese pension schemes supplement compulsory government administered pension plans which cover the entire population. As reported by the Economist, May, 1983 (p. 89) under, "Re-employment & Pension Plan-Aging of Japanese Social Security" in Japan, a pensioner on retirement at the age of 60 gets a maximum of 44.2% of their earnings in the year before they retire as against the persons retiring at the age of 65 years and getting between 44% and 41% of earning in West Germany, Sweden, Britain, and USA. Japanese have eight State run person insurance schemes. On these two biggest, one-known as the Employee's Pension Scheme-includes the employee of the companies with more than five workers, cover both workers and their dependents and account for 43% of the population. The other is organised on a rational basis,takes in the self-employed workers in small firms and all their dependents and covers 47% of the population. Rests are small funds schemes covering seamen, farm and fishery workers, teachers, employees of public corporations and so on.

Referring back to U.K. large companies provide for private pensions on the same line, more or less, as discussed in the case of Canada and USA. However, for those persons who are self-employed, private organisations run pension schemes which are different to those of Japan. The most common of these pension schemes are the two as discussed by Malcolm Craig in "Successful Investment Strategy" Woodhead-Faukner, Cambridge, 1984. First one is traditional plan 'with profit' pension scheme which offers steady growth and guarantee a basic pension in the retirement years; and the second one is "Unit Linked Scheme" which is major growth centre. The money paid into this scheme is reinvested by the funds investment managers into ordinary shares in U.K. and overseas, gilt-property, local authority bonds and other investments. These schemes are sold directly to public by market oriented institutions such a Abbey Life and Hambros. Besides over the past few years, the company pension market has been developing leaps and bounds as reported by Diana Wright in "Self-investment at a Premium" in Administrator, May, 1982. Favourable tax and other considerations viz. legislation have allowed 'Pension Industry' to grow fast. Small self-administered pension scheme in the corporate sector is better source of investible funds as low allow 50% of the funds to be utilised by the companies.

From the above discussions, it transpires that India lags much behind in the area of retirement benefits to the employees in government as well as in private sector. There is enough to be done and accomplished in the direction of introducing pension schemes by the private employers to their employees. On the part of the government too is required to relax retirement rules so that an employee may seek retirement prematurely on sound and attractive incentives and take up freely the commercial or industrial activity to add to GNP and create new avenues for employment. The public sector undertaking have to give lead to private sector particularly by quickly introducing retirement pension schemes on superannuation as well as on voluntary basis after completion of minimum period of service so that the people with will, zeal, experience and skill could take up production activity and add to the generation of new sources of GNP and employment in the economy.

SAIL have recently implemented the scheme of voluntary retirement for their employees. The basic objective of the scheme is to:

1. achieve optimum manpower utilisation.
2. improve the average-mix of the employees and
3. Improve the over all skill level.

The scheme is applicable to all regular/permanent employees of the company. Any regular employees who has completed 10 years of the service in the company or 40 years of age is eligible to seek voluntary retirement.

A retired employee is basically entitled to number of benefits. These are:

1. Full provident fund contribution of employer with accretion there to in the account of employee to provisions of Provident Fund Rules applicables to the employees.
2. Gratuity for each completed years of service or part there of as admissible under gratuity rules.
3. Leave salary for the unavailed earned leave. The quantum of leave salary will not exceeds the maximum limit to which earned leave can be accumulated under the leave rules applicable to the employee.
4. Transfer benefits for self and family as admissible under the TA rules on super annuation.
5. Ex-gratia payment equivalent to 45 days emoluments (Pay + DA) for each completed year of service or the monthly emoluments at the time or retirement multiplied by remaining months of service left before the normal date of retirement whichever is less. For example, an employee who has completed 24 years of service and has got only one year of service left for normal retirement, will get an ex-gratia of only 12 months of emoluments and not 36 months emoluments.
6. One month/three months notice pay as per service conditions: Other public sector units are also considering the above proposal for their employees.

In private sector, DCM has also introduced attractive scheme of voluntary retirement for the employees of the company.

With a view to boost India's economy to the stage of 'take off' of economic development to match the development and achievements of the developed nations, a new generation of entrepreneurs is required who may be innovating and imitating. The persons who could be released from jobs in private and public undertakings or Central or State Government services on pre-retirement plan could form an army of such entrepreneurs and besides creating avenues of new employment and new activities of productions could take the economy ahead to the aspirations of

"21 st" Century of electronic stage. Therefore, the government should bring effective legislation and take result bearing measures to ensure adoption of retirement benefits, inducement for premature retirements to aspirant employees who could be motivated to take up production activity on small or medium scale basis.

Future Projections and Provisions in the Accounts

Theoretically, a pension plan or other retirement benefit plan for an employee may be funded by a trust fund known as self-administered plan or by an insurance company known as insured pension plan or by a combination of both. Under the self-administered plan, contributions are paid to the trustee company who has full freedom and flexibility in investing the funds as per the provisions of the plan; whereas in the case of insured pension plan payments are directly made to a insurance company or to trustees for onward payment of premium to a insurance company. In U.S.A., maximum number of the companies follow self-administered plans. There are other types of plans in vogue in USA but this is the most familiar one which favourably compares to the plan which has been followed in these concerns where the provident fund and pension schemes have been statutorily implemented. Divestment of funds is the main attraction in the plan which keeps off the management from tampering with the funds.

Three broad factors affect the cost of a pension programme to a company according to J.B. Cohen and S.M. Robbins viz. (1) the nature of the benefits; (2) the cost of a programme may be affected by the method of funding employed; and (3) cost is influenced by the actual experience of the company in operating under the programme. In the first category the cost will depend upon the nature of benefits; i.e. more liberal the benefits, the greater will be the cost. "Pay-as-you-go pension plans" are the example of this type of plans. In these plans, costs, exclusive of administrative expenses, are the same as the amount of benefits disbursed. In the second category, advance funding arrangement is made and the costs of the benefits may be measured by the contributions the company makes in the form of premiums to an insurance company or payment to a trust fund.

James A. Hamilton and Dorrance C. Bronson in "Pensions" have discussed number of methods for funding the pension benefit schemes used by the companies as noted below:

(1) **Current disbursement method**: During the early years of the plan these disbursements start out at less than 1% of the active payroll and eventually reach a peak. The major drawback of this method is the absence of any reserve to provide a payment base in an emergency.

(2) **Terminal Funding method**: Funds are set aside to provide for an Immediate life time pension as each employee retires. Early payments under this method exceed actual pension requirements and thus a reserve is created which the company could use in an emergency which is not available under the first method. Company's later contributions to pension funds are below actual pension payments, as the company earn interest on the balances in the reserve. The main drawback of this method is that the reserve established in only applicable to the employee already retired and provides no projection to those still on the active pay-rolls who are looking forward to retirement in the future time.

(3) **Level Annual Method**: This method takes care of the above drawback visible in Terminal funding method. Company, as per this method, pays a level contribution at the beginning of each year to the pension fund or on an annuity contract. The payment is based on the age of the employees so that at the start of the plan i.e. one-year amount is needed for those reaching the year of retirement. Company's contribution are highest in the first years when the plan is installed and stabilise at a much lower level afterwards.

(4) **Past Service Reserve and Level Contributions for Future Service**: In this method the Company decides first to meet in full its past service liability. It does so by making a substantial extra payment in the first year of the plan. Thereafter, it funds its future costs as in the prior method by level contribution.

It transfers from the introduction of above methods that for any given pattern of benefits, payment will vary with the funding method selected. "Costs will be affected if benefits are increased and by the actual experience of the company. The death rate of active employees determines the number who eventually will receive the benefit while the rate among retired employees establishes the cut-off time for receipt of the benefits. The effect of mortality must be considered in conjunction with death benefits because increased retirement costs from a low death rate among active employees may be offset by reduced death benefits. Management must evaluate liberal death benefits in the light of the additional costs imposed. Besides, the turnover of employees also influences costs. In non-vested plans, the amount save through employee withdrawals either increases the benefit payments or lowers contribution costs. Because pension costs are reduced by the interest earned on the funds invested, a successful investment policy is of considerable importance."

Selection of method of funding: Finance manager has to select and recommend the method of funding a plan which will benefit to his company. He is guided in this decisional process by a number of bench marks. He has to consider of initial stage the importance of the pension plan as long-range programme with heavy costs upon the company in the later stage if no pre-arrangements are made. Therefore, advance funding is more desirable than pay-as-you-go-plan. For small companies self-administered plan are good as they cannot take advantage of buying individual policies from the insurance companies. Larger companies have a wider choice to make on relative advantage of each method.

Secondly the finance manager should consider the cost of acquisition and administration. The major acquisition item is the commission paid which is largest in individual contracts then group permanent contracts or group annuity contract. Similarly, administration expenses are higher in individual contract than the other categories.

Thirdly, managerial responsibilities be also taken into condera-tion which pension plan to create because specialised talents are required to develop and manage an investment portfolio.

Fourthly, tax aspects be taken into consideration with respect to tax incidence of qualified pension plans.

The Pension Plan Balance Sheet. Pension Plan Balance sheet provide information to the actuary to judge the cost of the plan. Pension Plan Balance Sheet looks as under:

Assets	*Liabilities*
PV Pension Fund	*PV* expected from Past service
PV contributions for future services	*PV* expected future service cost
Deficit/Surplus	
Total Assets	To *PV* expected Benefits-Total Liabilities

From the above Balance sheet, it may be observed that on the liabilities side, there are two principal liabilities i.e., (1) Pensions that have already been earned by current employees and retired employees; (2) Pension which are expected to be earned by the employees through their future service. The sum of these two numbers measures the present value of all the pension commitments.

On the asset side, there are two main assets viz., (1) the amount put aside by the company in the pension fund; (2) value of the regular contributions to the fund that the firm plans to make in the future for its current employees. If all goes well, the value of the fund and the planned contributions should be sufficient to cover the liabilities. But assets, will be less than liabilities in case either the pension benefits are increased or the investments in pension funds do not perform upto the desired level. This deficit will be the balancing item which the company will have to make some time.

Actuary does the entire accounting for pension funds and divides the plans liabilities into two parts:

PV expected benefits for past service

+ *PV* expected future service costs

= *PV* expected benefits

As per the definitions of what is due to past and what is due to future, the *PV* expected benefits are arrived at. Some actuaries like to think of the proportion of payments that have accrued as a result of past service. In that case "*PV* expected benefits for past service = *PV* accrued benefits". The other opinion could be that all employees have so far earned is the pension that they could secure if they left the company today and in that case "PV expected benefits for past services = PV vested accrued benefits." For these employees who are fully vested the two definitions are the same.

For employees who are only partially vested, their past service earns them less if they leave the firm today than if they stay on. Therefore, *PV* vested accrued benefits is less than *PV* accrued benefits.

On the assets side, first asset is "pension fund", which is a result of past contributions of a company. These funds are vested in trust and invested in a diversified portfolio of securities. These are generally reported as accounting costs as the market valuation of securities is controversial. Thus, the assets to the fund do not cover the benefits that have accrued, the company has an unfounded liability as under:

Unfunded liability = *PV* accrued benefits (–) *PV* Fund assets. This liability must be reported in a footnote to the company's Balance Sheet. The methods of calculating the unfunded liability may be different in different set-up and organisations.

The second assets in the pension plan balance sheet is the stream of contributions to cover future services. This is generally known as "normal costs". The pension fund should be large enough to cover any benefits resulting from past services and future normal costs should cover benefits resulting from future service. Accrued benefits costs method is recommended by actuaries with the idea that the company should contribute each year in present value of any benefit that have accrued in that year.

The above discussion relates to the normal situation when everything goes well which seldom happen. Things may go wrong viz. there may be decline in the value of securities in the pension funds; or employee turn-over may be lower than predicted; or union may negotiate increased pension benefits. In these circumstances, the actuary has to adjust the accounting by increasing the estimate or normal cost to bring the balance-sheet back into balance. If it is not done then balance sheet would show a deficit resulting from the excess of *PV* of expected benefits over *PV* of assets in the pension funds. Therefore, the actuary does the above adjustment.

One can imagine a system in which pension plans are not funded. The company does not make any provision but waits a person to retire and pay pension out of current income. This system can work so long company continues to grow or prosper but fails when the company is put into difficulties.

Funding

There are three principal approaches to funding:

1. **Pay-as-You-Go.** As the name implies, no advance provision is made for meeting the obligations of the plan. As each monthly pension payment falls due, funds are provided from corporate assets. This method is not widely used at present, principally because by postponing pension outlay, an organization may be building up an obligation which cannot conveniently be met. Secondly, money set aside for a qualified plan will earn tax-free interest, so that fewer employer dollars will be required to pay a specified benefit with advance funding.

2. **Terminal Funding.** As each employee retires, the single premium, or single sum, necessary to provide his retirement benefits on the basis of assumed mortality and interest rates (with or without provision for administrative expenses) is contributed to the fund implementing plan. This method has certain disadvantages. Since retirements may not occur evenly, the required annual outlay may fluctuate widely and the variation may be sufficient to produce irregular corporate earnings. Furthermore, funding in advance of retirement is less costly because more interest can be earned.

3. **Advance Funding.** Modern corporate plans are financed by making regular periodic payments during the employee's working years for the purpose of building up a fund from which benefits will be provided on his retirement. The periodic payments are usually referred to as "contributions," and there are two principal funding agencies with which the contributions may be deposited—the trust fund and the insurance company.

4. **Choice of Funding Medium.** There is no general agreement as to which of the two funding media mentioned above is the better method. Under a trust fund, all contributions are received by a bank, trust company, or other custodian of the fund, and benefit payments are withdrawn from the same fund as they fall due. Full advantage may be taken of investment opportunities; there has been, consequently, an opportunity to invest in equities to a greater extent than an insurance company is permitted to do under the laws of most states. (However, insurance companies in

most states are permitted to operate "separate accounts" with investment freedom comparable to that of a trust fund.) Moreover, greater flexibility in the matter of contributions and benefits is generally considered possible under a trust fund plan because the employer is limited only by restrictions of the IRS. Under an insured plan, the introduction of a new type of benefit or a change in amount or frequency of contributions would also require the consent of the insurance company. On retirement, the continuation of benefit payments depends on the continuing sufficiency of the fund which, in turn, depends on the continuing financial ability of the employer. Given proper investment and actuarial advice, a trust fund plan can be perfectly sound. Trust fund plans are also sometimes called "self-insured," "self- administered," or "uninsured," plans.

Proponents of the insured plan point to certain advantages, chief of which are the guarantees which only an insurance company can give. Once benefits are "purchased," their payment is absolutely guaranteed by the insurance company. (By "purchase" is meant the setting up of a definite reserve liability by the insurance company against the retirement benefit payment accrued for a specified individual.)

Also, the typical "deposit administration group annuity" provides that even before benefits are purchased, funds deposited with the insurance company are guaranteed a minimum interest return, and the fund is guaranteed against capital losses. However, the rate may be changed annually, after some specified initial period such as five years, and the employer loses a certain investment flexibility since, generally, he cannot withdraw funds once contributions have been made, except at a sacrifice.

Insurance companies offer four types of contracts, in addition to the "separate accounts" (where permitted by law) and "split funding:"

1. **Deposit Administration Group Annuity.** This contract consists of two parts: an active life fund and a retired life fund. Contributions are made by the employer to the active life fund in an amount calculated by a consulting actuary or the insurance company as necessary to provide the benefits promised. The fund is credited with interest each year.

The fund is charged with administrative expense and contributions toward general and special contingency reserves. On retirement, a transfer is made from the active life fund to the retired life fund of an amount necessary to purchase the accrued benefit for the retiring employee, such benefit being fully guaranteed from this point (but not before) by the insurance company. Because contributions are not definitely allocated to individuals until actual retirement, the deposit administration plan is quite versatile and adaptable to a wide variety of benefits.

Deposit administration contracts are usually subject to experience rating or dividend action by the insurance company. If the group covered is large, a variation known as "immediate participation guarantee" may be offered by the insurer. Under this method, each group stands squarely on its own experience as regards benefit payments and overhead expense—there is no pooling or risk sharing as in other insured plans. There are no guarantees; the insurance company simply manages the fund, receiving contributions, investing money, and making benefit payments. (However, "purchases" of guaranteed benefits for retired lives may be made if the fund becomes "thin".) The plan is usually restricted to groups large enough to have a fairly stable experience from year to year.

2. **"Conventional" Group Annuity.** The employer's contributions (and the employee's if required by the plan) are applied immediately on receipt or at the end of the contract year to purchase a deferred retirement benefit for each individual employee. This type of contract, while well suited to some of the older retirement plans, has largely given way to the deposit administration group annuity because of the greater flexibility and economy of this newer form.

3. **Individual Policy Plan.** A separate individual contract is required for each covered employee, and one or more additional contracts for each employee may be required if benefits increase after the original issue. The contract often provides life insurance benefits in addition to retirement benefits, and this is its chief advantage. However, if insurance benefits are provided, the individual employees must meet the applicable underwriting requirements of the insurance company. The plan is relatively expensive,

cumbersome, and inflexible, and is now generally recommended only when the group to be covered is too small to qualify for a group plan.

4. Group Permanent Plan. Group permanent insurance combines life insurance and annuity benefits in one group contract. It is similar, therefore, to combining in one contract the individual contracts under an individual policy plan. This type retains many of the disadvantages of the individual policy plan with few advantages. From the employer's point of view, the plan is relatively expensive in comparison with the cost of providing annuity and insurance benefits under a deposit administration plan and group term life insurance.

5. **Separate Accounts.** As the name indicates, funds deposited in separate accounts are segregated from the regular assets of the insurance company. The laws of some states require that funding by a separate account be limited to retirement plans qualified under Sections 401 and 404 of the Internal Revenue Code. This requirement must also be met if the Separate Account is to be exempt from regulation by the Securities and Exchange Commission. Upon the retirement of an employee, benefits are purchased by transferring the amount of the necessary single premium from the Separate Account to the General Account of the company. From this point on, the benefit to the employee is full guaranteed.

There are no guarantees prior to retirement; in this respect it differs from the deposit administration funds which have guarantees of a minimum interest return and no impairment of capital. The principal difference from the "immediate purchase guarantee" is that the latter is subject to state laws restricting investment to media specified for other regular insurance company funds.

Investment-only separate accounts are also available which, although they allow for the purchase of annuities at retirement, are usually not used for that purpose and instead are used only for the investment of funds.

6. **Split Funding.** Sometimes a combination of trust fund and insurance company is used. One such arrangement is to have employer contributions go to a trust fund but, on retirement, a sum is withdrawn from the fund to purchase an annuity from an insurance company. Or, a trust fund may be used to supplement a

conventional group annuity or individual policy plan in the event that the plan provides "final average," disability, or special benefits.

7. **Funding Techniques.** Because the liability for retirement plan benefits is often very large; most corporations prefer to set aside money currently, usually annually or more frequently. It is of the greatest importance to decide on a definite funding program and to determine periodically the sum which should be contributed annually.

The calculation of the required contribution is highly technical, and requires the services of an actuary. The pension payments have a "present value," that is, although they are deferred to normal retirement date, a one-sum dollar value can be calculated by use of assumed mortality and interest rates. Similarly, the amount of the required future contributions to the fund implementing the plan can be determined as that amount which will make the present value of contributions equal to the present value of the pension payments.

The calculation may or may not include an assumed rate of withdrawal other than by death, and should, in a "final average" plan, make some attempt to estimate final average salaries. The latter is usually done by projecting current salaries on the basis of certain assumed rates of salary increase. Without such a projection, there is a strong possibility that benefits (dependent on final salaries) will be understated, and as a result, the annual contributions actually required will be underestimated initially, leaving more to be made up in later years.

An important consideration in funding, once the assumptions have been decided upon, is the treatment of prior service. This generally means service with the employer before the plan was established, but for which pension credit is given. It can also mean service prior to the date on which a benefit increase became effective, or service prior to the date of valuation. Prior service may be calculated separately and funded separately, or it may be considered as an integral part of the total cost of the benefits (i.e., under an "aggregate method"). An advantage of funding methods which treat prior service separately is that it is possible to introduce flexibility into the funding program. Briefly, some of the more common funding methods are:

1. **Entry-Age-Normal-Cost.** The age at which service credit begins for each employee is recorded and a level annual contribution, level either as a percent of salary or as a dollar amount, is calculated, payable from "entry age" to normal retirement age, in an amount sufficient to provide his prospective benefit at retirement on the basis of the valuation assumptions. The level annual contribution is the "normal cost." The valuation is carried out at the attained age, thus creating an "actuarial deficiency," if service begins before the effective date, or if there have been increases in benefits, because the normal cost has been calculated at the entry age (i.e., an earlier age). This "actuarial deficiency" may be treated in several ways. It may be amortized over a stated period of years from the effective date of the plan (or from the date of a subsequent increase), or it may be funded at a specified rate (maximum rate, for purposes of Federal income tax is over ten years). Alternatively, interest only may be paid, in which case there is no reduction of the unfunded deficiency except through gains arising if actual experience is better than expected.

2. **Frozen Initial Liability Method.** As of the effective date of the plan, a calculation similar to entry age normal cost is made and an initial deficiency (or normal cost is made and an initial deficiency (or liability) is obtained. Later valuations are made on the basis of keeping this initial liability constant, and varying the current cost. The initial deficiency may be adjusted if there are later benefit increases.

3. **Single-Premium Method.** Single premium funding is adapted to benefit forms such as "career average," "unit purchase," and "money purchase." Each year benefits are purchased as they accrue, and "prior service"may be funded as in (1) above.

4. **Level Annual Premium Method.** A level annual premium is payable from date of entry. On a benefit increase, a new level annual premium for the increase is payable based on the attained age at date of increase. There is, consequently, no deficiency as in the entry-age-normal-cost method. The method is cumbersome and little used at present except with individual policies.

5. **Aggregate Method.** The present value of future pensions is found, less any assets in the fund, and less present value of future

salaries expected to be paid to normal retirement date or prior death or termination. An annual accrual rate is determined as the ratio of unfunded future pensions to future salaries. The annual contribution is the accrual rate times present salaries.

8

OCCUPATIONAL HEALTH AND SAFETY

OCCUPATIONAL Health is a collective term used to characterize all the various activities and disciplines devoted to maintaining and promoting the health, safety, and productivity of wage earners. This field, then includes, but is not necessarily limited to, occupational medicine, occupational health nursing, industrial hygiene, industrial accident prevention or safety engineering, and occupational health education. The earlier, almost synonymous, term, "Industrial Health," which was used when these efforts were largely limited to factories, mines, railroads, and other large or "heavy" industries, is also still in use. As these activities have been extended to mercantile, financial and other business institutions, and even to governmental agencies and other non-profit organizations, such as hospitals, the more accurate and broader term, "Occupational Health," is replacing it.

OCCUPATIONAL HEALTH ACTIVITIES

The growth of occupational health activities within the traditional industries listed, and their extension into the other institutions mentioned, reflect fundamental economic and social changes which have been steadily accelerating in the 35 years since the end of World War II. The perceived value of individual workers has risen as ever more complex businesses and industries have needed people with higher levels of skill and training; the unskilled common laborer hired for his simple muscular strength has become a rarity. At the same time, increasing rates of pay, triggered by union demands, have made more organizations "labor intensive" and increased the perceived value of employees collectively.

As the purely economic needs of wage earners have been better met, other rewards and benefits have received greater emphasis. Employers are expected to provide safer and more healthful working conditions, and government is expected to require them to do so. These trends culminated in enactment of the Federal Occupational Safety and Health Administration within the Department of Labor, in 1970. Briefly, the statute authorizes this new Administration to develop, encourage, and enforce uniform minimum national standards of health and safety in employment. The Act also created a National Institute of Occupational Safety and Health within the then, Department of Health, Education and Welfare to provide scientific advice and assistance to the new Administration. The activities and achievements of both these agencies remain highly controversial at the end of their first decade, but there can be no question that the Act itself has had a stimulating effect on the whole field of occupational health. It seems reasonable to hope that its impact will ultimately by beneficial.

Nevertheless, as of this writing, most of the occupational health services, outlines below under "Employee Health Services," are still provided by private enterprises to their employees on a voluntary basis, in the sense that only a few of these services are required by law. However, as a result of the adoption of the Act, a number of new private businesses organized to provide employers with those services which *are* required by law have arisen. Most of them tend to concentrate on the environmental control of hazards to health and safety and to provide minimal medical services, but a few provide a full range of occupational health services. In addition, some state and local governmental units within the Departments of Health or Labor have long provided some service, mostly in the form of inspections of work places to detect and correct violations of legal minimum health and safety standards. A few such units have also provided consultative, analytic, and other laboratory services to employers to help them control hazardous conditions. The new Federal agencies are continuing and expanding both these functions.

Occupational health workers give priority to preventing those illnesses and accidents which are directly attributable to, or associated with, the work performed. A few well-known examples, in addition to the notoriously high accident rates in the construction and transportation industries, are lead poisoning, asbestosis, insecticide poisoning, leukemia from ionizing radiation, and loss of hearing from excessive noise. Occupational health workers foster the productivity and general well-being of employees by providing relief of minor symptoms of non-occupational diseases and injuries during the work day.

Occupational health workers are also increasingly concerned with the prevention and control of diseases which, while not attributable to the work performed, affect the health and longevity of many workers in their most productive middle years, such as coronary heart disease, cancer, and off-the-job accidents. Efforts are also made to educate and motivate employees to develop better health habits and better utilize the services of their own doctors. Finally, there is increasing concern with certain diseases or conditions which are especially vulnerable to attach in a work setting. Alcoholism is the oldest example, but programs for the detection and control of high blood pressure, excessive weight, and cigarette smoking, are also being successfully developed.

Occupational Medicine

Occupational medicine may be defined as that branch of medicine which is concerned with the prevention and treatment of occupational injuries and diseases, and with the promotion for the optimal health, productivity, and social adjustment of gainfully employed people at all levels. It is the oldest discipline in occupational health, the others having developed as special non-medical skills were needed. It is also an ancient branch of medical knowledge in the sense that the relationships between certain diseases and certain kinds of work and between general health and productivity have been recognized and studied from earliest times—ancient writers from Hippocrates to Pliny described particular occupational diseases.

However, occupational medicine in the sense of a separate form of practice did not develop until the second decade of this century, with the passage of Workers' Compensation laws in every state. These laws make employers responsible for treating injuries and illnesses associated with work, and for a significant part of any consequent loss of wages. Employers are required to carry insurance against both these costs. As some private doctors began to concentrate on the treatment of such injuries, and some larger companies hired doctors to provide treatment directly, "industrial surgery" was born.

Many employers and their insurance carriers made efforts to reduce the frequency, severity, and consequent cost, of work injuries. A discipline of "safety engineering" within new "safety departments" appeared, and the National Safety Council was organized. Safety programs have been so successful that most workplace are now safer than the homes and recreational areas of workers. Industrial surgeons and company doctors gave these safety programs full support and cooperation from the beginning. However, they did not, and still do not, usually accept responsibility for their routine operation, but occupational safety and occupational rehabilitation remain vital concerns of occupational medicine.

As the administration of Workers' Compensation was refined and the safety movement became effective, occupational diseases, which were also covered under the compensation laws, drew more attention. They are of course, far more complex than occupational injuries, and far greater efforts were required to establish their causes, understand their mechanisms, treat their effects, and ultimately prevent their occurrence. Older ones, such as silicosis, lead poisoning, and the "bends" or decompression sickness were studied in much greater detail.

With the growth in the size and complexity of industry, particularly during and immediately after World War II, many new potentially toxic materials, such as plastics and pesicides, and new noxious agents, such as ionizing radiation and laser beams, also needed study. In addition, some noxious agents which had been unthinkingly accepted in the past, such as excessive noise, came under scrutiny and attack. Similarly, newer criteria for safety margins began to develop: it was no longer considered sufficient to prevent obvious disease; rather, it became desirable to prevent any detectable biological change in an exposed person, if possible. The broader medical knowledge needed to study, treat, and prevent these diseases made the title "Industrial Physician" more appropriate than the older one of "Industrial Surgeon." As this knowledge has been applied to all kinds of employees in all kinds of employment the title "Occupational Physician" has become even more accurate.

Most of the knowledge about occupational diseases has been acquired by physicians employed by private companies, but physicians associated with the Public Health Service and some state labor or health departments, have also made vital contributions. Increasingly, in recent decades academicians affiliated with Occupational Medical Departments in medical schools have conducted important research. Since the measurement of toxic substances and noxious agents is essential in evaluating the quantitative exposure of workmen, chemists and physicists were needed. And since the elimination or reduction of the offending agents required modification of buildings, equipment, and operations, engineers were also needed. The application of these pure and applied sciences to the control of occupational disease created the new discipline of "Industrial Hygiene."

By and large, industrial hygiene has been successful, especially in larger companies, in greatly reducing the exposure of workers and largely eliminating new cases of some of the worst of the older occupational diseases such as silicosis, decompression sickness, lead poisoning, and radium poisoning. As mortality and serious morbidity have decreased, more attention has been given to less dramatic agents, such as nuisance dusts and occupational skin diseases. As with industrial safety, occupational physicians do not usually accept direct responsibility for industrial hygiene, but occupational medicine remains concerned with its rationale, techniques, and effectiveness.

Second in priority only to the prevention and treatment of specific occupational diseases and injuries, occupational medicine is concerned with maintaining the immediate well-being and productivity of workers, as well as their long-term health. One way of doing so is the proper selection and placement of workers in terms of their physical, mental and emotional capacities. Applicants for new job, people being transferred to other jobs, and those returning from absences due to illness can be evaluated in these terms by techniques similar to those of any diagnostic medical evaluation. Since non occupational illnesses and accidents cause many times more absence from work and ineffectiveness at work than occupational ones, another way to maintain productivity and well-being is to provide some general medical care in the work place. Other efforts to promote general health concentrate on the early diagnosis of disease in its most reversible stage.

Every contact of an employee with a physician also provides an opportunity to educate and motivate him or her to develop better health habits and to make better use of community medical resources. All these therapeutic, diagnostic, and educational efforts are discussed below under "Employee Health Services."

Occupational Medical Practice

This practice is less standardized than any other medical or surgical specialty or sub-speciality. Like other specialties, it has developed a large body of knowledge, ethical and scientific principles, and many specific techniques. Postgraduate training programs of varying duration and intensity are available in a number of medical schools, and shorter courses in particular areas within the field are available through specialty and general medical associations.

Occupational physicians with each of these different educational backgrounds are found at every level of responsibility, achievement, and recognition. They usually seek full-time careers at a high level in private enterprise, an academic institution, or a government agency. However, a few establish, or participate as partners in, private practices, often called "Industrial Health Clinics" or "Occupational Health Clinics." These may provide a broad range of occupational medical services to a number of smaller employers, or to the smaller plants of larger employers in the nearby area. Some have office facilities in one or more large trailers which move from one industrial plant to another, operating as "mobile" industrial or occupational medical clinics. Private consulting practices in a special area of occupational medicine, such as epidemiology, toxicology, occupational skin diseases, or occupational lung diseases, are important, but rare.

Besides these certified specialists, there are even more physicians who work full time in occupational medicine without having sought formal training and certification. Some simply confine their private practices to the treatment of work injuries. Others may also examine candidates for employment or render some other limited employee health services.

Thus, the physicians who actually provide occupational medical services, and therefore may be said to practice occupational medicine, run a complete range from the general practitioner who occasionally treats a work injury, through the cardiologist who reads electrocardiograms on employees a few hours a week, to the highly trained and skilled Diplomate of the Board of Preventive Medicine in Occupational Medicine, with a Master's Degree in Public Health.

The day-to-day activities of an occupational medical practice will also vary widely, depending on which of the many forms of practice described is involved. They differ from other forms of practice in that they may include a role in the environmental control of occupational injuries and diseases, in the treatment and rehabilitation of work injuries and diseases; in job placement in terms of health, and in health maintenance by means of early diagnosis and health education. They may also include a role in special employee health services such as alcoholic rehabilitation, "troubled employee" counseling, hypertension control programs, and others, discussed under "Employee Health Services."

As employee health insurance to defray at least partially the cost of medical care has become almost universal, and as employers (voluntarily or through collective bargaining) have assumed a greater share of the premiums, occupational physicians have become involved in determining the benefits to be provided and the most effective way of administering them. They are also often asked for advice about other employee benefits, such as life insurance, supplemental sick pay, and pensions. While they do not ordinarily actually administer these employee benefits, they often participate in efforts at cost containment. In fact, a whole new paramedical, parapersonnel specialty in "Health Care Cost Containment" is developing.

As consumer advocates, environmentalists, government agencies, and the general public have become more concerned about the health effects of commercial products, intermediate products, by-products, and waste products, occupational physicians have become involved in these matters as they affect the corporations for which they work. They are frequently consulted, not only for their general knowledge of medicine and preventive medicine, but because the toxicology and epidemiology of substances in the workplace are so similar to those of substances in the general environment.

Finally, occupational physicians are often asked for advice about health-related corporate charitable contributions to local hospitals, local community funds, or local and national heart and cancer associations. They can be extremely useful in this area, helping to make sure that limited funds are wisely apportioned to the neediest and worthiest activity or organization.

Employee Health Service

Health services provided by employers in private business, government, and other nonprofit organizations are as variable as the practice occupational medicine. Workers' Compensation coverage, so important in the history of occupational medicine, is the practical minimum. The vast majority of employers, who of course employ only a few people each, usually provide nothing more, especially in the absence of serious, readily recognized hazards to safety or health. The many small stores, offices, and providers of personal of home services which fall into this category employ very many people in the aggregate. At the other extreme, some large international companies, with thousands of employees at many locations all over the world, such as large oil, steel or electronics companies, provide all the services to be briefly described, on a large scale.

Every combination is between can be found, depending on the nature of the work, the likelihood of injury or disease associated with that work, the size and prosperity of the organisation, and the attitudes of the employer, the employees, and their respective medical and legal advisors. The location at which services are given will depend on the location of the physician who provides them. Larger companies, especially at locations where they employ between one and five thousand people, are likely to provide them on the premises. Such "inplant" facilities are still often referred to as the "Medical Department," but there is an increasing tendency to call them the "Health Service" to stress their preventive function. The chief services which may be included can be summarized as follows, in approximate order of importance and frequency:

1. **Environmental Control.** The physician providing health services will frequently need the help of industrial hygienists and safety engineers, who, may be company employees or outside consultants. He or she should also be generally familiar with minimum legal health and safety requirements. Many states have long enforced certain safety standards, and the "factory inspectors" who do so are familiar figures, not only in India, but in England and on the continent. Some states, notably have also long had a series of occupational disease codes which set minimum standards for environmental control. The newer Federal Occupational Safety and Health Administration has already promulgated new standards for some hazardous materials and agents, has proposed but not yet adopted standards for others, and has temporarily used those of the older governmental agencies for the remainder.

2. **Emergency and Palliative Treatment.** This treatment for both occupational and non-occupational diseases and injuries, has become very common since the end of World War II in establishments of all kinds which employ more than 300 to 500 people. It is usually rendered by registered occupational health nurses. These nurses are usually provided with written standing orders by a physician for the treatment of common conditions. If there is a physician on the premises, he or she may supervise this activity more closely and will often amplify it. This is the kind of employee health activity which most employees most frequently encounter.

3. **Definitive Treatment of Occupational Injuries and Diseases.** Relatively minor injuries are often treated on the premises, if nurses and doctors are employed to provide other services as well. However, few individual plants employ enough people to keep a nurse or doctor busy with such cases alone. More serious occupational diseases and injuries are usually treated elsewhere, most frequently by private practitioners, since they are likely to need hospital facilities and the care of specialists, and involve absence from work. These are most important, but fortunately not very frequent, services.

4. Medical Evaluations or Examinations. "Examination," although a less exact term than "evaluation," is so well established that it will probably continue to predominate. "Examination" suggests primarily looking and touching, whereas "evaluation" is a broader term which also includes the history of current symptoms and prior illnesses and laboratory and X-ray determinations, as well as the interpretation of all the observations. The practical distinction is that 85% of diagnoses are very strongly suspected from the history alone, another 10% during the actual examination of the patient's body, and only a final 5% from laboratory studies. Many non-medical people, including employers wishing to obtain such services, think that this order is just reversed and mistakenly judge the thoroughness of an evaluation by the number of laboratory tests. Having made this important point, the word "examination" will be used for simplicity.

(a) *Placement or Preplacement Examinations.* Examinations of applicants for employment or for transfer to other jobs, are performed to ascertain that they are able to perform the new job effectively and without danger to themselves or fellow workers. Examples of conditions which may prevent their doing so are a serious uncorrectable hearing defect in a receptionist, an inguinal hernia in a heavy laborer, or epilepsy in a crane operator. Job restrictions of this kind should be realistic in order not to restrict unnecessarily any individual's job opportunities or the recruitment of otherwise well-qualified applicants. The restrictions must be individualized and carefully documented. Generalizations, such as that women are unable to perform heavy work, must not be used.

Recent Federal, state, and local regulation against discrimination in employment reinforce these principles.

A placement examination may also reveal ways in which the new employee can improve his health, through alterations in his daily habits, such as weight control, or by seeking treatment for a newly discovered abnormality, such as high blood pressure. Finally, such examinations give the health staff an initial contact with each employee, and provide a baseline of the new employee's physical, mental, and emotional characteristics which can facilitate later contacts. Until quite recently these placement examinations were also sometimes used to exclude applicants who were likely to be excessively absent or to use a disproportionate share of employee benefits, but the new regulations forbid selection on this basis.

(b) *Hazard Examinations*. This type of examination, also called "medical surveillance," may be necessary at regular intervals of people actually or potentially exposed to dangerous materials or agents, lest any undetected or temporary break in environmental controls have produced excessive exposure, or temporary, or even permanent damage. Such examinations are often limited to the particular tests which are most likely to be affected by the particular agent involved, such as chest X-rays for workers exposed to silica or asbestos, or hearing tests on those exposed to noise.

There is an increasing trend toward utilizing "biological markers" which show the earliest detectable biological alteration, even before any permanent or even temporary dysfunction occurs. Hazard examinations have long been provided, and even made mandatory, by more enlightened employers. Some recent federal standards promulgated by OSHA include requirements for particular kinds of examinations at specific intervals for workers exposed to particular hazards.

(c) *Return to Work or Clearance Examinations*. These may be performed on employees returning to work after any extended absence due to illness, leave of absence, or lay-off, to ascertain that they are again able to perform their work. The scope of these examinations and the duration of absence for which they are required are extremely variable. Brief questioning by an astute nurse is often sufficient, but in some cases quite detailed examinations may be needed, and information from the employee's own physician may be essential.

(d) *Separation Examinatioins*. Examinations on termination are required by only a few employers, usually where the employee may have been exposed to a material, agent, or situation which could lead to a later claim. Testing the hearing of an airplane mechanic who is leaving his job, but who will continue to work near noisy engines elsewhere, is a good example.

(e) *Periodic Prevention Medical Examinations*. These are second only to placement examinations in frequency and importance. They are often provided only for executive or management personnel, but they may be provided for all employees in some instances. Eligible employees are usually examined every year after the age of 40, but often less frequently at earlier ages. The scope of the examination also frequently varies with age, and sometimes with job level.

An adequate periodic examinations should lead to one of the three following conclusions, in decreasing order of frequency: (i) The individual is in good general health and needs no further medical study or treatment at the present time. (ii) The individual has certain definite diseases or conditions for which he should seek treatment from private physicians of his own choice. Or (iii) Certain abnormalities are detected which require additional medical study or consultation. These additional studies may also be provided in the Employee Health Service, but the employee is more often referred to his own private physician for them.

Most such periodic examinations are conducted by full-time occupational physicians in an Employees Health Service on the employer's premises, but some are performed by fixed or mobile occupational or industrial health clinics, and quite a few are done, especially at high executive levels, at sophisticated and prestigious medical centres. These are frequently connected with medical schools, sometimes at a considerable distance from the location of the business.

There is no evidence that these "fancier" examinations are more useful than the commoner kind. All kinds have become very popular with employers and employees, but recently their long-term value has been questioned by some physicians. Their value is difficult to measure; the crisis may focus too strongly on mortality and serious morbidity, whereas the recognition and relief of minor conditions may contribute greatly to productive and satisfying daily living at work and at home. Certainly periodic examinations have more value if they can be reinforced by more frequent contacts in selected cases, as well as by continuing efforts to improve health, such as the programs in the control of excessive weight, high blood pressure, and cigarette smoking discussed below.

5. **Rehabilitation.** Rehabilitation is an important employee health activity. Some large companies provide quite elaborate facilities and trained physical and occupational therapists on the premises to rehabilitate employees injured at work. These facili-

ties may also be made available for non-occupational cases when scheduling permits. More frequently rehabilitation of both occupational and non occupational cases is provided in community facilities. Even more frequent and far more important, is the rehabilitation of employees recovering from any illness or injury by means of temporary adjustment of their work assignments.

Ideally, the occupational physician or the occupational health nurse should begin to plan with the employee and his or her treating physician for the eventual return to work as soon as it becomes apparent that the patient will be ill long enough to need readjustment after recovery. Most frequently, a simple gradual increase in hours worked each day permits the employee to readjust to his or her previous job, but sometimes responsibility and effort cannot be directly measured in time, especially for executives. In these cases the employee must only gradually resume full responsibility, regardless of the number of hours put in. In some cases only a completely different, temporary, assignment will permit gradual resumption of full responsibility.

All necessary job limitations should be prescribed as exactly as possible. Vague directions like "take it easy," "don't overdo it," or "pace yourself," while popular with many doctors, are not helpful. They tend to prolong the time for full recovery of a fearful person and encourage a more adventurous one to exceed his capacity.

6. **Immunizations.** Protection against infectious diseases is frequently provided. Immunizations may be given for work-related purposes, such as tetanus toxoid for work injuries, or they may be provided for general purposes, such as recreational travel. They may also be given on a large scale to help control an epidemic, such as influenza. There is a trend in occupational medicine, as in general preventive medicine, to give only those "shots" which are clearly needed and effective. This more conservative attitude was intensified by the realization a few years ago that, with the worldwide eradication of smallpox, more people would become ill or die from smallpox vaccination than from the disease, if the old schedule of vaccination every three years were continued.

7. **Hypertension and Other Specific Disease Control Programs.** Control programs are increasingly frequent employee

health activities. An example of those controllable by drugs is high blood pressure. Lowering it with drugs has been clearly shown in recent years to avoid or delay complications and prolong life. Good control requires fairly frequent blood pressure determinations, and careful adjustment of the dosages of one, two, and sometimes more drugs which may produce inconvenient or even dangerous side effects. Once the diagnosis and need for control have been established, it is quite convenient for the patient to obtain the detailed observations and adjustments needed during brief visits to the Employee Health Service at his work place without absence from work, additional travel, or prolonged waiting.

It takes little additional time or expense for the occupational physician to conduct this preventive service. Some of the necessary observations can be made by occupational health nurses. The patient's own physician will usually welcome this help for his or her patient, provided that he (she) is initially consulted, kept regularly informed, and respectfully involved in all important decisions.

8. **Alcoholism and Other Behavioral Disorders.** The Employee Health Service must work as an equal partner with other departments of the organization to achieve good results in this area.

The existence of a drinking problem usually becomes apparent when the employee's attendance, or the quality and quantity of his work, or both, deteriorate. Once the supervisors and the personnel staff suspect alcoholism, the diagnosis should be confirmed medically, since excessive and compulsive drinking may be only a symptom of a more serious mental disorder which requires separate treatment. In addition, prolonged excessive drinking can produce physical disease, such as cirrhosis of the liver, which also requires active treatment.

Physicians can direct the alcoholic toward effective help, which almost always includes Alcoholics Anonymous. They can also help supervisors and the personnel staff monitor the employee's cooperation, which should always be made a condition of continued employment. The successful management of addiction to other drugs is analogous to that of alcoholism, but they are less frequently encountered in the work setting, and therefore formal programs are fewer and of lesser scope.

9. **Troubled Employee Programs.** These are a relatively new activity in which the Employee Health Service participates with other departments. Most of them have grown out of alcoholism programs, as it became apparent that deterioration in attendance and quality and quantity of work of many employees was due, not to excessive drinking, but to some other personal problem. Included are emotional disorders, family health problems, marital problems, child development and behavior problems, and financial problems.

Once the supervisor has established that an unexplained work deficiency exists, he or she, or a member of the personnel staff may suggest that the employee accept evaluation and counseling. In some programs the occupational physician then evaluates the problem, determining the presence and importance of medical factors, and recommends specific medical or psychiatric treatment, or some other kind of counseling. In other programs a counsellor interviews the employee first, using the occupational physician as a later consultant in developing a counseling program.

10. **Health Education and Motivation.** Every contact of an employee with the Health Service presents an opportunity for health education and motivation. No other technique is so effective as this kind of timely individual teaching and persuasion. Also worthwhile are posters and booklets, motion pictures, and lectures. Discussion groups can be extremely valuable if they are structured, focus on taking action rather than simply giving information, and deal with a single specific problems. Thus, groups to achieve weight reduction or stop cigarette smoking verge on formal group therapy and can be very effective.

Occupational Health Nursing

There are about 22,000 registered nurses in this country who devote all or part of their time to occupational health activities. The nursing subspecialty began almost contemporaneously with industrial surgery just before World War I, grew rapidly with industrial medicine after World War II, and has entered medicine after World War II, and has entered the current era as the most important partner of occupational medicine in the occupational health field.

Like occupational medicine, it has developed a large body of knowledge, special techniques, and educational curricula. A Master's degree in Occupational Health Nursing is awarded for formal postgraduate study, and many shorter courses in particular areas of interest are offered by academic institutions, government agencies, and professional nursing associations, especially the Association of Occupational Health Nurses. An independent and prestigious American Board of Occupational Health Nursing certifies knowledge and competence in the field.

Occupational health nurses participate in the detection and control of safety and health hazards in the wok place. To do so they must visit work areas and be familiar with work materials and processes, and with the working organization and interpersonal relationships. They almost always treat minor job-related illnesses and injuries, and monitor the treatment and progress of more serious ones. They very frequently also provide similar treatment for injuries and illnesses which are not job related. They may assess the health of workers exposed to specific health hazards, making some of the observations needed for "medical surveillance," and may also assess the general health of employees.

The nurses do a great deal of individual health counseling and guidance, both in terms of helping employees develop more healthful daily habits, and advising them of the need for specific medical investigation and treatment. Many nurses also do group teaching.

The legal limits of their activities are defined by Nurse Practice Acts in each State. In general they many diagnose and treat injuries and illnesses only under the direction of a particular physician who accepts responsibility for their actions, but they may undertake the preventive activities listed, such as hazard detection and control, health assessment, and health counseling, without specific medical direction.

The approximately 22,000 nurses engaged in occupational health work in about 8,500 organizations, only 1,500 of which are large enough to employ more than eight nurses. These are obviously the larger employers, and the other 7,000 units usually employ far fewer people. About one-third of the nurses work in units without any doctor on the premises, relying on written standing orders and telephone consultation for medical guidance.

A quarter work where there is at least one full-time doctor. The remaining 40% work in units where a doctor comes in a few hours a week.

Each of these forms of practice is useful and acceptable, if it is well suited to the health and safety problems encountered, and to the size and type of work unit involved. The occupational health nurse must of course be properly selected and trained, and management must understand and support her function. It is particularly important to obtain the services of a properly trained occupational health nurse in a smaller plant with fewer employees, where there will be no doctor on the premises, and where the doctors available for consultation and guidance may have little training or experience in occupational medicine. Unfortunately, it is under just these circumstances that the nurse is most likely to be selected on the basis of acquaintance and personal recommendation by someone in management or a local physician. Instead, management would be well-advised to seek consulation with a nearby local health agency or with one of the larger insurance companies, which frequently provide such service, both to determine the employee health activities needed and to select a well-qualified and preferably Certified Occupational Health Nurse.

Industrial Hygiene

This is the scientific discipline which seeks to ensure a safe and health full work environment. Engineers and chemists began to participate in such efforts very early in this century, but the specialty was widely recognized and named only during the burst of industrial and business growth following World War II. Like occupational medicine and occupational health nursing, industrial hygiene has developed a large body of knowledge, many highly refined techniques, and educational pre-requisites. An undergraduate degree in engineering, chemistry, physics, or one of the other basic science is essential. Master's degrees in Industrial Hygiene, Industrial Health, or Environmental Science are available from many academic institutions. There are also advanced courses available outside specific degree programs.

The Industrial Hygiene Association is the principal professional association, but industrial hygienists in government agencies and academic institutions usually also belong to the Conference of Governmental Industrial Hygienists. The American

Industrial Hygiene Association has also established a special Board which certifies the knowledge and competence of individuals in this field.

Industrial hygienists follow three basic sequential procedures. The first is the *recognition* of hazards by detailed inspection of the work place, which requires a thorough familiarity with innumerable materials and processes and with their possible safety hazards and toxic effects. The second is *evaluation* of the extent or degree of the hazard, which frequently involves chemical and physical measurements. analysis of the duration and intimacy of contact between individual workmen and the offending agent, and an estimation of the exact quantitative extent of the exposure of the workmen. The third and final procedure is *control,* which means lowering the exposure of individual workers to a safe level. A safe level should be one-tenth to one-hundredth of that level which could produce any ill effect in order to provide a margin of safety.

Control is achieved through four basic approaches. *Elimination* of the offending material, process or agent is obviously the most effective control if it is feasible: an example would be the prohibition of explosive or inflammable ingredients such as gasoline from home dry-cleaning agents. *Substitution* of a less toxic *agent* is advantageous, but still requires continued monitoring: an example would be the subsitution of perchlorethylene for carbon tetrachloride in commercial degreasing and cleaning processes. *Substitution* of one *process* for another may reduce the concentration of an offending substance to safe level; an example would be the substitution of wet grinding for dry grinding. *Enclosure* is another means of reducing the exposure of the individual worker; one can enclose the machine to reduce the noise it produces, but the use of earplugs really "encloses" the worker's ear in a different way. *Ventilation* is, of course, one of the most widely used and effective means of reducing the air concentration of toxic substances.

There are presently about 5,000 industrial hygienists. About 20% of them work for the Occupational Safety and Health Administration, probably another 20% work in other governmental agencies, academic institutions, or private consulting firms, and the remaining 60% are directly employed by private enterprises, extensive operations, and significant potential safety and health hazards, such as the larger oil, chemical, steel, mining and utility companies.

As stricter health and safety standards are adopted, and as more extensive environmental monitoring is required, more industrial hygienists will be needed in all these categories. A specific employer can get help in determining his need for an industrial hygienist, and in obtaining a well-qualified candidate, through the National Institutes of Occupational Safety and Health, his State Labor or Health Department, his insurance carrier, or one of the many private consulting firms in the field.

Other Occupational Health Disciplines

As the preceding discussion of occupational medical practice implies, some occupational physicians limit their interests and activities to special areas such as *Occupational Epidemiology, Toxicology, Radiation, Psychiatry, Dermatology,* as well as many others. Since these subspecialists almost always work with other general occupational physicians in larger, structured, employee health programs, detailed discussion of their fields appears unnecessary here.

"Physicians Assistants" and "Nurse Practitioners" have begun to enter the occupational health field during the last decade. These are people who have received limited medical training, almost always at a medical school, which qualifies them to perform simpler diagnostic and therapeutic procedures under the supervision of a licensed physician. Many of them were nurses, medical corpsmen in military service, or medical technicians of various kinds. They are well trained in the more common and routine medical procedures, and particularly trained to recognize unusual illnesses or injuries which must be brought to the attention of a fully trained and licensed physician promptly. They have proven extremely useful in performing routine examinations, treating simpler illnesses and injuries at work, and conducting preventive programs, such as the control of excessive weight or high blood pressure. Since the necessary supervision is relatively easily arranged in the work situation, the number of such practitioners may be expected to grow.

"Health Physicists" are the equivalent of Industrial Hygienists who concentrate on the control of hazards due to physical agents, particularly ionizing radiation from X-rays or radioactive materials. "Health educations" may be physicians, nurses, or specifically trained educators, who specialize in this area. "Administrators" in large Employee Health Services may have specific postgraduate training in medical or hospital administration. Finally, "Safety Engineers" and other safety workers, while of the greatest importance, have not developed so formal a discipline as other occupational health workers. Nevertheless, their efforts and their activities have undoubtedly prevented more discomfort, inconvenience, and disability among workers, and have saved more money for their employers and society, than any other group of workers in the field.

ADMINISTRATION

Costs and Benefits

Every employer must provide Workers' Compensation, and the number and scope of other occupational health services required by law are rapidly increasing. Management should provide as many other occupational health services as the company's size and resources permit, because it values its employees, wants their respect and cooperation, is genuinely concerned with their welfare, and wants the respect of business allies, competitors, and the community.

A company should not provide services in the expectation of any immediate financial benefit. Very few Employee Health Services can be shown to be cost-effective in the short-term accounting sense. They do reduce absence, increase productivity and morale, perhaps limit some employee medical benefits, and help attract and hold good employees, but so many of these factors are intangible, and there are such poor bases for comparisons, that any exact savings are difficult to measure.

Organizational Relationships

The Employee Health Service should serve as a staff function, providing information and advice to management in all matters relating to health and illness.

The individual in charge of the service, whether an occupational physician or an occupational health nurse, should have ready access to top management, such as the president of the company, a senior vice president, the local regional manager, another physician within the organization at a higher level, or some comparable official in other organizations. However, the occupational health worker should not accept direct responsibility for personnel, legal, or other management decisions.

Records

The results of all medical examinations, treatments, and other contacts of the health staff with each individual should be preserved in legible form and should be readily accessible at need. Medical details should be kept confidential and should not be revealed to management or anyone else without the employee's freely given permission.

However, the interpretation of the medical data may not be privileged if it is obtained outside a true doctor-patient relationship. For example, an applicant for employment understands that the physician will report his conclusions to management. Similarly, if an employee seeks authorization for absence, he knows that the physician will tell management whether he was indeed ill and whether he is able to work again. In other words, if an employee comes for a periodic preventive examination, or freely consults an occupational physician for some other reason, the information is confidential; but if the employee was sent to the physician for an administrative decision, the conclusion cannot be confidential.

Other records of individual employees, even though not purely medical, may be important for the health of the employee, and should be preserved with equal care. Job histories, especially with respect to actual or potential exposures to noxious agents, as well as environmental data on such agents, are very important. Finally, information about illnesses not actually seen in the Employee Health Service, or not even occurring during the period of employment, can be important.

All these quasi-medical observations can be especially valuable for statistical and epidemiological studies on the occupational diseases themselves, as well as on the individual employees exposed. For example, recent epidemiological studies on potential carcinogens draw on environmental data, complete work histories, and complete individual medical data, including illnesses after leaving employment, and the ultimate cause of death from Social Security files.

The volume of all these records becomes enormous, and systems for storing, sorting, and disposing of them when they become outmoded should be developed from the outset if they are to remain at all manageable. The automation of data, now common in larger companies, is of considerable help.

Until recently most records were made and kept by employers of their own volition, but law now requires the keeping of certain records, and prescribes the content and format of some. The first requirement was only for records of all job injuries, but both environmental and medical data are now required for some occupational disease hazards too. The Agency has also, as of this writing, promulgated a rule that medical and environmental data on all exposed individuals and hazardous situations must be preserved and readily available for 30 years, even if the affected employees are no longer employed and the hazard has been eliminated. The rule also gives the employee of his (her) authorized representative access to medical and environmental data. It further gives the staff of the Agency and of the national Institute for Occupational Safety and Health access to both kinds of data, even without the employee's permission. It gives union representatives access to environmental data, but not to the medical data, without the employee's permission.

The ethical problem of confidentiality of those medical records which are not in any way related to hazardous exposures, and the practical problem of preserving so much data in a readily accessible way, are too complex for discussion here. It is to be hoped that compromise and court interpretation will preserve the objective of free access to the specific information needed to study occupational disease and protect exposed workers' health without significantly compromising the value of the many preventive medical activities discussed, such as periodic and other diagnostic examinations, the treatment of minor nonoccupational illnesses, and the control of diseases like alcoholism and hypertension, which seem to require confidentiality.

Reports to Management

Budgets, expense reports, staffing justifications, personnel evaluations, and special requests are the same for the Employee Health Service as for any other staff units. Specialized reports which may be needed at times include: (1) Environmental surveys of work areas in terms of existing potential hazards, the effectiveness of control measures, and recommendations for improvement. (2) Health and illness summaries in terms of illnesses or injuries observed, absences recorded, or diseases found during routine examinations. (3) Statistical summaries of services rendered. (4) Narrative comment on any of the above statistics or about special problems and recommendations.

Internal Organization

Every Occupational Health Service or Medical Department is different, but some organizational guidelines have been developed out of experience. The size, type, and location of the physical facilities required, the number and kind of professional and clerical staff needed, the number and types of activities to be undertaken, the record system and budget, will depend on the size, function, and location of the company or other institution.

CONTROL PROBLEMS AND APPROACHES

The safety director is faced with two control problems. First, because of the interest in reducing trauma and damage to a socially and economically acceptable minimum, the safety director is faced with the problem of locating hazards and eliminating or controlling them in order to minimize unplanned events that may result in damage or trauma. Second, remedial control situations arise because, in spite of reasonable efforts, some unplanned events will occur and result in trauma or damage. In this section, we will discuss the problems associated with both preventive and remedial control. Before dealing with these two issues, however, we must discuss a problem that exists in both preventive and remedial control—assumptions concerning the factors that contribute to occupational damage and trauma.

Assumptions Concerning Factors That Contribute to Damage and Trauma

Single or Multiple Factors. Determining what factors have the greatest potential or contribute the most to unplanned events is a major problem for safety directors. Factors contributing to occupational safety and health hazards and therefore possibly to such unplanned events have been examined in two different ways. First, some persons have taken the position that occupational injuries and illnesses are largely the result of a single factor, while others have looked for multiple variable leading to such problems. Second, there has been some debate as to whether the hazards that lead to damage are unsafe acts, or both. The assumptions made concerning both of these issues will influence the types of problems identified and the type of approaches used to overcome such problems.

Historically, the view that a single factor is responsible for damage is the oldest. Under this assumption, the way to prevent unplanned events is fairly simple—remove the unsafe act or unsafe condition leading to the damage. For example, suppose one follows the single-contributing-factor view and also assumes that it is unsafe acts rather than unsafe conditions that result in unplanned events. If one were to observe an employee who has had a number of accidents, one might assume that removing the employee from the workplace would result in a reduction in the number of accidents occurring. The real cause, however, could be faulty machinery, and removal of the employee may do nothing to reduce the accident problem. The single-factor-analysis view is not widely held today except in some computer models (such as traffic record systems) in which only one main causal factor can be identified.

The multiple-variable viewpoint considers any unplanned even to be series of interrelated events. This view would evaluate an automobile accident as follows: A driver who is speeding (unsafe act), hits an icy spot in the road (unsafe condition), which should have been cleared by the road crew (unsafe act). The car spins, and a second driver coming from the other direction slams on the brakes (unsafe act), skids, and hits the first car. In this example, the single-factor theory might only consider the excessive speed of the first car as the cause of the accident. However, the multiple-factor view focuses attention on the fact that ultimate damage results from an interdependent series of prior events and coincidence.

Unsafe Acts. The assumption that unsafe acts are the sole contributor to damage focuses on individual behavior and therefore on individual values, attitudes, needs, personality, and so forth. Historically, proponents of the unsafe-act view held that certain individuals were accident prone and that through selection procedures they could be identified and not hired. This theory of accident proneness has fallen into disfavor due to the inability to find personality characteristics that are predictive of which employees are more likely to have accidents.

This is not to say that there is no such thing as accident proneness. Further, the concept does not provide a stable enough characteristic to make consistent measurement possible. In addition, the number of persons involved as accident repeaters is seldom large enough to justify expenditures to use "selection as a loss control method." One study found that in 27,000 industrial and 8000 non industrial accidents, accident repeaters accounted for only 0.5 percent of the cases, while 74 percent of the accidents were associated with a large number of individuals who had relatively infrequent accident experience. It has further been shown that the laws of chance alone will result in some people having more accidents than others.

It is unfortunate that the notion that unsafe acts of employees (through either accident proneness or negligence) is the prime or sole factor contributing to most damage has received a great deal of support. This view was presented by H.W. Heinrich in 1931 in his pioneering work, *Industrial Accident Prevention,* in which he asserted that 88 percent of accidents resulted from the unsafe acts of individuals, that 10 percent resulted from unsafe mechanical or physical conditions, and that only 2 percent were unpreventable.

This view has continued to be accepted by many persons involved in occupational safety and health as well as those in traffic safety. Unfortunately, this type of assessment focuses on only one aspect of the total problem. Thus, the belief of some safety directors seems to be: "I'll go after the 85% first and take care of the 15% after I get the carelessness thing licked. Why spend a lot of money first on only 15% of the job? I'm no that kind of sucker."

The fallacy of considering unsafe acts as the sole contributors to damage was pointed out by a study of 90,000 industrial accidents in Pennsylvania. This study looked beyond the unsafe- action question and found that unsafe conditions or mechanical problems underlay 89 percent of the damages. The study also found that in 83 percent of these cases the unsafe action by workers consisted of continuing to work under the unsafe conditions.

Unsafe Conditions. Assuming that unsafe conditions are the only important contributors to damage and trauma forces one to focus solely on factors in the physical environment (technology, machinery, noise, and so forth). This results in an engineering approach to safety and health that seeks to reduce damages by reducing technological hazards in the workplace. For example, continuous noise at 100 decibels day after day will produce permanent deafness. Redesigning equipment, machinery, and working procedures can prevent such traumas.

Some research has also shown that proper illumination can result in reduced accidents. However, the elimination or reduction of physical hazards over the years has had the unfortunate dysfunctional consequence of leading some people to blame employees for almost all accidents on the premise that their environments are free of hazards. As William W. Allison has stated, "Safety engineers have long felt that they must accept design concepts as logical and unalterable. Consequently they blame 85 percent of all accidents on the injured."

Since the late 1950s, there has been an increasing recognition that safety and health problems are often the result of multiple factors. Safety directors must consider unsafe acts, unsafe physical conditions, unsafe environmental conditions, and various combinations thereof in eliminating or reducing trauma in the workplace.

Problems and Approaches in Preventive Control

The major problem in preventive control is determining what factors have the greatest potential for contributing to damage and trauma. Here, safety directors have three major responsibilities. First, they conduct inspections to identify situations that are potentially hazardous because of unsafe conditions, unsafe acts, or both. Second, they recommend and develop specific programs aimed at eliminating or reducing these hazardous situations. Finally, no matter how "safe" a workplace is, safety directors must anticipate and recommend ways to reduce the consequences of unplanned events when they do occur.

Evaluating and Controlling Unsafe Conditions. The evaluation and control of unsafe conditions is an engineering problem encompassing "the four engineering aspects: design, construction, operation, and maintenance." Ideally, unsafe conditions are "designed out," or provisions are made for their control during the design phase. However, such ideal planning may not always exist, and unfortunately safety directors may have only limited input during the design and construction phases since the latter are often carried out in other locations.

Some hazardous conditions not detected during the design phase may be found and corrected during construction. However, additional hazardous conditions may also occur during the construction phase due to faulty workmanship, poor materials, or poor equipment. Later modifications to existing equipment may also result in the creation of hazardous conditions. Since these types of problems arise during the firm's operation, safety directors can make a major contribution by inspecting potentially hazardous conditions. In addition, safety directors can assist in maintenance control by assuring that facilities and equipment are being properly maintained.

One approach that safety directors can use in dealing with unsafe conditions is job safety analysis. This technique is similar to job analysis in that it involves breaking the job down into component parts. The potential hazards associated with each step of the job are identified and ways to eliminate or control them are developed. In general, however, the primary focus of the safety director's job in dealing with unsafe conditions is inspection of the workplace for potentially hazardous conditions.

These efforts must be continuous because conditions change. Further, some of the engineering relationships we think are true may in fact be erroneous. For example, since the time of Frederick W. Taylor, jobs have been designed around synchronized motions because of the greater efficiency that results. However, one study found that the safety of machine operators actually decreased because of the "complexity of synchronized movements required of the worker." Because conditions change and because additional research may increase our knowledge of unsafe conditions, safety directors must keep themselves appraised of such changes if the job is to be done effectively.

Reducing and Eliminating Unsafe Acts. Safety directors will often spend much of their time trying to eliminate and reduce unsafe acts. There are three basic approaches to accomplishing this goal: (1) avoiding the placement of workers possessing certain characteristics in jobs unsuited to them from a health and safety point of view, (2) training employees to behave in safer ways, (3) assisting employees personally in developing coping mechanisms which should reduce the incidence of unsafe acts.

Although the selection approach to safety has not proven as fruitful as the engineering approach, it is an important consideration in occupational safety and health. Physical examinations may identify some persons who have a high potential for certain types of illnesses or injuries which may be aggravated by certain job assignments. For example, a person with a history of respiratory problems should not be hired or placed in an environment in which there is constant, unavoidable exposure to dust. Similarly, workers with lower back problems should not be called on to lift heavy objects. Similarly, a pregnant employee should be reassigned to avoid the problem of contact with toxic materials suspected of posing dangers to fetuses.

The safety directors' approaches to dealing with unsafe acts through training consist of trying to make employees aware of potentially hazardous situations or behaviors. Safety education can assist employees in learning how such hazards can be avoided. Such efforts by safety (or training) directors aim at both teaching employees about unsafe acts and how to avoid them, and motivating employees to activity avoid such acts.

Safety directors will frequently use posters, contests, and training programs for these purposes. Posters are perhaps the simplest—although most limited—technique to remind employees of the need to engage in safe practices. The use of posters is the most limited technique, because in order to be effective such posters must be specific. For example, a large sign saying HIGHLY EXPLOSIVE FUMES—NO SMOKING will have a much greater impact on employee behavior than a sign which simply states WORK SAFELY. In addition, posters should be placed where they will be seen by employees and should be changed frequently in order to avoid boredom.

Contests are often used to keep employees aware of the need for safe actions. Such programs may reward individuals or entire departments that maintain the best safety and health records. Frequently such records are based on frequency or incidence rates.

A major problem with the use of contests is that there may be a letdown after a damaging or traumatic event, and the company may experience a rash of accidents. Further, if the damage results from an unsafe act, there may be resentment against the person(s) responsible.

One additional problem with accidents is that if the rewards are large enough, employees may falsify records, not report injuries, or not seek medical treatment when injuries do occur. In the last case, what might have been a minor injury may become a major one due to later complications. Finally, when contests are over, even the people or departments with the best records may revert to their previous patterns of behavior.

Safety directors may conduct or have others conduct training programs in an attempt to keep employees aware of the need to behave safely. Some programs may be training that makes individuals aware of specific dangers they may face (as opposed to programs offering general platitudes about being safe) is more likely to help eliminate or reduce the number of unsafe acts. The list below presents examples of good and bad training programs:

- At a number of weekly safety meetings, the safety director of a certain firm sermonized to first-line supervisors about how they had to not only "think safety" but "live safety." Before such meetings were over, several attendees could be seen dozing off—the message was irrelevant, repetitious, boring, and overgeneralized.
- Safety films depicting accidents in situations completely unlike those prevalent in a particular firm had often been shown to the firm's supervisors in safety meetings. Such training is irrelevant.
- The JIT method as used in industry specifically calls on trainers to make trainees aware of any potential trauma that may occur in each step of the job. This training is specific and highly effective if properly conducted.
- In one firm, supervisors from all three shifts were put into fire brigade groups. Fires were set in a vacant lot and a contest was conducted to see which group could react most quickly. As a result of the simulation, each supervisor practiced the use of fire extinguishers on each shift. Such training was effective because each department had someone

who knew what to do in case of a fire, (2) the training was specific, and (3) the program provided actual practice in dealing with hazards in the workplace.

The number of forms that safety training may take is large, and these examples are simple intended to suggest some appropriate and inappropriate forms of training. One other form of safety training that encompasses certain aspects of performance appraisal is worth mentioning. Petersen has suggested the use of *job safety observation* as an approach to "learn more about the work habits" of each employee. This approach also acts as a feedback mechanism to check on training effectiveness. Workers are observed, their actions recorded, and the results reviewed with each employee.

Employee Physical Fitness Programs. In recent years organizations have become increasingly aware that poor physical condition and excessive stress have adverse effects on worker productivity. As Kondrasuk has noted: "More than 132 million work days are lost per year due to employee illnesses and premature deaths; these lost work days translated to over Rs. 25 billion in lost revenue to industry." Such problems are costly to employers in other ways as well.

Employer Programs Aimed at Stress Management. Business firms have also developed programs to deal with the problems of job stress:

> At TRW...several steps to stress management and reduction were implemented such as: (a) crisis-counseling training sessions with the industrial relations staff, (b) increasing the employee's general awareness of stress and what they can do about it, (c) adding stress discussions to the supervisory training program, (d) adding a module on stress to middle-management programs, and (e) offering after-hours programs such as workshops in the use of biofeedback, meditation exercises, and other relaxation techniques.

Programs on stress management are aimed at reducing not only the incidence of coronary-related disease but also of health and safety problems connected with alcoholism, drug abuse, and so forth.

Glicken has suggested that stress management be included in crisis intervention programs following tragic accidents: "tragic accidents at the MGM and Hyatt-Regency Hotels, which killed and injured hundreds of guests and employees, emphasize the need for management to have on-going programs of crisis intervention for employees." Observes and those involved in the cleanup efforts of such catastrophes may experience future psychological and debilitating illnesses ranging from mild depression to "over-reliance on tranquilizing and mood elevating drugs" or "a severe increase in the use of alcohol." For this reason, employees who have witnessed such accidents are sometimes provided help through employee assistance programs (EAP) and/or private counseling in order to assist them in dealing with work-related trauma.

Biorhythms. On final issue involving individual coping mechanisms is the increased popularity of the biorhythm theory. The question has been raised in recent years as to whether a relationship exists between a person's biorhythm—his or her "good" or "bad" days—and the commission of unsafe acts. In one study of 300 accidents in four factories, the researchers found that 70 percent of the accidents occurred on biorhythmically critical days of the employees involved. However, other researchers have questioned the simple association posited on the basic of biorhythmic theory. Carvey and Nibler, for example, studied 150 work-related vehicular accidents and 210 job-related accidents which resulted in workers' compensation claims. Their findings were negative, and "the results of this analysis showed that no useful level of association existed for any cycle."

Our knowledge of the effects of personal fitness programs, stress management, employee assistance programs, and biorhythmic theory on occupational safety and health is still in the preliminary stages. As with knowledge of unsafe conditions, however, safety directors must keep themselves informed of new knowledge that may aid in the reduction of unsafe acts in the workplace. We believe that although controversy will exist over whether such issues are merely fads or are valuable aids to improving occupational safety and health, safety directors should continue to follow the literature in these areas.

Problems and Approaches in Remedial Control

In remedial control situations, safety directors face the problem of dealing with the sources of damage and trauma just as they do in preventive control. The basic difference is that in remedial control situations an unplanned event has already resulted in damage. Safety directors have, therefore, direct evidence as to which hazards will lead to which unplanned events, and which will lead to various types of damage.

In addition to investigating what factors contributed to the damage, the safety directors need to determine (1) the magnitude and potential for recurrence of such events in terms of both frequency and severity and (2) the costs or potential costs associated with the unplanned event. This information is needed for deciding the priorities by which hazards are to be eliminated or controlled. This information is also helpful in gaining support for health and safety programs.

SUPPORT PROBLEMS AND APPROACHES

As with all personnel functions, every organization member is responsible to some degree for the success or failure of the firm's occupational safety and health program. It is the safety director's responsibility, however, to make organization members aware of their specific responsibilities for safety and health efforts. More specifically, the safety director needs to gain the support of three groups within the organization—top management, supervisors, and non-managerial employees.

Top-Management Support

Although stating that top-management support is necessary if safety and health efforts are to succeed sounds trite, it cannot be overemphasized. Top management sets safety objectives and allocates funds necessary to carry out health and safety programs. Further, top management can set a climate in which safety directors gain the cooperation of supervisors and workers. For example, a great deal of support is provided if top management is willing to *"emphasize that one of the criteria for promotion is safe performance...whatever the individual's level in the corporate hierarchy."* By emphasizing the importance of occupational safety and health, top management can help create an organizational climate that is conducive to maintaining low levels of physical damage and trauma.

The importance of such support was pointed out in a study conducted by Yaghoub Shafai-Sahrai. He studies a pair of American companies in each of 11 different industries (22 firms in all). The firms were relatively small, ranging in size from 80 to 650 employees. Firms making up each study pair were of similar size and performed similar work, but differed greatly in their work-injury rates, which ranged from 12 to 173. The average pair frequency difference was 50, with the lowest difference being 11 and the highest difference being 129. He found that in the firms with the lower frequency and severity rates top management was highly interested and involved in the company's overall safety programs.

One way for safety directors to gain the support of top management is to appeal to their humanitarian values. Since top management sets the overall direction for the firm and the firm reflects their values, this approach may gain support for safety programs. A second approach is to emphasize the legal requirements for occupational safety and health. This approach may contribute to interest on the part of top management, but only to the extent of minimum compliance with Act of state laws. The third approach is to demonstrate that damage and trauma cost money and that safety and health efforts can help to decrease these financial drains.

Top managements generally respond much more quickly to cost information than to humanitarian appeals. For example, in the study of the matched pairs cited above, it was found that "the greater use of costs was one of the factors in which the pair members with better injury records differed from their 'twins'." As Ronald B. Blake stated in 1944, "The main driving force behind the industrial safety movement is the fact that accidents are expensive. Substantial savings can be had by preventing them." This simple fact has not changed in the past 40 years.

Supervisory Support

The support of supervisors is important because they are the connecting links between top management's objectives and the workers. Further, the supervisor is in the best position to influence worker behavior on a day-to-day basis. The important of supervisory attitudes toward safety was pointed out in one study by Hannaford. This research included data from a five-year period and involved 769 male employees from 47 firms with varying safety records. This study measured safety attitudes of the supervisors and found that those with poor attitudes tended to have a greater number of lost-time injuries per employee supervised than supervisors whose attitudes were more enthusiastic.

Additional support for the view that the supervisor can influence employees' desires to perform safely has also been provided in a study by Dunbar. This study found that "whether subordinates associates safety with their manager's safety related behavior may depend on the extent to which they perceive their general welfare. That is, through the support he or she provides, the manager may significantly influence the way subordinates thin about safety."

Safety directors can attempt to win supervisors' support in the same ways as were suggested for top management: humanitarian, legal, and cost. If the safety director has top management's support, it can also be made clear to supervisors that one aspect of their performance appraisal will be the safety and health records of their subordinates. In emphasizing this point, the safety director must make certain that supervisors understand the factors that contribute to a good record and the extent of their control over the factors that enter into the evaluation process.

Safety directors can also increase supervisory interest in safety and health efforts by providing supervisors with information about safety and health hazards. Such information may be given informally (during walks through the plant, at lunch, and so forth), or more formally by circulation articles from safety journals, news releases, and so forth, to all supervisory personnel. When safety directors become aware of specific hazards, they should immediately inform the supervisor, and is possible, allow time to correct the problem.

Safety directors can gain the support of supervisors by conducting effective training programs specifically for them. Such programs may motivate supervisors by showing the costs associated with damage and trauma, their obligations under the law, and ways to minimize hazards in the workplace.

Nonmanagerial Support

Attitudes of nonmanagerial employees toward safety and health are also important in minimizing damage and trauma. Hannaford, for example, found that the number of lost-time injuries increased as workers' safety attitudes became less favorable.

Safety directors can make employees more safety-conscious by providing training programs which stress the dangers and costs of unsafe acts. For example, safety should be built into all JIT training. In addition, programs that reward safe behavior can promote desired behaviors. For example, if management has discretion on how large merit raises will be safe performance can be rewarded in a way similar to that discussed with supervisory performance appraisal.

Finally, the safety director needs to remember that employees will behave in desired ways only if they see that the potential rewards for such behaviors are greater than the potential costs. For example, if blue-collar workers are being pushed for higher production by their supervisor, if they are on an incentive system, and if they see that higher production is possible if the safety guards are removed from the machines, they may motivated to remove the guards because the probable benefits appear to be greater than any possibilities of injury.

CONTINGENCIES INFLUENCING THE DECISIONS OF SAFETY DIRECTORS

We have already discussed a number of contingencies which influence the decisions of safety directors (for example, top- management support). In the remainder of this chapter we will consider three additional issues affecting what safety directors to regarding occupational safety and health: (1) firm size, (2) the industry in which a firm operates (which influences the technology used), and (3) the composition of the work force.

Firm Size

The firm size appears to be related to the incidence rate, with very small firms and very large firms having the lowest incidence rates as defined by OSHA. More importantly, these results tend to be fairly consistent across a wide variety of industries (See Fig. 1). A number of reasons for these findings have been suggested.

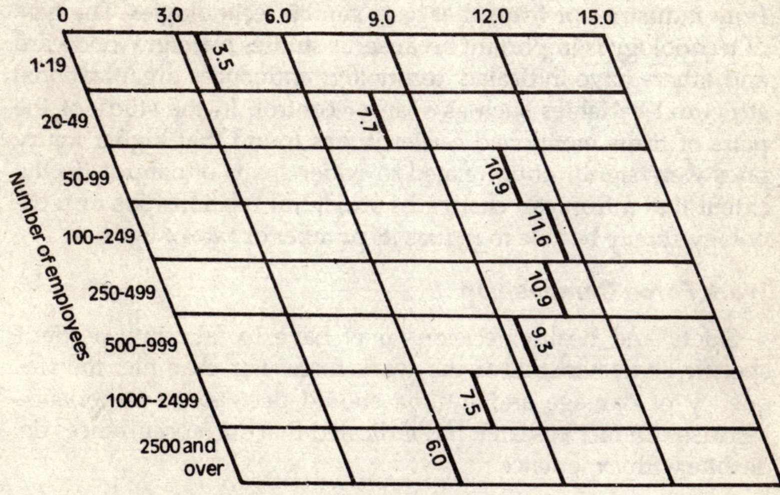

Fig. 1. Incidence rates per 100 full-time employees.

First, smaller firms may be less accurate in their reporting, since larger firms typically engage in better record keeping. Second, managers and supervisors in smaller firms may have closer personal contact with the operations and know when and where unsafe conditions exist. In addition, these managers may monitor the workers and processes more closely because even small losses could be disastrous to the organization.

Although such close contact may be lost in the largest firms, the greater resources of these companies allow them to hire specialists in occupational safety and health. The programs of such specialists may help reduce damage and trauma in the workplace. In addition, the largest firms can generally afford to hire more competent managers. Medium-size firms lack the advantages of both smallness and bigness, and therefore occupational safety and health problems occur with greater frequency.

Incidence in Industry

Incidence rates very considerably across industries. Some industries are inherently more dangerous than others. Safety directors must be aware of these differences and of the impact that certain types of technology can have. When comparisons are made to find out how well a firm is doing, data should be used from industries or firms that have similar technologies. The type of technology is important because, as studies by Joan Woodward and others have indicated, technology influences organizational structural variables such as span of control. In the study of the pairs of firms mentioned earlier it was found that higher injury rates were significantly related to wider spans of control. To the extent that a firm can change its structural relationships or technology, it may be able to reduce its number or rate of injuries.

Work Force Composition

Safety and health decisions may have to take into account specific characteristics of the work force. For example, the frequency of damage and trauma should decrease as experience increases. In fact, research has indicated that such occurrences do decline with experience.

Age, sex, and emotional stability have all been shown to be related to the likelihood of damage and trauma. The survey of 27,000 industrial and nonindustrial accidents cited earlier resulted in the following conclusions:

- ☐ Young people tend to have more accidents than older persons. Fifty percent of the nonindustrial accidents happened to people under age 24, and 70 percent to those under the age of 35. Further, the tendency to have accidents passes with age. In both the industrial and nonindustrial samples, the accident rate in the 20 to 24 age group was two and one-half times higher than in the 40 to 44 age group, four times higher than in the 50 to 54 age group, and nine times higher than in the 60 to 65 age group.
- ☐ Men are significantly more likely to have accidents than women. The ratio was two to one in the nonindustrial setting and even higher in the industrial setting.
- ☐ Accident proneness is not useful as a concept to deal with accident prevention. However, irresponsible and maladjusted people are significantly more likely to have accidents than responsible and normally adjusted people.

In addition, in one study the researchers found that in firms where a high percentage of the work force was married, the safety and health records were better than for firms is which only a small percentage was married. There is also some evidence that occupational safety and health statistics vary with economic conditions that influence the nature of the work force. As economic conditions are improved, more marginal workers are employed. This has been shown to contribute to an increase in injury rates. As Smith has noted, "The cyclical nature of work injury rates was first noted around 1940, and it has been estimated that in the postwar period a two percentage point reduction in the overall employment rate was associated with one additional (manufacturing) lost workday injury per million man-hours worked." This relationship may explain why frequency rates increased during the 1960s. Not only did more people in general enter the work force, more culturally disadvantaged individuals, who are less likely to be employed, also found jobs.

ACCIDENT ANALYSIS THROUGH INCIDENCE

The safety engineer is frequently confronted with the problem of expressing, in meaningful terms, the relative rankings, in accident experience, of various plants or departments. To meet this need, we have resorted to a simple statistical measure which we originally named the Accident Involvement Rate, but lately have called Incidence, in favor of brevity.

It is my considered opinion that this measure has value at the present time for comparative analyses. Furthermore, we believe this measure could have greater value and wide application as a U.S.A. Standard method, were statistics on Incidence available, similar to the national average accident frequency rates periodically published by the U.S. Bureau of Labor Statistics.

The insurance company safety engineer, who comprises a large segment of the profession, faces a problem of adverse selection. In this area lies one of the weaknesses, in application, of the present USASI method.

It is well established that the large employer enjoys lower accident rates than the small employer. "Available statistics show that two-thirds of all industrial injuries occur in businesses with fewer than one hundred workers. The accident frequency rate is more than double that of larger companies."

In the 1961 edition of *Accident Facts,* the frequency rates for all reporters to the N.S.C., engaged in manufacturing, relative to size of plant, were as follows: under 50 employees 12.82 to 100—10.94, 100 to 500—9.55 and over 500—3.57.

The superior performance of the large employer is probably due to his greater financial ability to provide safe environmental factors, expert management, and staff specialists such as the safety engineer. The tendency of the largest employers to be self-insured thus leaves the insurance companies as practitioners of the art of accident prevention with a residual, less safe class.

USASI Standard Weaknesses

Comparison of accident frequencies of this residual class with national averages is loaded against the small employer. A closer approximation of an objective could be attained by appropriate size subdivisions within the B.L.S. industry groupings.

Mere size, without reference to financial strength, mitigates against reliance on the present USASI Standard. With the present all-industry national average accident frequency rate at 15.2 the critical size would seem to be 33 employees, for a company in an industry of average hazard (It would be less for high hazard industries).

Such a company of critical size, which happened to experience one disabling injury in a given year would have a frequency rate equal to the national average. Two disabling injuries in the same year would result in a frequency twice the national average, which would certainly look bad. Whether in fact it would *be* bad is another question, one which I hope to explore more fully. At the very least, reliance on small sample frequencies is questionable, and their interpretation calls for considerable judgment.

Before further unfavorable comment on the present USA Standard method, we must say that it has met and probably will continue to meet a real need. Hopefully, my proposals will lead to refinements in the use of the present standard, and to improvement in the standard itself.

One area in which the present USA Standard methods falls short is where frequencies of 0.0 are encountered. How, in this area, does the safety engineer convince others of the need for action, or even generate much enthusiasm himself for the problem, conditioned as he is by traditional thinking in terms of frequency?

Consider the following hypothetical case of two plants of the same corporation, engaged in the same kind of operations.

PLANT A (1967): Frequency 0.0 for 120,000 Man-hours.

PLANT B (1967): Frequency 0.0 for 80,000 Man-hours.

If the above were the whole story, we could logically enough infer that plan A had the better performance, because its frequency of 0.0 was based on a significantly larger exposure to the hazards of the operation.

But if it were *not* the whole story; if, in fact, Plant A experienced 7, and Plant B experienced 4, non-disabling injuries in 1967, how do we interpret this additional data (which is usually ignored) and how do we present our interpretation meaningfully? Solution is easy by use of the following formula:

$$\text{Incidence} = \frac{\text{number of employees}}{\text{total work injuries}}$$

In an actual situation, we would know the number of employees, but for the purpose of this example we can presume 2,000 hours per employee per year, which is a nice round figure to work with, and which leads to the following comparison:

PLANT A (1967): Frequency 0.0; Incidence 8.6.

PLANT B (1967): Frequency 0.0; Incidence 10.0.

Taking into account all the data that is normally available, plant B is the winner. Note well that with Incidence, as opposed to frequency, a high score is good. The above figures express that in 1967, there was one accident for each 10 employees in plant B; and that there was one accident for each 8.6 employees in plant A. Obviously, plant B's performance is better. Notice that Incidence is always stated in terms of *one* accident. Observe that we have successfully compared plants with the Q.Q. frequency problem, in terms that can readily be understood. For reasons which will be made more apparent, we have also reduced the critical number of employees from 33 to 8.

Misleading for Analysis

My final and most serious objection to accident frequency as an analytical tool is that is misleading. Accident frequency is unreliable in that it focuses attention on symptoms rather than on causes. It is not, in my opinion , an adequate measure of accident experience, because it fails to tell the whole story or even enough of the story. Most seriously, it does not lead to fruitful analysis.

The extent of an industrial injury—*including whether or not it entailed a time loss from work*— is not normally predictable nor controllable Severity—*including temporary disability*—is largely a matter of chance Quoting from Heinrich, the first definitive authority on accident prevention, "When lost-time or so-called 'major' accidents are selected for study, therefore, as a basis for records and for guidance in prevention work, efforts are often misdirected, valuable data are ignored, and statistical exposure is unnecessarily limited."

To further illustrate the above reservations and objections to frequency, consider the following example from a recent study, showing departments of a certain plant ranked traditionally by frequency, and also by Incidence.

Department	*Frequency*	*Department*	*Incidence*
A	0.0	D	14.2
B	0.0	A	10.0
C	0.0	G	9.0
D	0.0	I	8.0
E	33.9	F	4.0
F	41.2	B	4.0
G	55.5	C	3.7
H	62.5	H	2.0
I	62.5	E	1.3
J	181.8	J	1.2

The above ranking by Incidence has several merits. It clearly identifies the major source of the accident problem as departments C, H, E, and J, which was not nearly so apparent from the frequency comparison. We know both where to concentrate our efforts and who to hold accountable. It is no coincidence that department J showed up poorly in both comparisons, or that department A appeared good in both. What may not be so clear is the large change in relative position of department I in the comparison, which is explained by the fact that department I experienced but one accident which happened to be disabling. We are getting a better answer because we are asking better question.

Other Rating Methods

Every objection we have voiced so far to Accident Frequency, Rate should be doubled, in spades, for Disabling Injury Severity Rate. Such considerations have their place, but in my opinion, they are best left to the casualty actuary and the statistician.

A recent attempt to overcome the inherent limitations of both frequency and severity is High Potential accident analysis. In my opinion there are practical difficulties in this approach, though it is not without merit. But any system which requires a supervisor to identify a particular accident as high potential and then have his accident record so charged is bound to be self-defeating. Perhaps a better approach would be to include one additional question on investigation forms: "In your opinion, could this accident have had serious consequences?"

The serious-injury accident is best handled by attention to *all* accidents (not that grave hazards should be overlooked) and by sustained management support of adequate planning, supervision, instruction, and inspection.

Before coming into general use and acceptance, Incidence will require thoughtful consideration and rigorous definition. We do not suggest that Incidence is a perfect tool, for it leaves out of consideration the majority of accidents which cause *no* injury, but as a practical matter, data on these is almost always absent. We submit that Incidence is a simple tool, and a better tool than frequency. It utilizes readily available data, it is applicable to the smallest employers, it presents a more complete picture, and it can lead to more successful accident prevention, especially in these days of generally reduced accident frequency rates.

We do not suggest that frequency be precipitately abandoned. It would be foolhardy to do so unless, and until, Incidence proves its superiority, and perhaps not even then. We do suggest for the time being that parallel computations of frequency and Incidence be made in all cases where frequency is presently employed. We further suggest the inclusion of Incidence within the USA Standard.

For the interested safety engineer, an all-industry Incidence can be considered as approximately 8.0. We have what is at this time only a suspicion that Incidence should be approximately 3.0 for construction, 10.0 for manufacturing, and perhaps as high as 50.0 for office workers.

In interpreting accident data, the safety engineer may wish to consider, though he cannot at this time quantitatively evaluate, the approximate all industry ratio of one disabling injury per four work injuries experienced.

LEGAL FRAMEWORK

Employer. The term "employer" defined by the Act means a person engaged in a business affecting commerce who has employees, but does not include the United States or any State or political subdivision of a state. The Act states:

(a) Each employer—

(1) shall furnish to each of his employees employment and a place of employment which are free from recognized hazards that are causing or are likely to cause death or serious physical harm to his employees.

(2) shall comply with occupational safety and health standards promulgated under this Act. An employer can be cited for violation of this section and fined.

Employees. The term "employee" defined by the Act means an employee who is employed in a business of his employer which affects commerce. The Act states:

(b) Each employee—

(1) shall comply with occupational safety and health standards and all rules, regulations, and orders issued persuant to this Act which are applicable to his own actions and conduct. There are no citations or penalties for violations.

It should be noted that the word *shall* indicates mandatory adherence, as opposed to "may" or "should," which connote permission to comply if desired. The word "shall" occurs many times both in the Act and in the *Federal Register* which contains the specific detailed standards which must be obeyed.

Purposes

Under the provisions of the Act, the Occupational Safety and Health Administration (OSHA) was created within the Department of Labor. While OSHA continually reviews and redefines specific standards and practices, its basic purposes remain constant—to assure safe and healthful working conditions for every worker in the nation. OSHA strives to implement its Congressional mandate fully and firmly with fairness to all concerned by:

(1) Encouraging employers and employees to reduce hazards in the work place and to implement new or improve existing safety and health programs.

(2) Establishing "separate but dependent responsibilities and rights" for employers and employees for the achievement of better safety and health conditions.

(3) Establishing reporting and record-keeping procedures to monitor job-related injuries and illnesses.

(4) Developing mandatory job safety and health standards and enforcing them effectively.

(5) Encouraging the states to assume the fullest responsibility for establishing and administering their own occupational safety and health programs, which must be "at least as effective as" the Federal program.

The mandatory job safety and health standards mentioned in (4) above are detailed in a publication known as the *Coded Federal Register.* This document contains in its many volumes the details of enacted legislation and records of other transactions, amendments, and notices. As an example Part 1910. *Occupational Safety and Health Standards* pertains to general industry. These standards cover every employer in a business affecting commerce who has one or more employees. They do not affect self-employed persons or family-owned and operated farms. They do not affect work places covered under other Federal laws such as Coal Mine Health and Safety Act, the Federal Aviation Administration. Railway Safety, Gas Pipelines Safety, Atomic Energy Acts, or the Metallic and Non-metallic Mine Safety Act. However, Federal Government employees are covered under separate provisions of the Act.

Regulations for Part 1910 contain nineteen subparts, sixteen of which contain references to the equipment, practices, environment, materials and substances found in work places. These subparts include:

D— Walking-Working Surfaces.
E— Means of Egress.
F— Powered Platforms, Manlifts and Vehicle-mounted Work Platforms
G— Occupational Health and Environmental Controls.
H— Hazardous Materials.
I— Personal Protective Equipment.
K— Medical and First Aid.
L— Fire Protection.
M— Compressed Gas and Compressed Air Equipment.
N— Materials Handling and Storage.
O— Machinery and Machine Guarding.
P— Hand and Portable Powered Tools and Other Hand-Held Equipment.
Q— Welding
R— Special Industries.
S— Electrical.

It is within these subparts that the specific procedures, mandatory inspections, prohibitions, and other applicable standards are detailed. It is the employers' responsibility to become familiar with the standards applicable to their establishments and to assure that employees have and use personal protective gear and equipment required for safety. Even in cases where OSHA has not promulgated specific standards, employers are responsible for following the intent of the Act's General Duty clause.

THE SCOPE AND MEASUREMENT OF OCCUPATIONAL SAFETY AND HEALTH

Because of the importance of statistics and numbers in increasing public interest in occupational safety and health, this section will present and discuss in detail data relating to occupational injuries. First we will consider the actual numbers involved, next the amount of time lost as a result of injuries, and finally the dollar costs involved. Unfortunately, data concerning occupational illnesses and disease cannot be presented in such detail because they have not been collected systematically or separately in the past.

There are a number of reasons for the lack of data concerning occupational health. First, it is only within the last few years that the extent to which toxic substances affect health problems has been recognized. For example, although exposure to asbestos was common place during World War II, the dangers connected with such exposure have only recently been recognized. This increased awareness of toxic substances in general has resulted from more accurate measuring instruments and from better record keeping. Improved record keeping is important because it permits locating employees who have been exposed to health hazards in the past to see if they have developed particular health problems. This type of analysis may reveal the extent of such problems as well as identify additional toxic substances which may create health difficulties.

A second reason for the lack of data concerning occupational health is that illnesses and diseases often do not appear immediately. Using the asbestos example, only recently have we come to recognize the long-term effects of exposure to this substance more than 40 years ago. Because diseases often do not appear immediately, it may be difficult to determine whether diseases or illnesses occurred from job-related activities or from other causes. In some cases, illnesses and diseases may have been counted as injuries, as in the case of the employee who became dizzy, fell and broke an arm.

9

HUMAN RELATIONS IN INDUSTRY

HUMAN Relations in Industry is a broad term applied in an embracive way to a concern on the part of management for the welfare of workers—viewing them as human beings possessing dignity and worth, and not merely as units of production. The underlying concept, which recognizes enlightened self-interest rather than sheer altruism, was early stated by ROBERT OWEN, a successful textile manufacturer in Scotland widely known as a social reformer. In his 1813 *Address to the Superintendents of Manufactories* he had this to say:

> If then due care as to the state of your inanimate machine can produce beneficial results, what may not be expected if you devote equal attention to your vital machines, which are far more wonderfully constructed? When you shall acquire a right knowledge of these, of their curious mechanism, of their self-adjusting powers; when their proper mainspring shall be applied to their varied movements, you will become conscious of their real value, and you will be readily induced to turn your thoughts more frequently from your inanimate to your living machines; you will discover that the latter may be easily trained and directed to procure a large increase of pecuniary gain, while you may also derive from them high and substantial gratification.

However, the term "human relations movement" as used in the literature today does not apply to earlier, experiences with "paternalism"—which in many cases failed to achieve desired results, as indicated blow—but rather covers the attempts to develop and apply a coherent and proven theory of worker motivation and behavior in order to channel the latter into desirable and productive patterns. The movement is based on the recognition that more than good physical working conditions and employee welfare program, and more than money incentive alone operate in the development of a responsive work force.

The Precursing Paternalism

Under the philosophy of paternalism, managements sought to raise employee morale by providing good working conditions, fringe benefits, employee services, and often (but not always) high wages. The rationale as stated by Strauss and Sayles [1] takes two forms, "native" and "subtle." The naive argument holds that if management is good to employees, they will work harder out of loyalty and gratitude. The more subtle argument ignores the question of gratitude; it holds that liberal benefits and good working conditions make for happy employees, and that happy employees work harder.

Naive paternalism had its heyday in the 1920s. In part, its fairly widespread adoption at that time was the result of a genuine concern on the part of employers for the welfare of their employees, but also to a significant degree a result of the rise of unionism during and immediately after World War I. In any case, as Strauss and Sayles point out, under the banner of the "New Industrial Relations," management became interested in a wide variety of projects, varying from cafeterias and recreation programs for employees to cooking classes for their wives. Some of the programs were designed to change the employees' personal lives as well as their on-the-job performance.

The early Ford Motor Company program embodied in its Sociology Department went farther than most, and is an example of the extreme form of such activity. Headed by a Protestant minister, the department at its peak was manned by 30 "investigators." Constructively, the latter functioned somewhat like the caseworker of a modern public welfare agency, visiting employees in their homes and giving advice on budgeting, hygiene, and home management. However, "hearsay as well as fact found its way into a card catalog where a record was kept of every worker's deviation, including 'earmarks of unwholesome living,' such as use of liquor, and reports of marital discord."

Ford's program was short-lived, but somewhat similar if less extreme programs were developed in other companies. However, Strauss Sayles point out that "there is little evidence that any of them were particularly successful in eliciting gratitude, in motivating workers to do a better job, or even in staving off the development of unions. In fact, some of the best companies with the best-known histories of paternalism late became scenes of bitter labor-management strife."

Modern Approaches

Ever since the mid 1920s, and especially as a concomitant of the social problems created by the Great Depression of the thirties, management has been increasingly preoccupied with the human side of its operations. It had seen that paternalism was not the answer to labour unrest, and began casting about for more effective answers to the problems of worker behavior. Important in this connection are the famous Hawthorne experiments of the Western Electric Company in 1923-1926 and 1927-1932, which triggered the human relations movement. This research produced the first purported objective truth of a positive correlation between employee participation in the decisions affecting him (her) and the work output produced. A major conclusion of the study was that the factory was a social system and that informal groupings in the work situation vitally affected human behavior. The corollary was that the worker could no longer be viewed solely as a factor of production. Rather, the employee was a human being with wants, desires, attitudes, and feelings, all of which influenced his or her productive usefulness.

In addition to the Hawthorne experiments and the subsequent (and continuing) research of behavioral scientists into the question of human motivation, several other factors also contributed to the human relations movement. Employment departments (later called personnel departments) were established by many organizations to handle employee selection, training, and turnover, to cope with increasing problems of trade unionism, and to research new areas of employee relations.

Prior to the Hawthorne experiments, industrial engineers had been seeking most of the answers to efficient operation in improved production processes and more refined budgeting and cost controls. This engineering approach had been sparked by the work of Frederick W. Taylor and other pioneers of the "scientific management" movement at the turn of the century. Although the benefits of that movement are well known, it has nevertheless come in for increasing criticism in the intervening years on the grounds that in its emphasis on efficiency of operations it was not sufficiently concerned with problems of individual worker motivation beyond financial incentives.

In all fairness to Taylor and his associates, however, as pointed out by Heckman, the scientific management movement did not designedly overlook the human element in industry. In fact, a prime concern of these pioneers was to increase the productivity of the worker with a commensurate decrease in his or her effort, fatigue, and other detriments to physical welfare. (The slogan was to "work smarter, not harder.") What was overlooked, however, was the relationship of the individual to the work group of which he (she) was a part. In other words, the worker was viewed solely as a production unit, and little, if any recognition was given to the complex social network that comprises any organization of human beings. It therefore remained for later investigators to demonstrate the tremendous influence of interpersonal relationships upon human behavior, and hence upon individual productivity.

Following the Hawthorne experiments there was a tremendous swing by management to a deep preoccupation with the human and social aspects of work. In industrial relations literature and from the platforms of management gatherings, the Hawthorne findings were quoted extensively. This is not, of course, to say that the swing was due solely to this work—but the findings did provide an apparent scientific basis for the arguments that were increasingly being advanced by socially conscious spokesmen for government, business, and academic circles. These arguments held that human relations had been a neglected factor in productivity; that too much attention had been given to money incentives and to impersonally engineered standards of performance; that management in general and supervisors in particular had to be much more concerned with "what made people tick," with problems of informal organization in any working group, and with problems of *communication, participation,* and *understanding.*

This new trend in management thinking had a marked influence on the type and content of supervisory training programs—and in many cases the preoccupation with the human reactions on the job led to rather extreme emphasis on psychological and even near-psychiatric approaches. While there was later a justified reaction against "analyzing" and giving advice to subordinates on alleged personality defects and a concomitant swing back to stressing performance on the job, the net result was a salutary concern in getting managers and supervisors to think about what constitutes effective leadership on the job; about effective techniques of communication and teaching, overcoming resistance to change, instilling pride in work, and achieving identification with company objectives.

Evolving Insights into Motivation

In the years under review, a great deal of attention has been given to the question of human motivation and behavior. Social scientists have sought to develop theories and predictive laws about the motivations, attitudes, actions, and reactions of people at work. These have been based on observations in controlled industrial situations, reports by clinical psychologists, reactions under controlled conditions of non-industry groups such as school children and military units, and laboratory studies of the behavior of birds and animals subjected to various stimuli. Inputs also were congruent inferences drawn from "real-life" examples furnished by the practitioners of work simplification, successful programs, such as the Lincoln incentive management plan, and experiences in participation gained from programs such as management by objectives and job enrichment and work effectiveness.

An outgrowth of the above activity has been a vast body of literature on worker motivation and behavior—shelves of books and reams of articles and papers in business and academic journals. (The diversity of subjects covered is indicated by the extensive cross references appended to this article). Unfortunately, this wealth of literature does not add up to a coherent, internally consistent whole, as will be indicated presently. However, a direct result has been that human relations has been a continuing prominent part in supervisor and management training courses. "How to Get Along with People," "How to Motivate Employees," "How to Develop a Responsive Work Force," "Job Enrichment," and more latterly "Behavior Management (or Modification)," or their equivalent, have been recurring session titles in management seminars.

Important among the concepts that have attained wide prominence are:

Maslow's Hierarchy of Needs. Dr. Maslow postulated five basic needs which, he said, are organized into successive levels. For example, hunger is a basic physiological need. But when there is plenty of food, higher needs emerge, such as safety needs, love needs (termed by some writers "social needs)," esteem needs, and the need for self-actualization, or self-fulfillment. When a higher need is satisfied, newer and still higher needs come to the fore, and so on. Thus, gratification becomes as important a concept in motivation as deprivation. A want that is satisfied is no longer a want.

Even if all of the first four needs are satisfied, we can still exact that a new discontent are restlessness will develop, unless the individual is doing what he is fitted for. People who are satisfied in all five levels of needs are basically satisfied people, and the theory states that it is from these that we can expect the fullest creativity and productivity. However, quite aside from the fifty level, the fourth, or esteem needs (also termed "egoistic" needs) are rarely completely satisfied in the typical industrial and commercial organization, and it is the recognition of this situation that has forced so much attention on ways to provide employees with a sense of participation.

The Maslow formulation is still frequently quoted in management literature despite the recent challenges indicated below.

McGregor's "Theory X" and "Theory Y." Douglas McGregor set forth six positive assumptions about worker attitudes, which he called "Theory Y." He contrasted these with commonly held negative assumptions about workers, which he termed "Theory X," the traditional view. The "X" assumption, he contended, form a block to constructive manager-employee relations.

Herzberg's Motivation-Hygiene Theory. This theory advanced by Dr. Frederick Herzberg underlies the development of the widely discussed and practiced technique of job enrichment. The motivation factors have to do with satisfaction from achievement and recognition, the task content of the job (variety of challenge, freedom of boredom), responsibility, and opportunities for growth and advancement. The "hygiene" factors (the term is borrowed from medical use as preventive and environmental), or potential dissatisfiers, are: salary, company policy and administration, working conditions, and interpersonal relations. A significant point made is that optimum hygiene factors merely *prevent dissatisfaction; for positive results,* the motivation factors, the *satisfiers,* must be brought into play.

The foregoing tie in with the continuing emphasis that has been given to the advantages of so-called "democratic" versus "authoritarian" supervision, and to the need for more "participative" management. A manager or supervisor who is "democratically oriented" is described as one who thinks of himself or herself as a coordinator of his group rather than "boss." He (she) believes subordinates should have more voice in running the department, listens to idea and suggestions from them, and passes adequate explanations on to subordinates when changes are made. He or she is ready on occasion to give in to a subordinate if there is disagreement on how something should be done.

Countermovement

The cumulative effect, in some companies, of all the emphasis on human relations was to swing the pendulum pretty far–to a "do-gooder'" philosophy of personnel administration. Inevitably there were second thoughts. Was all the talk about the human factor in industry taking on the aspects of a fad? Was "democratic" supervision simply "soft" supervision? Were all the interesting cases studies nothing more than anecdotes—isolated casebook material without any general significance? Participative management is all well and good, but should girls really be allowed to set conveyor speeds? Are we overly concerned with patting workers on the head, giving them expressions of approval to bolster their self-esteem? Do engineered performance standards really rob a worker of human dignity? Moreover, is there any proof that satisfied and happy workers are more productive?

To seek answers to questions such as these, numerous attempts were made to put a somewhat firmer scientific base under all the admonitions to encourage participation, to provide scope for individual goal setting, to consider social relationships, and the like. By and large the attempts to provide hard evidence based on strictly controlled situations proved disappointing, despite the undeniably positive results obtained with job enrichment programs in such companies as Texas Instruments and AT and T. (The interpretation of these has, as indicated below, been challenged by advocates of "behavior management" based on Skinnerian psychology.)

In the search for hard evidence, even the famed Hawthorne experiments came under critical review. In 1953, twenty years after the original Hawthorne reports, a British social scientist, Michael Argyle, published a paper entitled "The Relay Assembly Test Room in Retrospect". He carefully re-examined all the reported results, subjecting them to tests for statistical significance, evaluated the types of controls that had been set up, and reconsidered all the possible influences on the final measurements. He flatly stated that there was no quantitative evidence for the conclusions for which the study is famous, namely, the claim that the increase in worker output was due not to physical factors, but to social changes, and in particular to the new attitude of the girls toward supervision.

The British paper apparently made no significant impression upon American management literature, considering the continued frequent non-critical references over the years to the Hawthorne findings. However, Lawrence M. Miller, who is skeptical of the conclusions drawn from Hawthorne, quotes in his book, "Behavior Management" a report by H.M. Parsons documenting similar adverse findings from a re-examination of the Hawthorne studies.

Miller is an articulate representative of a school of thought that has come into prominence in recent years, which is in fundamental disagreement with the basic motivational assumptions of Maslow, Herzberg, McGregor, et al. Resting upon the theories propounded by the famed behavioral psychologist B.F. Skinner, the advocates of "behavior management" or "behavior modification" brush aside all interpretations of behavior that rely upon motivation. Knowledge of what goes on inside a person is in any event, they say, unavailable to another, and speculating upon it and hoping to change it is actually irrelevant to the problem of changing behavior. All that matters, they contend, is the outward observable behavior. Skinner's controlled laboratory experiments with rats and pigeons, they claim, show that desired behavior can be achieved by suitable positive or negative reinforcements (appropriate and appropriately timed rewards or the withholding of them), and by avoidance of "aversive" (threatening) controls.

As to job enrichment, Miller points out that most descriptions of such programs portray complex changes in the environment, and contends that it is very difficult, if not impossible, in most of these experiments to identify what change caused what effect on performance. And he sharply disagrees with a statement by Robert N. Ford, one of the first and most through researchers in job enrichment, made in Ford's "Motivation through the Work Itself." There Ford says, "A business owes the employee the most satisfying work it can give him within the limits of staying in business." Commenting on this, Miller clearly draws the line between the newer behaviorists and the earlier expounders of motivation and human relations theory:

> The implications of the concept that a "business owes the employee the most satisfying work it can give him within the limits of staying in business are profound. The manager who does accept this premise had best think this through to its logical conclusions, namely, that the business exists to provide satisfaction to the employee..." Efforts to prove satisfying work have often proved ineffective because they have assumed that, if a state of satisfaction exists, employees perform well. This places satisfaction exists, employees perform well. This places satisfaction first and performance second. Systems that have succeeded in improving performance and satisfaction have placed performance first, with satisfaction or rewards following and contingent upon the desired performance.

On Balance

Given the sharp differences of professional opinion regarding human motivation and behavior, how can the management practitioner arrive at a viable human relations philosophy as regards his own organization? The following observations may provide a workable rationale:

It must be remembered that the differing approaches and schools of thought highlighted in the foregoing do not mean that as one concept comes into prominence it completely negates all that went before. There is no succession of one "truth" following another. In real life, all the concepts live together: one approach is successfully applied in place A at the same time that another has been "proven" and is in successful operation in place B. Thus, a high degree of paternalism is still operative in many quarters—and management and employees may not even know about the theoretical and historical pitfalls involved. Job enrichment programs are flourishing in many companies where management is totally unaware that the advocates of behavior management have declared that the programs suffer from "inadequacies of theory." Many managers who have gone through a training seminar that stressed "Theory X" vs. "Theory Y" are as a result performing as better managers because they have a new confidence in the desire and ability of employees to take on new responsibilities and do a conscientious job without having to be driven or coerced, quite unaware that in some quarters the contention is that much of McGregor's Theory X does *not*, as he claimed, comprise assumptions widely held by management.

It should also be remarked that publications of conflicting approaches appear concurrently. At the same time that some books and academic papers report studies purportedly invalidating Hawthorne or job enrichment or participative goal setting, other books and articles appear that quote the Hawthorne findings or Herzberg or McGregor et al. as recognized authorities. Thus, in reading about any human relations concept such as presented in the numerous relevant entries in this Encyclopedia—whether on Taylorism or the Hawthorne experiments or whatever—the reader should automatically make the following assessments:

- ☐ When was this approach advocated? During what period was this experiment conducted or these observations made? For example, Miller referring to Theories X and Y, observes, "In defense of McGregor it must be said that he made his assumptions about X at a time when it was in vogue. Particularly in academia, to assume all good things about anonymous individuals, workers in particular, and to assume all negative things about 'the system,' business and management."

- ☐ Can I use the practical-sounding parts of the concept without necessarily having to acquiesce in all of it? For example, a manager can profit from the Skinnerian thesis about changing behavior through positive reinforcement—which in any case accords with practical experience—without going "whole hog" into acceptance of Skinner's radical determinism which makes *all* of a person's behavior the result of environmental and genetic influences to the total exclusion of free will and an inner motivational and decision-making apparatus.
- ☐ Have contradictory or countervailing theories been advanced since the one here advocated was propounded? If there is a demonstrated contradiction, can insights on both sides of the contradiction nevertheless be usefully applied? For example, one can couple the constructive and commonsense prescriptions based on the behavior-psychology approach with the insights into motivation based on the Herzberg formulation (even though the behaviorists insist that one need not postulate motivation at all).
- ☐ Is there a good probability that more causes than the one(s) set forth in the account were contributory to the effect(s) described? This is one of the criticisms leveled against the report of the Hawthorne experiments, and is an explanation offered for the success of many job enrichment programs.
- ☐ Are research findings or case example results advanced to provide a basis for a particular motivation-behavior theory or a new approach to management-employee relations based on sufficient evidence? How valid are the generalizations inferred from the findings reported?
- ☐ Does the policy or procedure advocated involve management's abdicating the right to manage? For example, the concept of "democratic supervision" is sound—within limits. Yes, if it means careful indoctrination of the workers by the supervisor on what is expected of them,

solicitation of suggestions, a voice by employees *to the extent feasible* in work allocation. Yes, if the supervisor knows that his (her) people are ready for it. No, if the supervisor has green help, or if methods in the department have undergone a significant change, or if the quality record is poor.

The Bottom Line

In the last analysis, the "bottom line" in all of this is that the manager must in the end devise and define his own consistent and coherent human relations philosophy, formulating it over the year by continuous and compatible accretions from all credible sources available.

LABOR RELATIONS AND SAFETY

Our search of literature has revealed a paucity of "management science" selections in both the fields of labor relations and safety. For this reason, we are grouping these two different "functional areas" of personnel together in this single chapter. This chapter includes:

1. Some ideas drawn from various sources are put forth relative to utilizing management science approaches in the field f labor; however, on selection on labor relation are included.
2. One section is included relative to quantitative measurement techniques in safety analysis and administration.

Labor Relations

Among the labor relations functions which the manager is called on to perform, two stand out as especially important: negotiating a contract with the union, the handling union complaints. From time to time in unionized firms, there are union complaints asserting that management has misinterpreted or violated a provision (or provisions) included in the existing union-management contract. Most contracts provide that when such a case arises, the union may file a grievance, and that if the combined efforts of management and the union cannot resolve the dispute, it will be submitted to an outside "impartial" arbitrator, whose decision is binding on both parties.

Viewing both contract negotiations and the grievance-arbitration process from an information-decision making view, we will now turn out attention to some possibilities as to how management science techniques may be applied in these areas.

Bueschel has suggested the possibility of simulation in labor-management negotiations. In such negotiations, the collective bargaining usually culminates in a contract in which both the initial management offer and union demands are subsequently compromised. Following up on this notion, an exploratory computerized simulation model of a small hypothetical firm was developed under the supervision of one of the authors of this text. It provides for the cost evaluation of various possible union demand alternatives in certain areas. In this simulation model:

1. One hundred hypothetical workers with different characteristics, such as seniority and wage rate, were included.
2. Given these workers, the computer can generate the cost of various union demand alternatives, such as increased hourly wage rates. For example, the program can print out the total costs to the hypothetical firm if the union were to demand, say a 5 per cent across-the-board wage increase, a ten-cent-an-hour increase, etc.

Several technical limitations still exist in the above model and it attempts to evaluate only a few types of union demand alternatives which can be coasted relatively easily. Much more difficult to accomplish would be a simulation evaluating the effects of certain less quantifiable union demands, such as certain work-rule changes. The basic values of any such labor- management simulation would be to provide management quickly with fairly reliable information regarding the impact of: (1) its own possible offer alternatives, and possible anticipated union demand alternatives *prior to* negotiations, for planning purposes; and (2) both its own offers, actual union demands, its own counter-offers, etc., *during* negotiations.

In the grievance-arbitration process, management science-oriented approaches also appear possible. For example, an exploratory probability model, aimed at providing a guide to management as to whether or not to proceed to arbitration, should no agreement be reached with the union on a particular type of grievance, has been developed under the supervision of one of the authors of this text. Based on the assumption that arbitrators often follow past precedents, and hence, that there is some consistency in their rulings for predictive purposes, a small sample of one type of discharge case rulings was analyzed. From these sample cases, certain key points, which management had to prove in order to obtain favorable arbitrator rulings, were extracted. Then, the notion was explored of relating the probability of obtaining favorable rulings in this class of cases to the costs involved in going to arbitration.

The particular model described above has several limitations. However, its focus does suggest the possibility of abstracting key data from different particular classes of prior arbitrator rulings; storing (and updating) such data on a computer for quick retrieval; and incorporating the data into a model relating probabilities to costs which may provide management with a guide to more effective decision making. One of the major problems in fully developing any such approach, would of course, be the quantification of data not readily amenable to quantification; and any attempts to do so would appear to necessitate subjective managerial probability estimates and other judgments.

Safety

Since the passage of workmen's compensation laws many companies have been held responsible for the safety of their employees at work both for work-incurred injuries and occupational diseases. Under these laws, a company's workmen's compensation costs are related to its safety experience, so that today there has become a strong incentive for organizations to improve their industrial safety and health performance.

One of the problems involved in the field of safety is that of *measuring* an organization's job-related accident performance. Two measurement tools widely utilized for such purposes are the so-called accident frequency and accident severity rates—both of which represent forms of ratio analysis. The accident frequency rate is defined as:

$$\frac{\text{Number of lost–time accidents} \times 1{,}000{,}000}{\text{Number of man-hours worked in period covered}}$$

while the accident severity rate is defined as:

$$\frac{\text{Number of days lost} \times 1{,}000{,}000}{\text{Number of man-hours worked in period covered}}$$

Hedian, criticizes these traditional measurement techniques on the grounds that they discriminate against smaller-sized companies; and that they are misleading since they consider only *disabling* injuries. The author then poses a new accident ratio measure, which he calls "incidence." Hedian does not suggest that the traditional accident frequency rate be "precipitately abandoned." Rather, he admits that his incidence approach is not a perfect tool; and suggests using incidence along with frequency, comparing the data obtained from each to determine their relative merits.

Hedian's *Addendum to Incidence* presents clarification of certain concepts in the original article, based on feedback which the author received from numerous "interested safety engineers and personnel men."

THE MANAGERIAL DECISION MAKING IN EMPLOYEE-MANAGEMENT RELATIONS

Management has three basic types of decisions to make regarding unionism: (1) to try to keep unions out; if unions win representation elections, (2) to bargain collectively with them and (3) to deal with discipline and other grievances through the negotiated grievance process. These decision-making processes are illustrated in Figure 1.

We will now first consider the important question, Why do individuals join or refrain from joining unions? then, after focusing attention on the three basic labor-management decision areas, we will conclude the chapter with a discussion of contingencies in employee-management relations.

Joining Unions

We now raise the question, Why have employees joined and continue to join unions; or conversely, why do many people *avoid* joining unions?

One basic reason why employees join unions is that they must do so. With the union shop, the union hiring hall in the building and construction trades, and sometimes agency shops, workers have no choice but to join a union (or in the agency shop to

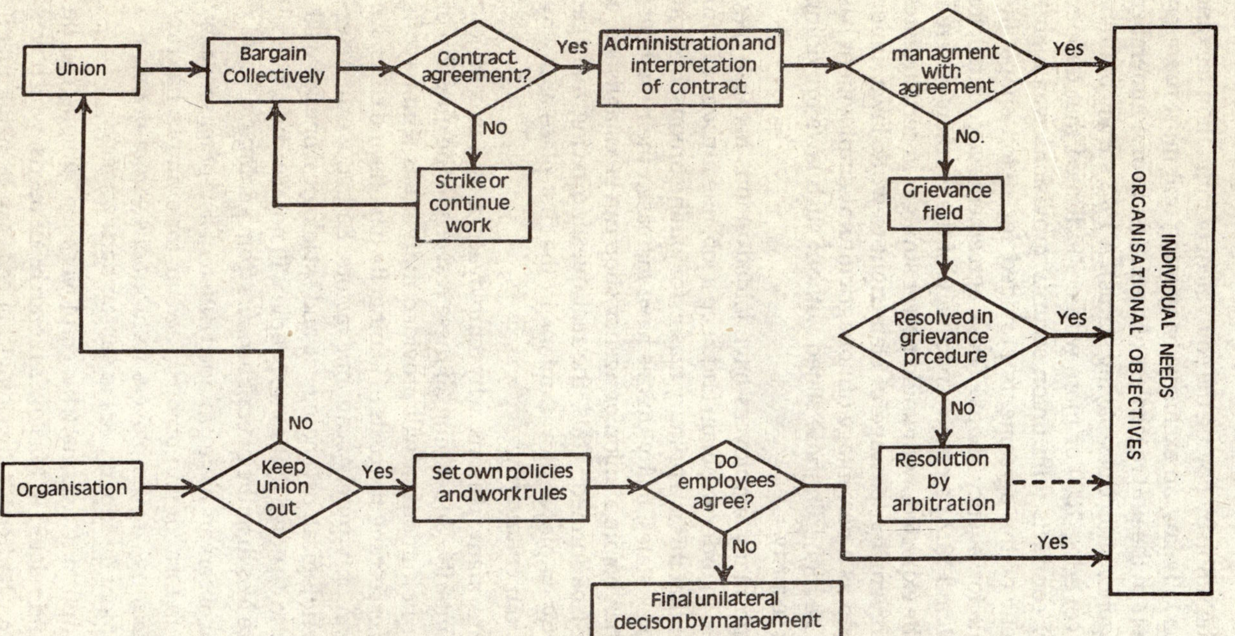

Fig. 1. Employee-management relations. The dashed assow is intended to illustrate that arbitrators' awards may please management, the union and employees, or none of these parties.

support the union by paying the equivalent of intimation fees and union dues). By law, an exclusive bargaining unit must represent all members in the unit regardless of membership or nonmembership (or agency shop dues-paying status). A 1973 survey of union contracts covering 1000 or more workers indicated that the percentage of contracts with union security provisions was high—72.5 percent of the agreements provided for union shops and 9.7 percent for agency shops. These agreements accounted for about 62.2 and 13.2 percent, respectively, of the workers covered. As might be expected, with union power stronger in certain states to help prevent the passage of state right-to-work laws, union membership as a percentage of nonagricultural employment has tended to be higher in those stated without such laws providing less union security.

Although many employees have joined unions because they have had to in order to obtain and keep a job, one must be careful not to infer that this is a primary reason for joining unions. Even in right-to-work states, many unions have increased their membership. Further, before a union or agency shop can be established, a union must be formed. Thus, the real question facing management is why employees form unions in the first place and why they often join voluntarily.

There are many reasons why employees may form or join union voluntarily. Underlying all these reasons in the question of whether or not unionism will provided individuals with payoffs or benefits exceeding the costs of joining. By payoffs and costs, we do not mean only purely economic factors. Rather, we are referring to physiological, psychological, and sociological ones as well. It should also be noted that some people will not pay dues, even if the dues are less than the overall benefits from joining.

Different observers have provided different lists of reasons why employees to form or join unions. Lawson, for example, has provided 15 reasons why employees form unions—from unfair and harsh treatment by supervisors to substandard wages.

Many important reasons why employees join unions can be classified and related to Maslow's hierarchy of needs, which was discussed in Chapter 12. Physiological needs can be better met if unions can improve the individual's wages. Further, unions may pressure management to improve working conditions in terms of occupational safety and health. Organized labor, for example, was strongly behind the passage of OSH Act.

Unions can help workers meet their safety and security needs to a greater extent. For example, employees cannot be arbitrarily discharged without reason by their supervisor under virtually all union contracts. Second, unions have been instrumental in helping to provide security be pressing for and obtaining such employee benefits as SUB, medical insurance, and pension plans. Finally, the seniority system provisions of contracts may provide workers with greater tenure protection from layoffs.

In some cases, unions have been able to meet employees' belongingness and esteem needs more fully. As Lawson has put it, many employees "believed that the union organization could relieve their feelings of frustration and boredom by giving them a chance to achieve prestige and social recognition." Actively participating in a union, such as being elected shop steward or local union president, may provide employees with considerable recognition among their fellow workers as well as help meet their self-actualization needs. In addition, with more and more companies hiring only college graduates for managerial and professional positions and no longer promoting rank-and-file workers into such jobs, many workers have come to believe (especially on assembly-line jobs) that there are no real opportunities to meet their esteem and self-actualization needs within the firm itself.

What about white-collar and professional unionism, which, represents the greatest area of growth today? Chamot has analyzed this phenomenon and pointed out several reasons for white-collar and professional unionism. College professors, for example, have become increasingly concerned about job security and look to unions as a vehicle for bargaining with college administrators who have taken on more and more power. The job security issue is perceived to be especially important since the widespread layoffs of engineers and other white-collar workers in the early 1970s and the continually poor job market for college graduates into the 1980s.

Furthermore, professionals are concerned with the administration's lack of concern with quality of services—for example, large classes in colleges or the quality of health care in hospitals. Finally, professionals who do not unionize lack a realistic grievance procedure. Should there be disagreement with upper management, the only choice may be to accept the unilateral decision of management or resign.

But why do employees refrain from joining unions even if it would improve their economic position or working conditions? One reason is that they fear a loss of status. This factor seems to be an important one, accounting for the reluctance of many professionals and salaried white-collar workers to join unions—they visualize a union as a blue-collar organization, representing hourly paid rather than salaried employees. They may also fear that there would be more constraints on their individual discretion if they joined a union. If a union had been chosen to represent this group, professors would have had to deal with their supervisors (the department heads, who were often long-time colleagues) on a much more formal basis, since the latter would have represented "management" and would not have been members of the bargaining unit.

Finally, with respect to unorganized professionals,

> a major reasons is that...[they]...frequently have a rather limited knowledge of what unions are and what they can do. They tend to think of unions in terms of not too accurate blue-collar stereotypes: complex and rigid work rules, excessive reliance on authority...dictatorial power in the hands of union leaders, and so on. They are unaware of the flexibility of collective bargaining...in short, they need realistic *models* for professional unions.

The growth of teacher unionism and militancy, however, seems to indicate that such perceptions by professionals are rapidly changing because of the factors indicated above.

Decision Strategies

There are three basic decision-making areas in which the firm may become involved with respect to unions. First, it may want to determine what strategies to take to discourage employees from voting for union representation. If the company is successful in such an endeavor, it will remain nonunionized and not become involved in the other two decision-making areas that unionized companies must face: contract negotiations and contract administration and interpretation. We will now consider each of these decision-making areas.

Unionization Campaigns. Many managements in non-unionized firms expend considerable efforts in attempting to prevent unions from organizing any of their employees. This is basically because unionization limits management's decision-making powers with respect to employee relations. Unionization, we should emphasize, is not necessarily "bad." Unions have negotiated with firms to provide better working conditions, more equitable disciplinary procedures, etc. These gains have, over the years, economically and socially improved the quality of work life for millions. Further, unions in some firms may actively collaborate with management to improve the position of both its members and the organization.

Some firms may have no objections to becoming unionized. As just indicated, (1) unions are not all bad from the point of view of the company, but (2) unionization may constrain management decision making to a considerable extent. Further, the unionized company faces incurring the costs of employing personnel to deal with the union—whether by retaining an outside labor relations specialist or hiring a voice president for labor relations (with a full-time staff).

In any organizing campaign the obvious focus of attention is union organizing drives and management's counterstrategies. Although these are often important in determining whether the union wins representation, it should be emphasized that the way in which management has been treating its employees prior to organization efforts is critical. As one writer has put it succinctly, "Unions are only necessary when management makes them so." "Harrison and Rachel conducted a questionnaire study in four firms and found that "employees who perceive their supervisor as one who is considerate and supportive are much more likely to vote against union representation than are employees who see their supervisor as nonsupportive."

In unionization drives the union is interested in winning the right to be the exclusive bargaining agent for all employees in any particular bargaining unit. Although there are different patterns of union strategies taken prior to representation elections, union activities such as the following are fairly typical.

Prior to the actual beginning of a unionization drive, the union usually attempts to obtain as much relevant information as possible. Union Organizers seek information about the company, the employees, and the community, often by studying published material about the firm and by talking to local labor leaders. Once they have such information, the organizers are ready for initial contact with the firm's employees.

Union organizers often try to seek out particular employees who are strongly interested in the union and who show potential as effective leaders. Next, the organizers attempt to get a sufficient number of employees in the proposed bargaining unit (at least 30 percent) to sign authorization cards or otherwise indicate their interest in unionization to have a representation election held. Union organizers typically communicate with both employees and their families, attempting to sell them on the benefits of unionization. Effective union organizers are likely to use a variety of communications methods in these efforts—letters, telephone conversations, calling at the employees' homes, etc.

Should the firm desire to prevent unionization, it will want to follow similar strategies—obtaining information about the union and communicating to its employees reasons why they should not unionize. Management may examine the organizing union's contracts with other companies, particularly those in the same industry. It may also obtain useful information from contracts of other unions in its geographical location. Such information may pinpoint weaknesses in union contracts from the employee's point of view which can be communicated to them. Further, it may provide management with some idea of the relative past success of the union's representation efforts with other firms. Management can also obtain information and assistance in preventing the unionization of its firm from management consulting firms that specialize in these types of endeavors.

It has been argued, however, that outsiders in organization campaigns may do more harm than good. With respect to outside consultants, for example:

- Their presence may signal to employee that the union is very powerful.
- Campaigns seem to change relatively few votes anyway.
- Outsiders may be very expensive.

- Bringing in outsiders may be regarded as a public admission that management is unable to communicate effectively with its employees.
- Unions lose over one-half of all elections anyway.

We relate these points not to discourage the use of outsiders, but rather to point out some of the potential hazards that management should know before deciding to go to an outside consultant.

To be effective in preventing unionization, management also needs to keep appraised of possible reasons why its employees might join the union. A firm may continually obtain information from its supervisors and nonmanagerial employees about problem areas in the company that might increase the probabilities of unionization. This information may enable the firm to resolve the problems so that unionization drives may never even start or, once started, may be rejected by the organization's employees.

With such information, management may communicate to its employees reasons for remaining nonunionized. In such communications, facts about the union (for example, a previous history of many long and bitter strikes) may be brought out that may induce those employees highly concerned with job security to reject unionization. Further, the company can present additional information as to the many employee benefits which it offers. Employees often do not appreciate some of their important benefits partially because they do not understand exactly what the organization offers. Gearing any such communications to its employees at their educational level is extremely important, for numerous studies have shown a tendency on the part of organizations to communicate with the employees at an educational level above that of many their rank-and-file workers. For example, one study showed that in one firm workers understood less than 25 percent of what their managers thought they did, while in another it was found that more than half the articles from company newspapers written for employees were on a readability level above the level of 67 to 95 percent of the adult population.

Decision-Making Processes in Negotiations

Once a firm has been unionized, the personnel or labor relations manager is confronted with two basic decision areas—preparing for and participating in contract negotiations, and dealing with grievances and arbitration. The personnel manager's contract negotiation responsibilities are continuous for the duration of the contract and are not just confined to the actual negotiations. It is being increasingly recognized that much preparatory work is required between contract negotiations if the firm is to be as successful as possible in dealing with the union. Further, proactive union leaders are continuously preparing for future negotiations throughout the duration of the contract.

Unions ordinarily initiate contract negotiations with a set of demands to be incorporated into the labor-management agreement. Increasingly, managements are prepared to present a series of counterdemands. Prior to this time, however, both the union and management should be actively preparing for the negotiations. This preparation involves two basic steps—gathering information in order to assess the other party's strengths and weaknesses, and building a factual basis for its own demands (or counterdemands). Unions also often expend considerable efforts in publicizing their demands to their workers through the steward system any by word of mouth, for ultimately it will be members of the local unions who accept or reject any agreement entered into by their bargaining representatives.

In many ways, the contract negotiation preparation efforts undertaken by the company parallel those of the union. Management attempts to assess the union's strength and anticipate the union's demands (and, whenever possible, cost them out), and it talks to its supervisors about problems that they have encountered in the existing contract and analyzes patterns of grievances that have arisen under the present contract. These two information sources assume that the company already has a contract and is not negotiating with a union for the first time. As Randle and Wortman have pointed out, "Management is seldom entirely satisfied with the way the contract has functioned over the past contract period and may be able to demonstrate that specific abuses have resulted. Possibly the seniority system has affected efficiency of operations or work-stoppages or illegal slow-downs have occurred." Management, in anticipating union demands, may also examine other recent labor-management agreements in its industry (or others), recognizing that the union may try to keep up with other union successes.

The union will, in turn, talk to its own members to see what issues are important to them, look to other recent labor-management contracts to see what their peers have obtained, analyze grievance patterns in the present contract, and assess the economic strength of the employer—trends in sales, profits, return on investment, etc.

Information such as this may provide the basis for both union and management proposals. Usually, both parties will incorporate more into their demands and counterdemands than they realistically expect. Since the final agreement may be the result of some "horse trading," both union and management proposals "usually contain from the start a certain number of built-in bargaining points that are intended to be thrown away, or swapped for something else, at the last moment."

The actual negotiation process varies considerably from one situation to another. However, certain guidelines have been put forth, which, if followed, may help facilitate the negotiation process. Privacy of the negotiations seems generally to be considered advisable because the presence of outsiders tends to inhibit negotiations. Davey has suggested a number of other successful resolution conditions. Some of the more important conditions include the following:

- ☐ Both negotiating committees should be reasonably small, which tends to decrease the probabilities of much irrelevant information being introduced.
- ☐ One person should be in charge of conducting the negotiations for each side so that an undivided from can be maintained.
- ☐ Exchange of demands by each side prior to actual negotiations will speed up the negotiations.
- ☐ Negotiators for both sides should have the power to make decisive commitments. Since in most cases the union's agreement must be ratified by its membership, this may create serious problems. In fact, trends in increasing membership, rejections in the past few decades have been reported.
- ☐ The negotiators should first resolve the less controversial issues and then proceed to the more difficult issues. This

narrows the areas of real conflict and hence may make ultimate agreement, usually based on compromises, easier.

- The difficult issues can be divided into those that involve monetary outlays and those that do not. The noneconomic issues may then be "negotiated individually in terms of their intrinsic merit rather than in terms of bargaining strength" of the two parties; and the parties must decide whether to bargain the monetary outlay issues one by one or all together as a package.

Davey has pointed out that nearly all management negotiators and most union negotiators favor the total-economic package approach. Often management may be indifferent as to the mix of wage increases as opposed to benefit increases—it is primarily concerned with the total outlay of funds it will have to make. Unions, on the other hand, may be much more interested in the monetary outlay mix. It is probable, for example, that in the 111-day 1977-1978 UMW strike, the miners rejected an agreement between the UMW and the coal producers more because of a concern about health insurance costs to them and pensions for retired miners than because of wage issues.

Both management and labor must estimate the impact of their respective decisions to permit a strike. Typically, when impasses are reached in negotiations, management must choose between accepting "excessive" union demands and losing profits if the plant has to be shut down. Further, management must decide under conditions of uncertainty, in which not only the possibility of a strike but also its duration is involved. Unions, on the other hand, also face a difficult choice: (1) accept management's not wholly satisfactory offer or (2) face the temporary loss of income during the strike and assume the even greater risks that management will replace the strikers with other workers or go out of business. Union members also face a difficult choice because their livelihoods are at stake.

Once management and labour have resolved their contract negotiation issues, with or without a strike or mediation, they must focus attention on contract interpretation and administration.

Contingencies

A major contingency concerning the way in which employee-management relations will function is whether or not the firm is unionized. Unionization not only constrains management's decisions with respect to unfair labor practices as spelled out in the Wagner Act, but management's decisions are also considerably influenced by union demands in the collective bargaining process. In nonunionized companies many of the decisions and approaches we have discussed throughout this text—the setting of rate ranges in wage and salary administration; the offering of profit sharing, pension, and health insurance plans; the provision of incentive standards—are made unilaterally. With unionization, the union may be in a position to force or at least pressure management to take action in many of these areas.

Whether a firm will be subjected to a unionization drive and, if so, what type of union is likely to gain representation by its employees are two factors also influenced by different conditions. First, one reason why employees join unions initially is that they believe their needs are not being met be management. Firms in which top management pays its employees well, provides them with opportunities for promotion and for self-actualization on the job when possible, and has adequate employee benefits (such as at the Lincoln Electric Company) are much less likely to be unionized in the first place than are firms which take less interest in their employees.

The type of technology predominating in an organization will also have an impact on both the probabilities of unionism and the type of union chosen. As pointed out earlier, firms in which skilled craft work predominates, such as in the building trades, if unionized, will be represented by craft unions, in which the number of grievances and cases taken to arbitration will be less than in mass production operations, which are typically represented by industrial unions.

Further technology *may* have an influence on the effectiveness of strikes as a weapon by unions. Although authorities disagree on the subject, we would tend to agree with the proposition that in highly automated, capital-intensive industries, automated equipment may permit management to maintain uninterrupted production with supervisory personnel, if required, due to strike by those nonmanagerial employees belonging to the union. Another contingency for the extent of unionization expected is that mentioned early in the chapter—geography—with greater union concentration in the highly industrialized East, Midwest, and West than in the South and Southwest. Finally, organization size seems to be a factor in whether or not unions will be organized. Although, as reported in 1978, there was one *national* union with less than 100 members (steel engravers), generally speaking, "the larger the firm, the more likely it is for employees to be organized." A basic reason for this is that the dollar organization costs per potential union member are generally less for larger firms than for very small ones.

10

THE FUTURE

THROUGHOUT this text, our another effort has been towards the direction that quantitative models, computerization, and information-decision making concepts and methods have much to offer the personnel manager in making more effective organizational decisions. Further, we envision that research in these areas will continue to expand and progress.

At the same time, however, it must be recognized that:

1. "Management science" does not now and probably never will provide the *only* means for attaining better personnel management practices, and
2. Management science is still in its infancy, especially in personnel. Hence, many of its techniques developed to date (and covered in this text), are exploratory, and "crude" in terms of what the "state of the art" is likely to be, say, five or ten years hence.

From a balanced point of view, then, we believe that "management science and personnel management" ought to be conceived of in a sense of "restrained optimism."

Throughout this book we have discussed the role of personnel managers as involving *decision makers operating in complex and open organizational systems.* At the very beginning we emphasized that in making those decisions, today's personnel managers must deal with a variety of interacting environmental variables: economic, political, sociopsychological, and legal. As we have seen time and time again, the strategy space of managers is constrained by both the internal and external environments in which they must operate.

In this concluding chapter we will consider those environmental changes which appear to be already in progress and which will pose decision problems for personnel managers in the remainder of this century. Such a discussion cannot and will not be complete. However, we will consider three issues which we believe impact directly on the processes discussed in this text: (1) the changing composition of tomorrow's work force, (2) the emerging role of women, and (3) the future of legislation and regulation in personnel decision making.

In discussing each of these three topics, we will look at the changes which are already under way, the effects of those changes on organizations, and some solutions which are already in place which seek to deal with these issues. Certainly nothing is as certain as change itself, and the future holds some dramatic changes for society at large and tomorrow's business organizations.

WORK FORCE OF COMING TIMES

There is no need to speculate about the composition of tomorrow's work force: Its members have already been born. In fact, the changes that are already occurring are creating concern for politicians and workers alike regarding the soundness of the social security system and the future direction(s) of government spending and taxation policies. The reason for these concerns is based upon one simple fact; the work force of tomorrow will be older—much older.

The baby boom which occurred immediately following World War II is now a middle-age boom. Between now and the year 2000, this group will continue to "gray" in age, experience, and expectations. By the year 1990, the average age of the American worker will be 40, and based upon current population statistics, by the year 2000 "persons aged 40 to 64 will comprise *half* of the population will represent the largest single age group in our workforce".

In addition to being older, tomorrow's worker will also be smarter—or at least better educated. Today's college graduates may already be asking themselves and their professors, "Where have all the jobs gone?" The jobs haven't gone anywhere—the applicant pools for those jobs have simply been filled with persons who are better educated than at any time in our history as a nation:

Accompanying a work force characterized by fewer younger workers and more and more older workers are projections of a continuing growing economy which will create nearly 50 million additional jobs by the year 2000. These new jobs will be created as a result of (1) continuing economic expansion and (2) the introduction of new technologies in the workplace. These changes have important implications for american businesses: "The labor force will continue to grow during these years, but at a slower rate, meaning American business will have a lot more jobs than people to fill them." The decision problem that will need to be resolved by personnel managers is, What can be done to deal with the problem of too few younger (entry-level) employees, and too many older (experienced) workers?

Alternatives and Solutions Already in Progress

This problem holds within itself the seeds of solution. All change is incremental, and companies today have already begun to seek solutions to the problems of untapped human resources and the need to make room at the top for aspiring younger employees. Since the state has decided to protect employees 40 to 70 years of age, many older workers have chosen to remain on the job out of either personal choice or financial necessity. In order to free up middle-and top-level management positions and still provide for the needs of employees, some firms have instituted creative and innovative programs which meet these dual needs.

The use older employees on a part-time basis is not limited to those persons in middle- and upper-level managerial or professional positions. Retirees from all levels of the organization provide a valuable source of skills for a variety of positions. TOPS, for example, "created a separate division of their temporary personnel services specifically for retirees." Lindroth has cited two examples which provide some insight into the ways in which the use of retirees can benefit both the employee and the firm:

> We have placed a person…who only works on Mondays. He handles the light maintenance of their automobile fleet, making sure the cars are gassed, washed, etc. After Monday he's through for the week. We have another person who serves as

hostess on their executive floor from 7 A.M until 2 P.M daily....This particular woman takes great pride in her job. She's been there over two years and has had a number of pay increases because they like her so much.

Such utilization of retired persons enables companies, individuals, and our society at large to meet organizational and personal goals.

Opportunities for the Handicapped and Disadvantaged

Projected labor shortages also provide the promise for opportunities for two other groups of currently underutilized citizens: the handicapped and the disadvantaged. As Lindroth has noted, "Hiring the handicapped is no longer going to be a question of Affirmative Action, it is going to be a necessity." In addition to recognizing the potential of handicapped employees, some firms have begun to expand programs for employees who are confined to their homes.

Control Data, for example, has instituted work alternatives for such employees by installing computer terminals in their homes and training them in "course development and design for the company's educational division." this creative approach to manpower planning and utilization provides direct benefits to the firm and has reduced the expense of disability insurances. As a result of the experiment, the firm "is now offering HOMEWORK to both the private and public sectors for use with disabled or able-bodied employees who wish to study and do programming at home".

Projected labor shortages afford potential opportunity for disadvantaged youth. For example, the unemployment rate for rural youth aged 18 to 22 exceeds 40 percent. The movement of fewer young people into the labor force over the next two decades may provide opportunities for these underutilized people to gain meaningful employment opportunity in the years ahead.

It must be emphasized, however, that such opportunities will become reality only with the cooperation of business and government in providing training opportunities aimed at increasing necessary skills. As with the utilization of the handicapped, the disabled, and other potential employees, the problem of a declining labor force can only be net by cooperative efforts to utilize those persons who are available but need to be made ready for the future.

Women in the Work Force

A second major change in the demographics of tomorrow's work force is the continuing dramatic increase of the numbers of women employees. In 1990, 18 per cent of the work force was female, and today more than half of all women in America are employed outside of the home. By the year 2000 more than 57 million women will be employee by businesses or government agencies.

There are many reasons for the dramatic increase in the numbers of women entering the labor market. One reason is financial. Women work because they have to. Seventy per cent of the women who work, over 25 million, are women who need the money to support their families, as they are either the sole wage earner, are married to husbands who earn less than Rs. 12,000 a year, or are single, divorced, or widowed.

We would hasten to add that in the decades of the 1980s and 1990s, many women who work also do so because they want to. Many women today seek careers within business and government which provide not only financial gain but personal satisfaction as well. For whichever reason(s) women seek to work, the result has been dramatic.

As more and more women enter the work force, organizations will fact the growing problem of dual-career couples. "Between 1947 and 1975 the number of working husbands increased 27 percent while the number of working wives increased 205 per cent." As more and more women view their jobs as careers and not simply jobs, "the impact of the dual career phenomenon on productivity and corporate philosophy is becoming 'enormous'". As a result of education, affirmative action programs, and choice, problems of dual-career families will pose a major decision problem for personnel managers in the next two decades.

A variety of personnel policies have already been affected by the dual-career phenomenon. In one 1980 survey of the top Fortune 100 industrial corporations and other Fortune companies, the researchers reported that firms with large percentages of females had adopted internal policies and procedures which were aimed